1000 Recipes
Mini Treats

igloobooks

igloobooks

Published in 2013
by Igloo Books Ltd
Cottage Farm
Sywell
Northants
NN6 0BJ
www.igloobooks.com

Copyright © 2013 Igloo Books Ltd

Food photography and recipe development: PhotoCuisine UK
Front and back cover images © PhotoCuisine UK

LEO002 0813
2 4 6 8 10 9 7 5 3 1
ISBN: 978-1-78197-437-7

Printed and manufactured in China

1000 Recipes
Mini Treats

CONTENTS

SWEET

MAKES 8

Almond and Raisin Moroccan Scones

PREPARATION TIME 10 MINUTES

COOKING TIME 15 MINUTES

INGREDIENTS

110 g / 4 oz / ⅔ cup raisins
75 ml / 3 fl. oz / ⅓ cup whole milk
55 g / 2 oz / ½ cup ground almonds
110 g / 4 oz / ⅔ cup plain
(all purpose) flour
a little plain (all purpose) flour,
for dusting
½ tsp cream of tartar
½ tsp bicarbonate of (baking) soda
1 tbsp flaked (slivered) almonds
1 tbsp sunflower oil
a pinch of salt

TO GARNISH

1 tsp caster (superfine) sugar

- Preheat the oven to 190°C (170° fan) / 375F / gas 5.
- Sift together the flour, cream of tartar and bicarbonate of soda into a large mixing bowl.
- Stir in the raisins, ground and chopped almonds.
- Pour the oil into the mixture, then gradually add the milk and mix with a wooden spoon until a dough starts to form.
- Briefly knead the dough on a floured surface, then roll out to 2 cm thickness.
- Use a 2" circular cutter to cut 8 rounds of dough.
- Grease and line a baking tray with greaseproof paper and arrange the dough spaced out on it.
- Bake for 12-16 minutes until cooked, risen and golden.
- Remove and allow to cool on a wire rack before serving stacked, sprinkled with caster sugar.

Rosewater and Almond Scones

- Add 1 tsp rosewater to the dough when you add the milk.

MAKES 12

Ricotta and Almond Madeleines

PREPARATION TIME 10 MINUTES

COOKING TIME 15 MINUTES

INGREDIENTS

125 g / 4 ½ oz / 1 cup icing
(confectioners') sugar, sifted
75 g / 3 oz / ⅓ cup unsalted butter,
melted and cooled
75 g / 3 oz / ½ cup plain (all purpose)
flour, sifted
75 g / 3 oz / ⅓ cup ricotta
55 g / 2 oz / ½ cup ground almonds
½ tsp baking powder
½ tsp almond extract
a pinch of salt

TO GARNISH

1 tbsp whole blanched almonds
½ lemon, zest julienned

- Preheat the oven to 180°C (160° fan) / 350F / gas 4.
- Grease a 12-hole madeleine tray.
- Beat together the eggs, icing sugar, ricotta, salt and almond extract in a large mixing bowl until thick and shiny.
- Fold in the flour and ground almonds in thirds, as well as the baking powder.
- Once all the flour has been added, fold in the melted butter until incorporated.
- Spoon into the moulds, leaving them about three-quarters full with the batter.
- Bake for 12-14 minutes until golden and risen.
- Remove and allow them to cool in the tray for a few minutes before turning out onto a wire rack to finish cooling.
- Garnish with almonds and lemon zest before serving.

Lemon Curd Madeleines

- Substitute the ricotta for lemon curd, beating it with the eggs and icing sugar; omit the almond extract.

5

SERVES 8

Crunchy Chocolate

- Grease and line a baking tray with greaseproof paper.
- Mix the sugar and water in a small saucepan and cook over a moderate heat until deep golden-brown in colour.
- Add the hazelnuts and swirl to coat before pouring onto the greaseproof paper and leaving to set.
- Once set, separate the nuts from the caramel.
- Grease and line 2 5" high rimmed baking trays with greaseproof paper.
- Place the chocolate in heatproof bowls set over saucepans of simmering water, stirring until melted.
- Pour the melted chocolates into the separate trays.
- Sprinkle as desired with almonds, caramelised hazelnuts and popping candy.
- Chill for 2 hours until set before turning out and serving.

PREPARATION TIME 10-15 MINUTES

COOKING TIME 15-20 MINUTES

INGREDIENTS

300 g / 10 ½ oz / 2 cups good-quality milk chocolate, chopped
300 g / 10 ½ oz / 2 cups good-quality dark chocolate, chopped
55 g / 2 oz / ⅓ cup coloured popping candy
55 g / 2 oz / ⅓ cup whole almonds, finely chopped
55 g / 2 oz / ½ cup blanched hazelnuts (cob nuts)
55 g / 2 oz / ¼ cup caster (superfine) sugar
2 tbsp cold water

Fruit and Nut Chocolate

6

- Mix together 75 g / 3 oz / ½ cup raisins with the chopped almonds and sprinkle all over the dark chocolate, omitting the hazelnuts.

7

MAKES 8

Chocolate and Ginger Mini Tartlets

- Preheat the oven to 180°C (160° fan) / 350F / gas 4.
- Roll the pastry out on a lightly floured surface.
- Cut out 8 rounds and line 8 fluted 2" tartlet cases.
- Trim any excess pastry and prick the bases with a fork.
- Line with greaseproof paper and baking beans and blind-bake for 12-15 minutes until golden at the edges.
- Remove from the oven and discard the greaseproof paper and baking beans.
- Return to the oven for 2-3 minutes to brown the bases.
- Melt the chocolate and ground ginger in a heatproof bowl set atop a saucepan of simmering water, stirring.
- Remove from the heat and leave to cool for 3 minutes before beating in the egg yolks.
- Turn out the tartlets from the cases and fill with a tablespoon of the chocolate mixture.
- Garnish with crystallised ginger before serving.

PREPARATION TIME 10 MINUTES

COOKING TIME 20 MINUTES

INGREDIENTS

350 g / 12 oz ready-made sweet shortcrust pastry
a little plain (all purpose) flour, for dusting
200 g / 7 oz / 1 ⅓ cups good-quality dark chocolate, chopped
2 large egg yolks
½ tsp ground ginger

TO GARNISH
30 g / 1 oz / 2 tbsp crystallised ginger

Chocolate and Sea Salt Tartlets

8

- Omit the ground ginger from the filling and garnish the tartlets with a pinch of flaked sea salt.

MAKES 12

Matcha Tea Sandwich Cookies

Cocoa Sandwich Cookies

10

- Replace the matcha tea powder with 30 g / 1 oz / 2 tbsp cocoa powder.

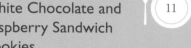

White Chocolate and Raspberry Sandwich Cookies

11

- Add 3 tbsp chopped freeze dried raspberries to the ganache mixture.

PREPARATION TIME 10-15 MINUTES

COOKING TIME 20 MINUTES

INGREDIENTS

FOR THE COOKIES
150 g / 5 oz / 1 cup plain (all purpose) flour, sifted
a little extra plain (all purpose) flour, for dusting
75 g / 3 oz / ¾ stick unsalted butter, chilled and cubed
60g / 2 oz / ½ cup icing (confectioners') sugar
2 tsp matcha tea powder
1 medium egg
1 medium egg yolk
½ tsp salt

FOR THE GANACHE
250 g / 9 oz / 1 ⅔ cups white chocolate, chopped
175 ml / 6 fl. oz / ¾ cup double (heavy) cream

- Mix together the icing sugar, cocoa powder, flour and salt in a large mixing bowl.
- Rub the butter into this mixture until it resembles fine breadcrumbs.
- Add the egg, egg yolk and matcha tea powder, mixing until a dough forms.
- Gather up and roll into a ball before wrapping in clingfilm and chilling for 30 minutes.
- Preheat the oven to 180°C (160° fan) / 350F / gas 4.
- Grease and line 2 baking trays with greaseproof paper.
- Roll the pastry out on a lightly floured work surface to ¾ cm thickness.
- Use a small square cookie cutter to stamp out 24 square.
- Arrange spaced out on the lined baking trays and bake for 12-14 minutes until set.
- Remove from the oven and allow to cool for 10 minuets on the trays before removing carefully to a wire rack to cool completely.
- Heat the cream in a saucepan until boiling then remove from the heat and whisk in the chocolate until smooth.
- Spoon into a piping bag fitted with a small straight-sided nozzle and leave to cool for 5 minutes.
- Pipe the ganache onto the base of 12 of the cookies and sandwich with the remaining 12 before serving.

SERVES 8

Chocolate, Toffee and Walnut Bars

- Preheat the oven to 180°C (160° fan) / 350F / gas 4.
- Grease and line a 12" x 9" x 3" baking tin with greaseproof paper.
- Melt the butter and syrup in a saucepan until runny.
- Remove from the heat and stir in the oats and salt, mixing gently but thoroughly.
- Spoon into the tin and bake for 25-30 minutes.
- Remove from the oven and leave to cool and harden.
- Melt the chocolates together in a heatproof bowl set atop a saucepan of simmering water.
- Once melted, pour evenly on top of the set flapjack and chill until firm.
- Warm the dulce de leche in a saucepan until runny before stirring in the walnuts.
- Leave to cool before pouring on top of the chocolate; chill until set before turning out and slicing.

Toffee, Peanut and Pecan Tartlets

13

- Substitute the chocolate for another 175 g / 6 oz / ¾ cup of dulce de leche, adding 75 g / 3 oz / ¾ cup peanuts to it at the same time as the walnuts.

PREPARATION TIME 10-15 MINUTES

COOKING TIME 10-15 MINUTES

INGREDIENTS

150 g / 5 oz / 2 cups rolled oats
150 g / 5 oz / ⅔ cup dulce de leche
125 g / 4 ½ oz / ⅓ cup Golden Syrup
110 g / 4 oz / ½ cup unsalted butter, softened
100 g / 3 ½ oz / ⅔ cup good-quality milk chocolate, chopped
100 g / 3 ½ oz / ⅔ cup good-quality dark chocolate, chopped
75 g / 3 oz / ¾ cup walnut halves
a pinch of salt

MAKES 6

Mini Marble Cakes

- Preheat the oven to 180°C (160° fan) / 350F / gas 4 and grease 6 mini loaf tins.
- Beat together all the ingredients for the chocolate batter in a large mixing bowl until smooth then repeat the process for the vanilla batter in a separate mixing bowl.
- Spoon half of the vanilla batter into the base of the loaf tins before following with half of the chocolate batter on top.
- Spoon the remaining vanilla batter on top of the chocolate batter and follow with the remaining chocolate batter before tapping the tins a few times to release any trapped air bubbles.
- Bake for 30-40 minutes; test with a wooden toothpick, if it comes out clean, they are done.
- Remove to a wire rack and allow to cool before serving.

Three Chocolate Marble Cakes

15

- Fold 100 g / 3 ½ oz / ⅔ cup dark chips into the vanilla batter before filling the tins and baking.

PREPARATION TIME 10 MINUTES

COOKING TIME 15 MINUTES

INGREDIENTS

FOR THE CHOCOLATE BATTER
150 g / 5 oz / 1 cup self-raising flour
150 g / 5 oz / ⅔ cup margarine, softened
150 g / 5 oz / ⅔ cup caster (superfine) sugar
30 g / 1 oz / 2 tbsp cocoa powder
30 ml / 1 fl. oz / 2 tbsp whole milk
3 large eggs
a pinch of salt

FOR THE VANILLA BATTER
150 g / 5 oz / 1 cup self-raising flour, sifted
150 g / 5 oz / ⅔ cup margarine, softened
150 g / 5 oz / ⅔ cup caster (superfine) sugar
3 large eggs
1 tbsp vanilla extract
a pinch of salt

16

MAKES 24

Florentines

PREPARATION TIME 10 MINUTES

COOKING TIME 15 MINUTES

INGREDIENTS

175 g / 6 oz / 1 cup dark chocolate, chopped
40 g / 1 ½ oz / 2 tbsp unsalted butter, softened
75 ml / 3 fl. oz / ⅓ cup double (heavy) cream
75 g / 3 oz / ⅓ cup caster (superfine) sugar
110 g / 4 oz / 1 cup flaked (slivered) almonds
30 g / 1 oz / 2 tbsp plain (all purpose) flour
30 g / 1 oz / 2 tbsp candied citrus peel, finely chopped

- Melt together 25 g of the butter, 10 g of plain flour and the sugar in a saucepan set over a low heat.
- Stir frequently until melted before adding the cream.
- Add the flaked almonds and candied citrus peel.
- Grease 2 baking trays with the remaining butter and spoon heaped tablespoons of the mixture onto them.
- Flatten the heaps of mixture with the back of a tablespoon before baking for 12-14 minutes.
- Remove from the oven and let sit for 3 minutes.
- Place the chopped chocolate in a heatproof bowl set over a saucepan of gently simmering water.
- Stir occasionally until melted, then put to one side.
- Using a pair of tongs to hold the Florentines, coat the undersides with melted chocolate then leave to set, inverted on wire racks.
- Store in an airtight container for up to 1 week.

Cherry Florentines

17

- Replace the candied citrus peel with glacé cherry and add at the same time as the flaked almonds.

18

MAKES 12

Cinnamon Flans

PREPARATION TIME 10 MINUTES

COOKING TIME 15 MINUTES

INGREDIENTS

400 g / 14 oz ready-made puff pastry, chilled
250 ml / 9 fl. oz / 1 cup whole milk
225 g / 8 oz / 1 cup caster (superfine) sugar
125 ml / 4 ½ fl. oz / ½ cup cold water
30 g / 1 oz / 4 tbsp unsalted butter, softened
30 g / 1 oz / 2 tbsp plain (all purpose) flour
1 tbsp cornflour (cornstarch)
½ tsp vanilla extract
3 large egg yolks
1 large egg
2 sticks of cinnamon
½ orange, sliced

TO GARNISH

1 tbsp icing (confectioners') sugar

- Combine the orange slices, sugar, cinnamon and water in a saucepan and simmer over a medium heat.
- Mix the flour, cornflour and vanilla extract in a jug with a little milk to make a smooth paste.
- Heat the remaining milk in a saucepan until simmering then combine with the paste, whisking simultaneously.
- Pour into a saucepan, cook over a medium heat.
- Discard the orange and cinnamon from the syrup and mix with the milk. Add the egg and yolks and mix, cook until simmering. Pour into a clean jug and chill.
- Preheat the oven to 220°C (200° fan) / 425F / gas 7.
- Roll the pastry out on a floured work surface. Cut the pastry in half, stack on top of each other and roll into a log. Cut 12 slices, and roll into 10 cm rounds.
- Grease a 12 hole muffin tin with butter and line with the pastry. Fill with custard and bake for 15-18 minutes.
- Leave to cool for 5 minutes. Garnish with icing sugar.

Cinnamon and Hazelnut Flans

19

- Add 2 tbsp chopped hazelnuts (cob nuts) to the pastry before filling with the custard.

20

MAKES 12

Coconut Cookies

Coconut and Peanut Cookies

 **21**

- Replace 75 g / 3 oz / 1 cup of the desiccated coconut with the same weight of chopped peanuts.

Coconut Chocolate Cookies

22

- When cooled dip the coconut cookies into melted chocolate and place on greaseproof paper to set.

PREPARATION TIME 5 MINUTES

COOKING TIME 10 MINUTES

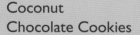

INGREDIENTS

225 g / 8 oz / 3 cups desiccated coconut
110 g / 4 oz / ½ cup caster (superfine) sugar
30 g / 1 oz / 2 tbsp ground almonds
2 large egg whites
¼ tsp cream of tartar
a pinch of salt

- Preheat the oven to 160°C (140° fan) / 325F / gas 3.
- Grease and line a large baking tray with greaseproof paper.
- Whisk the egg whites in a large, clean bowl until frothy, then add the cream of tartar and continue whisking until soft peaks form.
- Add the sugar a tablespoon at a time as you continue whisking until you have stiff peaks that are glossy.
- Add the ground almonds, salt and coconut, folding gently to mix well.
- Spoon 12 rounds of the mixture onto the baking tray and bake for 18-20 minutes until golden-brown in colour.
- Remove from the oven and allow to cool a little before serving.

Mini Cherry Rice Puddings

23

SERVES 4

PREPARATION TIME 5 MINUTES

COOKING TIME 15 MINUTES

INGREDIENTS

55 g / 2 oz / ¼ cup unsalted butter, softened
75 g / 3 oz / ⅓ cup pudding rice
55 g / 2 oz / ¼ cup caster (superfine) sugar
750 ml / 1 pint 6 fl. oz / 3 cups whole milk
225 g / 8 oz / 1 cup canned cherries, drained
a pinch of salt

TO SERVE

250 ml / 9 fl. oz / 1 cup good-quality vanilla custard

- Combine the milk and sugar in a saucepan simmer over a moderate heat, stirring frequently.
- Add the rice and cook for 45-50 minutes.
- Once the rice has absorbed most of the liquid and is creamy, add the cherries and half of the butter, stirring briefly.
- Preheat the oven to 180°C (160° fan) / 350F / gas 4.
- Grease the insides of 4 individual heatproof ramekins with the remaining butter before spooning the rice pudding into them.
- Bake for 18-20 minutes until the tops are golden in colour.
- Remove from the oven and turn out onto serving plates, using a sharp knife to help loosen them from the ramekins if necessary.
- Serve warm with the vanilla custard.

Chocolate and Cherry Rice Puddings

24

- Stir 100 g / 3 ½ oz / ⅔ cup of dark chocolate chips into the rice pudding before baking.

Star-Shaped Lemon Shortbread Cookies

25

MAKES 24

PREPARATION TIME 10 MINUTES

COOKING TIME 15 MINUTES

INGREDIENTS

300 g / 10 ½ oz / 2 cups plain (all purpose) flour
a little extra plain flour, for dusting
50 g / 2 oz / ⅓ cup cornflour (cornstarch)
225 g / 8 oz / 1 cup unsalted butter, cubed
75 g / 3 oz / 1 cup icing (confectioners') sugar
1 lemon, finely zested
a pinch of salt

TO GARNISH

55 g / 2 oz / ¼ cup caster (superfine) sugar

- Pulse together the flour, cornflour, salt, icing sugar, lemon zest and butter in a food processor until it comes together to form a dough.
- Remove the dough, knead gently and form into a ball.
- Wrap in clingfilm and chill for 60 minutes.
- Preheat the oven to 180°C (160° fan) / 350F / gas 4.
- Remove the dough from the fridge and roll out on a lightly floured surface to 1 cm thickness.
- Cut out shapes from the dough using a small star-shaped cookie cutter.
- Grease and line 2 baking trays with greaseproof paper.
- Arrange on the baking trays spaced apart then bake for 12-15 minutes until they just start to colour.
- Remove from the oven and sprinkle immediately with the caster sugar.
- Allow them to cool.

Mixed Citrus Shortbread Cookies

26

- Add the zest of 1 lime and ½ an orange before pulsing into a dough.

27

MAKES 4

Cherry Tartlets

- Preheat the oven to 180°C (160° fan) / 350F / gas 4.
- Roll the pastry out on a lightly floured surface.
- Cut out 4 rounds of pastry and use to line 4 individual 4" ramekins.
- Prick the bases and trim excess pastry. Chill until needed.
- Blitz together the ground almonds, sugar and butter in a food processor until creamy.
- Add the egg, egg white and kirsch and pulse until combined.
- Spoon into the pastry and bake for 25-30 minutes.
- Meanwhile, heat the cherry jam in a saucepan, then strain through a sieve into a jug.
- Remove tartlets from the oven and spoon glaze on top.
- Let it cool before garnishing with cherries.

Iced Cherry Tartlets

28

- Mix 65 g / 2 ½ oz / ½ cup icing (confectioners') sugar with 1-2 tbsp boiling water until you have a thick, pourable icing. Drizzle the tarts with the icing.

PREPARATION TIME 10 MINUTES

COOKING TIME 15-20 MINUTES

....

INGREDIENTS

300 g / 10 ½ oz / 2 cups ready-made shortcrust pastry
a little plain (all purpose) flour, for dusting
225 g / 8 oz / 2 cups ground almonds
110 g / 4 oz / ½ cup caster (superfine) sugar
110 g / 4 oz / ½ cup unsalted butter
2 small eggs
2 small egg whites
1 tbsp kirsch (optional)

FOR THE GLAZE
250 g / 9 oz / 1 cup cherry jam

TO GARNISH
a small handful of cherries, stems attached

29

SERVES 6

Chocolate Tart

- Grease and line a baking tray with greaseproof paper.
- Mix the water and sugar in a saucepan for the garnish.
- Cook over a moderate heat, swirling gently, until you have a dark caramel.
- Pour the caramel onto the tray and sprinkle with nuts.
- Preheat the oven to 180°C (160° fan) / 350F / gas 4.
- Roll the pastry out on a lightly floured surface.
- Line a 7" springform tart tin with the pastry. Prick the base with a fork and chill.
- Place the chocolate and butter in a heatproof bowl set atop a saucepan of simmering water.
- Stir until melted, remove from heat and beat in the eggs.
- Fold in the flour, then pour into the pastry case. Bake for 35-40 minutes until set.
- Crack the nut brittle into pieces before using to garnish the tart.

Chocolate and Peanut Brittle Tarts

30

- Replace almonds and hazelnuts with 110 g / 4 oz / 1 cup unsalted peanuts.

PREPARATION TIME 10 MINUTES

COOKING TIME 20 MINUTES

....

INGREDIENTS

250 g / 9 oz / 1 ⅔ cups ready-made shortcrust pastry
a little plain (all purpose) flour, for dusting
200 g / 7 oz / 1 ⅓ cups good-quality dark chocolate, chopped
55 g / 2 oz / ⅓ cup plain (all purpose) flour
55 g / 2 oz / ¼ cup unsalted butter
2 medium eggs

TO GARNISH
55 g / 2 oz / ⅓ cup whole almonds
55 g / 2 oz / ⅓ cup hazelnuts (cob nuts)
150 g / 5 oz / ⅔ cup caster (superfine) sugar
100 ml / 3 ½ fl. oz / ⅖ cup cold water

SERVES 4

Dark and White Chocolate Mousse

Chocolate and Hazelnut Mousse

32

- Top each mousse with 1 tbsp finely chopped hazelnuts (cob nuts) for a textural crunch to the mousses.

Chocolate Almond Mousse

33

- Add 1 tsp of almond essence to the mixture, and when set top with some flaked almonds.

PREPARATION TIME 10 MINUTES

COOKING TIME 15 MINUTES

INGREDIENTS

200 g / 7 oz / 1 ⅓ cups good-quality dark chocolate, chopped
150 ml / 5 fl. oz / ⅗ cup whipping cream
150 g / 5 oz / 1 cup white chocolate, chopped
125 ml / 4 ½ fl. oz / ½ cup double (heavy) cream

- Heat the heavy cream in a saucepan set over a medium heat until boiling.
- Remove from the heat and add the chopped white chocolate, whisking until smooth.
- Let the mixture cool a little before dividing between 4 serving cups and setting to one side.
- Melt the dark chocolate in a heatproof bowl set over a saucepan of simmering water.
- Whisk occasionally until melted them remove from the heat.
- Whisk the whipping cream until soft peaks form then add one third to the melted, cooled chocolate.
- Fold in the remaining cream in two parts, working quickly and carefully.
- Spoon the mousse on top of the white chocolate in the serving cups and serve immediately.

34

SERVES 4

Summer Fruit Tartlets

- Preheat the oven to 180°C (160° fan) / 350F / gas 4.
- Roll the pastry out on a lightly floured surface.
- Cut out 4 rounds of pastry to line 4 5" tartlet tins.
- Prick the bases and line with greaseproof paper.
- Trim the excess pastry and fill the lined tarts with baking beans.
- Blind-bake for 12-15 minutes until golden in colour.
- Remove from the oven and discard the greaseproof paper and baking beans.
- Whisk together the egg and milk in a small bowl.
- Return the tartlets to the oven for 3 minutes then brush with the egg wash. Set the pastry tarts to one side.
- Combine the summer fruit, sugar and vanilla extract and cook over a low heat for 5-7 minutes.
- Fill the tartlets with the berries before serving.

PREPARATION TIME 10 MINUTES

COOKING TIME 20 MINUTES

INGREDIENTS

250 g / 9 oz ready-made shortcrust pastry
a little (plain) flour, for dusting
450 g / 1 lb / 3 cups frozen summer berries
55 g / 2 oz / ¼ cup caster (superfine) sugar
½ tsp vanilla extract
1 large egg
1 tbsp whole milk

Summer Fruit Cream Tartlets

35

- Whip 250 ml / 9 fl. oz / 1 cup whipping cream with 65 g / 2 ½ oz / ½ cup icing (confectioners') sugar and use to top the tartlets before serving.

36

MAKES 4

Raspberry Tartlets

- Preheat the oven to 180°C (160° fan) / 350F / gas 4.
- Roll the pastry out on a lightly floured surface.
- Cut out 4 rounds of pastry and use to line 4 individual 4" ramekins.
- Prick the bases with a fork and trim any excess, overhanging pastry with a serrated knife.
- Chill until needed.
- Blitz together the ground almonds, sugar and butter in a food processor until creamy.
- Add the egg, egg white and framboise if using and pulse until combined.
- Spoon into the pastry and bake for 25-30 minutes until the edge of the pastry is golden brown in colour.
- Remove the tartlets from the oven and let them cool before garnishing with raspberries and dusting the outer rims with icing sugar.

PREPARATION TIME 10 MINUTES

COOKING TIME 15 MINUTES

INGREDIENTS

300 g / 10 ½ oz ready-made shortcrust pastry
a little plain (all purpose) flour, for dusting
225 g / 8 oz / 2 cups ground almonds
110 g / 4 oz / ½ cup caster (superfine) sugar
110 g / 4 oz / ½ cup unsalted butter
2 small eggs
2 small egg whites
1 tbsp framboise (optional)

TO GARNISH
300 g / 10 ½ oz / 2 cups raspberries
2 tbsp icing (confectioners') sugar

Raspberry and Almond Tartlets

37

- Replace 100 g / 3 ½ oz / 1 cup of the raspberries with the same weight of flaked (slivered) almonds for a nutty addition to the tartlets.

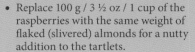

Chocolate Cookies

MAKES 12

38

PREPARATION TIME 5-10 MINUTES

COOKING TIME 15 MINUTES

INGREDIENTS

110 g / 4 oz / ⅔ cup plain (all purpose) flour, sifted
75 g / 3 oz / ¾ stick unsalted butter, chilled and cubed
60g / 2 oz / ½ cup icing (confectioners') sugar
55 g / 2 oz / ⅓ cup cocoa powder, sifted
110 g / 4 oz / ⅔ cup dark chocolate chips
1 large egg
½ tsp vanilla extract

- Mix the icing sugar, cocoa powder, flour and salt in a mixing bowl.
- Rub the butter into this mixture until it resembles fine breadcrumbs.
- Add the egg, dark chocolate chips and vanilla extract and mix until a stiff dough forms. Roll into a log shape with a diameter of 8-10 cm.
- Wrap in greaseproof paper and chill for 30 minutes.
- Preheat the oven to 180°C (160° fan) / 350F / gas 4.
- Grease and line a couple of baking trays with greaseproof paper.
- Use a knife to cut 1 cm thick cookies out of the dough.
- Arrange spaced out on the lined baking trays and bake for 12-14 minutes.
- Remove from the oven and allow to cool.

Chocolate and Banana Cookies

39

- Use 100 g / 3 ½ oz / 1 cup banana chips to stud the cookie dough before baking for a fruity addition to the cookies.

Strawberry and Pistachio Mini Tarts

MAKES 8

40

PREPARATION TIME 10-15 MINUTES

COOKING TIME 10-15 MINUTES

INGREDIENTS

110 g / 4 oz / ½ cup unsalted butter, softened
110 g / 4 oz / ½ cup caster (superfine) sugar
150 g / 5 oz / 1 cup plain (all purpose) flour
3 medium egg whites
½ tsp vanilla extract
¼ tsp salt
250 g / 9 oz / 1 ⅔ cups pistachios, shelled
55 g / 2 oz / ¼ cup caster (superfine) sugar
250 g / 9 oz / 1 ⅔ cups pistachios, shelled
24 strawberries, hulled
2 tbsp icing (confectioners') sugar

- Preheat the oven to 180°C (160° fan) / 350F / gas 4.
- Cream together the butter and sugar until pale.
- Beat in the egg whites one at a time, then fold in the flour and salt in thirds.
- Lightly grease a madeleine tray and carefully, thinly spread the batter into the moulds.
- Bake for 10-12 minutes until the tarts are golden-brown.
- Remove from the oven and let cool on a wire rack.
- Pulse the pistachios with the sugar in a food processor until they resemble rough breadcrumbs.
- Mix the icing sugar with boiling water until thick.
- Remove the tarts from the moulds and fill with the pistachio mixture.
- Spoon a little icing into the strawberries and secure upside-down on the pistachio.
- Dust with icing sugar before serving.

Peach and Pistachio Mini Tarts

41

- De-stone and dice 2 peaches and use in place of the strawberries on the tarts. Drizzle the icing sugar on top of the peaches before dusting with icing sugar.

42

MAKES 4

Orange Cream Tart

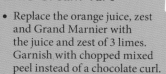

Lime Cream Tart   **43**

- Replace the orange juice, zest and Grand Marnier with the juice and zest of 3 limes. Garnish with chopped mixed peel instead of a chocolate curl.

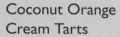

Coconut Orange Cream Tarts   **44**

- Before cooking sprinkle each of the tarts with 1-2 tsp of desiccated coconut.

PREPARATION TIME 10 MINUTES

COOKING TIME 15 MINUTES

INGREDIENTS

300 g / 10 ½ oz ready-made shortcrust pastry
a little plain (all purpose) flour, for dusting
225 g / 8 oz / 2 cups ground almonds
110 g / 4 oz / ½ cup caster (superfine) sugar
110 g / 4 oz / ½ cup unsalted butter
2 small eggs
2 small egg whites
1 orange, juiced and zested
1 tbsp Cointreau or Grand Marnier (optional)

TO GARNISH
4 white chocolate curls

- Preheat the oven to 180°C (160° fan) / 350F / gas 4.
- Roll the pastry out on a lightly floured surface to ½ cm thickness.
- Cut out 4 rounds of pastry and use to line 4 individual 5" tart cases.
- Prick the bases with a fork and trim any excess, overhanging pastry with a serrated knife.
- Chill until needed.
- Blitz together the ground almonds, sugar and butter in a food processor until creamy.
- Add the egg, egg white, orange juice, orange zest and Cointreau/Grand Marnier, if using and pulse until combined.
- Spoon into the pastry and bake for 30-35 minutes until the edge of the pastry is golden brown in colour and the filling is puffed up.
- Remove the tarts from the oven and let them cool on a wire rack.
- Turn the tarts out from the cases and bore a small hole in their centres.
- Place the chocolate curl in the holes before serving.

MAKES 4

Caramel Tarts

PREPARATION TIME 10 MINUTES

COOKING TIME 15-20 MINUTES

....

INGREDIENTS

250 g / 9 oz ready-made shortcrust
pastry
a little plain (all purpose) flour,
for dusting
300 g / 10 ½ oz / 1 ⅓ cups caster
(superfine) sugar
125 ml / 4 ½ fl. oz / ½ cup double
(heavy) cream
75 g / 3 oz / ⅓ cup butter, softened
55 ml / 2 fl. oz / ¼ cup Golden Syrup
30 ml / 1 fl. oz / 2 tbsp cold water
white icing pen

- Preheat the oven to 180°C (160° fan) / 350F / gas 4.
- Roll the pastry out on a lightly floured surface.
- Cut out 4 rounds to line 4 individual 5" tart cases. Prick the bases and trim any excess pastry.
- Line with greaseproof paper and fill with baking beans before blind-baking for 12-15 minutes until golden.
- Remove from the oven and discard the greaseproof paper and baking beans.
- Return to the oven for 3-4 minutes before cooling.
- Combine 150 g of the sugar and the water in a saucepan, cooking over a medium heat until light brown in colour.
- Remove the pan from the heat, add the butter and swirl.
- Add the remaining sugar, double cream and Golden Syrup and return to the heat, simmering for 3-4 minutes.
- Let the caramel cool before pouring into the pastry tarts.
- Once it starts to set, decorate with swirls using the icing

Caramel and White Chocolate Tarts 46

- Replace the white icing with 100 g / 3 ½ oz / ⅔ cup white chocolate chips.

 47

MAKES 4

White Chocolate Tarts with Cherry

PREPARATION TIME 10 MINUTES

COOKING TIME 15 MINUTES

....

INGREDIENTS

250 g / 9 oz ready-made shortcrust
pastry
a little plain (all purpose) flour,
for dusting
300 g / 10 ½ oz / 2 cups white
chocolate, chopped
175 ml / 6 fl. oz / ⅔ cup double
(heavy) cream
1 tbsp kirsch (optional)

TO GARNISH
4 cocktail cherries

- Preheat the oven to 180°C (160° fan) / 350F / gas 4.
- Roll the pastry out on a lightly floured surface.
- Cut out 4 rounds of pastry and line 4 5" tartlet cases.
- Prick the bases and trim any excess pastry.
- Line with greaseproof paper and fill with baking beans before blind-baking for 12-15 minutes.
- Remove from the oven and discard the greaseproof paper and baking beans.
- Return to the oven for 3-4 minutes to brown the base before removing to a wire rack to cool.
- Heat the cream in a saucepan until boiling, remove from the heat, and whisk in the chocolate and kirsch if using.
- Once smooth and thick, let it cool for 2 minutes before pouring into the pastry tarts.
- Garnish with a cocktail cherry before serving.

Dark Chocolate and Kirsch Tarts 48

- Chop 125 g / 4 ½ oz / 1 cup glacés cherries and fold into the chocolate and cream ganache with an additional 55 ml / 2 fl. oz / ¼ cup Kirsch.

49

MAKES 12

Moist Blueberry and Blackberry Buns

- Preheat the oven to 180°C (160° fan) / 350F / gas 4.
- Roll the pastry out on a lightly floured.
- Cut out 12 small rounds of pastry and use to line 12 individual 2" fluted bun moulds.
- Prick the bases with a fork and trim any excess, overhanging pastry with a serrated knife.
- Chill until needed.
- Blitz together the ground almonds, sugar and butter in a food processor until thick and creamy.
- Add the eggs and egg whites and pulse until combined.
- Spoon into the pastry and dot each with a few blueberries and blackberries.
- Bake for 20-25 minutes until the edge of the pastry is golden brown in colour and the filling is set.
- Remove from the oven and allow to cool before garnishing with a little golden caster sugar.

Raspberry Buns   **50**

- Replace the blueberries and blackberries with 200 g / 7 oz / 2 cups of raspberries, dotting them in the same way before baking.

PREPARATION TIME 10-15 MINUTES

COOKING TIME 15 MINUTES

INGREDIENTS

300 g / 10 ½ oz ready-made shortcrust pastry
a little plain (all purpose) flour, for dusting
225 g / 8 oz / 2 cups ground almonds
110 g / 4 oz / ½ cup caster (superfine) sugar
110 g / 4 oz / ½ cup unsalted butter
3 small eggs
2 small egg whites
110 g / 4 oz / 1 cup blueberries
110 g / 4 oz / 1 cup blackberries

TO GARNISH

1 tbsp golden caster (superfine) sugar

51

MAKES 4

Apple Bourdaloue Tarts

- Preheat the oven to 180°C (160° fan) / 350F / gas 4.
- Roll the pastry out on a lightly floured surface.
- Cut out 4 rounds of pastry and use to line 4 individual 5" tart cases.
- Prick the bases with a fork and trim any excess, overhanging pastry with a serrated knife.
- Chill until needed.
- Blitz together the ground almonds, sugar, flour and butter in a food processor until creamy.
- Add the eggs and calvados, pulsing until combined.
- Arrange the sliced apple in the pastry cases then spoon the almond mixture on top and around them.
- Bake for 30-35 minutes until the edge of the pastry is golden brown in colour and the filling is golden and set.
- Remove the tarts from the oven and let them cool on a wire rack before dusting with icing sugar and serving.

Pear Bourdaloue Tarts   **52**

- Instead of using apples, peel, core and slice 4 pears. If using the calvados, replace with pear eau de vie.

PREPARATION TIME 10-15 MINUTES

COOKING TIME 15 MINUTES

INGREDIENTS

250 g / 9 oz ready-made shortcrust pastry
a little plain (all purpose) flour, for dusting
110 g / 4 oz / ½ cup butter, softened
110 g / 4 oz / ½ cup caster (superfine) sugar
110 g / 4 oz / 1 ⅓ cups ground almonds
30 g / 1 oz / 2 tbsp plain (all purpose) flour
2 large eggs
1 tbsp calvados (optional)
4 Golden Delicious apples, peeled, cored and sliced

TO GARNISH

1 tbsp icing (confectioners') sugar

53

MAKES 8

Lunette Jam Biscuits

Lemon Curd
Lunette Biscuits
 54

- Replace the jam with the same weight of lemon curd to fill these biscuits.

Raspberry
Lunette Biscuits
55

- Replace the strawberry jam with raspberry jam to fill the biscuits.

PREPARATION TIME 10 MINUTES

COOKING TIME 15 MINUTES

INGREDIENTS

FOR THE BISCUITS
300 g / 10 ½ oz / 2 cups plain
(all purpose) flour
a little extra plain flour, for dusting
50 g / 2 oz / ⅓ cup cornflour
(cornstarch)
225 g / 8 oz / 1 cup unsalted butter,
cubed
65 g / 2 ½ oz / ½ cup icing
(confectioners') sugar
a pinch of salt

FOR THE FILLING
300 g / 10 ½ oz / 1 ⅓ cups seedless
strawberry jam, warmed

TO GARNISH
2 tbsp icing (confectioners') sugar

- Pulse together the flour, cornflour, salt, icing sugar and butter in a food processor until it comes together to form a dough.
- Remove the dough, knead gently and form into a ball.
- Wrap in clingfilm and chill for 60 minutes.
- Preheat the oven to 180°C (160° fan) / 350F / gas 4.
- Remove the dough from the fridge and roll out on a lightly floured surface to ½ cm thickness.
- Cut out 16 shapes from the dough using a fluted oval cutter.
- Grease and line 2 baking trays with greaseproof paper.
- Arrange on the baking trays spaced apart, then use a 1 cm straight-sided cutter to punch two holes out from 8 of the shapes.
- Bake for 12-15 minutes until they just start to colour.
- Remove to a wire rack to cool.
- Once cool, spread the 8 biscuits without holes with the warmed jam and dust the holed biscuits with icing sugar.
- Place these on top of the jam biscuits to complete.

56

MAKES 12

Raspberry Financiers

- Preheat the oven to 180°C (160° fan) / 350F / gas 4.
- Brown the butter in a saucepan until nutty in aroma.
- Strain through a fine sieve into a clean bowl, allowing it to cool.
- Combine the flour, almonds and sugar in a mixing bowl.
- Gently whisk the egg whites into this mixture and then fold through the cooled, melted butter.
- Chill for 30 minutes.
- Grease a 12-hole fluted bundt tin with unsalted butter.
- Arrange a few raspberries in each before pouring the batter into the moulds.
- Bake for 15-18 minutes until golden brown at the edges and risen.
- Remove from the oven and garnish with the flaked almonds.

Raspberry and Pistachio Financiers

57

- Fold 100 g / 3 ½ oz / 1 cup pistachios into the financier batter before spooning into the moulds.

PREPARATION TIME 10 MINUTES

COOKING TIME 15 MINUTES

INGREDIENTS

110 g / 4 oz / ½ cup caster (superfine) sugar
110 g / 4 oz / ½ cup slightly salted butter, softened
1 tbsp unsalted butter, softened
110 g / 4 oz / 1 cup ground almonds
30 g / 1 oz / 2 tbsp plain (all purpose) flour, sifted
3 medium egg whites
a pinch of salt
150 g / 5 oz / 1 ½ cups raspberries

TO GARNISH
30 g / 1 oz / 2 tbsp flaked (slivered) almonds

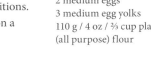

58

MAKES 4

Moist Chocolate Sponges

- Preheat the oven to 190°C (170° fan) / 375F / gas 5.
- Brush 4, 4" dariole moulds with a little melted butter.
- Chill for 15 mins then brush with another layer of melted butter.
- Dust the insides with cocoa powder then chill.
- Melt the chocolate and unsalted butter in a heatproof mixing bowl set atop a saucepan of simmering water.
- Once melted remove from the heat, stir, and cool.
- Whisk the eggs and yolks in a mixing bowl until thick.
- Sift the plain flour into the eggs and whisk until smooth.
- Pour the melted chocolate and butter mixture into the egg and flour in thirds, mixing well between additions.
- Spoon the batter evenly into the moulds and sit on a baking tray.
- Bake for 12-14 minutes until the tops are set.
- Remove and serve warm.

White and Dark Chocolate Sponges

59

- Chop 100 g / 3 ½ oz / ⅔ cup white chocolate and fold into the batter.

PREPARATION TIME 10 MINUTES

COOKING TIME 15 MINUTES

INGREDIENTS

30 g / 1 oz / 2 tbsp butter, melted
110 g / 4 oz / ⅔ cup good-quality dark chocolate, chopped
110 g / 4 oz / ½ cup unsalted butter, cubed
50 g / 2 oz / ⅓ cup good-quality cocoa powder
2 medium eggs
3 medium egg yolks
110 g / 4 oz / ⅔ cup plain (all purpose) flour

60
SERVES 4
Crunchy Pistachio Millefeuille

PREPARATION TIME 15 MINUTES

COOKING TIME 15 MINUTES

INGREDIENTS

FOR THE MILLEFEUILLE
110 g / 4 oz / ½ cup caster (superfine) sugar
100 g / 3 ½ oz / ⅔ cup plain (all purpose) flour
a few drops of vanilla extract
30 g / 1 oz / 2 tbsp unsalted butter, softened
2 medium egg whites

FOR THE PISTACHIO FILLING
375 ml / 13 fl. oz / 1 ½ cups crème fraîche
225 g / 8 oz / 1 ⅔ cups pistachios, shelled
65 g / 2 ½ oz / ½ cup icing (confectioners') sugar

TO GARNISH
1 tbsp pistachios, shelled and chopped

- Preheat the oven to 180°C (160° fan) / 350F / gas 4.
- Grease and line 2 baking trays with greaseproof paper.
- Beat the butter, vanilla extract and sugar in a mixing bowl until fluffy.
- Beat in the egg whites until incorporated, then sift in the flour and beat again until smooth.
- Spoon tablespoons of the mixture onto the baking trays and spread into circle shapes; you should aim for 24 rounds.
- Bake for 8-10 minutes until golden.
- Remove from the oven and let them cool on the trays.
- Pulse together the pistachios and icing sugar for the filling in a food processor.
- Remove to a bowl and fold in with the creme fraîche.
- Sandwich the tuiles on plates with the pistachio filling finishing with a tuile on top.
- Garnish with chopped pistachio on top before serving.

Crunchy Walnut Millefeuille

61

- Replace the pistachios with the same weight of chopped walnuts; add an additional 30 g / 1 oz / ¼ cup icing sugar to the filling.

62
MAKES 8
Orange Financiers

PREPARATION TIME 10 MINUTES

COOKING TIME 45 MINUTES

INGREDIENTS

FOR THE FINANCIERS
110 g / 4 oz / ½ cup caster (superfine) sugar
110 g / 4 oz / ½ cup slightly salted butter, softened
1 tbsp unsalted butter, softened
110 g / 4 oz / 1 cup ground almonds
30 g / 1 oz / 2 tbsp plain (all purpose) flour, sifted
2 large egg whites
1 orange, juiced and zested
1 tbsp Cointreau (optional)
a pinch of salt

TO GARNISH
candied orange slices

- Preheat the oven to 180°C (160° fan) / 350F / gas 4.
- Brown the butter in a saucepan.
- Strain through a fine sieve into a clean bowl, allowing it to cool.
- Combine the flour, almonds and sugar in a bowl.
- Gently whisk the egg whites into this mixture and then fold through the cooled, melted butter, orange juice, orange zest and Cointreau if using.
- Chill for 30 minutes.
- Grease 8 individual heart-shaped ramekins with the unsalted butter.
- Pour the batter into the moulds and bake for 18-20 minutes until golden-brown and risen.
- Remove from the oven and transfer to a wire rack.
- Turn out the financiers before garnishing with candied orange slices.

Orange and Lemon Financiers

63

- Replace half of the orange juice with lemon juice and half of the Cointreau with limoncello.

64

MAKES 4

Mini Lemon Tarts

Lemon and Lime Tarts 65

- Replace 125 ml / 4 ½ fl. oz / ½ cup of lemon juice with lime juice. Garnish with lime and lemon slices.

Chocolate Topped Lemon Tarts 66

- Sprinkle 2 tsp of grated white chocolate on top of the tarts.

PREPARATION TIME 10-15 MINUTES

COOKING TIME 20-25 MINUTES

INGREDIENTS

250 g / 9 oz ready-made shortcrust pastry
a little plain (all purpose) flour, for dusting
225 g / 8 oz / 1 cup caster (superfine) sugar
30 g / 1 oz / 2 tbsp cornflour (cornstarch)
250 ml / 9 fl. oz / 1 cup lemon juice
150 ml / 5 fl. oz / ⅔ cup water
175 g / 6 oz / ¾ cup butter, cubed
6 medium egg yolks
2 medium eggs

TO GARNISH
½ lemon, sliced thinly

- Preheat the oven to 180°C (160° fan) / 350F / gas 4.
- Roll the pastry out on a floured surface.
- Cut 4 rounds of pastry to line 4 5" tartlet cases.
- Prick the bases with a fork and trim any excess pastry.
- Line with greaseproof paper and fill with baking beans.
- Blind-bake for 12-15 minutes until golden at the edges.
- Remove from the oven and discard the greaseproof paper and baking beans.
- Return to the oven for 3-4 minutes to brown the base before removing to a wire rack.
- Combine the cornflour, sugar and in a saucepan.
- Gradually add the lemon juice, whisking simultaneously, then the water.
- Cook over a medium heat, stirring until thickened.
- Once the mixture starts to bubble, remove from the heat and beat in the butter by the cube.
- Whisk together the eggs and egg yolks in a separate jug and beat into the mixture.
- Return to the heat and stir constantly for a 4-6 minutes until the mixture drops from a spoon with a light tap.
- Remove from the heat and cool before spooning into the tart cases.
- Garnish with a lemon slice.

Melon and Chocolate Tartlets

67

MAKES 4

PREPARATION TIME 15 MINUTES

COOKING TIME 15 MINUTES

INGREDIENTS

200 g / 7 oz ready-made shortcrust pastry
a little plain (all purpose) flour, for dusting
250 g / 9 oz / 1 ⅔ cups good-quality dark chocolate, chopped
175 ml / 6 fl. oz / ¾ cup double (heavy) cream
½ Honeydew melon, peeled and sliced

TO GARNISH
1 tbsp desiccated coconut

- Preheat the oven to 180°C (160° fan) / 350F / gas 4.
- Roll the pastry out on a lightly floured surface to ½ cm thickness.
- Cut out 4 rounds of pastry and use to line 4 individual 4" fluted tartlet cases.
- Prick the bases with a fork and trim any excess, overhanging pastry.
- Line with greaseproof paper and fill with baking beans before blind-baking for 12-15 minutes until golden at the edges.
- Remove from the oven and discard the greaseproof paper and baking beans.
- Return to the oven for 3-4 minutes to brown the base before removing to a wire rack to cool.
- Heat the cream in a saucepan until boiling, remove from the heat, and whisk in the chocolate until smooth and thick.
- Pour into the tarts and layer the melon slices in the middle, overlapping slightly.
- Garnish with desiccated coconut before serving.

Mini Banana and Coconut Tart

68

MAKES 4

PREPARATION TIME 10-15 MINUTES

COOKING TIME 15 MINUTES

INGREDIENTS

250 g / 9 oz ready-made shortcrust pastry
a little plain (all purpose) flour, for dusting
110 g / 4 oz / 1 cup ground almonds
75 g / 3 oz / 1 cup desiccated coconut
110 g / 4 oz / ½ cup caster (superfine) sugar
110 g / 4 oz / ½ cup unsalted butter
2 small eggs
2 small egg whites
1 large banana, peeled and diced

TO GARNISH
1 tbsp desiccated coconut
1 tbsp icing (confectioners') sugar

- Preheat the oven to 180°C (160° fan) / 350F / gas 4.
- Roll the pastry out on a lightly floured surface to ½ cm thickness.
- Cut out 4 rounds of pastry and use to line 4 individual 5" fluted tart cases.
- Prick the bases with a fork and trim any excess, overhanging pastry with a serrated knife.
- Chill until needed.
- Blitz together the ground almonds, desiccated coconut, sugar and butter in a food processor until creamy.
- Add the egg and egg white and pulse again to incorporate.
- Spoon into the pastry and bake for 30-35 minutes until the edge of the pastry is golden brown in colour and the filling is puffed up.
- Remove the tarts from the oven and let them cool on a wire rack.
- Preheat the grill to hot.
- Top the tarts with banana and sprinkle with a little icing sugar before grilling for 1 minute.
- Remove and garnish with desiccated coconut before serving.

Mini Grape Tart

- Preheat the oven to 180°C (160° fan) / 350F / gas 4.
- Roll the pastry out on a lightly floured surface.
- Cut out 4 rounds of pastry and use to line 4 individual 5" tartlet cases.
- Prick the bases and trim excess pastry.
- Line with greaseproof paper and fill with baking beans before blind-baking for 12-15 minutes until golden.
- Remove from the oven and discard the greaseproof paper and baking beans.
- Return to the oven for 3-4 minutes to brown the base before removing to a wire rack to cool.
- Warm the grape jelly with 2 tbsp cold water in a saucepan set over medium heat.
- Add the grapes, swirl to coat in the liquid, then spoon into the tarts before serving.

PREPARATION TIME 10 MINUTES

COOKING TIME 15 MINUTES

INGREDIENTS

250 g / 9 oz ready-made shortcrust pastry
a little plain (all purpose) flour, for dusting
150 g / 5 oz / 1 ⅓ cups white seedless grapes
150 g / 5 oz / 1 ⅓ cups black seedless grapes
150 g / 5 oz / 1 ⅓ cups red seedless grapes
2 tbsp grape jelly
2 tbsp cold water

Almond Plum Tartlet

PREPARATION TIME 15 MINUTES

COOKING TIME 10 MINUTES

INGREDIENTS

900 g / 2 lb / 6 cups plums, de-stoned and halved
225 g / 8 oz / 1 cup caster (superfine) sugar
55 g / 2 oz / ⅓ cup plain (all purpose) flour
250 ml / 9 fl. oz / 1 cup whole milk
250 ml / 9 fl. oz / 1 cup double (heavy) cream
4 large egg yolks
4 large eggs
1 tbsp cherry brandy (optional)

- Preheat the oven to 160°C (140° fan) / 325F / gas 3.
- Combine the milk, cream and vanilla pod in a saucepan and simmer for 5 minutes.
- Remove from the heat and allow the flavours to infuse.
- In a large bowl, whisk together the egg yolks and eggs until light and frothy.
- Add the sugar and whisk until well blended.
- Fold in the flour and remove the vanilla pod from the milk.
- Gradually add to the egg mixture and whisk until smooth, then set to one side.
- Add the cherry brandy if using at this point.
- Pour the batter 4 individual fluted ramekins and stud with plum halves.
- Bake for 30-35 minutes until the filling is set and golden on top.
- Remove from the oven and serve hot.

Chocolate Madeleines

PREPARATION TIME 10 MINUTES

COOKING TIME 10 MINUTES

INGREDIENTS

125 g / 4 ½ oz / 1 cup icing (confectioners') sugar, sifted
125 g / 4 ½ oz / ½ cup unsalted butter, melted and cooled
100 g / 3 ½ oz / 1 cup plain (all purpose) flour, sifted
100 g / 3 ½ oz / ½ cup dark chocolate chips
½ tsp baking powder
½ tsp vanilla extract
a pinch of salt

- Preheat the oven to 180°C (160° fan) / 350F / gas 4.
- Grease a 12-hole madeleine tray.
- Beat together the eggs, icing sugar, salt and vanilla extract in a large mixing bowl with until thick and shiny.
- Add the flour, 25 g at a time, to the mixture, as well as the baking powder and fold in gently.
- Once all the flour has been incorporated, fold in the melted butter and then the chocolate chips.
- Spoon into the moulds, leaving them about three-quarters full with the batter.
- Bake for 12-14 minutes until golden and risen.
- Remove and allow them to cool in the tray for a few minutes before turning out onto a wire rack to finish cooling.
- Serve warm or cold.

72

MAKES 4

Chocolate and Coffee Tartlet

PREPARATION TIME 10 MINUTES

COOKING TIME 10-15 MINUTES

INGREDIENTS

200 g / 7 oz ready-made shortcrust pastry
a little plain (all purpose) flour, for dusting
200 g / 7 oz / 1 ⅓ cups good-quality dark chocolate, chopped
100 g / 3 ½ oz / ⅔ cup plain (all purpose) flour
55 g / 2 oz / ¼ cup unsalted butter
55 ml / 2 fl. oz / ¼ cup strong espresso
2 medium eggs

TO GARNISH

2 tbsp flaked (slivered) almonds
1 tsp icing (confectioners') sugar

- Preheat the oven to 180°C (160° fan) / 350F / gas 4.
- Roll the pastry out on a lightly floured surface to ½ cm thickness.
- Cut out 4 rounds and use to line 4 individual 4" fluted tartlet cases, trimming any excess pastry.
- Prick the bases with a fork and chill.
- Place the chocolate, espresso and butter in a heatproof bowl set atop a saucepan of simmering water.
- Stir until melted, remove from the heat and beat in the eggs after 2 minutes.
- Fold in the flour, then divide between the pastry cases.
- Bake for 35-40 minutes until the pastry is golden and the chocolate filling is set.
- Remove from the oven and garnish with flaked almonds and a very light dusting of icing sugar before serving.

Chocolate, Walnut and Coffee Tartlet

73

- Substitute the flaked almond garnish for 2-3 walnut halves on top of each tartlet.

74

SERVES 8

Dark Nougat

PREPARATION TIME 10 MINUTES

COOKING TIME 20-25 MINUTES

INGREDIENTS

750 g / 1 lb 10 ½ oz / 3 ½ cups almonds
500 g / 1 lb 2 oz / 1 ½ cups honey
175 g / 6 oz / ¾ cup caster (superfine) sugar
175 g / 6 oz / 1 ⅙ cups plain (all purpose) flour
175 ml / 6 fl. oz / ¾ cup red wine

ALSO NEEDED

2 12" x 4" rice paper

- Preheat the oven to 180°C (160° fan) / 350F / gas 4.
- Line a large baking tray with greaseproof paper and spread the almonds out on it.
- Toast in the oven for 5 minutes then remove.
- Line a 12" x 4" x 3" cake tin with one sheet of rice paper.
- Cook the honey and sugar in a saucepan for 3-4 minutes, then add the almonds and cook for 6-8 minutes, stirring constantly.
- Stir in the flour and continue to cook until the mixture is amber in colour and hard to stir.
- Stir in the red wine, then pour into the tin.
- Tap to level, then place the rice paper on top.
- Cover with a sheet of 12" x 4" greaseproof paper and weigh down with heavy books.
- Leave to set on a window sill overnight before turning out and cutting into slices.

Dark Raisin Nougat

75

- Substitute half of the almonds with the same weight of raisins.

MAKES 8 # Caramel and Nut Sticky Buns

- Dissolve the caster sugar and the yeast in the warm milk in a saucepan over a low heat.
- Add the salt and half of the flour and beat. Add the eggs and oil and continue beating for 1 minute.
- Add remaining flour until a dough pulls together.
- Turn the dough out and knead for 5-7 minutes.
- Place in an oiled bowl and cover with a tea towel.
- Allow to prove until doubled in size. Once proved, roll out into a log. Lightly oil a 13" x 9" baking tray.
- Cut the dough into 8 and arrange on the tray. Cover again with a tea towel and prove for 45 minutes.
- Preheat the oven to 180°C (160° fan) / 350F / gas 4. Bake for 25-30 minutes.
- Warm the dulce de leche in a saucepan, then add the walnuts.
- Drizzle over the rolls.

Pecan and Cinnamon Sticky Buns 77

- Substitute the walnuts for pecan halves and add ½ tsp ground cinnamon to the nut sauce before using.

PREPARATION TIME 10 MINUTES

COOKING TIME 45 MINUTES

INGREDIENTS

750 g / 1 lb 10 ½ oz / 5 cups plain (all purpose) flour
425 ml / 15 fl. oz / 1 ¾ cups whole milk, warmed to 45°C
110 g / 4 oz / ½ cup caster (superfine) sugar
55 ml / 2 fl. oz / ¼ cup vegetable oil
2 medium eggs
12 g dried active yeast
2 tsp salt

TO GARNISH

250 g / 9 oz / 1 cup dulce de leche
225 g / 8 oz / 2 cups walnut halves, roughly chopped

SERVES 6 # Sliced Chocolate and Almond Cake

- Preheat the oven to 180°C (160° fan) / 350F / gas 4.
- Grease and line a 2 lb circular loaf tin with greaseproof paper.
- Combine the flour, sugar, margarine, cocoa powder, eggs and salt in a large mixing bowl.
- Beat thoroughly until smooth; 2-3 minutes.
- Add the chopped almonds and fold through.
- Spoon into the loaf tin and bake for 40-45 minutes; test with a wooden toothpick, if it comes out clean, the cake is done.
- Remove from the oven and let the cake cool before turning out and slicing.
- Serve warm or cold.

Chocolate, Date and Almond Cake 79

- Stir a large handful of pitted dates into the batter before baking.

PREPARATION TIME 10 MINUTES

COOKING TIME 10 MINUTES

INGREDIENTS

150g / 5 oz / 1 cup self-raising flour
150 g / 5 oz / ⅔ cup margarine, softened
150 g / 5 oz / ⅔ cup golden caster (superfine) sugar
55 g / 2 oz / ⅓ cup good-quality cocoa powder
75 ml / 3 fl. oz / ⅓ cup whole milk
55 g / 2 oz / ¼ cup almonds, chopped
3 large eggs
a pinch of salt

80

MAKES 4

Rhubarb Meringue Pie

Blackberry Meringue Pies

81

- Toss 200 g / 7 oz / 2 cups blackberries with 55 g / 2 oz / ¼ cup of caster sugar and leave to macerate for 15 minutes before using in place of rhubarb.

Blueberry and Rhubarb Meringue Pie

82

- Replace 100 g rhubarb with blueberries and add before topping with meringue.

PREPARATION TIME 10-15 MINUTES

COOKING TIME 20-25 MINUTES

INGREDIENTS

FOR THE PASTRY AND FILLING
250 g / 9 oz ready-made shortcrust pastry
a little plain (all purpose) flour, for dusting
675 g / 1 lb 8 oz / 5 cups rhubarb, trimmed and sliced
75 g / 3 oz / ⅓ cup caster (superfine) sugar
60 ml / 2 fl. oz / ¼ cup cold water

FOR THE MERINGUE
2 medium egg whites
110 g / 4 oz / ½ cup caster (superfine) sugar
¼ tsp cream of tartar
a pinch of salt

TO GARNISH
1 tbsp icing (confectioners') sugar

- Preheat the oven to 180°C (160° fan) / 350F / gas 4.
- Roll the pastry out on a lightly floured surface.
- Cut out 4 rounds of pastry and line 4 5" fluted cases.
- Prick the bases and trim excess pastry.
- Line with greaseproof paper and fill with baking beans before blind-baking for 12-15 minutes until golden.
- Remove from the oven, discard greaseproof paper and baking beans then return to the oven for 3-4 minutes..
- Remove to a wire rack to cool.
- Combine the rhubarb, sugar and water in a saucepan and cook over a medium heat, covered, until soft.
- Drain and cool to one side.
- Whisk the egg whites with the salt in a large, clean mixing bowl until soft peaks form.
- Add the cream of tartar and the sugar, 1 tablespoon at a time, beating well until you have a glossy meringue. Spoon into a piping bag.
- Increase the oven to 220°C (200° fan) / 425F / gas 7.
- Fill the pastry with the rhubarb and pipe the meringue on top in blobs.
- Bake for 8-10 minutes until the meringue is browned, then remove from the oven.
- Dust with icing sugar before serving.

83

MAKES 4

Salted Butter Caramel Toffee Apples

- Combine the condensed milk, sugar and butter in a saucepan.
- Cook the mixture over a medium heat, until simmering, stirring until the sugar has dissolved.
- Continue to cook the caramel until thickened and golden brown in colour.
- Remove from the heat and season to taste using the sea salt.
- Line a baking tray with a sheet of greaseproof paper.
- Pour the crushed biscuit into a tall cup and pour the caramel into a tall jug.
- Skewer the apples with the lolly sticks then dunk into the caramel, halfway.
- Coat the caramel with the crushed biscuit before leaving to set on the greaseproof paper.
- Serve once the caramel has set.

PREPARATION TIME 10 MINUTES

COOKING TIME 10 MINUTES

INGREDIENTS

4 Braeburn apples
400 g / 14 oz / 1 ⅔ cups condensed milk
110 g / 4 oz / ½ cup golden caster (superfine) sugar
110 g / 4 oz / ½ cup salted butter
½ tsp of flaked sea salt

TO GARNISH
75 g / 3 oz / ½ cup digestive (graham cracker) biscuits, crushed

ALSO NEEDED
4 wooden lolly sticks

Salted Butter Caramel Toffee Pears

 84

- Use 4 Conference pears instead of the apples.

85

MAKES 24

Raspberry and Pistachio Financiers

- Preheat the oven to 180°C (160° fan) / 350F / gas 4.
- Brown the butter in a saucepan until lightly nutty in aroma.
- Strain through a fine sieve into a clean bowl, allowing it to cool.
- Combine the flour, almonds and sugar in a mixing bowl.
- Gently whisk the egg whites into this mixture and then fold through the cooled, melted butter.
- Chill for 30 minutes.
- Grease 2, 12-hole financier tins with unsalted butter.
- Pour the batter into the moulds, dot each with 2 raspberries and 4-5 pistachios.
- Bake for 12-15 minutes until golden brown at the edges and risen.
- Remove from the oven and cool on a wire rack before serving.

PREPARATION TIME 10-15 MINUTES

COOKING TIME 15 MINUTES

INGREDIENTS

110 g / 4 oz / ½ cup caster (superfine) sugar
110 g / 4 oz / ½ cup slightly salted butter, softened
1 tbsp unsalted butter, softened
110 g / 4 oz / 1 cup ground almonds
30 g / 1 oz / 2 tbsp plain (all purpose) flour, sifted
3 medium egg whites
a pinch of salt
220 g / 8 oz / 2 cups raspberries
100 g / 3 ½ oz / ⅔ cup pistachios, shelled

Redcurrant Financiers

 **86**

- Omit the pistachios and use redcurrants instead of raspberries in the financier batter.

SERVES 4

Sponge and Gingerbread Ice-Cream

87

PREPARATION TIME 10 MINUTES

COOKING TIME 15 MINUTES

FREEZING TIME: 2 HOURS

INGREDIENTS

FOR THE ICE-CREAM
500 ml / 18 fl. oz / 2 cups good-quality vanilla ice-cream, softened
150 g / 5 oz / 1 cup ready-made gingerbread, chopped

FOR THE SPONGE FINGERS
110 g / 4 oz / ⅔ cup self-raising flour
110 g / 4 oz / ½ cup caster (superfine) sugar
110 g / 4 oz / ½ cup margarine
2 large eggs
½ tsp vanilla extract
¼ tsp ground ginger

- Preheat the oven to 180°C (160° fan) / 350F / gas 4.
- Grease a 12-hole sponge finger mould.
- Combine all the ingredients for the sponge fingers in a large mixing bowl and beat until smooth; approximately 2-3 minutes.
- Spoon the batter into the mould and bake for 15-18 minutes; test with a wooden toothpick, if it comes out clean, the cake is done.
- Remove from the oven and leave to cool on a wire rack.
- Place the softened ice-cream in a food processor and pulse until smooth and creamy.
- Add the chopped gingerbread and pulse again until combined.
- Spoon into a freezer tub and freeze for at least 2 hours before serving with the sponge fingers.

Marsala and Gingerbread Ice-Cream

88

- Soak the sponge fingers in Marsala before serving with the ice cream.

SERVES 4

Hazelnut Cream Chouqettes

89

PREPARATION TIME 10-15 MINUTES

COOKING TIME 20-25 MINUTES

INGREDIENTS

FOR THE CHOUQUETTES
110 g / 4 oz / ⅔ cup plain (all purpose) flour
110 g / 4 oz / ½ cup unsalted butter, cold and cubed
250 ml / 9 fl. oz / 1 cup whole milk
4 large eggs
1 tsp caster (superfine) sugar

FOR THE CHOCOLATE TOPPING
225 g / 8 oz / 1 ½ cups good-quality dark chocolate, chopped
55 g / 2 oz / ¼ cup unsalted butter

FOR THE BUTTERCREAM
500 g / 1 lb 2 oz / 4 cups icing (confectioners') sugar
450 g / 1 lb / 2 cups butter, softened
200 g / 7 oz / 2 cups hazelnuts (cob nuts), blanched

- Sift together flour and sugar in a mixing bowl. Combine the butter and milk in a saucepan.
- Add the flour and stir until a smooth dough forms. Beat the dough until it pulls away from the saucepan.
- Remove from the heat and add the eggs, one at a time, beating well until shiny. Spoon into a piping bag.
- Preheat the oven to 200°C (180° fan) / 400F / gas 6.
- Grease and line 2 baking trays with greaseproof paper. Pipe blobs of the pastry onto the sheets, spaced apart.
- Bake for 15-18 minutes then remove to a wire rack.
- Melt the butter and chocolate in a heatproof bowl.
- Blitz the hazelnuts in a food processor, add the butter and blitz until smooth. Add the icing sugar in two batches, pulsing until smooth.
- Remove the tops of the buns, fill with buttercream and reassemble. Top with the chocolate sauce.

Almond Cream Chouquettes

90

- Substitute the hazelnuts for flaked (slivered) almonds in the buttercream.

91

MAKES 8

Chocolate and Pink Peppercorn Tartlets

Chocolate and Chilli Tartlets

92

- Substitute the crushed peppercorn garnish for a pinch of chilli (chili) powder on each tartlet.

Salted Chocolate Tartlets

93

- Garnish with a generous pinch of flaked sea salt before chilling.

PREPARATION TIME 10-15 MINUTES

COOKING TIME 15-20 MINUTES

....

INGREDIENTS

300 g / 10 ½ oz / 2 cups plain (all purpose) flour
a little extra plain flour, for dusting
50 g / 2 oz / ⅓ cup cornflour (cornstarch)
225 g / 8 oz / 1 cup unsalted butter
75 g / 3 oz / 1 cup icing (confectioners') sugar
a pinch of salt
200 g / 7 oz / 1 ⅓ cups good-quality dark chocolate, chopped
55 g / 2 oz / ⅓ cup plain (all purpose) flour
55 g / 2 oz / ¼ cup unsalted butter
2 medium eggs
¼ tsp pink peppercorns, ground
1 tbsp pink peppercorns, crushed
2 tbsp chocolate curls

- Pulse together the flour, cornflour, salt, icing sugar, lemon zest and butter in a food processor until it comes together to form a dough.
- Remove the dough, knead gently and form into a ball.
- Wrap in clingfilm and chill for 60 minutes.
- Preheat the oven to 180°C (160° fan) / 350F / gas 4.
- Remove the dough from the fridge and divide into 12.
- Roll out on a lightly floured surface to ½ cm thickness and use to line a 12-hole fluted financier mould.
- Bake for 12-15 minutes until lightly coloured then remove from the oven and let them cool in the mould.
- Place the chocolate and butter in a heatproof bowl set atop a saucepan of simmering water.
- Stir until melted, remove from the heat and beat in the eggs after 2 minutes.
- Fold in the flour and ground pepper, then pour into the shortbread cases.
- Chill until set then garnish with the crushed peppercorns and chocolate curls before serving.

94

SERVES 8

Strawberry Nougat

PREPARATION TIME 15 MINUTES

COOKING TIME 20 MINUTES

INGREDIENTS

FOR THE STRAWBERRY
NOUGAT

275 g / 10 oz / 1 ¼ cups caster
(superfine) sugar
250 g / 9 oz / 1 cup glucose
100 g / 3 ⅓ oz / 1 cup whole almonds,
blanched
50 ml / 2 fl. oz / ¼ cup cold water
1 large egg white, at room
temperature
1 tsp strawberry flavouring / extract

ALSO NEEDED

sugar thermometer
electric whisk/mixer

- Preheat the oven to 160°C (140° fan) / 325F / gas 3.
- Grease and line a 8" x 4" x 2" pan with greaseproof paper.
- Combine the sugar, water and glucose in a saucepan, cooking over a medium heat.
- Beat the egg white in a separate mixing bowl until soft peaks form.
- Once the sugar mixture reaches 136-138°C, remove from the heat and beat into the egg white.
- Keep whisking for 2-3 minutes until thick and glossy.
- Stir in the almonds and vanilla extract, then spoon into the pan, levelling the mixture with a wet spoon.
- Cover with a sheet of oiled greaseproof and gently weigh down; leave the nougat to set for at least 6 hours.

Chocolate Nougat

95

- Substitute the strawberry flavouring for concentrated chocolate flavouring.

96

MAKES 4

Brownie Tartlets with Mixed Berries

PREPARATION TIME 10-15
MINUTES

COOKING TIME 15 MINUTES

INGREDIENTS

175 g / 6 oz / 1 ¼ cups good-quality
dark chocolate, chopped
110 g / 4 oz / ½ cup unsalted butter
110 g / 4 oz / ½ cup caster (superfine)
sugar
110 g / 4 oz / ⅔ cup plain
(all purpose) flour
3 large eggs
1 tsp baking powder
a pinch of salt

TO GARNISH

250 ml / 9 fl. oz / 1 cup vanilla ice-
cream, softened
100 g / 3 ½ oz / 1 cup blueberries
100 g / 3 ½ oz / 1 cup raspberries
100 g / 3 ½ oz / 1 cup redcurrants
80 g / 3 oz / ¾ cup strawberries,
hulled and diced
2 tbsp icing (confectioners') sugar

- Preheat the oven to 160°C (140° fan) / 325F / gas 3.
- Grease 4 round straight-sided cake moulds.
- Melt the chocolate and butter together in a saucepan over a medium-low heat, stirring occasionally.
- Remove from the heat and allow to cool.
- In a large mixing bowl, whisk the eggs until thick then add the sugar and continue to whisk until glossy.
- Beat in the melted chocolate mixture, then fold in the flour and baking powder until incorporated.
- Pour into the moulds and tap to release air bubbles.
- Bake for 30-35 minutes.
- Dust the sides with icing sugar and arrange on plates.
- Top with a mixture of the berries, leaving 4 raspberries.
- Quenelle scoops of ice cream between two tablespoons and sit on top of the fruit. Top the ice cream with a raspberry.

Walnut Brownie Tartlets
with Berries

97

- Stir 75 g / 3 oz / ¾ cup walnut halves into the brownie batter before baking.

98

SERVES 4

Chocolate and Pistachio Nests

- Finely grind 100 g of the pistachios in a food processor.
- Place a small upturned sieve on a lined baking tray.
- Melt the chocolate in a heatproof bowl set atop a saucepan of simmering water.
- Stir occasionally until melted then remove from the heat and let it cool for 1 minute.
- Drizzle the melted chocolate in a circular motion on top of the sieve until you have a rough nest shape.
- Let the chocolate set before removing it.
- Repeat for the remaining nests.
- Once you have 4 set nests, brush the dark chocolate mini eggs with glucose using a damp pastry brush, then roll in the ground pistachios to coat.
- Fill the base of the nests with the remaining shelled pistachios and top with the pistachio and chocolate eggs and white chocolate fish before serving.

Mini Egg Nests

99

- Fill each chocolate nest with 1 tablespoon of mini chocolate eggs instead of pistachios and chocolate fish.

PREPARATION TIME 10-15 MINUTES

COOKING TIME 20 MINUTES

INGREDIENTS

300 g / 10 ½ oz / 2 cups good-quality dark chocolate, chopped
100 g / 3 ½ oz / ⅔ cup pistachios, shelled

TO GARNISH

200 g / 7 oz / 1 ⅓ cups dark chocolate mini eggs
100 g / 3 ½ oz / ½ cup liquid glucose, warmed
100 g / 3 ½ oz / 1 cup pistachios, shelled
50 g / 2 oz / ⅓ cup white chocolate fish

100

MAKES 12

Pistachio and Passionfruit Macaroons

- Preheat the oven to 180°C (160° fan) / 350F / gas 4. Grease and line 2 baking trays with greaseproof paper.
- Combine the ground almonds, cocoa powder and icing sugar in a large mixing bowl.
- Beat the egg whites with salt until stiff peaks form.
- Fold the egg whites into the ground almond mixture then spoon into piping a bag. Pipe 24 3-4 cm rounds onto the baking trays.
- Sprinkle with chopped pistachios, leave for 15 minutes, then bake for 8-10 minutes until just set and allow to cool.
- Melt the chocolate and butter in a heatproof bowl set atop a saucepan of simmering water.
- Remove and cool before blitzing with the butter in a food processor.
- Spread half the macaroons with the filling and sandwich with the other halves.

Chocolate, Hazelnut and Passionfruit Macaroons

101

- Substitute the pistachios for chopped blanched hazelnuts (cob nuts).

PREPARATION TIME 15 MINUTES

COOKING TIME 20-25 MINUTES

INGREDIENTS

FOR THE MACAROONS
225 g / 8 oz / 1 ¾ cups icing (confectioners') sugar, sifted
150 g / 5 oz / 2 cups ground almonds
30 g / 1 oz / 2 tbsp good-quality cocoa powder, sifted
55 g / 2 oz / ⅓ cup pistachios, shelled
2 medium egg whites
a pinch of salt

FOR THE FILLING
300 g / 10 ½ oz / 2 cups good-quality dark chocolate, chopped
125 ml / 4 ½ fl. oz / ½ cup passionfruit puree
225 g / 8 oz / 1 cup butter, softened

102

MAKES 24

Apricot Confit Tartlets

Plum Confit Tartlets   103

- Substitute the apricots in the tartlets for pitted halved plums.

Cinnamon Apricot Tartlets   104

- Add 1 tsp ground cinnamon when cooking the apricots for a spicy finish.

PREPARATION TIME 10 MINUTES

COOKING TIME 20-25 MINUTES

INGREDIENTS

24 ready-made mini tartlet cases
12 apricots
500 ml / 18 fl. oz / 2 cups cold water
225 g / 8 oz / 1 cup caster (superfine) sugar
30 ml / 1 fl. oz / 2 tbsp apricot brandy (optional)

- Blanche the apricots in a saucepan of boiling water.
- Refresh in a bowl of iced water, then peel, halve and de-stone.
- Combine the sugar, water and brandy if using in a saucepan.
- Cook over a medium heat, stirring until the sugar has dissolved then add the apricot halves and simmer until the liquid is syrupy and reduced.
- Let the apricots cool before spooning into the tartlet cases.

105

SERVES 8

Dark Chocolate and Pistachio Marquise

- Melt the chocolate in a heatproof bowl set atop a saucepan of simmering water, stirring until melted.
- Beat together the butter and half of the sugar in a separate bowl until light and creamy.
- Add the cocoa powder and beat again.
- Beat together the egg yolks with the remaining sugar in a separate mixing bowl until pale and thick.
- Whip the cream in another bowl until soft peaks form.
- Pour the cooled chocolate into the butter and sugar mixture, stirring until well combined.
- Fold through the egg mixture, then the whipped cream.
- Line a shallow 2 lb loaf tin with clingfilm before spooning the mixture into it. Level the top and sprinkle with the chopped pistachios.
- Cover with clingfilm before chilling overnight.
- Cut into portions using a hot knife.

PREPARATION TIME 10-15 MINUTES

COOKING TIME 15 MINUTES

INGREDIENTS

225 g / 8 oz / 1 ½ cups good-quality dark chocolate, chopped
110 g / 4 oz / ½ cup caster (superfine) sugar
110 g / 4 oz / ½ cup unsalted butter, softened
30 g / 1 oz / 2 tbsp cocoa powder
4 medium egg yolks
4 medium egg whites
325 ml / 11 fl. oz / 1 ⅓ cups double (heavy) cream
75 g / 3 oz / ½ cup pistachios, shelled and chopped

Dark Chocolate and Raspberry Marquise

106

- Sprinkle raspberries on top of the marquise before setting instead of pistachios.

107

MAKES 4

Peach and Apricot Sweet Pizzas

- Preheat the oven to 180°C (160° fan) / 350F / gas 4.
- Grease and line a baking tray with greaseproof paper.
- Roll the pastry out on a lightly floured work surface to ½ cm thickness.
- Cut out 4 rounds approximately 4" in diameter.
- Transfer to the baking tray and bake for 12-15 minutes until lightly golden in colour.
- Remove from the oven and brush with melted butter, then arrange the fruit slices in a fan shape on top.
- Dust with sugar and return to the oven for 2-3 minutes.
- Remove from the oven and season with the black pepper before serving.

PREPARATION TIME 10 MINUTES

COOKING TIME 10-15 MINUTES

INGREDIENTS

200 g / 7 oz ready-made sweet shortcrust pastry
a little plain (all purpose) flour, for dusting
2 peaches, halved, de-stoned and sliced into segments
2 apricots, halved, de-stoned and sliced into segments
2 tbsp unsalted butter, melted
2 tbsp caster (superfine) sugar
¼ tsp finely ground black pepper

Sweet Strawberry Pizzas

108

- Substitute the peaches and apricots for sliced strawberries on the pizzas.

109

MAKES 12

Fruit and Nuts Mendiants

PREPARATION TIME 5-10
MINUTES

COOKING TIME 15 MINUTES

INGREDIENTS

110 g / 4 oz / ⅔ cup plain
(all purpose) flour, sifted
110 g / 4 oz / ½ cup unsalted butter
55 g / 2 oz / icing (confectioners')
sugar
55 g / 2 oz / ⅓ cup cocoa powder
100 g / 3 ½ oz / 1 cup blanched
almonds
75 g / 3 oz / ¾ cup hazelnuts
(cob nuts)
75 g / 3 oz / ½ cup pistachios,
shelled and chopped
55 g / 2 oz / ⅓ cup dried figs,
chopped
30 g / 1 oz / 2 tbsp raisins
30 g / 1 oz / 2 tbsp candied peel
1 large egg
½ tsp vanilla extract

- Mix together the icing sugar, cocoa powder and flour.
- Rub the butter into this mixture.
- Add the egg and vanilla extract and mix until a stiff dough forms. Gather up and roll into a log shape.
- Wrap in greaseproof paper and chill in the fridge.
- Grease and line a couple of baking trays with greaseproof paper.
- Preheat the oven to 180°C (160° fan) / 350F / gas 4.
- Grease and line a couple of baking trays with greaseproof paper.
- Cut 1 cm thick cookies out of the cookie dough.
- Arrange spaced out on the lined baking trays and bake for 12-14 minutes until just set.
- Remove from the oven and stud immediately with a mixture of the nuts and dried fruit before they harden.
- Let them cool before serving.

Candied Citrus Mendiants

 110

- Substitute the nuts, figs and raisins for and extra 150 g / 5 oz / 1 cup candied mixed peel.

111

MAKES 4

Lemon and Strawberry Tartlets

PREPARATION TIME 10 MINUTES

COOKING TIME 15 MINUTES

INGREDIENTS

250 g / 9 oz ready-made shortcrust
pastry
a little plain (all purpose) flour,
for dusting
300 g / 10 ½ oz / 3 cups strawberries,
hulled and halved
225 g / 8 oz / 1 cup lemon curd

TO GARNISH
1 tbsp icing (confectioners') sugar

- Preheat the oven to 180°C (160° fan) / 350F / gas 4.
- Roll the pastry out on a lightly floured surface to ½ cm thickness.
- Cut out 4 rounds of pastry and use to line 4 individual 5" fluted tartlet cases.
- Prick the bases with a fork and trim any excess, overhanging pastry.
- Line with greaseproof paper and fill with baking beans before blind-baking for 12-15 minutes until golden at the edges.
- Remove from the oven and discard the greaseproof paper and baking beans.
- Return to the oven for 3-4 minutes to brown the base before removing to a wire rack to cool.
- Once cool, fill with lemon curd and top with the strawberry halves.
- Dust with icing sugar before serving.

Orange and Raspberry Tartlets

112

- Substitute the lemon curd for orange curd and use raspberries instead of strawberries.

MAKES 4 113

Lemon and Chocolate Tarts

Lemon and White Chocolate Tartlets 114

- Substitute the dark chocolate for white chocolate in the sauce.

Lemon Loganberry Tartlets 115

- Replace the lemon zest with loganberries to top the tarts.

PREPARATION TIME 10-15 MINUTES

COOKING TIME 20 MINUTES

INGREDIENTS

225 g / 8 oz ready-made shortcrust pastry
a little plain (all purpose) flour, for dusting
4 medium eggs
1 medium egg yolk
110 g / 4 oz / ½ cup caster (superfine) sugar
425 ml / 15 fl. oz / 1 ¾ cups double (heavy) cream
2 tbsp cornflour
2 lemons, juiced

FOR THE CHOCOLATE SAUCE

150 g / 5 oz / 1 cup good-quality dark chocolate, chopped
125 ml / 4 ½ fl. oz / ½ cup double (heavy) cream

TO GARNISH

1 lemon, zested

- Preheat the oven to 180°C (160° fan) / 350F / gas 4.
- Roll the pastry out on a lightly floured surface.
- Cut out 4 rounds of pastry and line 4 5" tartlet cases.
- Prick the bases and trim excess pastry.
- Line with greaseproof paper and fill with baking beans before blind-baking for 12-15 minutes until golden.
- Remove from the oven and discard the greaseproof paper and baking beans.
- Return to the oven for 3-4 minutes to brown the base before removing to a wire rack to cool.
- Whisk together the eggs, egg yolk, caster sugar and cornflour in a large mixing bowl.
- Add the double cream and lemon juice and stir well.
- Pass through a fine sieve into a jug and pour into the pastry cases.
- Reduce the oven to 150°C (130° fan) / 300F / gas 2 and bake for 30-35 minutes. Remove from the oven to a wire rack.
- Heat the cream in a saucepan until boiling, remove from the heat and whisk in the chocolate until smooth.
- Allow to cool before topping the tarts with it and garnishing with lemon zest.

116

MAKES 16

Chocolate Chip Cookies

PREPARATION TIME 5-10 MINUTES

COOKING TIME 10 MINUTES

....

INGREDIENTS

225 g / 8 oz / 1 ½ cups plain (all purpose) flour, sifted
150 g / 5 oz / ⅔ cup unsalted butter, chilled and cubed
110 g / 4 oz / ½ cup caster (superfine) sugar
175 g / 6 oz / 1 ¼ cups dark chocolate chips
2 medium eggs
½ tsp vanilla extract
½ tsp salt

- Mix the sugar, flour and salt in a mixing bowl.
- Rub the butter into this mixture.
- Add the eggs, dark chocolate chips and vanilla extract and mix until a stiff dough forms.
- Gather up and roll into a log shape.
- Wrap in greaseproof paper and chill in the fridge for at least 30 minutes.
- Grease and line 2 baking trays with greaseproof paper.
- Preheat the oven to 180°C (160° fan) / 350F / gas 4.
- Use a sharp knife to cut ½ cm thick cookies out of the cookie dough.
- Arrange spaced out on the lined baking trays and bake for 10-12 minutes until just set.
- Remove from the oven and allow to cool on the trays before removing carefully to a wire rack to cool.

Chocolate and Raisin Cookies

 117

- Substitute half of the chocolate chips for the same weight of raisins in the cookie dough.

118

MAKES 12

Summer Fruit Cream-Filled Biscuits

PREPARATION TIME 10-15 MINUTES

COOKING TIME 15 MINUTES

....

INGREDIENTS

FOR THE BISCUITS
250 g / 9 oz / 1 ⅔ cups plain (all purpose) flour
a little extra plain flour, for dusting
50 g / 2 oz / ⅓ cup cornflour (cornstarch)
225 g / 8 oz / 1 cup unsalted butter, cubed
90 g / 3 ½ oz / ¾ cup icing (confectioners') sugar
a pinch of salt

FOR THE FILLING
500 ml / 18 fl. oz / 2 cups double (heavy) cream
150 g / 5 oz / ⅔ cup strawberry jam
150 g / 5 oz / ⅔ cup cherry jam

- Pulse together the flour, cornflour, salt, icing sugar and butter in a food processor until it comes together.
- Remove the dough, knead gently and form into a ball. Wrap in clingfilm and chill for 60 minutes.
- Preheat the oven to 180°C (160° fan) / 350F / gas 4.
- Remove the dough from the fridge and roll out on a lightly floured surface to ½ cm thickness.
- Cut out 24 rounds using a 2" diameter cutter.
- Grease and line 2 baking trays with greaseproof paper.
- Arrange on the baking trays and bake for 12-15 minutes.
- Remove to a wire rack to cool.
- Once cool, whip the cream to soft peaks then gently fold in the jams until incorporated.
- Once the biscuits have cooled, spoon 1 tablespoon of cream on top of 12 of the biscuits and use the remaining 12 to sandwich them with.

Lemon Cream-Filled Biscuits

119

- Use 250 g / 9 oz / 1 cup lemon curd instead of the jams in the cream filling.

120
SERVES 4

Passionfruit Chouquettes

- Sift together flour and sugar in a mixing bowl.
- Combine the butter and milk in a saucepan and heat gently until the butter melts.
- Add the flour and stir until a smooth dough forms.
- Beat the dough until it pulls away from the saucepan.
- Remove from the heat and add the eggs, one at a time, beating well between each addition until shiny.
- Spoon the dough into a piping bag.
- Preheat the oven to 200°C (180° fan) / 400F / gas 6.
- Grease and line 2 baking trays with greaseproof paper.
- Pipe blobs of the pastry onto the sheets, spaced apart.
- Dot with the sugar nibs and bake for 15-18 minutes.
- Whip the cream with the icing sugar until soft peaks form; remove the tops of the buns, fill with cream and top with passionfruit pulp.
- Replace the tops and serve on plates.

Orange Croquettes
 121

- Finely dice 1 large segmented orange and use on top of the passionfruit pulp.

PREPARATION TIME 10-15 MINUTES

COOKING TIME 20 MINUTES

INGREDIENTS

FOR THE CHOUX PASTRY
110 g / 4 oz / ⅔ cup plain (all purpose) flour
110 g / 4 oz / ½ cup unsalted butter, cold and cubed
250 ml / 9 fl. oz / 1 cup whole milk
4 large eggs
1 tsp caster (superfine) sugar
2 tbsp sugar nibs

FOR THE FILLING
375 ml / 13 fl. oz / 1 ½ cups double (heavy) cream
65 g / 2 ½ oz / ½ cup icing (confectioners') sugar
2 passionfruit, halved with pulp scooped out

122
MAKES 4

Blackberry and Lemon Tartlets

- Preheat the oven to 180°C (160° fan) / 350F / gas 4.
- Roll the pastry out on a lightly floured surface to ½ cm thickness.
- Cut out 4 rounds of pastry and use to line 4 individual 5" tartlet cases.
- Prick the bases with a fork and trim any excess, overhanging pastry.
- Line with greaseproof paper and fill with baking beans before blind-baking for 12-15 minutes until golden at the edges.
- Remove from the oven and discard the greaseproof paper and baking beans.
- Return to the oven for 3-4 minutes to brown the base before removing to a wire rack to cool.
- Fill with the lemon curd and garnish with blackberries before dusting with icing sugar and serving.

Blueberry and Lemon Tartlets
 123

- Use blueberries to garnish instead of blackberries.

PREPARATION TIME 10 MINUTES

COOKING TIME 15 MINUTES

INGREDIENTS

250 g / 9 oz ready-made shortcrust pastry
a little plain (all purpose) flour, for dusting
300 g / 10 ½ oz / 1 ⅓ cups lemon curd
350 g / 12 oz / 3 cups blackberries

TO GARNISH
1 tbsp icing (confectioners') sugar

124

MAKES 4

Almond-Flavoured Chocolate Tartlet

Chocolate and Brandy Tartlets

125

- Substitute the almond extract for 30 ml / 1 fl. oz / 2 tbsp brandy.

Chocolate Grand Marnier Tartlets

126

- Substitute the almond extract for 30 ml / 1 fl. oz / 2 tbsp Grand Marnier liqueur.

PREPARATION TIME 10 MINUTES

COOKING TIME 15 MINUTES

INGREDIENTS

250 g / 9 oz ready-made shortcrust pastry
a little plain (all purpose) flour, for dusting
300 g / 10 ½ oz / 2 cups good-quality dark chocolate, chopped
175 ml / 6 fl. oz / ⅔ cup double (heavy) cream
2 tsp almond extract

TO GARNISH

1 tbsp cocoa powder

- Preheat the oven to 180°C (160° fan) / 350F / gas 4.
- Roll the pastry out on a lightly floured surface to ½ cm thickness.
- Cut out 4 rounds of pastry and use to line 4 individual 5" tartlet cases.
- Prick the bases with a fork and trim any excess, overhanging pastry.
- Line with greaseproof paper and fill with baking beans before blind-baking for 12-15 minutes until golden at the edges.
- Remove from the oven and discard the greaseproof paper and baking beans.
- Return to the oven for 3-4 minutes to brown the base before removing to a wire rack to cool.
- Heat the cream in a saucepan until boiling, remove from the heat, and whisk in the chocolate and almond extract.
- Once smooth and thick, pour into the pastry tarts and let the filling cool before dusting with cocoa powder.

127
MAKES 24

Almond and Lemon Shortbread

- Pulse together all the ingredients in a food processor until they come together as a dough.
- Remove the dough and knead gently for 30 seconds.
- Divide in 2 and roll into log shapes approximately 3 cm in diameter.
- Wrap in greaseproof paper and chill for 60 minutes.
- Grease and line 2 baking trays with greaseproof paper.
- Use a sharp knife to cut discs 1 cm thick.
- Arrange on the baking sheets spaced apart.
- Bake for 12-15 minutes until they just start to colour then remove from the oven.
- Allow them to cool on the sheets before transferring to a wire rack to cool completely.

PREPARATION TIME 10 MINUTES

COOKING TIME 10 MINUTES

INGREDIENTS

225 g / 8 oz / 1 ½ cups plain (all purpose) flour
50 g / 2 oz / ⅓ cup cornflour (cornstarch)
75 g / 3 oz / ¾ cup ground almonds
225 g / 8 oz / 1 cup unsalted butter, cubed
85 g / 3 ½ oz / ⅔ cup icing (confectioners') sugar
½ tsp salt
1 lemon, juiced and zested

Orange and Lime Shortbread

 128

- Juice and zest 1 lime and ½ an orange, using in place of the lemon juice and zest.

129
MAKES 4

Kiwi and Honey Tartlets

- Preheat the oven to 180°C (160° fan) / 350F / gas 4.
- Roll the pastry out on a lightly floured surface.
- Cut out 4 rounds of pastry and line 4 4" pastry rings, pressing the pastry into the base and sides well.
- Transfer to a baking tray lined with greaseproof paper.
- Prick the bases and trim excess pastry.
- Line with greaseproof paper and fill with baking beans before blind-baking for 12-15 minutes until golden.
- Remove from the oven and discard the greaseproof paper and baking beans.
- Return to the oven for 2-3 minutes to brown the base before removing to a wire rack to cool.
- Once cool, warm the honey gently in a saucepan set over a low heat, then brush the insides of the tartlets with it.
- Layer the slices of kiwi inside and glaze with honey.

PREPARATION TIME 10-15 MINUTES

COOKING TIME 15 MINUTES

INGREDIENTS

200 g / 7 oz ready-made shortcrust pastry
a little plain (all purpose) flour, for dusting
4 kiwis, peeled and sliced
150 g / 5 fl. oz / ⅔ cup orange blossom honey

Clementine and Honey Tartlets

 130

- Segment 4 clementines and use the segments to line the pastries, instead of the kiwi, before brushing with honey.

MAKES 12

Matcha Tea Madeleines

PREPARATION TIME 10 MINUTES

COOKING TIME 15 MINUTES

INGREDIENTS

125 g / 4 ½ oz / 1 cup icing (confectioners') sugar, sifted
115 g / 4 oz / ½ cup unsalted butter, melted and cooled
100 g / 3 ½ oz / ⅔ cup plain (all purpose) flour, sifted
½ tsp baking powder
½ tsp matcha tea powder
a pinch of salt

- Preheat the oven to 180°C (160° fan) / 350F / gas 4.
- Grease a 12-hole madeleine tray.
- Beat together the eggs, salt and icing sugar in a large mixing bowl until thick and shiny.
- Fold in the flour, 25 g at a time, as well as the baking powder and matcha tea powder.
- Once all the flour has been added, fold in the melted butter until incorporated.
- Spoon into the moulds, leaving them about three-quarters full with the batter.
- Bake for 12-14 minutes until golden and risen.
- Remove and allow them to cool in the tray for a few minutes before turning out onto a wire rack to finish cooling.
- Dust with icing sugar before serving.

Earl Grey Madeleines

- Add 85 ml / 3 fl. oz / ⅓ cup cold, strong Earl Grey tea and an additional 50 g / 2 oz / ⅓ cup plain flour to the batter.

MAKES 8

Pistachio Cookies with Strawberries

PREPARATION TIME 10-15 MINUTES

COOKING TIME 15-20 MINUTES

INGREDIENTS

225 g / 8 oz / 1 ½ cups plain (all purpose) flour
a little extra plain (all purpose) flour, for dusting
55 g / 2 oz / ⅓ cup cornflour (cornstarch)
225 g / 8 oz / 1 cup unsalted butter, cubed
110 g / 4 oz / ⅔ cup shelled pistachios, finely chopped
75 g / 3 oz / ⅔ cup icing (confectioners') sugar
½ tsp salt
125 ml / 4 ½ fl. oz / ½ cup whipping cream
4 large strawberries, tops removed and quartered
1 tbsp shelled pistachios, shelled and chopped

- Pulse the flour, cornflour, pistachios, salt, icing sugar and butter in a processor until it comes together.
- Gently knead the dough on a floured work surface, wrap in clingfilm and chill for 60 minutes.
- Preheat the oven to 170°C (150°C fan) / 325F / gas 3.
- Grease and line a baking tray with greaseproof paper.
- Remove the dough from the fridge and roll out on a lightly floured work surface to 1 cm thickness.
- Use a 3" fluted cookie cutter to stamp out 8 rounds of dough before lifting carefully onto the baking tray.
- Bake for 18-20 minutes until the cookies start to colour.
- Remove to a wire rack to cool.
- Whip the cream until soft peaks form before serving with a couple of cookies and some quartered strawberries on top.
- Garnish with chopped pistachios.

Almond Cookies with Raspberries

- Substitute the pistachios in the recipe for blanched almonds and use raspberries instead of strawberries.

135

MAKES 4

White Chocolate Tartlets

Dark Chocolate Tartlets 136

- Replace the white chocolate with the same weight of dark chocolate.

Milk Chocolate and Mint Tarts 137

- Replace the white chocolate with the same weight of milk chocolate and add 1 tsp peppermint essence.

PREPARATION TIME 10 MINUTES

COOKING TIME 15 MINUTES

....

INGREDIENTS

200 g / 7 oz ready-made shortcrust pastry
a little plain (all purpose) flour, for dusting
300 g / 10 ½ oz / 2 cups white chocolate, chopped
175 ml / 6 fl. oz / ⅔ cup double (heavy) cream

TO GARNISH
4 raspberries

- Preheat the oven to 180°C (160° fan) / 350F / gas 4.
- Roll the pastry out on a lightly floured surface to ½ cm thickness.
- Cut out 4 rounds of pastry and use to line 4 individual 4" fluted tartlet cases.
- Prick the bases with a fork and trim any excess, overhanging pastry.
- Line with greaseproof paper and fill with baking beans before blind-baking for 12-15 minutes until golden at the edges.
- Remove from the oven and discard the greaseproof paper and baking beans.
- Return to the oven for 3-4 minutes to brown the base before removing to a wire rack to cool.
- Heat the cream in a saucepan until boiling, remove from the heat, and whisk in the chocolate.
- Once smooth and thick, let it cool for 2 minutes before pouring into the pastry tarts.
- Garnish with a raspberry before serving.

138

MAKES 12

Lemon and Coconut Cookies

PREPARATION TIME 10-15 MINUTES

COOKING TIME 40-50 MINUTES

INGREDIENTS

FOR THE BISCUIT BASE
110 g / 4 oz / ⅔ cup plain flour
110 g / 4 oz / 1 cup icing sugar
110 g / 4 oz / ½ cup butter, softened
1 tbsp cornflour
2 large egg whites, a pinch of salt
225 g / 8 oz / 1 cup caster sugar

FOR THE LEMON CURD
30 g / 1 oz / 2 tbsp cornflour
250 ml / 9 fl. oz / 1 cup lemon juice
150 ml / 5 fl. oz / ⅔ cup water
175 g / 6 oz / ¾ cup butter, cubed
6 medium egg yolks
2 medium eggs
110 g / 4 oz / 1 ½ cups desiccated coconut
55 g / 2 oz / ¼ cup caster sugar
2 limes, zest finely grated

- Preheat the oven to 200°C (180°C fan) / 400°F / gas 6.
- Grease and line a cake tin with greaseproof paper.
- Combine the butter, sugar and vanilla for the biscuit base and beat until pale and fluffy. Add the egg whites, one at a time, beating well. Fold through the flour.
- Spoon the mixture into the base and spread evenly. Bake for 6-8 minutes.
- Remove from the oven and leave to cool.
- To prepare the lemon curd, combine the cornflour and sugar in a saucepan.
- Gradually add the lemon juice, whisking as you pour, then add 150 ml water.
- Cook over a medium heat until it thickens. Once it bubbles, remove from the heat and beat in the butter.
- Whisk the eggs and egg yolks and beat into the mixture.
- Return to the heat and stir constantly for a 4-6 minutes.
- Remove from the heat and let cool slightly.
- Pour over the cooled biscuit base and spread evenly before chilling briefly.
- Combine the sugar, lime zest and desiccated coconut.
- Sprinkle the coconut mixture on top of the lemon curd.
- Cut into square portions before serving.

139

SERVES 4

Chocolate Verrines

PREPARATION TIME 15 MINUTES

COOKING TIME 40 MINUTES

INGREDIENTS

400 g / 14 oz / 2 ⅔ cups dark chocolate, roughly chopped
cooking spray
110 g / 4 oz / ½ cup unsalted butter
110 g / 4 oz / ½ cup caster (superfine) sugar
110 g / 4 oz / ⅔ cup self-raising flour
1 tsp vanilla extract
2 large eggs
100 g / 3 ½ oz / ⅔ cup pistachios, shelled and chopped
150 g / 5 oz / 1 ½ cups raspberries

- Melt the chocolate in a large heatproof bowl set over a pan of gently simmering water.
- Spray 12 7.5 cm x 5 cm x 5 cm disposable aluminium dariole moulds with cooking spray on the insides.
- Use a pastry brush to paint the insides of the moulds with the melted chocolate.
- Make several coats of the chocolate and place in the freezer to solidify.
- Preheat the oven to 180°C (160° fan) / 350F / gas 4. Grease and line a 8 inch springform cake tin.
- Prepare the sponge by whisking together the butter, sugar, eggs, self-raising flour and vanilla extract.
- Whisk until smooth and then spoon into the prepared cake tin. Bake for 15-20 minutes.
- Remove from the oven and turn onto a wire rack to cool.
- Remove the chocolate cups and allow to thaw a little.
- Cut the cake into sections and pulse in a food processor for a few seconds.
- Peel the foil carefully away from the solid chocolate cups and fill them with a combination of the raspberries, pistachios and crumbled sponge cakes.

140

MAKES 6

Plum and Coffee Tartlets

- Preheat the oven to 180°C (160° fan) / 350F / gas 4.
- Roll the pastry out on a lightly floured surface to ½ cm thickness.
- Cut out 4 rounds of pastry and use to line 6 individual 4" tartlet cases.
- Prick the bases with a fork and chill until needed.
- Blitz together the ground almonds, sugar and butter in a food processor until creamy.
- Add the egg, egg white and espresso and pulse until combined.
- Spoon into the pastry and bake for 30-35 minutes until the edge of the pastry is golden brown in colour and the filling is puffed up.
- Remove the tarts and top with the plum slices.
- Grill under a hot grill for 1 minute before removing and serving.

PREPARATION TIME 10 MINUTES

COOKING TIME 15 MINUTES

INGREDIENTS

300 g / 10 ½ oz ready-made shortcrust pastry
a little plain (all purpose) flour, for dusting
225 g / 8 oz / 2 cups ground almonds
110 g / 4 oz / ½ cup caster (superfine) sugar
110 g / 4 oz / ½ cup unsalted butter
2 small eggs
2 small egg whites
55 ml / 2 fl. oz / ¼ cup strong espresso, cold
6 plums, de-stoned and sliced

White Almond Nougat

141

SERVES 4

PREPARATION TIME 15 MINUTES

COOKING TIME 20 MINUTES

SETTING TIME 6 HOURS

INGREDIENTS

FOR THE ALMOND NOUGAT
275 g / 10 oz / 1 ¼ cups caster (superfine) sugar

250 g / 9 oz / 1 cup glucose
200 g / 7 oz / 2 cups whole almonds, blanched
50 ml / 2 fl. oz / ¼ cup cold water
1 large egg white, at room temperature
1 tsp vanilla extract

ALSO NEEDED
sugar thermometer
electric whisk/mixer

- Preheat the oven to 160°C (140° fan) / 325F / gas 3.
- Grease and line a 8" x 4" x 2" pan with greaseproof paper.
- Combine the sugar, water and glucose in a saucepan, cooking over a medium heat until the sugar has dissolved.
- Cook until the mixture registers 120°C on the thermometer, then start to beat the egg white in a separate mixing bowl until soft peaks form.
- Once the sugar mixture reaches 136-138°C, remove from the heat and beat into the egg white in a slow, steady stream until fully incorporated.
- Keep whisking for 2-3 minutes until thick and glossy.
- Stir in the almonds and vanilla extract, then spoon into the pan, levelling the mixture with a wet spoon.
- Cover with a sheet of oiled greaseproof and gently weigh down; leave the nougat to set for at least 6 hours until firm.
- Once firm, turn out and cut into portions.

Vanilla Shortbread

142

SERVES 24

PREPARATION TIME 10 MINUTES

COOKING TIME 15-20 MINUTES

INGREDIENTS

300 g / 10 ½ oz / 2 cups plain (all purpose) flour
50 g / 2 oz / ⅓ cup cornflour (cornstarch)

225 g / 8 oz / 1 cup unsalted butter,
325 g / 11 oz / 2 ⅔ cup icing (confectioners') sugar,
50-75 ml / 2-3 fl. oz / ¼-⅓ cup hot water
a few drops of red food colouring
24 silver dragee balls

- Pulse together the flour, cornflour, 75 g of the icing sugar, lemon zest and butter in a food processor until it forms a dough.
- Remove the dough, knead gently and form into a ball. Wrap in clingfilm and chill for 60 minutes.
- Preheat the oven to 180°C (160° fan) / 350F / gas 4.
- Remove the dough from the fridge and roll out on a floured surface.
- Grease and line 2 baking trays with greaseproof paper.
- Cut out 24 shapes from the dough. Arrange on the baking trays spaced apart then bake for 12-15 minutes. Allow to cool.
- Whisk together the icing sugar with enough hot water to make a spreadable icing.
- Divide the icing in two and colour one with drops of the red colouring, whisking until pink.
- Spread half of the cookies with white icing and the remaining with pink icing, garnishing each with a dragee ball.

143

MAKES 16

Cinnamon and Ginger Mini Buns

PREPARATION TIME 10 MINUTES

COOKING TIME 10-15 MINUTES

INGREDIENTS

500 g / 1 lb 2 oz ready-made puff pastry
a little plain (all purpose) flour, for dusting
175 g / 6 oz / ¾ cup caster (superfine) sugar
110 g / 4 oz / ½ cup butter, melted and cooled
2 tsp ground ginger
2 tsp ground cinnamon

TO GARNISH

55 g / 2 oz / ¼ cup caster (superfine) sugar

- Combine the sugar, ground ginger and ground cinnamon in a bowl.
- Roll the pastry out on a lightly floured surface.
- Brush all over with some melted butter and sprinkle the sugar mixture on top.
- Roll into a log and wrap in greaseproof paper. Chill for 30 minutes.
- Preheat the oven to 180°C (160° fan) / 350F / gas 4.
- Grease and line 2 baking trays with greaseproof paper.
- Remove the pastry roll and cut into 16 slices.
- Arrange flat on the baking trays and brush with the remaining butter. Bake for 12-15 minutes.
- Remove from the oven and dust immediately with the additional sugar.
- Cool on a wire rack before serving.

Cinnamon Apple Mini Buns

144

- Remove the ginger from the sugar mixture and spread the pastry with the same amount of apple puree instead of butter.

145

MAKES 48

Grand-Marnier and Chocolate Truffles

PREPARATION TIME 10 MINUTES

COOKING TIME 20 MINUTES

INGREDIENTS

100 ml / 3 ½ fl. oz / ½ cup Grand Marnier
300 g / 10 ½ oz / 2 cups good-quality dark chocolate, roughly chopped
300 ml / 10 ½ fl. oz / 1 ¼ cups double (heavy) cream
60 g / 2 oz / ¼ cup unsalted butter

FOR THE GARNISH

40 g / 1 ½ oz / ½ cup desiccated coconut
40 g / 1 ½ oz / ⅓ cup Brazil nuts, finely chopped
25 g / 1 oz / 2 tbsp cocoa powder

- Place the chocolate in a large heatproof mixing bowl.
- Place the cream and butter in a saucepan and bring to a simmer over a moderate heat.
- Once the butter has fully melted and the mixture is simmering, pour it over the chocolate.
- Whisk until you have a smooth mixture, then beat in the Grand Marnier. Cover the bowl and chill for 4 hours.
- Take out scoops of the truffle mixture. Using lightly oiled hands, roll into truffle shapes, then roll a third of the truffles in the desiccated coconut.
- Leave to set on a baking tray.
- Roll another third in the chopped Brazil nuts and leave to set.
- Roll the remaining truffles in the cocoa powder, shaking off any excess.
- Leave to set on a baking tray.

Tia Maria Truffles

146

- Replace the Grand-Marnier with Tia Maria for a coffee flavoured truffle.

147

SERVES 8

Walnut and Chocolate Flapjacks

- Preheat the oven to 180°C (160° fan) / 350F / gas 4.
- Grease and line a 12" x 9" x 3" baking tin with greaseproof paper.
- Melt the butter and syrup together in a large saucepan until runny.
- Remove from the heat and stir in the oats, walnuts, blackcurrants and salt, mixing gently but thoroughly.
- Spoon into the tin and bake for 25-30 minutes until set and golden on top.
- Remove from the oven and leave to cool and harden a little.
- Melt the chocolates together in a heatproof bowl set atop a saucepan of simmering water.
- Once melted, pour evenly on top of the set flapjack and chill until firm.
- Remove the flapjack once the chocolate has set.

PREPARATION TIME 10 MINUTES

COOKING TIME 10 MINUTES

INGREDIENTS

300 g / 10 ½ oz / 4 cups rolled oats
225 g / 8 oz / 1 cup unsalted butter, softened
125 g / 4 ½ oz / ⅓ cup Golden Syrup
150 g / 5 oz / 1 cup good-quality milk chocolate, chopped
150 g / 5 oz / 1 cup good-quality dark chocolate, chopped
55 g / 2 oz / ⅔ cup walnut halves, finely chopped
55 g / 2 oz / ½ cup blackcurrants
a pinch of salt

Pecan, Chocolate and Cherry Flapjacks

148

- Replace the walnuts and blackcurrants with the same weight of pecans and dried cherries.

149

MAKES 4

Passion Fruit Tartlets

- Preheat the oven to 180°C (160° fan) / 350F / gas 4.
- Roll the pastry out on a lightly floured surface.
- Cut out 4 rounds of pastry and use to line 4 individual 5" fluted tartlet cases.
- Prick the bases with a fork and trim any excess, overhanging pastry.
- Line with greaseproof paper and fill with baking beans before blind-baking for 12-15 minutes until golden at the edges.
- Remove from the oven and discard the greaseproof paper and baking beans.
- Return to the oven for 3-4 minutes to brown the base before removing to a wire rack to cool.
- Once cool, sweeten the fromage frais with the icing sugar and use to fill the tartlets.
- Top with the passion fruit pulp and seeds before serving.

PREPARATION TIME 10 MINUTES

COOKING TIME 15 MINUTES

INGREDIENTS

250 g / 9 oz ready-made shortcrust pastry
a little plain (all purpose) flour, for dusting
375 ml / 13 fl. oz / 1 ½ cups fromage frais
30 g / 1 oz / ¼ cup icing (confectioners') sugar
2 passion fruit, pulp and seeds scooped out

Pineapple Tartlets

150

- Replace the passion fruit with 300 g / 10 ½ oz / 2 cups chopped pineapple in the tartlets.

151

SERVES 8

Pistachio and Chocolate Brownie

Chocolate and Raisin Brownies

152

- Replace the pistachios with the same weight of raisins and omit the cranberries as well.

Pecan Cinnamon Brownies

153

- Replace the pistachios with chopped pecan nuts, and add 1 tsp ground cinnamon to the batter mixture.

PREPARATION TIME 10-15 MINUTES

COOKING TIME 15 MINUTES

INGREDIENTS

350 g / 12 oz / 2 ⅓ cups good-quality dark chocolate, chopped
225 g / 8 oz / 1 cup unsalted butter, softened
250 g / 9 oz / 1 ⅓ cups light soft brown sugar
150 g / 5 oz / 1 cup shelled pistachios, chopped
110 g / 4 oz / ⅔ cup plain (all purpose) flour
110 g / 4 oz / 1 cup digestive biscuits, chopped
55 g / 2 oz / ⅓ cup dried cranberries
4 large eggs
1 tsp baking powder
a pinch of salt

TO GARNISH
30 g / 1 oz / 2 tbsp good-quality cocoa powder

- Preheat the oven to 170°C (150°C fan) / 325°F / gas 3.
- Grease and line a 5" square baking tray with greaseproof paper.
- Melt the chocolate and butter in a saucepan over a medium-low heat, stirring occasionally until smooth.
- Remove from the heat and allow to cool a little.
- In a large mixing bowl, whisk the eggs until they are thick then add the sugar and continue to whisk until glossy.
- Beat in the melted chocolate mixture, then fold in the flour and baking powder until incorporated.
- Add the pistachios, digestive biscuits and cranberries and stir well.
- Pour into the baking tray and tap lightly a few times to release any trapped air bubbles.
- Bake for 35-40 minutes until the surface has set; test with a wooden toothpick, if it comes out almost clean, the brownie is done.
- Remove and let the brownie cool before turning out, cutting and dusting with cocoa powder.

154

MAKES 24

Mini Raspberry and Blackberry Tartlets

- Preheat the oven to 180°C (160° fan) / 350F / gas 4.
- Roll the pastry out to ¾ cm thickness on a lightly floured surface.
- Cut out 24 rounds of pastry and use to line a 24-hole mini cupcake tin.
- Fill with small rounds of greaseproof paper and fill with baking beans or dry rice.
- Blind-bake for 12-14 minutes, then remove from the oven and discard the greaseproof paper and the baking beans/dry rice.
- Leave to cool before whipping the cream with the icing sugar until soft peaks form.
- Spoon into the cooled pastry tartlets and top half with a raspberry and the other half with a blackberry.
- Dust with icing sugar before serving.

PREPARATION TIME 10 MINUTES

COOKING TIME 15 MINUTES

INGREDIENTS

450 g / 1 lb ready-made shortcrust pastry
a little plain (all purpose) flour, for dusting
500 ml / 18 fl. oz / 2 cups double (heavy) cream
125 g / 4 ½ oz / 1 cup icing (confectioners') sugar
12 raspberries
12 blackberries

TO GARNISH
2 tbsp icing (confectioners') sugar

Cocoa-Dusted Mini Tartlets

 155

- Dust the tartlets with good-quality cocoa powder instead of icing sugar before serving.

156

MAKES 4

Pine Nut Tartlets

- Preheat the oven to 180°C (160° fan) / 350F / gas 4.
- Roll the pastry out on a lightly floured surface.
- Cut out 4 rounds of pastry and line 4 5" fluted cases.
- Prick the bases and trim excess pastry.
- Line with greaseproof paper and fill with baking beans before blind-baking for 12-15 minutes.
- Remove from the oven and discard the greaseproof paper and baking beans.
- Return to the oven for 3-4 minutes to brown the base before removing to a wire rack to cool.
- Whisk together the eggs with the milk and creme fraîche until smooth.
- Pour into the cases and reduce the oven to 160°C (140° fan) / 325F / gas 3. Bake for 25-30 minutes.
- Remove from the oven and top with pine nuts and a tablespoon of jam.

PREPARATION TIME 10 MINUTES

COOKING TIME 15 MINUTES

INGREDIENTS

300 g / 10 ½ oz ready-made shortcrust pastry
a little plain (all purpose) flour, for dusting
250 ml / 9 fl. oz / 1 cup whole milk
250 ml / 9 fl. oz / 1 cup crème fraîche
3 large eggs, beaten
55 g / 2 oz / ½ cup pine nuts
salt and pepper

TO GARNISH
4 tbsp apricot jam

Pistachio Tartlets

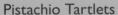 **157**

- Replace the pine nuts with toasted pistachios and use strawberry jam instead of apricot.

158

SERVES 6

Chocolate, Hazelnut and Fudge Moelleux

PREPARATION TIME 10 MINUTES

COOKING TIME 10 MINUTES

INGREDIENTS

30 g / 1 oz / 2 tbsp butter, melted
110 g / 4 oz / ⅔ cup good-quality dark chocolate, chopped
110 g / 4 oz / ½ cup unsalted butter, cubed
75 g / 3 oz / ½ cup fudge, chopped
75 g / 3 oz / ½ cup plain (all purpose) flour
30 g / 1 oz / 2 tbsp good-quality cocoa powder
30 g / 1 oz / 2 tbsp cup ground hazelnuts (cob nuts)
2 medium eggs
2 medium egg yolks

- Preheat the oven to 190°C (170° fan) / 375F / gas 5.
- Brush 6 mini ramekins with some of the melted butter.
- Chill the ramekins for 15 mins then brush with another layer of melted butter.
- Dust the insides with the cocoa powder.
- Chill until ready to fill with the batter.
- Prepare the batter by melting together the chocolate and cubed butter in a heatproof mixing bowl set over a pan of gently simmering water.
- Once melted, remove from the heat and allow to cool.
- Meanwhile, whisk together the eggs and egg yolks in a separate mixing bowl until thick.
- Sift in the plain flour and whisk until smooth, then fold in the ground hazelnuts and fudge and then the melted chocolate and butter.
- Spoon into the ramekins and bake for 10-12 minutes.

Chocolate Orange Moelleux 159

- Omit the fudge and use 1 tsp orange extract as well as 2 tbsp Cointreau in the batter.

160

SERVES 4

Coconut Baked Egg Custard

PREPARATION TIME 10 MINUTES

COOKING TIME 10 MINUTES

INGREDIENTS

8 medium egg yolks
75 g / 3 oz / ⅓ cup caster (superfine) sugar
250 ml / 9 fl. oz / 1 cup whipping cream
250 ml / 9 fl. oz / 1 cup coconut milk
2 tbsp desiccated coconut
1 tbsp cornflour

TO GARNISH

1 tbsp desiccated coconut

- Preheat the oven to 160°C (140°C fan) / 300°F / gas 2.
- Whisk together the egg yolks, cornflour and sugar until pale and thick.
- Add the cream and coconut milk and mix well before passing through a fine sieve into a saucepan.
- Heat over a medium heat to blood temperature, stirring all the time.
- Pour the custard carefully into individual heatproof, fluted ramekins and arrange on a baking tray.
- Carefully transfer to the oven and bake for 25-30 minutes until the custard is set and the edges are starting to colour.
- Remove once ready and sprinkle with desiccated coconut before serving.

Lemon Baked Custards 161

- Replace the coconut milk with 250 ml / 9 fl. oz / 1 cup whole milk and replace the desiccated coconut with 2 tbsp limoncello.

162

SERVES 4

Samosa Pancakes with Summer Fruit

Samosa Pancakes with Nutella

163

- Replace the jam filling with Nutella for a chocolate take on the samosas. Serve with banana instead of berries.

Citrus Samosa Pancakes

164

- Instead of jam, use lemon curd and serve with segments of tangerine instead of summer fruits.

PREPARATION TIME 10-15 MINUTES

COOKING TIME 10 MINUTES

INGREDIENTS

FOR THE PANCAKES
200 g / 7 oz / 1 ⅓ cups plain (all purpose) flour
500 ml / 18 fl. oz / 2 cups whole milk
55 g / 2 oz / ¼ cup unsalted butter, melted
2 large eggs

FOR THE FILLING
110 g / 4 oz / ½ cup strawberry jam
110 g / 4 oz / ½ cup raspberry jam

TO GARNISH
55 g / 2 oz / ½ cup redcurrants
55 g / 2 oz / ½ cup strawberries
55 g / 2 oz / ½ cup raspberries
55 g / 2 oz / ½ cup blackberries

- Sift the flour into a large bowl and whisk the eggs and milk in a jug until smooth.
- Pour half of the egg and milk mixture onto the flour and whisk until you have a smooth, thick batter.
- Add the remaining wet mixture and whisk until smooth.
- Add small tablespoons of the melted butter to a non-stick frying pan and heat over a medium heat.
- Fry the pancake batter making sure you tilt the pan to coat the surface as soon as you have added it.
- Flip and cook the other side of the pancake once one side is set.
- Continue cooking them in this way until you have used up all the batter; keep the cooked pancakes on a plate covered loosely with aluminium foil.
- Spread the cooked pancakes with the jam and shape into cones, before pushing the top of the cone back into the centre to make the samosas.
- Serve with an assortment of the berries.

165

MAKES 4

Fromage Blanc Tartlets

PREPARATION TIME 10 MINUTES

COOKING TIME 15-20 MINUTES

INGREDIENTS

200 g / 7 oz ready-made shortcrust pastry
a little plain (all purpose) flour, for dusting
3 large egg whites
2 large egg yolks
250 g / 9 oz / 1 cup fromage blance
85 g / 3 ½ oz / ⅓ cup caster (superfine) sugar
1 tbsp cornflour (cornstarch)
a pinch of salt

TO GARNISH

1 tbsp icing (confectioners') sugar

- Preheat the oven to 190°C (170° fan) / 375F / gas 5.
- Roll the pastry out to ½ cm thickness and cut out 4 rounds.
- Line 4 individual canele moulds with the pastry.
- Chill until needed.
- Cream together the egg yolks and butter until smooth, then whisk in the fromage blanc.
- Whisk the egg whites in a separate, clean bowl with a pinch of salt until stiff peaks form.
- Whisk in the sugar, 1 tablespoon at a time until thick.
- Fold 1 third of the mixture into the fromage black mixture, then fold in the remaining meringue until just incorporated.
- Spoon into the pastry cases and level the tops.
- Bake for 18-20 minutes until risen.
- Remove from the oven and let the tartlets cool.

Lemon Fromage Blanc Tartlets **166**

- Add the juice and zest of 1 lemon to the fromage blanc mixture before spooning into the pastry and baking.

167

MAKES 4

Amandine and Grape Tartlets

PREPARATION TIME 10 MINUTES

COOKING TIME 15 MINUTES

INGREDIENTS

300 g / 10 ½ oz ready-made shortcrust pastry
a little plain (all purpose) flour, for dusting
225 g / 8 oz / 2 cups ground almonds
110 g / 4 oz / ½ cup caster (superfine) sugar
110 g / 4 oz / ½ cup unsalted butter
2 small eggs
2 small egg whites
100 g / 3 ½ oz / 1 cup black seedless grapes
100 g / 3 ½ oz / 1 cup green seedless grapes

- Preheat the oven to 180°C (160° fan) / 350F / gas 4.
- Roll the pastry out on a lightly floured surface to ½ cm thickness.
- Cut out 4 rounds of pastry and use to line 4 individual 5" tart cases.
- Prick the bases with a fork and trim any excess, overhanging pastry with a serrated knife.
- Chill until needed.
- Blitz together the ground almonds, sugar and butter in a food processor until creamy.
- Add the egg and egg white and pulse until combined.
- Spoon into the pastry and dot with the grapes.
- Bake for 30-35 minutes until the edge of the pastry is golden brown in colour and the filling is golden.
- Remove the tarts from the oven and let them cool on a wire rack before serving.

Amandine and Apricot Tartlets **168**

- Roughly chop 150 g / 5 oz / 1 cup dried apricot halves and use in place of the grapes.

169

MAKES 4

Chilled Summer Fruit Charlottes

- Line 4 large individual ramekins with sheets of clingfilm.
- Brush the insides with melted butter and line each with 14 savoiardi biscuits, stacked neatly around the perimeter.
- Whip the cream to soft peaks, then fold through the jam and fromage frais until incorporated.
- Spoon into the ramekins and chill.
- Combine the blackcurrants, redcurrants and sugar in a saucepan and heat over a low heat until the fruit starts to release some juice.
- Remove the Charlottes from the fridge and carefully turn out onto serving plates.
- Top with the fruit before serving.

PREPARATION TIME 10-15 MINUTES

COOKING TIME 15-20 MINUTES

INGREDIENTS

56 savoiardi biscuit fingers
55 g / 2 oz / ¼ cup unsalted butter, melted
30 g / 1 oz / ¼ cup icing (confectioners') sugar
150 g / 5 oz / ½ cup seedless strawberry jam
125 ml / 4 ½ fl. oz / ½ cup whipping cream
250 ml / 9 fl. oz / 1 cup fromage frais
100 g / 3 ½ oz / 1 cup blackcurrants
100 g / 3 ½ oz / 1 cup redcurrants
2 tbsp caster (superfine) sugar

Chilled Apple Charlottes

170

- Replace the strawberry jam with the same weight of apple puree and garnish with diced apple on top.

171

MAKES 4

Pink Praline Tartlets

- Preheat the oven to 180°C (160° fan) / 350F / gas 4.
- Roll the pastry out on a lightly floured surface.
- Cut out 4 rounds of pastry and line 4 5" tartlet cases.
- Prick the bases and trim excess pastry.
- Line with greaseproof paper and fill with baking beans before blind-baking for 12-15 minutes until golden.
- Remove from the oven and discard the greaseproof paper and baking beans.
- Return to the oven for 3-4 minutes to brown the base.
- Blitz the pralines in a food processor until fine then transfer to a saucepan.
- Add the cream and cook over a medium heat.
- Reduce to a steady simmer for 10 minutes.
- Remove from the heat and stir through the glucose before spooning into the tartlets.
- Chill until the filling is firm.

PREPARATION TIME 10 MINUTES

COOKING TIME 20 MINUTES

INGREDIENTS

250 g / 9 oz ready-made shortcrust pastry
a little plain (all purpose) flour, for dusting
250 g / 9 oz / 1 ½ cups pink pralines, crushed
250 ml / 9 fl. oz / 1 cup single cream
1 tbsp liquid glucose

Praline and Cream Tarts

172

- Top the chilled tarts with 1 tbsp of whipped, sweetened cream before serving.

173

SERVES 6

Thin Melon Tarts

Thin Apricot Tarts

174

- Instead of melon use apricot slices.

Thin Pear and Chocolate Tarts

175

- Instead of melon use thin pear slices, and top with chocolate shavings before baking.

PREPARATION TIME 10-15 MINUTES

COOKING TIME 15 MINUTES

INGREDIENTS

300 g / 10 ½ oz ready-made shortcrust pastry
a little plain (all purpose) flour, for dusting
1 Galia melon, peeled and thinly sliced
55 g / 2 oz / ¼ cup honey, warmed
55 g / 2 oz / ½ cup flaked (slivered) almonds

- Preheat the oven to 180°C (160° fan) / 350F / gas 4.
- Roll the pastry out on a lightly floured surface to ½ cm thickness.
- Cut out 6 rounds of pastry and use to line 6 individual 4" fluted tartlet cases.
- Prick the bases with a fork and trim any excess, overhanging pastry.
- Line with greaseproof paper and fill with baking beans before blind-baking for 12-15 minutes until golden at the edges.
- Remove from the oven and discard the greaseproof paper and baking beans.
- Return to the oven for 3-4 minutes to brown the base before removing to a wire rack to cool.
- Arrange the melon slices in concentric circles inside the pastry, leaving a space in the middle.
- Brush with the warmed honey and fill the centres with the flaked almonds.

176

SERVES 4

Small Creamy Heart-Shaped Cake

- Preheat the oven to 180°C (160° fan) / 350F / gas 4.
- Grease and line a 1 lb heart-shaped cake tin with greaseproof paper on the base.
- Beat together the sugar, margarine, flour, eggs, vanilla extract and salt in a mixing bowl until smooth.
- Spoon into the cake tin and bake for 20-25 minutes; test with a wooden toothpick, if it comes out clean, the cake is done.
- Remove from the oven and leave to cool in the tin.
- Beat together the butter and icing sugar until soft and creamy before adding drops of green food colouring, beating between additions, until you have a pale green buttercream.
- Turn the cake out from the tin and spread the top and sides with the buttercream.
- Serve with the ice-cream on the side.

Chocolate Heart-Shaped Cake

177

- Add 30 g / 1 oz / 2 tbsp cocoa powder and 2 tbsp whole milk to the batter instead of the vanilla extract.

PREPARATION TIME 10 MINUTES

COOKING TIME 10-15 MINUTES

INGREDIENTS

110 g / 4 oz / ½ cup caster (superfine) sugar
110 g / 4 oz / ½ cup margarine
110 g / 4 oz / ⅔ cup plain (all purpose) flour
2 large eggs
1 tsp vanilla extract
a pinch of salt
250 g / 9 oz / 2 cups icing (confectioners') sugar
225 g / 8 oz / 1 cup butter, softened
½ tsp green food colouring

TO GARNISH
250 ml / 9 fl. oz / 2 cups strawberry ice-cream

178

SERVES 4

Chouquettes Filled with Mango Sorbet

- Sift together flour and sugar in a mixing bowl.
- Combine the butter and milk in a saucepan.
- Add the flour and stir until a smooth dough forms.
- Beat the dough until it pulls away from the saucepan.
- Remove from the heat and add the eggs, one at a time, beating well between each addition until shiny.
- Spoon the dough into a piping bag.
- Preheat the oven to 200°C (180° fan) / 400F / gas 6. Grease and line 2 baking trays with greaseproof paper.
- Pipe blobs of the pastry onto the sheets, spaced apart.
- Bake for 15-18 minutes until puffed and golden.
- Melt the butter and chocolate in a heatproof bowl.
- Remove the tops of the buns, fill with balls of mango sorbet and reassemble.
- Top with the chocolate sauce, then the chopped nuts. Garnish with mint leaves.

Neopolitan Chouquettes

179

- Replace the mango sorbet with balls of Neopolitan ice cream.

PREPARATION TIME 10-15 MINUTES

COOKING TIME 20 MINUTES

INGREDIENTS

FOR THE CHOUQUETTES
110 g / 4 oz / ⅔ cup plain (all purpose) flour
110 g / 4 oz / ½ cup unsalted butter, cold and cubed
250 ml / 9 fl. oz / 1 cup whole milk
4 large eggs
1 tsp caster (superfine) sugar
500 ml / 18 fl. oz / 2 cups good-quality mango sorbet

FOR THE CHOCOLATE TOPPING
225 g / 8 oz / 1 ½ cups good-quality dark chocolate, chopped
55 g / 2 oz / ¼ cup unsalted butter

TO GARNISH
2 tbsp chopped nuts
a few sprigs of mint leaves

180

MAKES 12

Matcha Tea Financiers

PREPARATION TIME 10 MINUTES

COOKING TIME 15 MINUTES

INGREDIENTS

110 g / 4 oz / ½ cup caster (superfine) sugar
110 g / 4 oz / ½ cup slightly salted butter, softened
1 tbsp unsalted butter, softened
110 g / 4 oz / 1 cup ground almonds
30 g / 1 oz / 2 tbsp plain (all purpose) flour, sifted
3 medium egg whites
a pinch of salt
2 tsp matcha tea powder

- Preheat the oven to 180°C (160° fan) / 350F / gas 4.
- Brown the butter in a saucepan until nutty in aroma.
- Strain through a fine sieve into a clean bowl, allowing it to cool.
- Combine the flour, almonds, salt, matcha tea powder and sugar in a mixing bowl.
- Gently whisk the egg whites into this mixture and then fold through the cooled, melted butter.
- Chill for 30 minutes.
- Grease a 12-hole financier tin with unsalted butter and fill with the batter.
- Bake for 15-18 minutes until golden brown at the edges and risen.
- Remove from the oven and cool on a wire rack before serving.

Cocoa Financiers

181

- Replace the tea powder with 2 tbsp good-quality cocoa powder. Dust with icing sugar before serving.

182

SERVES 8

Mini Cherry Savarins

PREPARATION TIME 10-15 MINUTES

COOKING TIME 15-20 MINUTES

INGREDIENTS

FOR THE SAVARINS
225 g / 8 oz / 1 ½ cups strong white plain (all purpose) flour, sifted
125 ml / 4 ½ fl. oz / ½ cup whole milk, warmed
60 g / 2 oz / ¼ cup butter, softened
2 tsp dried active yeast
a pinch of salt
2 tbsp caster (superfine) sugar
2 large eggs

TO GARNISH
250 ml / 9 fl. oz / 1 cup double (heavy) cream
12 canned cherries in syrup

- Combine the flour, yeast, sugar and salt in a large mixing bowl and whisk together the eggs and milk.
- Add to the flour mixture in a slow, steady stream, whisking simultaneously until smooth and thick.
- Dot the butter all over the surface off the batter, cover with a damp tea towel and prove for 30-40 minutes.
- Beat the butter into the batter then spoon into 12 mini savarin moulds.
- Cover with lightly-oiled clingfilm and prove in a warm place for 20 minutes.
- Preheat the oven to 220°C (200° fan) / 425F / gas 7.
- Remove the clingfilm and bake for 10-12 minutes.
- Remove from the oven and allow to cool on a wire rack.
- Whip the cream to soft peaks and spoon into a piping bag.
- Sit the savarin in serving cups and glaze with the cherry syrup. Pipe cream onto the savarins and top with a cherry.

Ice-Cream Savarins

183

- Replace the cream with small balls of vanilla ice-cream and garnish in the same fashion.

184

SERVES 4

Moist Chocolate and Pear Tarts

Moist Cinnamon and Pear Tarts

 185

- Add 1 tsp of ground cinnamon to the batter mixture for a spicy flavour.

Moist Ginger and Pear Tarts

186

- Add 1 tsp of ground ginger to the batter mixture for an exotic flavour.

PREPARATION TIME 10-15 MINUTES

COOKING TIME 25-40 MINUTES

INGREDIENTS

2 large, ripe eating pears, halved
150 ml / 5 fl. oz / ⅔ cup whole milk
150 ml / 5 fl. oz / ⅔ cup double cream
3 medium egg yolks
2 medium eggs
110 g / 4 oz / ½ cup caster sugar
30 g / 1 oz / 2 tbsp plain flour
30 g / 1 oz / 2 tbsp good-quality cocoa powder
a pinch of salt

- Preheat the oven to 160°C (140°C fan) / 300°F / gas 2.
- Line a large cupcake tray with 4 large moulds.
- Prepare the batter by combining the milk and cream in a saucepan and bringing to a simmer over a medium heat.
- Remove from the heat and set to one side.
- In a large bowl, whisk together the egg yolks and eggs until light and frothy.
- Add the sugar and whisk until well blended.
- Sieve the flour and cocoa powder into the mixture and fold through thoroughly.
- Gradually add to the egg mixture, whisking until smooth.
- Divide the batter between the cases, positioning a pear half in the middle of the batter with their cut sides facing upwards.
- Bake for 25-30 minutes until the batter has set.
- Remove from the oven and serve immediately.

187

MAKES 12

Melted Chocolate Madeleines

PREPARATION TIME 10 MINUTES

COOKING TIME 15 MINUTES

INGREDIENTS

125 g / 4 ½ oz / 1 cup icing
(confectioners') sugar, sifted
115 g / 4 oz / ½ cup unsalted butter,
melted and cooled
100 g / 3 ½ oz / ⅔ cup plain
(all purpose) flour, sifted
½ tsp baking powder
½ tsp vanilla extract
a pinch of salt
150 g / 5 oz / 1 cup good-quality dark
chocolate, chopped

- Preheat the oven to 180°C (160° fan) / 350F / gas 4.
- Grease a 12-hole madeleine tray.
- Beat together the eggs, icing sugar, salt and vanilla extract in a large mixing bowl until thick and shiny.
- Fold in the flour, 25 g at a time, and the baking powder.
- Once all the flour has been added, fold in the melted butter until incorporated.
- Spoon into the moulds, leaving them about three-quarters full with the batter.
- Bake for 12-14 minutes until golden and risen.
- Remove and allow them to cool in the tray for a few minutes before turning out onto a wire rack.
- Melt the chocolate in a heatproof bowl set atop a saucepan of simmering water, stirring occasionally.
- Let the chocolate cool a little before spooning over the madeleines.

White Chocolate Madeleines 188

- Use the same weight of melted white chocolate instead of dark chocolate to coat the madeleines.

189

SERVES 8

Chocolate-Coated Walnuts

PREPARATION TIME 10 MINUTES

COOKING TIME 10 MINUTES

INGREDIENTS

450 g / 1 lb / 3 cups good-quality
dark chocolate, chopped
225 g / 8 oz / 2 cups shelled walnuts

- Line a baking tray with greaseproof paper.
- Melt the chocolate in a large heatproof bowl set atop a saucepan of simmering water, stirring occasionally until melted.
- Remove from the heat and leave to cool for 2 minutes.
- Dip the walnuts into the melted chocolate, coating well before transferring to the baking tray to set.

Chocolate and 190
Biscuit-Coated Walnuts

- Finely grind 75 g / 3 oz / ½ cup digestive biscuits and sprinkle on top.

191

MAKES 4

Grapefruit Tartlet

- Preheat the oven to 180°C (160° fan) / 350F / gas 4.
- Roll the pastry out on a lightly floured surface.
- Cut out 4 rounds of pastry and line 4 5" tartlet cases.
- Prick the bases with a fork and trim the excess pastry.
- Line with greaseproof paper and fill with baking beans before blind-baking for 12-15 minutes until golden.
- Remove from the oven and discard the greaseproof paper and baking beans.
- Return to the oven for 3 minutes to brown the base.
- Reduce the oven to 160°C (140°C fan) / 300°F / gas 2.
- Whisk together the egg yolks, cornflour and sugar.
- Add the cream and milk, before passing through a sieve into a saucepan. Heat over a medium heat.
- Pour the custard into the pastry cases and bake for 25-30 minutes.
- Top with grapefruit segments and desiccated coconut.

PREPARATION TIME 10-15 MINUTES

COOKING TIME 15-20 MINUTES

INGREDIENTS

250 g / 9 oz ready-made shortcrust pastry
a little plain (all purpose) flour, for dusting
6 medium egg yolks
75 g / 3 oz / ⅓ cup caster (superfine) sugar
250 ml / 9 fl. oz / 1 cup whipping cream
200 ml / 7 fl. oz / ⅘ cup whole milk
2 tsp cornflour (cornstarch)

TO GARNISH
2 pink grapefruit, segmented
2 tbsp desiccated coconut

Orange Tartlet

192

- Replace the grapefruit segments with orange segments. Garnish with icing sugar instead of desiccated coconut.

193

MAKES 12

Ginger and Hazelnut Cookies

- Preheat the oven to 180°C (160°C fan) / 350F / gas 4.
- Grease and line 2 baking trays with greaseproof paper.
- Cream together the butter and sugar in a mixing bowl.
- Add the honey, egg and vanilla extract and beat again.
- In a separate mixing bowl, sift together the flour, salt, bicarbonate of soda, ground ginger and hazelnuts.
- Beat into the creamed butter and sugar mixture until you have an even cookie dough.
- Fold in the rolled oats until incorporated then chill for 30 minutes.
- Roll the chilled dough out to 1 cm thickness on a floured work surface and cut out 12 shapes.
- Arrange on the baking trays, spaced apart, and bake for 16-18 minutes until golden-brown all over.
- Remove from the oven and allow to cool. Garnish with heart-shaped candies before serving.

PREPARATION TIME 10-15 MINUTES

COOKING TIME 15 MINUTES

INGREDIENTS

350 g / 12 oz / 3 cups rolled oats
225 g / 8 oz / 1 ½ cups plain (all purpose) flour, sifted
175 g / 6 oz / ¾ cup unsalted butter, softened
175 g / 6 oz / 1 cup soft brown sugar
100 g / 3 ½ oz / 1 cup hazelnuts (cob nuts), finely chopped
1 tsp vanilla extract
1 large egg
1 tbsp honey
1 tsp ground ginger
½ tsp salt

TO GARNISH
1 tbsp small heart-shaped candies

Allspice Cookies

194

- Replace the ground ginger with 2 tsp ground allspice and use finely chopped almonds instead of hazelnuts.

195

SERVES 2

Cherry Heart Pie

196

Strawberry Heart Pies

- Replace the cherries with tinned strawberries.

197

Raspberry Heart Pies

- Replace the cherries with tinned raspberries.

PREPARATION TIME 10-15 MINUTES

COOKING TIME 15-20 MINUTES

INGREDIENTS

250 g / 9 oz ready-made sweet shortcrust pastry
a little plain (all purpose) flour, for dusting
400 g / 14 oz / 2 cups canned cherries
75 g / 3 oz / ⅓ cup caster (superfine) sugar
1 lemon, juiced
1 small egg, beaten

- Roll half the pastry out on a lightly floured surface.
- Cut rounds of pastry that will line the base and sides of two individual ceramic pie dishes.
- Roll the other half of pastry out on a floured surface and cut 2 rounds as the lids.
- Use a heart-shaped cookie cutter to stamp heart shapes of the centre of the pastry lids; reserve them.
- Chill all the pastry.
- Combine the cherries lemon juice and sugar in a saucepan.
- Bring to a simmer over a medium heat, then remove from the heat, stirring frequently as you do.
- Remove the pastry from the fridge and prick the bases.
- Once the cherry mixture has cooled sufficiently, divide between to the two pie dishes.
- Drape the pastry lids on top and crimp the edges using the tines of a fork.
- Transfer carefully to lined baking sheets and chill for 15 minutes.
- Preheat the oven to 190°C (170° fan) / 375F / gas 5.
- Egg wash all the exposed pieces of pastry, including the heart shapes of pastry.
- Bake everything for 25-30 minutes.
- Replace the heart shape of pastry in the centre.

198

SERVES 2

Heart Cake with Rose Jam

- Preheat the oven to 180°C (160° fan) / 340F / gas 4.
- Grease and line 2 heart-shaped cake moulds.
- Combine the flour, margarine, sugar, eggs and rosewater and whisk until smooth. Spoon into the moulds and bake for 15-20 minutes.
- Combine the strawberry jam and rosewater.
- Heat until simmering, then remove and stir well.
- Once the sponges are cool, spread jam on the top of each. Sandwich them together.
- Roll the marzipan out on a dusted surface.
- Use one of the heart-shaped cake moulds as a template to cut out a thin layer of the marzipan.
- Drape the marzipan heart on top and press down gently.
- Combine the icing sugar and boiling water and whisk.
- Spread evenly on top of the marzipan and allow to set.
- Decorate with a sugar rose.

Heart Shaped Violet Sponge

199

- Replace the rosewater with 5-6 drops of violet essence and top with a candied violet instead of a sugar rose.

PREPARATION TIME 20 MINUTES

COOKING TIME 45-50 MINUTES

INGREDIENTS

FOR THE SPONGE

110 g / 4 oz / ⅔ cup self-raising flour, sifted
110 g / 4 oz / ½ cup margarine
110 g / 4 oz / ½ cup caster (superfine) sugar
2 medium eggs
½ tsp rosewater

FOR THE JAM

100 g / 3 ½ oz / ½ cup strawberry jam
1 tsp rosewater

FOR THE ICING AND GARNISH

50 g / 2 oz / ¼ cup marzipan
125 g / 4 ½ oz / 1 cup icing (confectioners') sugar, for dusting
100 g icing (confectioners') sugar
30 ml / 1 fl. oz / 2 tbsp boiling water
sugar rose, to decorate

200

MAKES 12

Rosebud Pastry Tartlets

- Preheat the oven to 190°C (170° fan) / 375F / gas 5.
- Roll the pastry out to ½ cm thickness on a lightly floured surface.
- Cut out 12 rounds 5 cm in diameter.
- Use to line 12 mini tartlet cases, pricking the bases with a fork.
- Brush the thin apple slices with a little melted butter and shape into rosebud shapes by layering in concentric circles.
- Place inside the pastry-lined tartlet cases and brush with more melted butter.
- Bake for 10-12 minutes until the pastry is golden-brown in colour.
- Remove from the oven and leave to cool on wire racks.
- Mix the pink sugar crystals and the icing sugar and use to dust the tartlets before serving.

Pear Rosebud Tartlets

201

- Replace the apple slices with thinly sliced pear before shaping into rosebuds. Dust with only icing sugar.

PREPARATION TIME 15 MINUTES

COOKING TIME 20 MINUTES

INGREDIENTS

150 g / 5 oz ready-made puff pastry
a little plain (all purpose) flour, for dusting
55 g / 2 oz / ¼ cup unsalted butter, melted and cooled
4 eating apples, peeled, cored and thinly sliced

TO GARNISH

1 tbsp pink sugar crystals
1 tbsp icing (confectioners') sugar

MAKES 12 · 202

Cranberry and Honey Madeleines

PREPARATION TIME 10 MINUTES

COOKING TIME 15 MINUTES

INGREDIENTS

75 g / 3 oz / ⅔ cup icing
(confectioners') sugar, sifted
55 g / 2 oz / ¼ cup orange blossom
honey
115 g / 4 oz / ½ cup unsalted butter,
melted and cooled
100 g / 3 ½ oz / ⅔ cup plain
(all purpose) flour, sifted
55 g / 2 oz / ⅓ cup cranberries
½ tsp baking powder
½ tsp vanilla extract
a pinch of salt

- Preheat the oven to 180°C (160° fan) / 350F / gas 4.
- Grease a 12-hole mini muffin tin.
- Beat together the eggs, icing sugar, salt, honey and vanilla extract in a large mixing bowl until thick and shiny.
- Fold in the flour, 25 g at a time, as well as the baking powder.
- Once all the flour has been added, fold in the melted butter until incorporated.
- Spoon into the moulds, dotting each with a few cranberries.
- Bake for 14-16 minutes until golden and risen.
- Remove and allow them to cool in the tin for a few minutes before turning out onto a wire rack to finish cooling.

Raspberry and Honey Madeleines 203

- Replace the cranberries with 100 g / 3 ½ oz / 1 cup raspberries.

MAKES 12 · 204

Mint Madeleines

PREPARATION TIME 10 MINUTES

COOKING TIME 15 MINUTES

INGREDIENTS

125 g / 4 ½ oz / 1 cup icing
(confectioners') sugar, sifted
115 g / 4 oz / ½ cup unsalted butter,
melted and cooled
100 g / 3 ½ oz / ⅔ cup plain
(all purpose) flour, sifted
1 tsp peppermint extract
½ tsp baking powder
a pinch of salt

TO GARNISH
a few mint leaves

- Preheat the oven to 180°C (160° fan) / 350F / gas 4.
- Grease a 12-hole round madeleine tin.
- Beat together the eggs, icing sugar, salt and peppermint extract in a large mixing bowl until thick and shiny.
- Fold in the flour, 25 g at a time, as well as the baking powder.
- Once all the flour has been added, fold in the melted butter until incorporated.
- Spoon into the madeleine tin and bake for 12-14 minutes until golden and risen.
- Remove and allow them to cool in the tin for a few minutes before turning out onto a wire rack to finish cooling.
- Garnish with mint leaves before serving.

Mint and Orange Madeleines 205

- Add ½ tsp orange flower water to the batter before baking.

206

MAKES 12

Milk Chocolate Financiers

Dark and White Chocolate Financiers **207**

- Replace the milk chocolate with dark chocolate chips and fold through 55 g / 2 oz / ⅓ cup chopped white chocolate into the batter.

Chocolate Blueberry Financiers **208**

- Press 5 blueberries into the top of each financier before cooking.

PREPARATION TIME 10 MINUTES

COOKING TIME 15 MINUTES

INGREDIENTS

55 g / 2 oz / ¼ cup caster (superfine) sugar
100 g / 3 ½ oz / ⅔ cup milk chocolate chips
110 g / 4 oz / ½ cup slightly salted butter, softened
1 tbsp unsalted butter, softened
110 g / 4 oz / 1 cup ground almonds
30 g / 1 oz / 2 tbsp plain (all purpose) flour, sifted
3 medium egg whites
a pinch of salt

- Preheat the oven to 180°C (160° fan) / 350F / gas 4.
- Brown the butter in a saucepan until nutty in aroma.
- Strain through a fine sieve into a clean bowl, allowing it to cool.
- Melt the chocolate in a heatproof bowl set atop a saucepan of simmering water, stirring occasionally.
- Remove once melted and leave to cool.
- Combine the flour, almonds, salt and sugar in a mixing bowl.
- Gently whisk the egg whites into this mixture and then fold through the cooled, melted butter and the melted chocolate.
- Grease a 12-hole financier tin with unsalted butter and fill with the batter.
- Bake for 15-18 minutes; test with a wooden toothpick, if it comes out clean, they are ready.
- Remove from the oven and cool on a wire rack before turning out and serving

209

MAKES 12

Raspberry Madeleines

PREPARATION TIME 10 MINUTES

COOKING TIME 15 MINUTES

....

INGREDIENTS

115 g / 4 oz / ½ cup unsalted butter,
melted and cooled
100 g / 3 ½ oz / ⅔ cup plain
(all purpose) flour, sifted
100 g / 3 ½ oz / ½ cup raspberry
puree
65 g / 2 ½ oz / ½ cup icing
(confectioners') sugar, sifted
½ tsp baking powder
½ tsp vanilla extract
a pinch of salt

TO GARNISH
a small handful of raspberries

- Preheat the oven to 180°C (160° fan) / 350F / gas 4.
- Grease a 12-hole madeleine tray.
- Beat together the eggs, icing sugar, salt and vanilla extract in a large mixing bowl until thick and shiny.
- Fold in the flour, 25 g at a time, as well as the baking powder.
- Once all the flour has been added, fold in the melted butter until incorporated.
- Spoon into the moulds, leaving them about three-quarters full with the batter.
- Bake for 12-14 minutes until golden and risen.
- Remove and allow them to cool in the tray for a few minutes before turning out onto a wire rack to finish cooling.
- Serve with raspberries.

210

MAKES 12

Pistachio Macaroons with Chocolate Filling

PREPARATION TIME 10-15
MINUTES

COOKING TIME 20 MINUTES

....

INGREDIENTS

300 g / 10 ½ / 2 ⅓ cups icing
(confectioners') sugar, sifted
200 g / 10 ½ oz / 2 cups pistachios,
shelled
55 g / 2 oz / ⅓ cup shelled pistachios,
chopped
3 medium egg whites
a pinch of salt
250 g / 9 oz / 1 ⅔ cups good-quality
dark chocolate, chopped
250 ml / 9 fl. oz / 1 cup double
(heavy) cream

- Preheat the oven to 180°C (160° fan) / 350F / gas 4.
- Blitz the pistachios in a food processor until finely ground.
- Grease and line 2 baking trays with greaseproof paper.
- Combine the ground pistachios and icing sugar in a large mixing bowl.
- Beat the egg whites in a separate, clean mixing bowl with a pinch
of salt until stiff peaks form.
- Fold the egg whites into the ground pistachio mixture then spoon into a piping bags fitted with straight-sided 3 cm nozzle.
- Pipe 24 rounds onto the baking trays, spaced apart, and sprinkle with the finely chopped pistachios.
- Leave for 15 minutes, then bake for 8-10 minutes until just set.
- Remove from the oven and allow to cool on the trays for 10 minutes before moving to a wire rack.
- Heat the cream in a saucepan over a moderate heat until boiling.
- Remove the saucepan from the heat and stir in the chocolate, until smooth and thick.
- Let the ganache cool before spreading on top of half the macaroon rounds.
- Reassemble using the remaining rounds before serving.

211

SERVES 4

Individual Lemon Meringue Pies

- Preheat the oven to 190°C (170° fan) / 375F / gas 5.
- Roll the pastry out on a lightly floured surface.
- Cut out 4 rounds of pastry and line 4 5" tartlet cases.
- Prick the bases and trim excess pastry.
- Line with greaseproof paper and fill with baking beans before blind-baking for 12-15 minutes until golden.
- Remove from the oven and discard the greaseproof paper and baking beans.
- Return to the oven for 3-4 minutes to brown the base before removing to a wire rack to cool.
- Whisk the egg white with the salt until stiff peaks form.
- Add the cream of tartar and the sugar, 1 tablespoon at a time, beating well between additions until thick and glossy.
- Fill the pastry with lemon curd and top with the meringue before baking for 8-10 minutes.

PREPARATION TIME 10-15 MINUTES

COOKING TIME 20 MINUTES

INGREDIENTS

250 g / 9 oz ready-made shortcrust pastry
a little plain (all purpose) flour, for dusting
450 g / 1 lb / 2 cups lemon curd
1 medium egg white
55 g / 2 oz / ¼ cup caster (superfine) sugar
a pinch of salt
½ tsp cream of tartar

212

MAKES 24

Coffee Truffles

PREPARATION TIME 5-10 MINUTES

COOKING TIME 10-15 MINUTES

INGREDIENTS

300 g / 10 ½ oz / 2 cups good-quality dark chocolate, chopped
300 ml / 10 ½ fl. oz / 1 ⅓ cups double (heavy) cream
55 g / 2 oz / ¼ cup unsalted butter
55 g / 2 oz / ⅓ cup cocoa powder
2 tsp instant coffee granules
30 ml / 1 fl. oz / 2 tbsp Kahlua
a little sunflower oil
½ tsp caster (superfine) sugar

- Place the chocolate in a large heatproof mixing bowl.
- Place the cream, butter, instant coffee granules and Kahlua if using in a saucepan and heat over a moderate heat until simmering.
- Once the butter has fully melted and the mixture is simmering, remove from the heat and pour over the chocolate.
- Beat until you have a smooth mixture, then cover the bowl and chill for 4 hours.
- To make the truffles, remove the chocolate mixture from the fridge and let sit at room temperature for 10 minutes.
- Use a melon baller to take out scoops of the truffle mixture.
- Using lightly oiled hands, roll into truffle shapes then roll in the cocoa powder to lightly coat.
- Shake off any excess before serving.

213

MAKES 4

Gluten and Dairy-Free Tarts

PREPARATION TIME 10 MINUTES

COOKING TIME 10 MINUTES

INGREDIENTS

450 g / 1 lb / 3 cups lactose-free chocolate, chopped
250 ml / 9 fl. oz / 1 cup coconut milk
55 g / 2 oz / ⅓ cup shelled pistachios, chopped
55 g / 2 oz / ½ cup hazelnuts (cob nuts), finely chopped
30 g / 1 oz / 2 tbsp mixed candied peel
1 tbsp raisins

- Pulse half of the pistachios in a food processor and set to one side.
- Heat together the chocolate and coconut in a saucepan, stirring until melted and smooth.
- Pour into individual ramekins and chill overnight.
- Garnish the tarts with the hazelnuts, ground and chopped pistachios, mixed candied peel and raisins before serving.

214

SERVES 4

Mini Raspberry Macaroon Charlottes

PREPARATION TIME 10-15 MINUTES

COOKING TIME 20 MINUTES

INGREDIENTS

250 g / 9 oz / 2 cups icing (confectioners') sugar
150 g / 5 oz / 1 ½ cups ground almonds
4 medium egg whites
1 tsp red food colouring
1 tsp raspberry flavouring
1 tbsp Framboise (optional)
400 ml / 14 fl. oz / 1 ¾ cups fromage frais
250 ml / 9 fl. oz / 1 cup whipping cream
125 g / 4 ½ oz / 1 cup icing (confectioners') sugar
150 g / 5 oz / ⅔ cup seedless raspberry jam
12 raspberries

- Preheat the oven to 180°C (160°C fan) / 350°F / gas 4. Line 2 baking trays with greaseproof paper.
- Combine the ground almonds and icing sugar.
- Beat the egg whites in a bowl until stiff peaks form.
- Fold the egg whites into the ground almond and icing sugar until incorporated.
- Add the raspberry flavouring, red food colouring and Framboise and fold until incorporated.
- Spoon into a piping bag and pipe 36 1" rounds onto the baking trays. Leave to set for 15 minutes, then bake for 8-10 minutes.
- Whip cream with the icing sugar. Beat the fromage frais with jam, then fold mixtures together.
- Arrange 4, 4" pastry rings on a line baking tray and arrange 9 macaroon rounds around the perimeters.
- Fill with the cream mixture and chill overnight. Remove the rings and garnish with raspberries.

Pistachio and Raspberry Macaroon Charlottes

215

- Replace the raspberry flavouring and Framboise with 55 g / 2 oz / ½ cup finely ground pistachios.

216

SERVES 4

Crème Brûlée Tartlets

PREPARATION TIME 10-15 MINUTES

COOKING TIME 20 MINUTES

INGREDIENTS

250 g / 9 oz ready-made shortcrust pastry
a little plain (all purpose) flour, for dusting
250 ml / 9 fl. oz / 1 cup whole milk
250 ml / 9 fl. oz / 1 cup double (heavy) cream
6 large egg yolks
110 g / 4 oz / ½ cup caster (superfine) sugar
1 vanilla pod, split in half lengthways

TO GARNISH

55 g / 2 oz / ⅓ cup soft light brown sugar

- Preheat the oven to 180°C (160° fan) / 350F / gas 4.
- Roll the pastry out on a lightly floured surface.
- Cut out 4 rounds of pastry and line 4 4" tartlet cases.
- Prick the bases with a fork and trim any excess pastry.
- Line with greaseproof paper and fill with baking beans before blind-baking for 12-15 minutes until golden.
- Remove and discard the greaseproof paper and beans.
- Return to the oven for 3 minutes.
- Reduce the oven to 150°C (130° fan) / 300F / gas 2.
- Combine milk, cream and vanilla pod in a saucepan and heat over a moderate heat until simmering.
- Whisk together the egg yolks and sugar in a mixing bowl. Pour the milk and cream in a slow stream.
- Pour into the pastry cases and bake for 25-30 minutes.
- Remove from the oven and sprinkle the tops with the brown sugar before caramelising under a hot grill.

Orange Crème Brûlée Tartlets

217

- Add 2 tsp orange flower water to the milk and cream when simmering, omitting the vanilla pod.

218

MAKES 24

Chocolate Toffee Delicacies

- Beat together the butter, salt and dulce de leche until soft and creamy.
- Spoon into a piping bag fitted with a 3 cm star-shaped nozzle.
- Pipe into the petit fours cups, leaving a tail on top.
- Sprinkle with grated chocolate before serving.

PREPARATION TIME 5 MINUTES

COOKING TIME 10 MINUTES

INGREDIENTS

24 chocolate petit fours cups
450 g / 1 lb / 2 cups butter, softened
250 g / 9 oz / 1 cup dulce de leche
a pinch of salt

TO GARNISH

100 g / 3 ½ oz / ⅔ cup dark chocolate, grated

Peanut Butter Cups

  219

- Beat 525 g / 1 lb 3 oz / 3 cups peanut butter and pipe into the chocolate cups instead of the toffee buttercream. Garnish with chopped peanuts.

220

SERVES 4

Rose de Reims Biscuit Trifles

- Preheat the oven to 180°C (160° fan) / 350F / gas 4.
- Grease and line a large baking tray.
- Beat the egg yolk, caster sugar and vanilla extract in a mixing bowl for 2 minutes.
- Add a few drops of food dye and beat until pink.
- Fold the flour and cornflour into the mixture. Whisk the egg whites then fold into the sugar mixture.
- Spoon into a piping bag and pipe lines onto the baking tray, spaced apart.
- Bake for 8-10 minutes until set and dry.
- Beat the Greek yoghurt and jam, then whip the cream until soft peaks form. Fold mixtures together.
- Break up the biscuits and arrange some in the jars.
- Spoon the raspberry mixture on top before topping with more crushed biscuit.
- Garnish each with 2 raspberries.

PREPARATION TIME 10-15 MINUTES

COOKING TIME 20 MINUTES

INGREDIENTS

FOR THE BISCUITS
110 g / 4 oz / ½ cup caster (superfine) sugar
110 g / 4 oz / ⅔ cup plain (all purpose) flour, sifted
110 g / 4 oz / ½ cup butter, melted
2 large egg white
2 large egg yolks
1 tbsp cornflour (cornstarch), sifted
½ tsp vanilla extract
½ tsp red food colouring

FOR THE FILLING
250 ml / 9 fl. oz / 1 cup whipping cream
125 g / 4 ½ oz / ½ cup Greek yoghurt
100 g / 3 ½ oz / ½ cup seedless raspberry jam

TO GARNISH
8 raspberries

Blackcurrant Biscuit Trifles

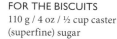 **221**

- Replace the jam in the filling with blackcurrant jam and garnish with small bunches of blackcurrants on top.

69

Summer Fruit Muffins and Cakes

Mixed Currant Muffins and Cakes

223

- Replace the redcurrant and raspberries in the recipe with sultanas and currants.

Blackcurrant and Blackberry Cakes and Muffins

224

- Replace the redcurrants with black currants, and replace the raspberries with blackberries.

PREPARATION TIME 10-15 MINUTES

COOKING TIME 20-25 MINUTES

....

INGREDIENTS

250 g / 9 / 1 ⅔ cups plain
(all purpose) flour, sifted
110 g / 4 oz / ½ cup caster (superfine) sugar
125 ml / 4 ½ fl. oz/ ½ cup plain yoghurt
75 g / 3 oz / ⅓ cup butter, melted and cooled
100 g / 3 ½ oz / 1 cup redcurrants
1 medium egg, 1 tsp vanilla extract
1 tsp baking powder, salt
110 g / 4 oz / ½ cup caster (superfine) sugar
110 g / 4 oz / ½ cup margarine
110 g / 4 oz / ⅔ cup self-raising flour
2 eggs
1 tsp vanilla extract
100 g / 3 ½ oz / 1 cup raspberries
100 g / 3 ½ oz / 1 cup redcurrants

- Preheat the oven to 180°C (160° fan) / 350F / gas 4.
- Grease and line a 12-hole muffin tin with 8 cases.
- Grease and line 8 mini loaf tins with greaseproof paper.
- For the muffins, combine the flour, sugar, salt and baking powder in a large mixing bowl.
- In a separate mixing bowl, whisk together the butter, yoghurt, eggs and vanilla extract until smooth.
- Add to the dry ingredients and mix until just incorporated.
- Spoon into the cases and dot the tops with redcurrants.
- Bake 18-20 minutes until risen, golden and risen; test with a wooden toothpick, if it comes out clean, they are ready.
- Remove and transfer to a wire rack to cool.
- Beat together all the ingredients for the cakes except the raspberries and redcurrants until smooth; 2-3 minutes.
- Fold in the raspberries and spoon into the loaf tins.
- Top with redcurrants and bake for 18-20 minutes; test with a wooden toothpick, if it comes out clean, they are ready.
- Remove to a wire rack to cool before turning out and serving with the muffins.

225

MAKES 6

Chocolate and Hazelnut Mini Loafs

- Preheat the oven to 180°C (160° fan) / 350F / gas 4.
- Grease 4 disposable mini loaf cases.
- Beat together the flour, sugar, margarine, eggs, cocoa powder and milk until smooth; 2-3 minutes.
- Fold in the chopped hazelnuts and spoon into the loaf cases.
- Arrange on a baking tray and bake for 18-20 minutes until risen; test with a wooden toothpick, if it comes out clean, the loafs are ready.
- Remove from the oven and leave to cool on a wire rack before serving.

PREPARATION TIME 10 MINUTES

COOKING TIME 10 MINUTES

INGREDIENTS

110 g / 4 oz / ½ cup caster (superfine) sugar
110 g / 4 oz / ½ cup margarine
110 g / 4 oz / ⅔ cup self-raising flour
100 g / 3 ½ oz / 1 cup hazelnuts (cob nuts) roughly chopped
2 large eggs
30 g / 1 oz / 2 tbsp cocoa powder
2 tbsp whole milk

Two Chocolate and Hazelnut Cakes

 226

- Stir 100 g / 3 ½ oz / ⅔ cup chopped white chocolate into the batter.

227

MAKES 12

Chocolate and Hazelnut Bites

- Grease and line a baking tray with greaseproof paper.
- Mix the sugar and water in a pan until deep golden-brown.
- Add 2 tablespoons of hazelnuts and swirl to coat before pouring onto the greaseproof paper and leaving to set.
- Preheat the oven to 180°C (160° fan) / 350F / gas 4. Grease and line a 12-hole mini cupcake tin with cases.
- Blitz the remaining hazelnuts and oats in a food processor until finely ground.
- Melt the butter and syrup together in a large saucepan.
- Add the ground oats mixture and stir well.
- Spoon into the cases and bake for 20-25 minutes.
- Melt the chocolate in a heatproof bowl set atop a saucepan of simmering water, until melted.
- Remove from the heat and coat with the chocolate.
- Top with candied hazelnuts before the chocolate sets.

PREPARATION TIME 10 MINUTES

COOKING TIME 15-20 MINUTES

INGREDIENTS

450 g / 1 lb / 3 cups good-quality puffed rice chocolate, chopped
150 g / 5 oz / 1 ½ cups hazelnuts (cob nuts)
150 g / 5 oz / 2 cups rolled oats
225 g / 8 oz / 1 cup unsalted butter, softened
125 g / 4 ½ oz / ⅓ cup Golden Syrup
55 g / 2 oz / ¼ cup caster (superfine) sugar
2 tbsp cold water

Chocolate and Raisin Bites

 228

- Replace the hazelnut topping with 4-5 raisins before the chocolate sets.

229

SERVES 8

Rosewater-Flavoured Nougat

PREPARATION TIME 15 MINUTES

COOKING TIME 20 MINUTES

SETTING TIME 6 HOURS

INGREDIENTS

FOR THE ALMOND NOUGAT

275 g / 10 oz / 1 ¼ cups caster (superfine) sugar
250 g / 9 oz / 1 cup glucose
200 g / 7 oz / 2 cups whole almonds, blanched
50 g / 2 oz / ½ cup pistachios, shelled
50 ml / 2 fl. oz / ¼ cup cold water
1 large egg white, at room temperature
2 tsp rosewater

ALSO NEEDED

sugar thermometer
electric whisk/mixer
2 12" x 4" pink rice paper (use white if pink is not available)

- Line a 12" x 4" x 3" jelly roll pan or cake tin with one of the sheets of rice paper.
- Combine the sugar, water and glucose in a saucepan, over a medium heat until the sugar has dissolved.
- Cook until the mixture registers 120°C on the thermometer, then start to beat the egg white in a separate mixing bowl until soft peaks form.
- Once the sugar mixture reaches 136-138°C, remove from the heat and beat into the egg white in a slow, steady stream until fully incorporated.
- Keep whisking for 2-3 minutes until thick and glossy.
- Stir in the almonds, pistachios and rosewater, then spoon into the pan, levelling the mixture with a wet spoon.
- Cover with the other sheet of rice paper and gently weigh down, leaving to set for at least 6 hours.

Orange-Flavoured Nougat

230

- Replace the rosewater with 2 tsp orange flower water and omit the pistachios.

231

MAKES 4

Individual Apple Pies

PREPARATION TIME 10 MINUTES

COOKING TIME 15-20 MINUTES

INGREDIENTS

200 g / 7 oz ready-made shortcrust pastry
180 g / 6 ½ oz ready-made puff pastry
a little plain (all purpose) flour, for dusting
800 g / 1 lb 12 oz / 3 ¼ cups cooking apples, peeled and diced
110 g / 4 oz / ½ cup caster (superfine) sugar
55 ml / 2 fl. oz / ¼ cup cold water
½ tsp ground cinnamon
1 large egg, beaten

- Preheat the oven to 190°C (170° fan) / 375F / gas 5.
- Combine the apple, sugar, cinnamon and water in a saucepan over a medium heat until the apple is soft.
- Roll out the shortcrust pastry on a floured surface.
- Cut 4 rounds of pastry and line 4 deep 4" tartlet cases. Prick the bases and trim excess pastry.
- Line with greaseproof paper and fill with baking beans before blind-baking for 10-12 minutes.
- Remove and discard the greaseproof paper and beans. Brush the bases with a little of the beaten egg.
- Roll the puff pastry out on a floured surface.
- Cut out 4 rounds 4" in diameter; wet the rims of the shortcrust pastry and fill with apple.
- Lay the puff pastry rounds on top and seal well before poking a hole on top.
- Brush the tops with beaten egg and bake for 12-15 minutes.

Spiced Apple Pies

232

- Add 1 tsp ground allspices and ½ tsp ground cloves to the apple filling.

233

SERVES 8

Mango and Blueberry Tartlets

Blueberry and Raspberry Tarts

234

- Replace the mango with 350g raspberries.

Peach and Blueberry Tarts

235

- Replace the mangos with slices of ripe peaches (6-7 peaches).

PREPARATION TIME 10-15 MINUTES

COOKING TIME 35-45 MINUTES

INGREDIENTS

320 g / 11 oz ready-made shortcrust pastry
a little plain (all purpose) flour, for dusting
4 ripe mangoes, destoned and cut into strips
350 g / 12 oz / 3 cups blueberries

FOR THE CRÈME PATISSERIE

350 ml / 12 fl. oz / 1 ½ cups whole milk
1 vanilla pod, split lengthwise
4 medium egg yolks
55 g / 2 oz / ¼ cup caster (superfine) sugar
25 g / 1 oz / 2 tbsp plain (all purpose) flour
25 g / 1 oz / 2 tbsp cornflour (cornstarch)

- Preheat the oven to 180°C (160°C fan) / 350°F / gas 4.
- Roll the pastry out on a lightly floured work surface.
- Cut out 8 rounds to line 8 fluted tartlet tins.
- Press the pastry into the base and sides well, then remove excess pastry. Prick the bases with a fork.
- Line with greaseproof paper and fill with baking beans.
- Blind bake for 12-15 minutes until they start to colour.
- Remove from the oven and discard the greaseproof paper and baking beans.
- Return to the oven to brown the bases for 3-4 minutes.
- Remove from the oven and let cool.
- Place the split vanilla pod and milk in a saucepan and bring to the boil, then set to one side to cool a little.
- In a mixing bowl, whisk the egg yolks and sugar until thick then sift in the flour and cornflour, whisking until smooth.
- Pour the milk and vanilla onto this mixture.
- Pour back into the saucepan and cook on a medium heat for about 2 minutes.
- Transfer to a clean bowl and cover with clingfilm.
- Once the pastry tartlet cases are cool, fill with generous tablespoons of the crème patisserie.
- Arrange the blueberries and strips of mango in each tartlet.

236

SERVES 6

Gluten-Free Chocolate Cakes

PREPARATION TIME 10-15
MINUTES

COOKING TIME 15 MINUTES

INGREDIENTS

100 g / 3 ½ oz / ⅔ cup dark
chocolate chips
110 g / 4 oz / ½ cup slightly salted
butter, softened
110 g / 4 oz / 1 cup ground almonds
55 g / 2 oz / ¼ cup caster (superfine)
sugar
2 tbsp cornflour (cornstarch)
2 medium egg whites
a pinch of salt

TO GARNISH

500 ml / 18 fl. oz / 2 cups pistachio
ice-cream, softened
50 g / 2 oz / ⅓ cup dark chocolate,
grated
25 g / 1 oz / ¼ cup pistachios,
finely chopped

- Preheat the oven to 180°C (160° fan) / 350F / gas 4.
- Grease a 6-hole Yorkshire pudding tray.
- Melt together the butter, sugar and chocolate chips in a saucepan set over a medium heat, stirring until smooth.
- Whisk the egg whites with a pinch of salt until stiff peaks form.
- Fold the ground almonds and cornstarch into the chocolate mixture.
- Spoon into the Yorkshire pudding tray and bake for 15-18 minutes; test with a wooden toothpick, if it comes out clean, the cakes are ready.
- Remove from the oven and leave to cool in the tray before turning out.
- Serve with balls of pistachio ice cream, garnish with chopped pistachios and sprinkled with grated chocolate.

Gluten-Free Chocolate Walnut Cakes

 237

- Add 50 g / 2 oz / ½ cup chopped walnut halves to the batter before baking.

238

MAKES 6

Pistachio Tartlets

PREPARATION TIME 10 MINUTES

COOKING TIME 15 MINUTES

INGREDIENTS

300 g / 10 ½ oz ready-made
shortcrust pastry
a little plain (all purpose) flour,
for dusting
225 g / 8 oz / 2 cups shelled
pistachios, chopped
110 g / 4 oz / ½ cup caster (superfine)
sugar
110 g / 4 oz / ½ cup unsalted butter
2 small eggs

TO GARNISH

55 g / 2 oz / ⅓ cup pistachios, shelled
and chopped

- Preheat the oven to 180°C (160° fan) / 350F / gas 4.
- Roll the pastry out on a lightly floured surface.
- Cut out 4 rounds of pastry and line 6 3" tartlet cases.
- Prick the bases with a fork and trim any excess, overhanging pastry with a serrated knife.
- Chill until needed.
- Blitz the pistachios in a food processor until finely ground, then add the butter and sugar and blitz until creamy.
- Add the eggs and pulse until incorporated.
- Spoon into the pastry and bake for 25-30 minutes until the edge of the pastry is golden brown in colour and the filling is puffed up a little.
- Remove the tartlets from the oven and let them cool on a wire rack.
- Garnish with chopped pistachios.

Pistachio and Orange Tartlets

239

- Add 2 tsp orange flower water to the food processor at the same time as the eggs.

240
MAKES 4

Mirabelle Plum Tartlets

- Preheat the oven to 180°C (160° fan) / 350F / gas 4.
- Roll the pastry out on a lightly floured surface.
- Cut out 4 rounds of pastry and line 4 5" tartlet cases.
- Prick the bases and trim excess pastry.
- Line with greaseproof paper and fill with baking beans before blind-baking for 12-15 minutes until golden.
- Remove from the oven and discard the greaseproof paper and baking beans.
- Return to the oven for 3 minutes to brown the base before removing to a wire rack to cool.
- Combine the plums, sugar, brandy and water in a saucepan and cook over a medium heat for 6-8 minutes until the fruit is soft. Preheat the grill to hot.
- Spoon the plums into the pastry cases and dust with icing sugar before grilling for 1-2 minutes.
- Remove from the grill before serving.

Plum and Orange Tartlets   241

- Replace 150 g of the plums with 1 segmented orange, adding the finely grated zest from the orange to the saucepan.

PREPARATION TIME 10-15 MINUTES

COOKING TIME 20 MINUTES

INGREDIENTS

250 g / 9 oz ready-made shortcrust pastry
a little plain (all purpose) flour, for dusting
600 g / 1 lb 5 oz / 4 cups Mirabelle plums, de-stoned and halved
110 g / 4 oz / ½ cup golden caster (superfine) sugar
55 ml / 2 fl. oz / ¼ cup cold water
30 ml / 1 fl. oz / 2 tbsp brandy (optional)

TO GARNISH
2 tbsp icing (confectioners') sugar

242
MAKES 4

Summer Fruit and Cream Shortcake

- Preheat the oven to 190°C (170° fan) / 375F / gas 5.
- Combine the flour, salt, baking powder and sugar in a food processor.
- Add the cubed butter and pulse.
- Add the buttermilk and pulse until a dough forms.
- Turn out on a work surface and knead until even. Roll the dough out and cut out 8 rounds.
- Grease and line 2 baking trays with greaseproof paper and arrange the rounds spaced apart on them.
- Bake for 10-12 minutes until golden-brown.
- Whip the cream with the icing sugar and vanilla extract until soft peaks form.
- Spoon the cream on 4 of the shortcakes and top with the raspberries and blackberries.
- Sandwich with the remaining shortcakes and dust with icing sugar.

Blackcurrant Cream Shortcakes   243

- Fold 200 g / 7 oz / 2 cups blackcurrants into the whipped cream instead of using raspberries and blackberries.

PREPARATION TIME 10 MINUTES

COOKING TIME 15-20 MINUTES

INGREDIENTS

150 g / 5 oz / 1 cup plain (all purpose) flour
55 ml / 2 fl. oz / ¼ cup buttermilk
30 g / 1 oz / 2 tbsp unsalted butter, cold and cubed
30 g / 1 oz / 2 tbsp caster (superfine) sugar
a little extra plain (all purpose) flour, for dusting
1 tsp baking powder
a pinch of salt
250 ml / 9 fl. oz / 1 cup whipping cream
2 tbsp icing (confectioners') sugar
1 tsp vanilla extract
100 g / 3 ½ oz / 1 cup raspberries
100 g / 3 ½ oz / 1 cup blackberries
1 tbsp icing (confectioners') sugar

244

SERVES 4

Chocolate and Chilli Pepper Fondant

Two Chocolate and Chilli Fondants

245

- Add 55 g / 2 oz / ⅓ cup chopped white chocolate to the batter before baking.

Salted Chocolate Fondants

246

- Replace the chilli powder with 1 tsp of flaked sea salt. Garnish with a pinch of salt flakes.

PREPARATION TIME 10 MINUTES

COOKING TIME 10 MINUTES

INGREDIENTS

30 g / 1 oz / 2 tbsp butter, melted
110 g / 4 oz / ⅔ cup good-quality dark chocolate, chopped
110 g / 4 oz / ½ cup unsalted butter, cubed
75 g / 3 oz / ½ cup plain (all purpose) flour
30 g / 1 oz / 2 tbsp good-quality cocoa powder
2 medium eggs
2 medium egg yolks
½ tsp chilli (chili) powder

TO GARNISH

1 tbsp icing (confectioners') sugar
4 red chilli (chili) peppers

- Preheat the oven to 190°C (170° fan) / 375F / gas 5.
- Brush 4 individual ramekins with some of the melted butter, making sure to use upwards strokes with a pastry brush.
- Chill the ramekins for 15 mins then brush with another layer of melted butter.
- Dust the insides with the cocoa powder, tapping lightly to get rid of any excess.
- Chill until ready to fill with the batter.
- Prepare the batter by melting together the chocolate and cubed butter in a heatproof mixing bowl set over a pan of gently simmering water.
- Once melted, remove from the heat and allow to cool for 5 minutes.
- Meanwhile, whisk together the eggs and egg yolks in a separate mixing bowl until thick.
- Sift the plain flour and chilli powder into the eggs and whisk until smooth.
- Fold into the melted chocolate and butter until even.
- Spoon into the ramekins and bake for 12-14 minutes until just set and starting to come away from the sides.
- Serve immediately with a dusting of icing sugar and a chilli pepper.

MAKES 10-12 # Chocolate Smartie Cookies

- Pre-heat the oven to 180 degrees.
- In a large mixing bowl, combine the flour, cocoa powder, baking powder, bicarbonate of soda and salt.
- In a separate bowl, whisk the butter and sugars using an electric whisk until light and fluffy.
- Gradually add the beaten egg by the tablespoon whilst whisking simultaneously.
- Fold in the flour mixture until incorporated.
- Take large tablespoons of the mixture and roll into balls.
- Line and grease two baking trays and arrange the balls of dough, spaced well apart.
- Flatten each ball a little and stud with a few Smarties.
- Bake for 10-12 minutes.
- Remove from the oven and cool on a wire rack.
- Serve stacked on plates.

PREPARATION TIME 20 MINUTES

COOKING TIME 20 MINUTES

INGREDIENTS

180 g / 6 oz / 1 ¼ cups plain (all purpose) flour
25 g / 1 oz / 2 tbsp cocoa powder
½ tsp baking powder
½ tsp bicarbonate of (baking) soda
½ tsp salt
80 g / 3 oz / ⅓ cup unsalted butter, softened
45 g / 1 ½ oz / ¼ cup soft light brown sugar
55 g / 2 oz / ¼ cup caster (superfine) sugar
1 egg, lightly beaten
100 g / 3 ½ oz / ½ cup Smarties

Chocolate Raisin Cookies

- Stud each cookie with 1-2 tsp of raisins before baking.

SERVES 4 # Chocolate and Almond Fondant

- Preheat the oven to 180°C (160° fan) / 350F / gas 4.
- Brush 4 ramekins with some melted butter.
- Chill, then brush with another layer of melted butter.
- Dust the insides with the cocoa powder then chill again.
- Melt together the chocolate and cubed butter in a heatproof mixing bowl set over a pan of simmering water.
- Meanwhile, whisk the eggs and egg yolks until light.
- Sift the plain flour into the eggs and whisk, then fold in the ground almonds.
- Pour the melted chocolate mixture into the egg and flour mixture in thirds, mixing well.
- Divide the fondant batter between the moulds and arrange on a baking tray.
- Bake in the oven for 10-12 minutes.
- Garnish with the flaked almonds.

PREPARATION TIME 10 MINUTES

COOKING TIME 45 MINUTES

INGREDIENTS

1 tbsp butter, melted
100 g / 3 ½ oz / ⅔ cup dark chocolate, chopped
100 g / 3 ½ oz / ½ cup unsalted butter, cubed
30 g / 1 oz / 2 tbsp cocoa powder
2 medium eggs
2 medium egg yolks
75 g / 3 oz / ½ cup plain (all purpose) flour
25 g / 1 oz / ¼ cup ground almonds
a few tbsp flaked almonds, to garnish

Chocolate and Hazelnut Fondants 250

- Replace the almonds with ground and crushed hazelnuts.

251

MAKES 6

Mendiant Tartlet

PREPARATION TIME 10-15
MINUTES

COOKING TIME 15-20 MINUTES

INGREDIENTS

300 g / 10 ½ oz ready-made
shortcrust pastry
a little plain (all purpose) flour,
for dusting
350 g / 12 oz / 2 ⅓ cups good-quality
dark chocolate, chopped
250 ml / 9 fl. oz / 1 cup double
(heavy) cream
55 g / 2 oz / ½ cup whole almonds,
blanched
55 g / 2 oz / ½ cup hazelnuts
(cob nuts)
55 g / 2 oz / ⅓ cup dried fig halves
30 g / 1 oz / ¼ cup pistachios, shelled
and finely chopped
30 g / 1 oz / ¼ cup walnut halves

- Preheat the oven to 180°C (160° fan) / 350F / gas 4.
- Roll the pastry out on a lightly floured surface.
- Cut out 6 rounds of pastry and line 6 3" fluted cases.
- Prick the bases and trim excess pastry.
- Line with greaseproof paper and fill with baking beans before blind-baking for 12-14 minutes until golden.
- Remove from the oven and discard the greaseproof paper and baking beans.
- Return to the oven for 2 minutes to brown the base before removing to a wire rack to cool.
- Heat the cream in a large saucepan set over a moderate heat until boiling, then add the chocolate and whisk until smooth.
- Pour into the tartlet cases and stud with a mixture of the nuts and dried fig halves.
- Chill until set before turning out and serving.

Dried Fruit Tartlets **252**

- Substitute the nuts with the same weight of raisins, sultanas and currants.

253

MAKES 16

Lemon Curd Macaroon Biscuits

PREPARATION TIME 10-15
MINUTES

COOKING TIME 20-25 MINUTES

INGREDIENTS

FOR THE MACAROON MIXTURE
225 g / 8 oz / 1 ¾ cups icing
(confectioners') sugar, sifted
225 g / 8 oz / 1 cup caster (superfine)
sugar
300 g / 10 ½ oz / 3 cups ground
almonds
225 g / 8 oz / 1 cup lemon curd
4 medium egg whites
a pinch of salt

- Preheat the oven to 180°C (160° fan) / 350F / gas 4.
- Grease and line 2 baking trays with greaseproof paper.
- Combine the ground almonds, icing sugar and caster sugar in a large mixing bowl.
- Beat the egg whites in a separate, clean mixing bowl with a pinch of salt until stiff peaks form.
- Fold the egg whites into the ground almond mixture and spoon into a large piping bag fitted with a 3 cm straight-sided nozzle.
- Pipe 32 rounds of each mixture onto the baking trays, spaced apart.
- Leave for 15 minutes, then bake for 8-10 minutes.
- Remove from the oven and allow to cool.
- Spoon a generous teaspoon of lemon curd onto 16 of the rounds before reassembling with the other 16 rounds.

Coconut and Lemon **254**
Curd Macaroons

- Replace 100 g / 3 ½ oz / 1 cup of the ground almonds with the same amount of desiccated coconut.

MAKES 4

SWEET

Redcurrant Tartlets

Blackcurrant Tartlets **256**
- Replace the redcurrant with blackcurrants.

Mixed Berry Tartlets **257**
- Swap ⅓ of the redcurrants for blackcurrants, and ⅓ of the redcurrants for white currants.

PREPARATION TIME 10 MINUTES

COOKING TIME 20-25 MINUTES

INGREDIENTS

250 g / 9 oz ready-made shortcrust pastry
a little plain (all purpose) flour, for dusting
300 g / 10 ½ oz / 3 cups redcurrants
55 g / 2 oz / ¼ cup caster (superfine) sugar
1 tbsp lemon juice
2 sheets of gelatin

TO GARNISH

150 g / 5 oz / 1 ½ cups redcurrants
1 tbsp icing (confectioners') sugar

- Preheat the oven to 180°C (160° fan) / 350F / gas 4.
- Roll the pastry out on a lightly floured surface to ½ cm thickness.
- Cut out 4 rounds of pastry and use to line 4 individual 4" fluted tartlet cases.
- Prick the bases with a fork and trim any excess, overhanging pastry.
- Line with greaseproof paper and fill with baking beans before blind-baking for 12-15 minutes until golden at the edges.
- Remove from the oven and discard the greaseproof paper and baking beans.
- Return to the oven for 3 minutes before removing to a wire rack to cool.
- Soak the gelatin in a bowl of cold water.
- Toss together the redcurrants, lemon juice and sugar in bowl then cook in a saucepan over a medium heat, stirring occasionally, until softened.
- Puree the redcurrants in a food processor and transfer back to the saucepan.
- Squeeze the excess water from the gelatin and add to the hot redcurrant puree, whisking well.
- Spoon into the pastry cases and chill for 2 hours.
- Top with redcurrants and dust with icing sugar.

258

MAKES 4

Chocolate Banana Tartlets

PREPARATION TIME 10 MINUTES

COOKING TIME 15 MINUTES

INGREDIENTS

250 g / 9 oz ready-made shortcrust pastry
a little plain (all purpose) flour, for dusting
300 g / 10 ½ oz / 2 cups good-quality dark chocolate, chopped
175 ml / 6 fl. oz / ⅔ cup double (heavy) cream

TO GARNISH

1 large banana, peeled and sliced

- Preheat the oven to 180°C (160° fan) / 350F / gas 4.
- Roll the pastry out on a lightly floured surface.
- Cut out 4 rounds of pastry and line 4 5" tartlet cases.
- Prick the bases and trim excess pastry.
- Line with greaseproof paper and fill with baking beans before blind-baking for 12-15 minutes until golden.
- Remove from the oven and discard the greaseproof paper and baking beans.
- Return to the oven for 3-4 minutes to brown the base before removing to a wire rack to cool.
- Heat the cream in a saucepan until boiling, remove from the heat, and whisk in the chocolate and kirsch.
- Once smooth and thick, let it cool for 2 minutes before pouring into the pastry tarts.
- Garnish with the sliced banana before serving.

Chocolate and Mango Tartlets

259

- Garnish the tartlets with sliced mango instead of banana.

260

MAKES 4

Blueberry Tartlets

PREPARATION TIME 10 MINUTES

COOKING TIME 20 MINUTES

INGREDIENTS

250 g / 9 oz ready-made shortcrust pastry
a little plain (all purpose) flour, for dusting
400 g / 14 oz / 4 cups blueberries
75 g / 3 oz / ⅓ cup caster (superfine) sugar
½ lemon, juiced

TO GARNISH

1 tbsp icing (confectioners') sugar

- Preheat the oven to 180°C (160° fan) / 350F / gas 4.
- Roll the pastry out on a lightly floured surface.
- Cut out 4 rounds of pastry and line 4 4" fluted cases.
- Prick the bases and trim excess pastry.
- Line with greaseproof paper and fill with baking beans before blind-baking for 12-15 minutes until golden.
- Remove from the oven and discard the greaseproof paper and baking beans.
- Return to the oven for 3-4 minutes to brown the base before removing to a wire rack to cool.
- Combine 200 g of the blueberries, the sugar and lemon juice in a saucepan and cook over a medium heat until the fruit softens and is easily mashed.
- Let it cool before spooning into the tartlet cases.
- Top with the remaining blueberries and garnish with a dusting of icing sugar before serving.

Raspberry and Blueberry Tartlets

261

- Substitute the whole blueberries on top of the tartlets with the same weight of raspberries.

262

MAKES 4

Blackberry Tartlets

- Preheat the oven to 180°C (160° fan) / 350F / gas 4.
- Roll the pastry out on a lightly floured surface.
- Cut out 4 rounds of pastry and use to line 4 individual 4" fluted tartlet cases.
- Prick the bases and trim excess pastry.
- Line with greaseproof paper and fill with baking beans before blind-baking for 12-15 minutes until golden at the edges.
- Remove from the oven and discard the greaseproof paper and baking beans.
- Return to the oven for 3-4 minutes to brown the base before removing to a wire rack to cool.
- Warm the blackberry jam in a small saucepan over a low heat before spooning into the tartlet cases.
- Top with the blackberries and garnish with a light dusting of icing sugar before serving.

PREPARATION TIME 10 MINUTES

COOKING TIME 15-20 MINUTES

INGREDIENTS

250 g / 9 oz ready-made shortcrust pastry
a little plain (all purpose) flour, for dusting
225 g / 8 oz / 1 cup blackberry jam
200 g / 7 oz / 2 cups blackberries
55 g / 2 oz / ¼ cup caster (superfine) sugar

TO GARNISH

1 tbsp icing (confectioners') sugar

Blackberry and Damson Tartlets

 263

- Replace the blackberry jam with the same amount of damson jam, warmed through.

264

MAKES 4

Mascarpone, Strawberry and Mint Tartlets

- Preheat the oven to 180°C (160° fan) / 350F / gas 4.
- Roll the pastry out on a lightly floured surface.
- Cut out 4 rounds of pastry and line 4 4" fluted cases.
- Prick the bases and trim excess pastry.
- Line with greaseproof paper and fill with baking beans before blind-baking for 12-15 minutes until golden.
- Remove from the oven and discard the greaseproof paper and baking beans.
- Return to the oven for 3-4 minutes to brown the base before removing to a wire rack to cool.
- Beat together the mascarpone and icing sugar in a mixing bowl until smooth and creamy.
- Stir in the diced strawberries and spoon into the pastry cases.
- Garnish with the sliced strawberries, pumpkin seeds and sprigs of mint before serving.

PREPARATION TIME 10-15 MINUTES

COOKING TIME 20 MINUTES

INGREDIENTS

250 g / 9 oz ready-made shortcrust pastry
a little plain (all purpose) flour, for dusting
400 g / 14 oz / 2 cups mascarpone
65 g / 2 ½ oz / ½ cup icing (confectioners') sugar
200 g / 7 oz / 2 cups strawberries, hulled and diced

TO GARNISH

4 strawberries, tops removed and sliced thinly
1 tbsp pumpkin seeds
a few sprigs of mint leaves

Mascarpone, Melon and Pistachio Tartlets

265

- Replace the strawberries with the same weight of diced melon. Garnish with chopped pistachios.

266

MAKES 4

Mini Cheesecake

Peppermint Cheesecakes

267

- Replace the vanilla extract with peppermint extract.

Strawberry and Lemon Individual Cheesecakes

268

- Replace the raspberries with halved strawberries and add another 1 tbsp of lemon juice to the mixture.

PREPARATION TIME 10-15 MINUTES

COOKING TIME 15-20 MINUTES

....

INGREDIENTS

150 g / 5 oz / 1 cup digestive (graham cracker) biscuits, pulsed into fine crumbs
50 g / 2 oz / ¼ cup unsalted butter, melted
400 g / 14 oz / 2 cups cream cheese
125 ml / 4 ½ fl. oz / ½ cup sour cream
110 g / 4 oz / ½ cup caster (superfine) sugar
2 large eggs
1 large egg yolk
1 tbsp vanilla extract
1 tbsp lemon juice
1 tbsp cornflour (cornstarch)

TO GARNISH

8 raspberries
1 tbsp julienned lemon zest

- Preheat the oven to 150°C (130° fan) / 300F / gas 2.
- Combine the biscuits and melted butter until they resemble wet sand then press into 4 springform individual cheesecake moulds.
- Beat the cream cheese in a mixing bowl until smooth and creamy.
- Add the caster sugar and the cornflour and mix again for 1 minute.
- Add the vanilla extract, lemon juice, eggs and egg yolk, one at a time, beating well between additions.
- Add the sour cream and mix again until smooth.
- Pour on top of the biscuit base in the moulds and arrange in a roasting tray.
- Half-fill the roasting tray with boiling water and move the tray to the oven.
- Bake the cheesecakes for 45-55 minutes; test with a wooden toothpick, if it comes out clean, the cheesecakes are ready.
- Remove from the oven and chill for at least 3 hours.
- Before serving, preheat a grill to hot.
- Carefully turn out the cheesecakes and flash under the grill for 1 minute.
- Remove and garnish with raspberries and lemon zest.

269

MAKES 4

Individual Orange Sponge Cakes

- Preheat the oven to 180°C (160° fan) / 350F / gas 4.
- Boil the zest three times in a saucepan, using fresh water each time in order to remove bitterness.
- Strain the zest and reserve to one side.
- Place 50 g of sugar and 100 ml of water in a saucepan and bring to a simmer, stirring gently to dissolve the sugar.
- Simmer for 4-5 minutes, add the boiled zest and simmer for a further 5 minutes.
- Strain the candied zest and allow to dry.
- Meanwhile, beat together the butter, sugar, flour, eggs and orange flower water in a large mixing bowl.
- Grease the inside of cardboard mini loaf moulds and spoon the batter into them evenly.
- Bake on a baking sheet for 15-20 minutes.
- Remove and allow to cool. Peel away the moulds.

PREPARATION TIME 25 MINUTES

COOKING TIME 40 MINUTES

INGREDIENTS

110 g / 4 oz / ½ cup unsalted butter
110 g / 4 oz / ⅔ cup self-raising flour
110 g / 4 oz / ½ cup caster (superfine) sugar
1 tsp orange flower water
2 large eggs

FOR THE GARNISH
orange zest, julienned
50 g / 2 oz / ¼ cup caster (superfine) sugar
wedge of orange, to garnish

Chocolate Orange Sponge Cakes

270

- Add 100g chocolate chips to the batter before cooking.

271

MAKES 4

Pear and Flaked Almond Pizzas

- Preheat the oven to 220°C (200° fan) / 425F / gas 7.
- Grease and line a large baking tray with greaseproof paper.
- Combine the flour, yeast and sugar in a large mixing bowl.
- Add the oil and water, bring together to form a rough dough.
- Knead on a lightly floured surface for 1 minute.
- Divide the dough into 4 small balls and roll out on a lightly floured work surface to 1 cm thickness and 5 cm in diameter.
- Arrange on baking trays and prick with a fork.
- Top with the jam and peach slices before baking for 15-18 minutes until the dough is cooked through and starting to colour.
- Remove and garnish with flaked almonds before serving.

PREPARATION TIME 10-15 MINUTES

COOKING TIME 15 MINUTES

INGREDIENTS

FOR THE DOUGH
200 g / 7 oz / 1 ⅓ cups plain (all purpose) flour
a little extra plain (all purpose) flour, for dusting
30 ml / 1 fl. oz / 2 tbsp olive oil
125 ml / 4 ½ fl. oz / ½ cup warm water (45°C / 113F)
1 tsp dried active yeast
1 tbsp caster (superfine) sugar

FOR THE TOPPING
110 g / 4 oz / ½ cup apricot jam
1 large peach, de-stoned and sliced

TO GARNISH
30 g / 1 oz / 2 tbsp flaked (slivered) almonds

Pear and Pistachio Pizzas

272

- Replace the peach with pear slices and garnish with chopped pistachios instead of flaked almonds.

MAKES 4

Raspberry Linzer Tarts

PREPARATION TIME 10-15 MINUTES

COOKING TIME 20 MINUTES

....

INGREDIENTS

300 g / 10 ½ oz ready-made sweet shortcrust pastry
a little plain (all purpose) flour, for dusting
400 g / 14 oz / 1 ¾ cups raspberry jam
1 large egg, beaten
1 tbsp whole milk
1 tsp caster (superfine) sugar

- Preheat the oven to 180°C (160° fan) / 350F / gas 4.
- Roll the pastry out on a lightly floured surface.
- Cut out 4 rounds of pastry and line 4 4" fluted cases.
- Prick the bases and trim excess pastry, gathering it into a ball and setting to one side.
- Line with greaseproof paper and fill with baking beans before blind-baking for 12-15 minutes until golden.
- Remove from the oven and discard the greaseproof paper and baking beans.
- Brush with the beaten egg and cool on a wire rack.
- Roll the reserved pastry to ½ cm thickness and cut out 16 strips that are 4" x ½" x ½" in diameter.
- Fill the tartlets with raspberry jam and drape the pastry strips in a hash pattern on top.
- Brush the top with milk and return to the oven for 12-14 minutes.

Strawberry Linzer Tarts

274

- Replace the raspberry jam with the same amount of strawberry jam.

MAKES 6

Sticky Toffee Mini Loafs

PREPARATION TIME 10 MINUTES

COOKING TIME 10 MINUTES

....

INGREDIENTS

150 g / 5 oz / 1 cup self-raising flour, sifted
150 g / 5 oz / ⅔ cup caster (superfine) sugar
150 g / 5 oz / ⅔ cup margarine, softened
125 g / 4 ½ oz / ⅓ cup treacle
125 g / 4 ½ oz / ½ cup dulce de leche
3 large eggs
½ tsp vanilla extract

- Preheat the oven to 180°C (160° fan) / 350F / gas 4.
- Grease and line 6 mini loaf tins with greaseproof paper.
- Beat together the flour, sugar, margarine, eggs, treacle and vanilla extract in a large mixing bowl until smooth.
- Spoon into the loaf tins and bake for 20-25 minutes; test with a wooden toothpick, if it comes out clean, they are done.
- Remove from the oven and prick the tops a few times with a skewer.
- Glaze the tops with a tablespoon of the dulce de leche and let them sit for 10 minutes before turning out and serving.

Sticky Date Mini Loafs

276

- Add 100 g / 3 ½ oz / ⅔ cup chopped pitted dates to the batter.

MAKES 4 — 277

Banana Custard Tartlets

Banana Chocolate Custard Tartlets — 278

- Garnish the tartlets with grated chocolate before serving.

Pineapple Custard Tartlets — 279

- Replace the banana with 300 g drained crushed pineapple.

PREPARATION TIME 10-15 MINUTES

COOKING TIME 20-25 MINUTES

....

INGREDIENTS

250 g / 9 oz ready-made shortcrust pastry
a little plain (all purpose) flour, for dusting
6 medium egg yolks
75 g / 3 oz / ⅓ cup caster (superfine) sugar
250 ml / 9 fl. oz / 1 cup whipping cream
250 ml / 9 fl. oz / 1 cup coconut milk
2 tbsp desiccated coconut
1 tbsp cornflour
2 bananas, peeled and sliced

TO GARNISH
1 tbsp desiccated coconut

- Preheat the oven to 180°C (160° fan) / 350F / gas 4.
- Roll the pastry out on a lightly floured surface.
- Cut out 4 rounds of pastry and line 4 5" fluted cases.
- Prick the bases and trim excess pastry.
- Line with greaseproof paper and fill with baking beans before blind-baking for 12-15 minutes until golden.
- Remove from the oven and discard the greaseproof paper and baking beans.
- Return to the oven for 3 minutes to brown the base before removing to a wire rack to cool.
- Reduce the oven to 160°C (140°C fan) / 300°F / gas 2.
- Whisk together the egg yolks, cornflour and sugar until pale and thick.
- Add the cream and coconut milk and mix well before passing through a fine sieve into a saucepan.
- Cook over a medium-low heat, stirring constantly for 2 minutes.
- Arrange banana slices in the pastry and cover with the custard mixture.
- Carefully transfer to the oven and bake for 20-25 minutes until the custard is set and starting to colour.
- Remove and sprinkle with desiccated coconut before serving.

280

MAKES 4

Banana Tartlets

PREPARATION TIME 10-15 MINUTES

COOKING TIME 30-35 MINUTES

INGREDIENTS

200 g / 7 oz ready-made sweet shortcrust pastry
a little plain (all purpose) flour, for dusting
1 small egg, beaten
2 large bananas, finely sliced on the diagonal (roughly ½cm thick slices)
30 ml / 1 fl. oz / 2 tbsp runny honey

- Preheat the oven to 190°C (170°C fan) / 375F / gas 5.
- Roll the pastry out on a lightly floured work surface.
- Cut into 4 rounds and line 8-10cm fluted tartlet tins. Press the pastry into the tins.
- Prick the bases and trim excess pastry.
- Line the pastry with greaseproof paper and fill with baking beans.
- Blind bake the pastry for 10-15 minutes.
- Remove from the oven and discard the greaseproof paper and baking beans.
- Return to the oven for a few minutes to lightly brown the bases.
- Brush the base and sides with the beaten egg and return to the oven to glaze for 1-2 minutes.
- Remove the tartlets and let them cool.
- Meanwhile, warm the honey in a small saucepan set over a low heat.
- Brush the insides of the pastry with some of the honey, then layer the inside with the banana slices, overlapping then in a circular pattern.
- Brush the banana tops with more honey and leave to cool a little before serving.

281

SERVES 6

Chocolate and Coconut Bavarian

PREPARATION TIME 10-15 MINUTES

COOKING TIME 20 MINUTES

INGREDIENTS

FOR THE CRUST
300 g / 10 ½ oz / 4 cups rolled oats
150 g / 5 oz / 2 cups desiccated coconut
150 g / 5 oz / ⅔ cup butter, softened
150 g / 5 oz / ½ cup Golden Syrup

FOR THE FILLING
300 g / 10 ½ oz / 2 cups good-quality dark chocolate, chopped
125 ml / 4 ½ fl. oz / ½ cup coconut milk
125 ml / 4 ½ fl. oz / ½ cup double (heavy) cream

TO GARNISH
1 tbsp dark chocolate, grated
1 tbsp coconut, grated

- Melt together the butter and Golden Syrup in a saucepan set over a medium heat, stirring occasionally.
- Add the oats and desiccated coconut and stir well.
- Press into a 6" springform cake tin, creating a 1" border along the base and sides.
- Chill until ready to fill.
- Place the chocolate, coconut milk and double cream in a heatproof bowl set atop a saucepan of simmering water.
- Stir occasionally until smooth.
- Remove from the heat and leave to cool for 2 minutes.
- Pour into the oat and coconut crust and return to the fridge to chill until set.
- Garnish with grated coconut and chocolate before serving.

282
MAKES 4

Pecan and Pumpkin Tartlets

- Preheat the oven to 190°C (170°C fan) / 375°F / gas 5.
- Roll the pastry out on a floured work surface cut out 6 rounds to line fluted tartlet moulds.
- Line the moulds with pastry and trim excess pastry. Prick the bases all over with a fork.
- Line with greaseproof paper and fill with baking beans before blind-baking for 10-12 minutes.
- Remove and discard the paper and beans.
- Return to the oven to brown the bases for 2-3 minutes.
- Reduce the oven to 160°C (140°C fan) / 300°F / gas 2.
- Puree the canned pumpkin in a food processor.
- Scrape into a mixing bowl and combine with the condensed milk, beaten eggs and spices, whisking well.
- Pour into pastry shells and bake in the oven for 35-40 minutes.
- Arrange the pecan halves and drizzle with maple syrup.

PREPARATION TIME 10 MINUTES

COOKING TIME 1 HOUR 5-10 MINUTES

INGREDIENTS

225 g / 8 oz shortcrust pastry
450 g / 1 lb / 2 cups canned pumpkin
500 ml / 18 fl. oz / 2 cups condensed milk
2 large eggs, beaten
1 tsp ground cinnamon
½ tsp ground ginger
½ tsp ground nutmeg
½ tsp salt
110 g / 4 oz / 1 cup pecan halves
110 ml / 4 fl. oz / ½ cup maple syrup

283
MAKES 6

Mini Kugelhofs

PREPARATION TIME 10-15 MINUTES

COOKING TIME 15-20 MINUTES

INGREDIENTS

300 g / 10 ½ oz / 2 cups plain (all purpose) flour
a little extra plain (all purpose) flour,

125 ml / 4 ½ fl. oz / ½ cup whole milk, lukewarm
110 g / 4 oz / ½ cup butter, softened
50 g / 2 oz / ¼ cup caster (superfine) sugar
3 medium eggs, beaten
1 tbsp fresh yeast
¼ tsp table salt
1 tbsp icing (confectioners') sugar

- Stir together the flour and sugar in a mixing bowl.
- Briefly stir together the yeast and milk in a jug then add to the flour and sugar. Add the eggs and mix until you have a rough dough.
- Knead on a floured surface for 10 minutes, then add a little of the butter at a time, kneading well between additions until incorporated.
- Transfer to a lightly oiled bowl and cover with a damp tea towel.
- Let it rise in a warm place for 30-40 minutes, then knock the dough back before kneading again for 2 minutes.
- Grease 6 mini kugelhof moulds and arrange the dough in them. Prove for 60 minutes.
- Preheat the oven to 180°C (160°C fan) / 350F / gas 4.
- Bake the kugelhof for 30-40 minutes; test with a wooden toothpick, if it comes out clean, they are done.
- Remove from the oven and leave to cool in the moulds before turning out and dusting with icing sugar.

284
MAKES 4

Strawberry Pistachio Tartlets

PREPARATION TIME 10 MINUTES

COOKING TIME 15-20 MINUTES

INGREDIENTS

250 g / 9 oz ready-made shortcrust pastry
a little plain (all purpose) flour, for dusting
100 g / 3 ½ oz / 1 cup pistachios, shelled
400 g / 14 oz / 1 ⅔ cups fromage blanc
65 g / 2 ½ oz / ½ cup icing (confectioners') sugar

TO GARNISH

150 g / 5 oz / 1 ½ cups strawberries, hulled and sliced
30 g / 1 oz / ¼ cup pistachios, shelled and chopped

- Preheat the oven to 180°C (160° fan) / 350F / gas 4.
- Roll the pastry out on a lightly floured surface to ½ cm thickness.
- Cut out 4 rounds of pastry and use to line 4 individual 5" tartlet cases.
- Prick the bases with a fork and trim any excess, overhanging pastry.
- Line with greaseproof paper and fill with baking beans before blind-baking for 12-15 minutes until golden at the edges.
- Remove from the oven and discard the greaseproof paper and baking beans.
- Return to the oven for 3-4 minutes to brown the base before removing to a wire rack.
- Blitz together the icing sugar and pistachios in a food processor until very finely ground.
- Add the fromage blanc and pulse until incorporated.
- Spoon into the cases and top with sliced strawberries.
- Garnish with chopped pistachios.

285

MAKES 4

Pistachio Cream and Cherry Tartlets

PREPARATION TIME 10-15 MINUTES

COOKING TIME 15-20 MINUTES

INGREDIENTS

200 g / 7 oz ready-made shortcrust pastry
a little plain (all purpose) flour, for dusting
250 ml / 9 fl. oz / 1 cup whipping cream
150 g / 5 oz / 1 cup shelled pistachios, chopped
300 g / 10 ½ oz / 3 cups cherries, pitted and halved
65 g / 2 ½ oz / ½ cup icing (confectioners') sugar

TO GARNISH
50 g / 2 oz / ½ cup pistachios, shelled and chopped

- Preheat the oven to 180°C (160° fan) / 350F / gas 4.
- Grease and line a baking tray with greaseproof paper.
- Roll the pastry out on a lightly floured surface to ½ cm thickness.
- Cut out 4 rounds of pastry using a fluted 4" cookie cutter and transfer to the baking tray, pricking a few times with a fork.
- Bake for 15-18 minutes until golden on top.
- Remove from the oven and leave to cool on a wire rack.
- Blitz the pistachios and icing sugar together in a food processor until fine then transfer to a bowl.
- Whip the cream in a separate mixing bowl until soft peaks form, then fold through the pistachio mixture.
- Spoon on top of the pastry rounds and top with cherry halves.
- Garnish with the chopped pistachios before serving.

Pistachio Cream and Apricot Tartlets

 286

- Use halved, de-stoned apricots instead of cherries on top of the pistachio cream.

287

MAKES 4

Pine Nut Tartlets

PREPARATION TIME 10 MINUTES

COOKING TIME 15 MINUTES

INGREDIENTS

250 g / 9 oz ready-made shortcrust pastry
a little plain (all purpose) flour, for dusting
225 g / 8 oz / 2 cups ground almonds
150 g / 5 oz / 1 ½ cups pine nuts
110 g / 4 oz / ½ cup caster (superfine) sugar
110 g / 4 oz / ½ cup unsalted butter
2 small eggs
2 small egg whites
30 g / 1 oz / 2 tbsp white fondant icing

TO GARNISH
4 glacés cherries

- Preheat the oven to 180°C (160° fan) / 350F / gas 4.
- Roll the pastry out on a lightly floured surface.
- Cut out 4 rounds of pastry and use to line 4 individual 5" tart cases.
- Prick the bases with a fork and trim any excess, overhanging pastry with a serrated knife.
- Chill until needed.
- Blitz together the ground almonds, sugar and butter in a food processor until creamy.
- Add the egg and egg white and pulse until combined.
- Spoon into the pastry and top with a teaspoon of fondant icing in the centre, followed by the pine nuts all over.
- Bake for 30-35 minutes.
- Remove the tarts from the oven and let them cool on a wire rack before garnishing with a glacé cherry.

Walnut Tartlets

288

- Replace the pine nuts with walnut halves.

289

SERVES 4

Lemon Meringue Pies

- Preheat the oven to 190°C (170° fan) / 375F / gas 5.
- Roll the pastry out on a lightly floured surface.
- Cut out 4 rounds of pastry and line 4 5" tartlet cases.
- Prick the bases and trim excess pastry.
- Line with greaseproof paper and fill with baking beans before blind-baking for 12-15 minutes until golden.
- Remove and discard the paper and beans.
- Return to the oven for 3-4 minutes to brown the base before removing to a wire rack to cool.
- Whisk the egg whites with the salt until stiff peaks form.
- Add the cream of tartar and the sugar, 1 tablespoon at a time, beating well between additions until glossy. Spoon into a piping bag.
- Fill the pastry with lemon curd and pipe the meringue on top before baking for 10-12 minutes.

PREPARATION TIME 10-15 MINUTES

COOKING TIME 20 MINUTES

....

INGREDIENTS

250 g / 9 oz ready-made shortcrust pastry
a little plain (all purpose) flour, for dusting
450 g / 1 lb / 2 cups lemon curd
110 g / 4 oz / ½ cup caster (superfine) sugar
2 medium egg whites
a pinch of salt
½ tsp cream of tartar

Orange Curd Pies

 290

- Use orange curd in place of the lemon curd.

291

MAKES 4

Mini Raspberry and Apple Pies

- Preheat the oven to 180°C (160° fan) / 350F / gas 4.
- Cook the apple, sugar and water in a saucepan until the apple is soft.
- Drain and spoon into individual 5" ceramic dishes.
- Dot with raspberries and roll the pastry out to ½ cm thickness on a lightly floured work surface.
- Cut out 5" rounds and drape over the fruit in the dishes.
- Bake for 20-25 minutes until golden then remove from the oven and sprinkle immediately with caster sugar.
- Garnish with a raspberry before serving.

PREPARATION TIME 10-15 MINUTES

COOKING TIME 15 MINUTES

....

INGREDIENTS

200 g / 7 oz ready-made shortcrust pastry
a little plain (all purpose) flour, for dusting
450 g / 1 lb / 1 ¾ cups cooking apples, peeled and diced
275 g / 9 ½ oz / 2 ¾ cups raspberries
75 g / 3 oz / ⅓ cup caster (superfine) sugar
1 tbsp cold water

TO GARNISH

4 raspberries
1 tbsp caster (superfine) sugar

Apple and Raisin Pies

 292

- Replace the raspberries with 100 g / 3 ½ oz / ⅔ cup raisins in the filling.

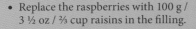

MAKES 4

Heart-Shaped Summer Fruit Tartlets

Summer Fruit and White Chocolate Tartlets

294

- Once cooled, top each tartlet with a generous tablespoon of white chocolate shavings.

Summer Fruit and Dark Chocolate Tartlets

295

- Once cooled, top each tartlet with a generous tablespoon of dark 70% cocoa chocolate shavings.

PREPARATION TIME 10 MINUTES

COOKING TIME 15 MINUTES

INGREDIENTS

160 g / 5 oz ready-made sweet shortcrust pastry
a little plain (all-purpose) flour, for dusting
150 ml / 5 fl. oz / ⅔ cup whole milk
150 ml / 5 fl. oz / ⅔ cup double cream
110 g / 4 oz / ½ cup caster (superfine) sugar
30 g / 1 oz / 2 tbsp plain (all-purpose) flour
3 small egg yolks
2 small whole eggs
110 g / 4 oz / ⅔ cup raspberries
55 g / 2 oz / ⅓ cup blueberries
55 g / 2 oz / ⅓ cup blackberries
30 g / 1 oz / 2 tbsp redcurrants

TO GARNISH

1 tbsp granulated sugar
1 tbsp icing (confectioners') sugar

- Preheat the oven to 180°C (160°C) / 350°F / gas 4.
- Dust a work surface with flour and roll the pastry out.
- Cut 4 even rounds of pastry from the sheet of pastry.
- Use the rounds to line 4, heart-shaped tartlet moulds, pressing the pastry carefully into the base and sides.
- Prick the bases all over and line with greaseproof paper. Fill with baking beans and chill for 15 minutes.
- Prepare the filling by combining the milk and cream in a saucepan and bringing to a simmer.
- Once simmering, remove the saucepan from the heat.
- In a large bowl, whisk together the egg yolks and eggs.
- Add the sugar and whisk until well blended, then sift in the flour and whisk.
- Gradually add the milk and cream to the egg mixture and whisk until smooth, then set to one side.
- Remove the pastry from the fridge and arrange the moulds on a baking sheet. Blind bake for 12-15 minutes.
- Remove from the oven and discard the greaseproof paper and the baking beans.
- Fill the pastries with the a mixture of the fruits, then pour the batter evenly on top.
- Reduce the oven to 160°C. Bake for 15-20 minutes.
- Let the tartlets cool on a wire rack. Dust with the icing and granulated sugars.

Dried Fruit Cookie Sandwiches

- Cream the butter, ground cloves and sugars together.
- Beat in one egg at a time, mixing well.
- Beat in the flour in thirds with a pinch of salt.
- Roll into a Swiss roll shape and wrap in parchment paper. Chill until firm; roughly 1 hour.
- Preheat the oven to 180°C (160° fan) / 350F / gas 4.
- Cut discs of dough roughly 1 cm thick.
- Arrange on a greased and lined baking tray, then sprinkle the chopped hazelnuts and sultanas on top.
- Bake for 15-20 minutes until golden brown.
- Whip the double cream until it form soft peaks.
- Fold into the chestnut puree. Spoon into a piping bag.
- Once the cookies are cool, pipe the chestnut cream onto the bottom of half of the cookies.
- Place the bottom half of the other cookies on top of the filling.

Raisin and Almond Cookies
297

- Replace the sultanas with raisins and replace the hazelnuts with chopped almonds.

PREPARATION TIME 10-15 MINUTES

COOKING TIME 40-45 MINUTES

INGREDIENTS

FOR THE COOKIE DOUGH
600 g / 1 lb 5 oz / 4 cups plain (all purpose) flour
250 g / 9 oz / 1 cup unsalted butter
110 g / 4 oz / ½ cup caster (superfine) sugar
80 g / 3 oz / ½ cup soft light brown sugar
2 small eggs
55 g / 2 oz / ⅓ cup golden sultanas
50 g / 2 oz / ½ cup blanched hazelnuts
1 tsp ground cloves
pinch of salt

FOR THE FILLING
200 ml / 7 fl. oz / ¾ cup double (heavy) cream
200 g / 7 oz / ¾ cup sweetened chestnut puree

Rose Cookie and Raspberry Jam Whoopies

- Sift the flour, icing sugar and cornflour for the biscuits. Add the softened butter and rose water and beat.
- Shape the dough into a ball and wrap in film. Chill for 45 minutes. Preheat the oven to 180°C (160°C) / 350°F / gas 4. Grease and line 2 baking trays.
- Remove the dough from the fridge once firm and roll out on a lightly floured work surface to ½cm thickness.
- Use a flower-shaped cookie cutter to cut out shapes. Arrange on the trays and bake for 10-12 minutes.
- Sift the icing sugar into a large mixing bowl.
- Combine a few drops of the red food colouring and the rosewater with about 100-150 ml of boiling water.
- Pour a little of the water into the icing sugar and whisk.
- Spread the tops of half of the cookies with the jam.
- Spread the icing on the tops of the remaining cookies and sprinkle over the popping candy. Sandwich them on top of the jam-topped cookies.

Orange Blossom and Raspberry Cookies
299

- Replace the rosewater with orange blossom water and colour icing orange.

PREPARATION TIME 15 MINUTES

COOKING TIME 40-50 MINUTES

INGREDIENTS

FOR THE ROSE COOKIES
250 g / 9 oz / 1 cup unsalted butter, softened
75 g / 3 oz / ⅔ cup icing (confectioners') sugar
225 g / 8 oz / 1 ½ cups plain (all purpose) flour
75 g / 3 oz / ½ cup cornflour (cornstarch)
½ tsp rosewater
a little extra plain (all purpose) flour, for dusting

FOR THE FILLING AND ICING
165 g / 5 ½ oz / ⅔ cup smooth raspberry jam
110 g / 4 oz / 1 cup icing sugar
boiling water
a few drops of rosewater
a few drops of red food colouring
1 small bag strawberry flavoured popping candy

300

MAKES 6

Almond and Lemon Whoopie Pies

PREPARATION TIME 10-15 MINUTES

COOKING TIME 15-20 MINUTES

INGREDIENTS

240 g / 8 oz / 1 ½ cups plain (all purpose) flour, sifted
175 g / 6 oz / ¾ cup margarine, softened
75 g / 3 oz / ⅓ cup caster (superfine) sugar
30 g / 1 oz / ¼ cup ground almonds
½ tsp almond extract
½ tsp bicarbonate (baking) of soda
50 g / 2 oz / ½ cup flaked (slivered) almonds
a pinch of salt
125 g / 4 ½ oz / 1 cup icing (confectioners') sugar
125 g / 4 ½ oz / ½ cup lemon curd
30-55 ml / 1-2 fl. oz / 2 tbsp - ¼ cup boiling water
1 lime, zested

- Preheat the oven to 170°C (150°C fan) / 325F / gas 3. Grease and line 2 baking trays with greaseproof paper.
- Cream together the margarine and sugar.
- Beat in the flour, bicarbonate of soda and almond extract until you have a rough dough.
- Knead the dough before rolling out on a floured surface.
- Use a 3" cookie cutter to cut out 12 rounds before carefully lifting onto the baking trays, spaced apart.
- Stud each cookie with ½ tablespoon of flaked almonds before baking for 15-18 minutes. Remove from the oven to a wire rack to cool.
- Whisk together the icing sugar, lime zest and enough boiling water to make runny icing.
- Whisk in the lemon curd before spooning generous tablespoons onto the back of 6 of the cookies.
- Sandwich with the remaining cookies before serving.

Vanilla and Lemon Whoopie Pies 301

- Replace the almond extract with 1 tbsp vanilla extract and omit the flaked almonds.

302

SERVES 4

Chocolate, Orange and Nut Fondant

PREPARATION TIME 10 MINUTES

COOKING TIME 15 MINUTES

INGREDIENTS

30 g / 1 oz / 2 tbsp butter, melted
150 g / 5 oz / 1 cup good-quality dark chocolate, chopped
110 g / 4 oz / ½ cup unsalted butter, cubed
75 g / 3 oz / ½ cup plain (all purpose) flour
30 g / 1 oz / 2 tbsp good-quality cocoa powder
75 g / 3 oz / ½ cup sultanas
75 g / 3 oz / ¾ cup Brazil nuts, chopped
30 g / 1 oz / 2 tbsp raisins
2 medium eggs
2 medium egg yolks
2 tsp orange flower water

TO GARNISH

2 tbsp grated white chocolate
1 tbsp sultanas
1 tbsp raisin

- Preheat the oven to 190°C (170° fan) / 375F / gas 5.
- Brush 4 ramekins with some of the melted butter.
- Chill the ramekins then brush with another layer of melted butter.
- Dust the insides with the cocoa powder. Chill until ready to fill with the batter.
- Prepare the batter by melting together the chocolate and cubed butter in a heatproof mixing bowl set over a pan of gently simmering water.
- Once melted, remove from the heat and allow to cool.
- Whisk together the eggs and yolks until thick.
- Sift the plain flour into the eggs and whisk.
- Fold into the melted chocolate and butter, then add the raisins, sultanas, Brazil nuts and orange flower water.
- Spoon into the ramekins and bake for 16-18 minutes. Remove from the oven and to cool.

Chocolate and Nut Fondants 303

- Replace the dried fruit with 100 g / 3 ½ oz / 1 cup chopped mixed nuts. Omit the orange flower water.

304

MAKES 4

Peach and Raspberry Tartlets

Raspberry, Peach and Strawberry Tartlets

305

- Replace the peach yoghurt with raspberry yoghurt and use sliced strawberries to garnish on top.

Apricot and Raspberry Tartlets

306

- Replace the peaches with tinned apricots, and replace the peach yoghurt with apricot yoghurt.

PREPARATION TIME 10 MINUTES

COOKING TIME 10 MINUTES

INGREDIENTS

250 g / 9 oz / 1 ⅔ cups digestive (graham cracker) biscuits
400 g / 14 oz / 1 ¾ cups peach yoghurt
400 g / 14 oz / 2 cups canned peach slices, drained

TO GARNISH

150 g / 5 oz / 1 ½ cups raspberries

- Roughly mash the peach slices until broken up and pulp-like.
- Break the biscuits into bite-sized pieces, as evenly as possible.
- Use to line the base and sides of 4 individual 4" ceramic shallow ramekins.
- Top with the peach yoghurt, smoothing level before topping with the peach.
- Garnish with raspberries before serving.

307

SERVES 4

Chocolate Fondant

PREPARATION TIME 10 MINUTES

COOKING TIME 10 MINUTES

INGREDIENTS

30 g / 1 oz / 2 tbsp butter, melted
110 g / 4 oz / ⅔ cup good-quality
dark chocolate, chopped
110 g / 4 oz / ½ cup unsalted butter,
cubed
75 g / 3 oz / ½ cup plain (all purpose)
flour
30 g / 1 oz / 2 tbsp caster (superfine)
sugar
2 medium eggs
2 medium egg yolks

TO GARNISH

8 clementine segments
1 tbsp icing (confectioners') sugar
basil, to garnish

- Preheat the oven to 190°C (170° fan) / 375F / gas 5.
- Brush 4 individual ramekins with some of the melted butter. Chill the ramekins then brush with another layer of melted butter.
- Dust the insides with the sugar. Chill until ready to fill with the batter.
- Prepare the batter by melting together the chocolate and cubed butter in a heatproof mixing bowl set over a pan of gently simmering water.
- Once melted, remove from the heat and allow to cool.
- Whisk together the eggs and yolks until thick.
- Sift the plain flour and into the eggs and whisk.
- Fold into the melted chocolate until even then spoon into the ramekins and bake for 12-14 minutes.
- Leave to cool before garnishing with clementine segments on top and a dusting of icing sugar.

White Chocolate Fondant

308

- Replace the dark chocolate with 150 g / 5 oz / 1 cup chopped white chocolate.

309

MAKES 4

Chocolate Pastry Tartlets

PREPARATION TIME 10-15
MINUTES

COOKING TIME 20 MINUTES

INGREDIENTS

250 g / 9 oz / cups ready-made
shortcrust pastry
a little plain (all purpose) flour,
for dusting
200 g / 7 oz / 1 ⅓ cups good-quality
dark chocolate, chopped
55 g / 2 oz / ⅓ cup plain (all purpose)
flour
55 g / 2 oz / ¼ cup unsalted butter
2 medium eggs

TO GARNISH

8 small strawberries, hulled
4 sprigs of mint leaves

- Preheat the oven to 180°C (160° fan) / 350F / gas 4.
- Roll the pastry out on a lightly floured surface.
- Cut out 4 rounds of pastry to line 4 individual 4" fluted tartlet cases.
- Trim any excess, overhanging pastry and prick the bases with a fork. Chill until ready to fill.
- Place the chocolate and butter in a heatproof bowl set atop a saucepan of simmering water.
- Stir until melted, remove from the heat and beat in the eggs after 2 minutes.
- Fold in the flour, then pour into the pastry cases.
- Bake for 30-35 minutes until the pastry is golden and the chocolate filling is set.
- Remove from the oven and allow to cool before chilling.
- Serve garnished with a couple of strawberries and a sprig of mint leaves.

Chocolate and Rum Tartlets

310

- Add 55 ml / 2 fl. oz / ¼ cup dark rum to the chocolate and butter before melting.

311

MAKES 4

Toffee Tartlets

- Preheat the oven to 180°C (160° fan) / 350F / gas 4.
- Roll the pastry out on a lightly floured surface.
- Cut out 4 rounds of pastry and line 4 4" tartlet cases.
- Prick the bases and trim excess pastry.
- Line with greaseproof paper and fill with baking beans before blind-baking for 12-15 minutes until golden at the edges.
- Remove from the oven and discard the greaseproof paper and baking beans.
- Return to the oven for 3 minutes to brown the base before removing to a wire rack to cool.
- Combine the sugar and water in a saucepan, and cook over a medium heat, swirling occasionally, until golden-brown in colour.
- Remove from the heat and gradually whisk in the butter.
- Pour into the pastry cases and leave to cool.

PREPARATION TIME 10-15 MINUTES

COOKING TIME 20 MINUTES

INGREDIENTS

250 g / 9 oz / ready-made shortcrust pastry
a little plain (all purpose) flour, for dusting
300 g / 10 ½ oz / 1 ⅓ cups caster (superfine) sugar
100 ml / 3 ½ fl. oz / ⅖ cup cold water
55 g / 2 oz / ¼ cup butter, cubed

Toffee and Raisin Tartlets

 312

- Stir 100 g / 3 ½ oz / ⅔ cup raisins into the toffee sauce before filling the tartlets.

313

SERVES 4-6

Lemon Bavarian

- Prepare the jelly. Place the water in a saucepan and sprinkle the gelatine on top. Heat to dissolve it.
- Remove from the heat then add the lemon juice and sugar. Stir well to dissolve the sugar.
- Divide the lemon jelly mixture between 2 x 4 inch bavarois moulds. Chill for 2-3 hours until set.
- Prepare the bavarois mixture. Cover the gelatine leaves with cold water and soak.
- Beat the egg yolks and caster sugar together. Place the milk in a saucepan.
- Bring to the boil, then remove from the heat.
- Pour the milk onto the egg yolk mixture, then return to the saucepan.
- Cook over a low heat, stirring until thickened.
- Remove the gelatine leaves from the water and squeeze out any excess water.
- Add to custard and whisk until the gelatine dissolves.
- Leave the mixture to cool. Whip the double cream in a separate bowl until it forms soft peaks.
- Fold the whipped cream into the custard.
- Pour the bavarois mixture on top of the set lemon jelly in the moulds. Chill overnight until set.
- Warm the outsides of the moulds using a warm cloth.
- Turn the Bavarians out and serve with the lemon wedges on the side.

PREPARATION TIME 10 MINUTES

COOKING TIME 45 MINUTES

INGREDIENTS

FOR THE BAVAROIS MIXTURE
450 ml / 16 fl. oz / 2 cups whole milk
225 ml / 8 fl. oz / 1 cup double (heavy) cream
75 g / 3 oz / ⅓ cup golden caster (superfine) sugar
3 large egg yolks
1 vanilla pod, split lengthwise with seeds scraped out
2 ½ sheets leaf gelatine

FOR THE LEMON JELLY MIXTURE
juice of 4 lemons
450 ml / 16 fl. oz / 2 cups water
4 tsp gelatine powder
4 tsp caster (superfine) sugar
1 lemon, cut into thin wedges to garnish

314

SERVES 4

Mini Sour Griotte Cherry Pies

Cherry and Blueberry Pies

315

- Add 1 tbsp of blueberries to each pie before baking.

Boozy Cherry Pies

316

- Soak the cherries in kirsch for an hour before adding them to the pie cases and cooking.

Cherry and Raspberry Pies

317

- Add 1 tbsp of raspberries to each pie before baking.

PREPARATION TIME 10 MINUTES

COOKING TIME 40-45 MINUTES

INGREDIENTS

200 g / 7 oz ready-made sweet shortcrust pastry
a little plain (all purpose) flour, for dusting
300 g / 10 ½ oz / 1 ½ cup canned griotte cherries, drained
30 ml / 1 fl. oz / 2 tbsp whole milk
1 tbsp caster sugar

- Roll half the pastry out on a lightly floured surface.
- Cut 4 rounds of pastry that will line the base and sides of the moulds of a cupcake tin.
- Line 4 moulds of a cupcake tin with the pastry and trim any excess pastry. Prick the base and chill for 15 minutes.
- Preheat the oven to 180°C (160° fan) / 350F / gas 4.
- Roll the other half of pastry out on a lightly floured surface and cut rounds 5 cm in diameter.
- Prick the pastry lids a few times with a fork.
- Remove the chilled pastry from the fridge and spoon the drained griotte cherries into them.
- Wet the rims of the pastry in the moulds with a little water.
- Carefully place the pastry lids on top and crimp the edges together to secure.
- Bake the pies for 25-30 minutes until the pastry is cooked and starting to colour.
- Meanwhile, whisk together the milk and sugar until the sugar has dissolved to make a glaze.
- Remove the pies from the oven and brush the tops with the glaze. Return to the oven for a few minutes to glaze.
- Remove from the oven once glazed and leave to cool.

MAKES 6 Chocolate and Coffee Mini Cakes

- Preheat the oven to 180°C (160° fan) / 350F / gas 4.
- Grease and line 6 mini loaf tins with greaseproof paper.
- Blitz the chocolate in a food processor until very fine then remove and set to one side.
- Blitz the espresso beans until very finely ground and add to the chocolate.
- Beat together the flour, sugar, margarine, eggs and vanilla extract in a large mixing bowl until smooth.
- Add the chocolate and coffee mixture and beat again thoroughly.
- Spoon into the loaf tins and bake for 20-25 minutes; test with a wooden toothpick, if it comes out clean, they are done.
- Remove from the oven and leave to cool in the tins before turning out and serving.

PREPARATION TIME 10 MINUTES

COOKING TIME 15 MINUTES

INGREDIENTS

150 g / 5 oz / 1 cup self-raising flour, sifted
150 g / 5 oz / ⅔ cup caster (superfine) sugar
150 g / 5 oz / ⅔ cup margarine, softened
100 g / 3 ½ oz / ⅔ cup good-quality dark chocolate, cold
1 tbsp espresso beans
3 large eggs
½ tsp vanilla extract

Chocolate and Fudge Mini Loafs 319

- Replace the ground espresso beans with 75 g / 3 oz / ½ cup chopped fudge in the batter.

MAKES 12 Fig Shortbread Cookies

- Pulse together the flour, cornflour, salt, icing sugar and butter in a food processor until it forms a dough.
- Remove the dough, knead gently and form into a ball.
- Wrap in clingfilm and chill for 60 minutes.
- Preheat the oven to 180°C (160° fan) / 350F / gas 4.
- Remove the ends of each fig then cut the remaining part of the fruit into 3 slices.
- Grease and line 2 baking trays with greaseproof paper.
- Remove the dough from the fridge and roll out on a lightly floured surface to ½ cm thickness.
- Cut out 12 rounds from the dough using a fluted cutter.
- Arrange on the baking trays and bake for 10-12 minutes.
- Remove from the oven and top each with a slice of fig.
- Sprinkle with fennel seeds and return to the oven for 4-5 minutes.

PREPARATION TIME 10 MINUTES

COOKING TIME 15-20 MINUTES

INGREDIENTS

200 g / 7 oz / 1 ⅓ cups plain (all purpose) flour
a little extra plain flour, for dusting
150 g / 5 oz / ⅔ cup unsalted butter, cubed
65 g / 2 ½ oz / ½ cup icing (confectioners') sugar
30 g / 1 oz / 2 tbsp cornflour (cornstarch)
30 g / 1 oz / 2 tbsp fennel seeds
4 figs
a pinch of salt

Peach Shortbread Cookies 321

- Thinly slice 2 peaches and use in place of the figs, omitting the fennel seeds as well.

322

MAKES 4

Plum, Sesame and Almond Tartlets

PREPARATION TIME 10-15 MINUTES

COOKING TIME 20-25 MINUTES

INGREDIENTS

250 g / 9 oz ready-made shortcrust pastry
a little plain (all purpose) flour
450 g / 1 lb / 3 cups plums, de-stoned and diced
250 ml / 9 fl. oz / 1 cup whipping cream
250 ml / 9 fl. oz / 1 cup whole milk
75 g / 3 oz / ⅓ cup caster (superfine) sugar
30 g / 1 oz / 1 cup mint leaves, chopped
6 medium egg yolks
1 tbsp cornflour

TO GARNISH

50 g / 2 oz / ½ cup flaked (slivered) almonds, toasted
50 g / 2 oz / ⅓ cup sesame seeds

- Preheat the oven to 180°C (160° fan) / 350F / gas 4.
- Roll the pastry out on a lightly floured surface.
- Cut out 4 rounds of pastry and line 4 4" tartlet cases.
- Prick the bases with a fork and trim the excess pastry.
- Line with greaseproof paper and fill with baking beans before blind-baking for 12-15 minutes until golden.
- Remove and discard the paper and beans. Return to the oven for 3 minutes to brown the base.
- Reduce the oven to 160°C (140°C fan) / 300°F / gas 2.
- Whisk together the egg yolks, cornflour and sugar.
- Add the cream and milk, mixing well before passing through a sieve into a saucepan.
- Heat over a medium heat then add the mint and plum.
- Pour custard into the pastry and bake for 25-30 minutes.
- Garnish with flaked almonds and sesame seeds.

Plum and Tarragon Tartlets

 323

- Replace the mint with half the weight of chopped tarragon leaves.

324

MAKES 4

Coconut Milk Panna Cottas

PREPARATION TIME 5-10 MINUTES

COOKING TIME 15 MINUTES

INGREDIENTS

500 ml / 18 fl. oz / 2 cups coconut milk
55 g / 2 oz / ¼ cup caster (superfine) sugar
3 sheets of gelatine

TO GARNISH

1 lime, finely zested

- Soak the gelatine sheets in a small bowl of cold water.
- Combine the sugar and coconut milk in a saucepan and cook over a medium heat until the sugar has dissolved.
- Remove the gelatine, squeezing out the excess water before adding to the hot coconut milk mixture.
- Whisk briefly until the gelatine has dissolved before setting to one side.
- Once cool, pour into 4 cannele moulds, cover with clingfilm and chill overnight.
- Before serving, warm the outsides of the moulds with a hot tea towel before inverting onto plates until the panna cottas drop.
- Garnish with lime zest on top.

Coconut and Rum Panna Cottas

 325

- Add 55 ml / 2 fl. oz / ¼ cup white rum to the coconut milk before heating.

326

MAKES 4

Mixed Fruit Tartlets

Mixed Fruit and Nut Tartlets

 327

- Substitute the agar-agar jelly beans for 100 g / 3 ½ oz / 1 cup chopped mixed nuts.

White Chocolate and Fruit Tartlets

328

- Substitute the jelly beans with generous shavings of white chocolate.

PREPARATION TIME 15 MINUTES

COOKING TIME 10-15 MINUTES

INGREDIENTS

250 g / 9 oz ready-made shortcrust pastry
a little plain (all purpose) flour, for dusting
50 g / 2 oz / ½ cup pine nuts, toasted
1 large red eating apple, cored and sliced
1 banana, peeled and sliced
1 orange, segmented
1 kiwi fruit, peeled and thinly sliced
2 tbsp agar-agar red jelly beans
2 tbsp blackberries
2 tbsp strawberries, hulled and chopped
2 tbsp apricot glaze, warmed
1 tbsp green seedless grapes, sliced

- Preheat the oven to 180°C (160° fan) / 350F / gas 4.
- Roll the pastry out on a lightly floured surface to ½ cm thickness.
- Cut out 4 rounds of pastry and use to line 4 individual 4" fluted tartlet cases.
- Prick the bases with a fork and trim any excess, overhanging pastry.
- Line with greaseproof paper and fill with baking beans before blind-baking for 12-15 minutes until golden at the edges.
- Remove from the oven and discard the greaseproof paper and baking beans.
- Return to the oven for 3-4 minutes to brown the base before removing to a wire rack to cool.
- Toss together the fruits in a large mixing bowl.
- Brush the bases of the tartlets with the apricot glaze then fill with the fruit mixture.
- Sprinkle the agar-agar jelly beans and pine nuts on top before serving.

329

SERVES 4

Chiboust Tartlets

PREPARATION TIME 10-15
MINUTES

COOKING TIME 20-25 MINUTES

....

INGREDIENTS

250 g / 9 oz ready-made sweet
shortcrust pastry
a little plain (all purpose) flour,
for dusting
375 ml / 13 fl. oz / 1 ½ cups whole
milk
50 g / 2 oz / ¼ cup caster (superfine)
sugar
1 vanilla pod, split lengthwise
4 medium egg yolks
1 tbsp plain (all purpose) flour
1 tbsp cornflour
2 medium egg whites
110 g / 4 oz / ½ cup caster (superfine)
sugar
a pinch of salt
30 g / 1 oz / 2 tbsp demerara sugar

- Preheat the oven to 180°C (160° fan) / 350F / gas 4.
- Roll the pastry out on a lightly floured surface. Cut out
  4 rounds of pastry and line 4 4" tartlet cases. Prick the
  bases and trim excess pastry.
- Line with greaseproof paper and fill with baking beans
  before blind-baking for 12-15 minutes.
- Discard the paper and beans. Bake for 2 minutes to
  brown. Place vanilla pod and milk in a pan and boil.
- Whisk together egg yolks and sugar until thick then
  sift in the flour and cornflour.
- Add the milk, then pour into the pan and cook for 2
  minutes. Spoon into a bowl, cover and chill.
- Reduce the oven to 130°C (110° fan) / 250F / gas ½.
- Whisk egg whites with then whisk.
- Spoon into a piping bag. Pipe 4 rounds onto a lined
  baking tray. Bake for 1 hour 30-40 minutes.
- Fill the tartlets with cream and top with meringue.
  Sprinkle demerara sugar on top and grill.

Raspberry Chiboust Tartlets 330

- Dot the pastry cream in the tartlets
  with a few raspberries before placing
  the meringue on top.

331

SERVES 6

Apricot Tartlets

PREPARATION TIME 10-15
MINUTES

COOKING TIME 45-50 MINUTES

....

INGREDIENTS

250 g / 9 oz ready-made shortcrust
pastry
a little plain (all purpose) flour, for
dusting
125 g / 4 ½ oz / ½ cup caster
(superfine) sugar
125 g / 4 ½ oz / ½ cup unsalted
butter, softened
125 g / 4 ½ oz / 1 ¼ cup ground
almonds
3 large eggs
1 tsp almond extract
400 g / 14 oz / 2 cups canned apricot
halves, drained
55 g / 2 oz / ¼ cup apricot jam

- Preheat the oven to 190°C (170° fan) / 375F / gas 5.
- Roll the pastry out on a lightly floured surface. Cut into
  6 rounds and line 10 cm flan tins.
- Line with greaseproof paper and baking beans. Blind
  bake for 10-12 minutes.
- Remove and discard the greaseproof paper and beans.
- Return to the oven for 4-5 minutes to brown the bases.
- Blitz together the ground almonds, sugar and butter.
- Add the eggs and almond extract and continue to pulse.
- Pour into pastry cases then stud with 3 apricot halves.
- Reduce the heat and bake the tartlets for 15-20 minutes.
- Meanwhile, warm the apricot jam and strain.
- Brush the tartlets with the jam.

Tangerine and Almond Tartlets 332

- Replace the apricots with peeled tangerine
  segments and glaze with warm marmalade
  instead of apricot jam.

333

MAKES 8

Lemon Curd Whoopies

- Preheat the oven to 170°C (150°C fan) / 325F / gas 3.
- Grease and line 2 baking trays with greaseproof paper.
- Cream together the margarine and sugar in a large mixing bowl until pale and fluffy.
- Beat in the flour, bicarbonate of soda and lemon extract until you have a rough dough, then add the food colouring and mix until the dough is yellow.
- Knead the dough briefly before rolling out on a lightly floured surface to ½ cm thickness.
- Use a 2" cookie cutter to cut out 16 rounds before carefully lifting onto the baking trays, spaced apart.
- Bake for 15-18 minutes. Remove to a wire rack to cool.
- Once cool, spoon the lemon curd onto the base of half of the cookies and sandwich with the remaining halves.
- Julienne the pared lemon zest before using to garnish the pies.

Lemon and Lime Whoopie Pies

 334

- Replace the lemon curd with lime curd.

PREPARATION TIME 10-15 MINUTES

COOKING TIME 15-20 MINUTES

INGREDIENTS

FOR THE COOKIES
250 g / 9 oz / 1 ½ cups plain (all purpose) flour, sifted
a little extra plain (all purpose) flour, for dusting
175 g / 6 oz / ¾ cup margarine, softened
75 g / 3 oz / ⅓ cup caster (superfine) sugar
½ tsp lemon extract
½ tsp bicarbonate (baking) of soda
a pinch of salt
a few drops of yellow food colouring

FOR THE FILLING
250 g / 9 oz / 1 cup lemon curd

TO GARNISH
1 lemon, pared

335

MAKES 4

Chocolate and Ginger Tartlets

- Preheat the oven to 180°C (160° fan) / 350F / gas 4.
- Roll the pastry out on a lightly floured surface.
- Cut out 4 rounds of pastry and line 4 5" tartlet cases.
- Prick the bases and trim excess pastry.
- Line with greaseproof paper and fill with baking beans before blind-baking for 12-15 minutes until golden.
- Remove and discard the greaseproof paper and beans. Return to the oven for 3-4 minutes to brown the base.
- Melt together the chocolate and cubed butter in a heatproof bowl set atop a saucepan of simmering water.
- Once melted, remove from the heat and allow to cool.
- Meanwhile, whisk together the eggs and egg yolks.
- Sift the plain flour into the eggs and whisk until smooth.
- Fold into the melted chocolate and butter with the stem ginger then spoon into the pastry cases. Bake for 12-15 minutes.

Chocolate and Honeycomb Tartlets

 336

- Replace the stem ginger with chopped honeycomb.

PREPARATION TIME 10 MINUTES

COOKING TIME 15 MINUTES

INGREDIENTS

250 g / 9 oz ready-made shortcrust pastry
a little plain (all purpose) flour, for dusting
110 g / 4 oz / ⅔ cup good-quality dark chocolate, chopped
110 g / 4 oz / ½ cup unsalted butter, cubed
75 g / 3 oz / ½ cup plain (all purpose) flour
30 g / 1 oz / 2 tbsp caster (superfine) sugar
2 medium eggs
2 medium egg yolks
2 pieces of stem ginger in syrup, finely chopped

TO GARNISH
1 tbsp crystallised ginger

337

MAKES 6

Raspberry Mini Vacherins

Mixed Fruit Vacherins

338

- Replace the pistachios with 100 g / 4 oz / 1 cup diced strawberries.

White Chocolate Pistachio Vacherin

339

- Replace the raspberries with 75 g of chopped white chocolate and mix into the whipped cream.

PREPARATION TIME 10 MINUTES

COOKING TIME 10-15 MINUTES

....

INGREDIENTS

FOR THE MERINGUE
2 medium egg whites
110 g / 4 oz / ½ cup caster (superfine) sugar
a pinch of salt

FOR THE TOPPING
250 ml / 9 fl. oz / 1 cup double (heavy) cream
12 raspberries
30 g / 1 oz / ¼ cup shelled pistachios, chopped

TO GARNISH
1 tbsp icing (confectioners') sugar

- Preheat the oven to 130°C (110° fan) / 250F / gas ½.
- Grease and line a large baking tray with greaseproof paper.
- Whisk the egg whites with a pinch of salt in a large mixing bowl until soft peaks form.
- Whisk in the sugar, 1 tablespoon at a time, beating well between additions until thick and glossy.
- Spoon into a piping bag fitted with a medium straight-sided nozzle.
- Pipe wave-like mounds onto the baking tray before baking for 2 hours until set.
- Open the oven door and let the meringues cool in the oven before removing to a wire rack.
- Whip the cream until soft peaks form them use to top the meringues with.
- Dot with 2 raspberries and sprinkle the chopped pistachios on top before serving.

340

MAKES 12-14 # Almond Shortbread Cookies

- Pulse together the flour, cornflour, ground almonds, salt, icing sugar and butter in a food processor until it comes together to form a dough in the machine.
- Gently knead the dough on a lightly floured work surface before wrapping in clingfilm or greaseproof paper and chilling for 1 hour.
- Preheat the oven to 170°C (150°C fan) / 325°F / gas 3 after 1 hour.
- Remove the dough from the fridge and roll out on a lightly floured work surface to 1 cm thickness.
- Use a 5-6 cm diameter cookie cutter to punch out 12-14 rounds of the dough.
- Transfer to baking sheets and light brush their tops with the milk before studding each with an almond on top.
- Bake for 15-18 minutes until the cookies start to colour.
- Remove from the oven and let the cookies cool.

PREPARATION TIME 10 MINUTES

COOKING TIME 25-30 MINUTES

INGREDIENTS

225 g / 8 oz / 1 ½ cups plain (all purpose) flour
a little extra plain flour, for dusting
55 g / 2 oz / ⅓ cup cornflour
75 g / 3 oz / ⅔ cup ground almonds
225 g / 8 oz / 2 sticks unsalted butter, cubed
75 g / 3 oz / ⅔ cup icing (confectioners') sugar
½ tsp salt
30 ml / 1 fl. oz / 2 tbsp whole milk
12-14 whole almonds

Hazelnut Cookies

 341

- Replace the ground almonds with ground hazelnuts, and use whole hazelnuts to stud the tops.

342

MAKES 4 # Chocolate, Almond and Pear Verrines

- Melt the cream and chocolate in a heatproof set atop a saucepan of simmering water.
- Stir occasionally until melted then remove to one side and allow to cool.
- Divide two-thirds of the pear into the base of 4 serving glasses.
- Top with a generous tablespoon of the melted chocolate cream and top with the remaining pear.
- Spoon the remaining chocolate evenly on top before garnishing with flaked almonds, grated chocolate and coconut shavings.
- Serve immediately.

PREPARATION TIME 10-15 MINUTES

COOKING TIME 10-15 MINUTES

INGREDIENTS

4 large pears, diced
200 g / 7 oz / 1 ⅓ cup good-quality dark chocolate
125 ml / 4 ½ fl. oz / ½ cup double (heavy) cream

TO GARNISH
30 g / 1 oz / ¼ cup flaked (slivered) almonds
1 tbsp grated dark chocolate
1 tbsp coconut shavings or chips

Raspberry Verrines

 343

- Replace the pear in the recipe with 300 g / 10 ½ oz / 3 cups of raspberries.

344

MAKES 4

Easter Nest Cake

PREPARATION TIME 10-15
MINUTES

COOKING TIME 15-20 MINUTES

INGREDIENTS

FOR THE SPONGE

110 g / 4 oz / ½ cup caster (superfine)
sugar
110 g / 4 oz / ½ cup margarine
110 g / 4 oz / ⅔ cup self-raising flour
2 large eggs
1 tsp vanilla extract

FOR THE BUTTERCREAM

225 g / 8 oz / 1 cup butter, softened
125 g / 4 ½ oz / 1 cup icing
(confectioners') sugar
2 tsp almond extract
1 tsp vanilla extract

TO GARNISH

225 g / 8 oz / 1 cup chopped
mixed nuts
16 mini chocolate eggs

- Preheat the oven to 180°C (160° fan) / 350F / gas 4.
- Grease and line 4 individual cake moulds with greaseproof paper.
- Combine all the ingredients for the sponge in a large mixing bowl and beat thoroughly for 2-3 minutes.
- Spoon into the cake moulds and bake for 15-18 minutes until risen.
- Remove from the oven to a wire rack to cool.
- Blitz together all the ingredients for the buttercream in a food processor until smooth.
- Once the cakes are cool, turn them out and spread the outsides with buttercream, reserving a little and spooning into a small piping bag.
- Roll the outsides of the cakes in the nuts to coat.
- Pipe small circles of buttercream on top and garnish with mini chocolate eggs before serving.

Coffee Easter Egg Cakes

345

- Replace the vanilla and almond extract with 30 ml / 1 fl. oz / 2 tbsp strong cold espresso in the buttercream.

346

MAKES 6

Jam Tartlets

PREPARATION TIME 10 MINUTES

COOKING TIME 15 MINUTES

INGREDIENTS

400 g / 14 oz ready-made shortcrust
pastry
a little plain (all purpose) flour,
for dusting
110 g / 4 oz / ½ cup apricot jam
1 tbsp whole milk
1 tsp caster (superfine) sugar

- Preheat the oven to 180°C (160° fan) / 350F / gas 4.
- Grease and line 2 baking trays with greaseproof paper.
- Roll the pastry out on a lightly floured surface to 1 cm thickness.
- Use a 4" fluted cookie cutter to stamp out 6 rounds from the pastry and arrange on the baking trays.
- Flatten the centres slightly with the back of a tablespoon to make a round indent.
- Gather the remaining pastry into a ball and re-roll to ¾ cm thickness.
- Cut out strips that will act as the lattice pastry top.
- Spoon the jam into the indents and arrange the strips of pastry into lattice patterns over the jam, securing them into the edges of the pastry.
- Briefly whisk together the milk and sugar and brush the edges with the glaze before baking for 20-25 minutes.

Cherry Lattice Tartlets

347

- Substitute the apricot jam with red or black cherry jam for the filling.

348

MAKES 6

Mini Almond and Chocolate Cakes

Almond and Cherry Cakes

349

- Add 50 g / 2 oz / ⅓ cup chopped glacés cherries to the batter before baking.

White Chocolate Almond Mini Cakes

350

- Replace the dark chocolate with white chocolate for a sweeter finish.

PREPARATION TIME 10-15 MINUTES

COOKING TIME 15 MINUTES

....

INGREDIENTS

FOR THE CAKES
150 g / 5 oz / 1 cup self-raising flour, sifted
150 g / 5 oz / ⅔ cup caster (superfine) sugar
150 g / 5 oz / ⅔ cup margarine, softened
30 g / 1 oz / ⅓ cup ground almonds
3 large eggs
½ tsp vanilla extract
½ tsp almond extract

TO GARNISH
100 g / 3 ½ oz / ⅔ cup good-quality dark chocolate, chopped
1 tbsp flaked (slivered) almonds

- Preheat the oven to 180°C (160° fan) / 350F / gas 4.
- Grease and line 6 mini loaf tins with greaseproof paper.
- Beat together the flour, sugar, margarine, ground almonds, eggs, almond and vanilla extracts in a large mixing bowl until smooth.
- Spoon into the loaf tins and bake for 20-25 minutes; test with a wooden toothpick, if it comes out clean, they are done.
- Remove from the oven to a wire rack to cool.
- Once cool, turn out and arrange on serving plates.
- Melt the chocolate in a heatproof bowl set atop a saucepan of simmering water, stirring occasionally.
- Drizzle over the mini cakes and garnish with flaked almonds before serving.

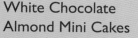

351

MAKES 4

Rhubarb Meringue Pie

Mandarin Meringue Pie

352

- Drain 400 g / 14 oz / 2 cups canned mandarin segments and use in place of the rhubarb.

Gooseberry Meringue Pies

353

- Replace the rhubarb with 400 g gooseberries.

PREPARATION TIME 10-15 MINUTES

COOKING TIME 20-25 MINUTES

....

INGREDIENTS

FOR THE PASTRY AND FILLING
250 g / 9 oz ready-made shortcrust pastry
a little plain (all purpose) flour, for dusting
675 g / 1 lb 8 oz / 5 cups rhubarb, trimmed and sliced
75 g / 3 oz / ⅓ cup caster (superfine) sugar
60 ml / 2 fl. oz / ¼ cup cold water

FOR THE MERINGUE
1 large egg white
55 g / 2 oz / ¼ cup caster (superfine) sugar
¼ tsp cream of tartar
a pinch of salt

- Preheat the oven to 180°C (160° fan) / 350F / gas 4.
- Roll the pastry out on a lightly floured surface.
- Cut out 4 rounds of pastry and line 4 5" fluted cases.
- Prick the bases and trim excess pastry.
- Line with greaseproof paper and fill with baking beans before blind-baking for 12-15 minutes until golden.
- Remove from the oven, discard the greaseproof paper and baking beans then return to the oven for 3-4 minutes to brown the base.
- Remove to a wire rack to cool.
- Combine the rhubarb, sugar and water in a saucepan and cook over a medium heat, covered, until soft.
- Drain and cool to one side.
- Whisk the egg white with salt in a large, clean mixing bowl until soft peaks form.
- Add the cream of tartar and the sugar, 1 tablespoon at time, beating well until you have a thick, glossy meringue. Spoon into a piping bag.
- Increase the oven to 220°C (200° fan) / 425F / gas 7.
- Fill the pastry with the rhubarb and pipe the meringue on top in a swirl.
- Bake for 8-10 minutes.

MAKES 12

Pineapple-Filled Shortbread Cookies

- Pulse together the flour, cornflour, salt, icing sugar and butter in a food processor until it forms a dough.
- Remove the dough, knead gently and form into a ball.
- Wrap in clingfilm and chill for 60 minutes.
- Reduce the pineapple juice in a saucepan.
- Preheat the oven to 180°C (160° fan) / 350F / gas 4.
- Remove the dough and divide into 12 even balls.
- Roll the balls out into rounds on a floured surface and place 1 tsp of pineapple in their centres.
- Bring the edges of the dough over towards the centre on top of the pineapple, securing the seams.
- Grease and line a baking tray with greaseproof paper.
- Arrange the filled shortbread on it and stud the tops with a clove.
- Spoon over a little pineapple juice and bake for 15-18 minutes.

PREPARATION TIME 10-15 MINUTES

COOKING TIME 20 MINUTES

INGREDIENTS

300 g / 10 ½ oz / 2 cups plain (all purpose) flour
a little extra plain flour, for dusting
50 g / 2 oz / ⅓ cup cornflour (cornstarch)
225 g / 8 oz / 1 cup unsalted butter, cubed
75 g / 3 oz / 1 cup icing (confectioners') sugar
125 g / 4 ½ oz / 1 ¼ cups dried pineapple
125 ml / 4 ½ fl. oz / ½ cup pineapple juice
12 cloves

Fig-Filled Shortbread

355

- Replace the pineapple with the same weight of dried fig in the centres.

356

SERVES 4

Nectarine and Ginger Tartlets

- Preheat the oven to 190°C (170° fan) / 375F / gas 5.
- Grease and line a large baking tray with greaseproof paper.
- Roll the pastry out on a lightly floured surface to ½ cm thickness.
- Use a 2" rectangular cutter to stamp out 12 squares and arrange on the baking tray.
- Mix together the ginger and sugar and sprinkle a little over the squares.
- Lay 3 nectarine slices across the pastry squares and sprinkle the remaining ginger sugar on top.
- Bake for 12-15 minutes until the pastry is cooked through.
- Remove from the oven and leave to cool on the tray before serving.

PREPARATION TIME 10-15 MINUTES

COOKING TIME 10 MINUTES

INGREDIENTS

200 g / 7 oz ready-made shortcrust pastry
a little plain (all purpose) flour, for dusting
55 g / 2 oz / ¼ cup golden granulated sugar
1 tsp ground ginger
3 nectarines, de-stoned and cut into 36 thin slices

Apple and Cinnamon Tartlets

357

- Substitute the nectarine for apple slices and use ground cinnamon instead of ginger.

SERVES 6

Chocolate and Hazelnut Croquants

PREPARATION TIME 10-15 MINUTES

COOKING TIME 15 MINUTES

INGREDIENTS

250 g / 9 oz / 1 ⅔ cups plain (all purpose) flour
a little extra plain (all purpose) flour, for dusting
225 g / 8 oz / 1 cup caster (superfine) sugar
100 g / 3 ½ oz / ⅔ cup dark chocolate chips
100 g / 3 ½ oz / 1 cup blanched hazelnuts (cob nuts), chopped
75 g / 3 oz / ½ cup good-quality cocoa powder
1 tsp baking powder
3 large eggs
a pinch of salt

- Preheat the oven to 180°C (160° fan) / 350F / gas 4.
- Grease and line a large baking tray with greaseproof paper.
- Sift together the flour, cocoa powder, salt and baking powder into a large mixing bowl.
- Beat together the eggs and sugar in a separate bowl then stir into the dry ingredients until you have a dough.
- Add the hazelnuts and chocolate chips and turn the dough out onto a lightly floured surface.
- Knead gently for 1 minute then roll into a log shape before moving to the baking tray.
- Flatten the top slightly and bake for 25 minutes.
- Remove and cut on the bias into 3 cm thick slices.
- Return to the baking tray, laying the slices on their sides and bake for an additional 20-25 minutes until firm.

Fruit and Nut Croquants 359

- Substitute half of the hazelnuts with 75 g / 3 oz / ½ cup raisins.

MAKES 6

White Chocolate and Pistachio Yoghurts

PREPARATION TIME 10 MINUTES

COOKING TIME 10 MINUTES

INGREDIENTS

500 ml / 18 fl. oz / 2 cups plain yoghurt
250 ml / 9 fl. oz / 1 cup whipping cream
100 g / 3 ½ oz / ⅔ cup white chocolate, chopped
75 g / 3 oz / ¾ cup shelled pistachios, chopped

- Melt together the chocolate and cream in a heatproof bowl set atop a saucepan of simmering water, stirring occasionally.
- Once melted, remove to one side to cool for 5 minutes.
- Stir into the yoghurt then spoon into 6 individual serving pots.
- Chill until ready to serve before garnishing with chopped pistachios on top.

White Chocolate and Mango Yoghurts 361

- Stir 1 diced mango into the yoghurt and chocolate mixture before pouring into the serving pots.

362

MAKES 6

Mini Christmas Loafs

Almond and Mini Fruit Loaf

363

Almond and Mixed Fruit Loaf

- Add 55 g / 2 oz / ½ cup ground almonds to the batter before spooning everything into a lined 1 lb loaf tin. Bake for 45-55 minutes until ready.

Hazelnut and Fruit Christmas Loaf

364

- Add 55 g / 2 oz / ½ cup ground hazelnuts to the batter and stud each mini loaf top with a whole hazelnut.

PREPARATION TIME 10 MINUTES

COOKING TIME 10 MINUTES

....

INGREDIENTS

150 g / 5 oz / 1 cup self-raising flour, sifted
150 g / 5 oz / ⅔ cup caster (superfine) sugar
150 g / 5 oz / ⅔ cup margarine, softened
75 g / 3 oz / ½ cup raisins
30 g / 1 oz / 2 tbsp mixed chopped peel
3 large eggs
1 tbsp treacle
1 tbsp brandy
½ tsp vanilla extract

TO GARNISH
1 tbsp icing (confectioners') sugar

- Preheat the oven to 180°C (160° fan) / 350F / gas 4.
- Grease and line 6 mini loaf tins with greaseproof paper.
- Beat together the flour, sugar, margarine, eggs, treacle and vanilla extract in a large mixing bowl until smooth.
- Fold through the brandy, raisins and mixed chopped peel.
- Spoon into the loaf tins and bake for 20-25 minutes; test with a wooden toothpick, if it comes out clean, they are done.
- Remove from the oven and leave to cool in the tins before dusting with icing sugar and serving.

PARTY FOOD

365

MAKES 8

Strawberry and Cream Pastry Boats

PREPARATION TIME 15 MINUTES

COOKING TIME 20-25 MINUTES

INGREDIENTS

FOR THE BOATS
350 g / 12 oz ready-made shortcrust pastry
a little plain (all purpose) flour, for dusting
250 ml / 9 fl. oz / 1 cup whipping cream
250 g / 9 oz / 2 ½ cups strawberries, halved
65 g / 2 ½ oz / ½ cup icing (confectioners') sugar
½ tsp vanilla extract

TO GARNISH
100 g / 3 ½ oz / 1 cup shelled pistachios, crushed
1 tbsp icing (confectioners') sugar
a few sprigs of fresh mint

- Preheat the oven to 180°C (160° fan) / 350F / gas 4.
- Roll the pastry out to ½ cm thickness and cut out 8 ovals; use them to line 8 individual boat tartlet moulds.
- Trim any excess pastry and prick the bases with a fork.
- Line with greaseproof paper and baking beans and blind-bake for 12-15 minutes until golden at the edges.
- Remove and discard the greaseproof paper and baking beans.
- Return to the oven for 3-4 minutes to brown the bases.
- Whip the cream with the icing sugar and vanilla extract in a mixing bowl until soft peaks form.
- Spoon into a piping bag.
- Remove the tartlets from the moulds and fill with swirls of whipped cream.
- Top with 3-4 upright strawberry halves and garnish with crushed pistachios, icing sugar and basil leaf sprigs.

Forest Fruit Cream Boats **366**

- Thaw 200 g / 7 oz / 1 cup frozen mixed berries and use in place of the strawberries on top of the cream.

367

MAKES 24

Prune and Muesli Truffles

PREPARATION TIME 10 MINUTES

COOKING TIME 15-20 MINUTES

INGREDIENTS

300 g / 10 ½ oz / 2 cups good-quality dark chocolate, chopped
250 ml / 9 fl. oz / 1 cup double (heavy) cream
150 g / 5 oz / 2 cups muesli
150 g / 5 oz / 1 cup dried prunes, finely chopped
55 g / 2 oz / ¼ cup unsalted butter

- Place the chocolate in a large heatproof mixing bowl.
- Place the cream and butter in a saucepan and bring to a simmer over a moderate heat.
- Once the butter has fully melted and the mixture is simmering, remove from the heat and pour over the chocolate.
- Beat until you have a smooth mixture, then stir in the prunes.
- Cover the bowl and chill for 4 hours.
- To make the truffles, remove the chocolate mixture from the fridge and let sit at room temperature for 10 minutes.
- Use a melon baller to scoop the truffle mixture.
- Using lightly oiled hands, roll into truffle shapes making sure they are slightly soft and warmed.
- Roll in the muesli to coat.

Coconut Muesli Truffles **368**

- Substitute the chopped prunes in the truffle mixture for 75 g / 3 oz / 1 cup desiccated coconut, stirring it in at the same time as you would with the prunes.

369

MAKES 10

Chocolate Profiteroles

- Sift together flour and sugar in a mixing bowl.
- Combine the butter and milk in a saucepan and heat gently until the butter melts.
- Add the flour and stir until a smooth dough forms.
- Beat the dough until it pulls away from the saucepan.
- Remove from the heat and add the eggs, one at a time, beating well between each addition until shiny.
- Spoon the dough into a piping bag.
- Preheat the oven to 200°C (180° fan) / 400F / gas 6.
- Grease and line 2 baking trays with greaseproof paper.
- Pipe blobs of the pastry onto the sheets, spaced apart. Bake for 15-18 minutes.
- Combine the butter and chocolate for the sauce in a heatproof bowl, set atop a saucepan of simmering water.
- Remove the tops of the buns, fill with scoops of ice cream and reassemble.
- Garnish with the sauce and hazelnuts.

Two Chocolate Profiteroles   **370**

- Replace half of the dark chocolate with white chocolate for a marbled chocolate sauce.

PREPARATION TIME 10-15 MINUTES

COOKING TIME 20 MINUTES

INGREDIENTS

FOR THE CHOUX PASTRY
110 g / 4 oz / ⅔ cup plain
(all purpose) flour
110 g / 4 oz / ½ cup unsalted butter,
cold and cubed
250 ml / 9 fl. oz / 1 cup whole milk
4 large egg
1 tsp caster (superfine) sugar

FOR THE CHOCOLATE SAUCE
225 g / 8 oz / 1 ½ cups good-quality
dark chocolate, chopped
55 g / 2 oz / ¼ cup unsalted butter

FOR THE FILLING
500 ml / 18 fl. oz / 3 cups good-
quality vanilla ice cream
55 g / 2 oz / ⅓ cup hazelnuts
(cobnuts), finely chopped

371

MAKES 12

Opera Iced Chocolate Cakes

- Preheat the oven to 180°C (160° fan) / 350F / gas 4.
- Grease and line a 8" x 4" x 3" springform tin with greaseproof paper.
- Combine the all the cake ingredients apart from the hazelnuts in a mixing bowl.
- Beat until smooth then fold in the hazelnuts.
- Spoon into the tin and bake for 20-25 minutes.
- Remove from the oven and cool to one side.
- Prepare the white ganache by heating the cream in a saucepan until boiling.
- Remove from the heat and whisk in the white chocolate and butter until smooth before cooling for 5 minutes.
- Pour onto the cake and chill until set.
- Repeat the method with the dark ganache, before cooling and pouring on top of the set white ganache.
- Chill until set.

Chocolate Orange Opera Cakes   **372**

- Finely chop 55 g / 2 oz / ⅓ cup candied orange peel and use to garnish the tops of the cakes.

PREPARATION TIME 10-15 MINUTES

COOKING TIME 15 MINUTES

INGREDIENTS

110 g / 4 oz / ½ cup margarine
110 g / 4 oz / ½ cup caster (superfine) sugar
110 g / 4 oz / ⅔ cup self-raising flour
50 g / 2 oz / ⅓ cup hazelnuts
(cob nuts), roughly chopped
30 g / 1 oz / 2 tbsp cocoa powder
30 ml / 1 fl. oz / 2 tbsp whole milk
salt
2 large eggs
250 g / 9 oz / 1 ⅔ cups white chocolate, chopped
200 ml / 7 fl. oz / ⅘ cup double (heavy) cream
1 tbsp unsalted butter, softened
225 g / 8 oz / 1 ½ cups dark chocolate
175 ml / 6 fl. oz / ¾ cup double (heavy) cream
1 tbsp unsalted butter, softened

373

MAKES 8

Small Semolina and Coconut Cakes

Semolina, Coconut and Spice Cakes

374

- Add ½ tsp mixed all spice and ¼ tsp ground cinnamon at the same time as the ground cardamom.

Orange, Semolina and Coconut Cakes

375

- Replace the cardamom with 1 tbsp of grated orange zest, and add 1 tsp of orange extract / essence.

PREPARATION TIME 10 MINUTES

COOKING TIME 10-15 MINUTES

INGREDIENTS

175 g / 6 oz / ¾ cup caster (superfine) sugar
150 g / 5 oz / 1 cup self-raising flour
150 g / 5 oz / ⅔ cup unsalted butter, softened
125 ml / 4 ½ fl. oz / ½ cup coconut milk
110 g / 4 oz / 1 ½ cups desiccated coconut
110 g / 4 oz / ⅔ cup semolina
30 ml / 1 fl. oz / 2 tbsp sunflower oil
2 medium eggs
8 cardamom pods, lightly crushed
a pinch of salt

TO GARNISH
small handful of cardamom pods

- Preheat the oven to 180°C (160° fan) / 350F / gas 4.
- Grease 8 individual bundt tins with sunflower oil.
- Remove the seeds from the cardamom pods and grind in a mortar and pestle.
- Cream the butter and sugar in a mixing bowl until pale and fluffy.
- Beat in the eggs, one at a time, then fold through the flour, semolina, ground cardamom and coconut milk.
- Add the desiccated coconut and mix well.
- Spoon into the ramekins and bake for 18-22 minutes; test with a wooden toothpick, if it comes out clean, the cakes are done.
- Remove the cakes to a wire rack and let them cool before turning out.
- Garnish with cardamom pods before serving.

MAKES 12 — Custard Tarts with Icing Sugar

- Simmer the sugar, cinnamon sticks and water in a pan.
- Mix the flour, cornflour and vanilla extract in a jug with a little milk to make a smooth paste.
- Heat the remaining milk in a saucepan until simmering then combine with the paste, whisking simultaneously.
- Pour into a saucepan, cooking over a medium heat.
- Discard the cinnamon and combine with the thickened milk. Add the egg and yolks, cooking until simmering.
- Pour into a jug, covering the surface before chilling.
- Preheat the oven to 220°C (200° fan) / 425F / gas 7.
- Roll the puff pastry out on a floured work surface.
- Cut pastry in half, stack on top of each other and roll into a log. Cut 12 slices and roll into 10 cm rounds.
- Grease a 12 hole muffin tin with the butter and line with pastry.
- Fill with custard and bake for 15-18 minutes. Garnish with icing sugar and cinnamon.

Orange Custard Tarts   377

- Replace the vanilla extract with 1 tsp orange extract for a fruity take on this tart.

PREPARATION TIME 10-15 MINUTES

COOKING TIME 15 MINUTES

INGREDIENTS

400 g / 14 oz / 2 ⅔ cups ready-made puff pastry, chilled
250 ml / 9 fl. oz / 1 cup whole milk
225 g / 8 oz / 1 cup caster (superfine) sugar
125 ml / 4 ½ fl. oz / ½ cup cold water
30 g / 1 oz / 2 tbsp unsalted butter, softened
30 g / 1 oz / 2 tbsp plain (all purpose) flour
15 g / ½ oz / 1 tbsp cornflour (cornstarch)
½ tsp vanilla extract
3 large egg yolks
1 large egg
2 sticks of cinnamon

TO GARNISH

1 tbsp icing (confectioners') sugar
1 tsp ground cinnamon

MAKES 20 — Financiers with Grapefruit Syrup

- Preheat the oven to 180°C (160° fan) / 350F / gas 4.
- Brown the butter in a saucepan. Strain through a fine sieve into a clean bowl.
- Combine the flour, almonds and sugar.
- Whisk the egg whites into this mixture and then fold through the cooled, melted butter. Chill for 30 minutes.
- Grease 2, 12-hole financier tins with unsalted butter.
- Pour the batter into the moulds and bake for 12-15 minutes until golden brown at the edges and risen.
- Prepare the syrup by mixing the sugar, water, grapefruit and lemon juice in a saucepan.
- Julienne half of the grapefruit and lemon zest.
- Simmer and stir until the sugar has dissolved, then add the zests and reduce for a further 5 minutes.
- Spoon the syrup and peanuts on top.

Financiers with Lime Syrup   379

- Replace the yellow grapefruit and lemon juice with the juice of 5 limes and the zest of 2 of them.

PREPARATION TIME 10-15 MINUTES

COOKING TIME 15 MINUTES

INGREDIENTS

110 g / 4 oz / ½ cup caster (superfine) sugar
110 g / 4 oz / ½ cup slightly salted butter, softened
1 tbsp unsalted butter, softened
110 g / 4 oz / ⅔ cup ground almonds
30 g / 1 oz / 2 tbsp plain (all purpose) flour, sifted
3 medium egg whites
a pinch of salt

FOR THE GRAPEFRUIT SYRUP

125 ml / 4 ½ fl. oz / ½ cup cold water
75 g / 3 oz / ⅓ cup caster (superfine) sugar
2 yellow grapefruits, juiced and zested
1 lemon, juiced and zested
1 tsp peanuts, finely chopped

MAKES 4

Toffee Apples

380

PREPARATION TIME 5 MINUTES

COOKING TIME 10 MINUTES

INGREDIENTS

4 eating apples (Braeburn or Gala for example)
225 g / 8 oz / 1 cup caster (superfine) sugar
55 ml / 2 fl. oz / ¼ cup cold water
2 tbsp Golden Syrup
½ tsp distilled vinegar

ALSO NEEDED

4 wooden sticks or skewers
sugar thermometer

- Place the apples in a large bowl of boiling water, letting them sit for 30 seconds.
- Remove and dry thoroughly, before removing any stalks.
- Push a wooden stick or skewer through the centre of the apples but not all the way through.
- Grease and line a baking tray with greaseproof paper.
- Combine the sugar and water in a saucepan and cook until the sugar dissolves; approximately 4 minutes.
- Add the syrup and vinegar, stir once, then cook until the mixture reaches 140°C on a sugar thermometer.
- Carefully and quickly dip the apples in the mixture, coating thoroughly, then leave to dry and harden on the lined baking tray.
- Serve once the toffee is hard and dry to the touch.

Chocolate Toffee Apples

381

- Melt 150 g / 5 oz / 1 cup good-quality dark chocolate and drizzle the toffee apples with it. Let the chocolate set before serving.

MAKES 16

Coffee-Flavoured Fudge

382

PREPARATION TIME 5 MINUTES

COOKING TIME 20 MINUTES

INGREDIENTS

400 g / 14 oz / 1 ⅗ cups condensed milk
100 ml / 3 ½ fl. oz / ⅔ cup whole milk
55 ml / 2 fl. oz / ¼ cup strong espresso
450 g / 1 lb / 2 cups demerara sugar
110 g / 4 oz / ½ cup butter, softened

ALSO NEEDED

sugar thermometer

- Grease and line a 7" square tin with greaseproof paper.
- Combine all the ingredients in a large saucepan.
- Cook over a low heat, stirring frequently, until the sugar dissolves.
- Simmer for 10-12 minutes until thickened and the temperature reaches 118°C on a sugar thermometer.
- Remove the fudge from the heat and continue to beat until it starts to set; approximately 8 minutes.
- Pour the fudge into the prepared tin and leave to cool and set.
- Once set, cut into squares and serve.

Vanilla and Raisin Fudge

383

- Replace the espresso with 1 tbsp vanilla extract; add 100 g / 3 ½ oz / ⅔ cup raisins to the fudge when you beat it until it sets.

384

MAKES 12

Plain Chocolate Shortbread Cookies

Plain Chocolate and Pecan Cookies

385

- Roughly chop 100 g / 3 ½ oz / 2/3 cup pecans and stud the cookies with them before baking.

Double Chocolate Dipped Cookies

386

- When set dip the other half of the cookies in melted white chocolate.

PREPARATION TIME 10 MINUTES

COOKING TIME 15 MINUTES

INGREDIENTS

250 g / 9 oz / 1 ⅔ cups plain (all purpose) flour
a little extra plain (all purpose) flour, for dusting
1 tsp baking powder
75 g / 3 oz / ⅓ cup butter, cubed
55 g / 2 oz / ¼ cup caster (superfine) sugar
1 large egg
½ tsp vanilla extract
a pinch of salt
2 tbsp whole milk
200 g / 7 oz / 1 ⅓ cups good-quality dark chocolate, chopped

- Preheat the oven to 180°C (160° fan) / 350F / gas 4.
- Pulse together the flour, salt, baking powder and butter in a food processor until they resemble breadcrumbs.
- Combine the egg, milk and vanilla extract in a jug then add to the food processor, little by little, pulsing simultaneously until a dough forms.
- Turn out and knead gently for 10 seconds before rolling out on a lightly floured surface to 1" thickness.
- Grease and line a large baking tray with greaseproof paper.
- Use an 2" oval cookie cutter to make the shortbread cookie shapes out of the dough.
- Arrange spaced apart on the tray and bake for 20-25 minutes until golden.
- Remove from the oven and cool on a wire rack; melt the chocolate in a heatproof bowl set atop a saucepan of simmering water.
- Stir until melted, remove from the heat and set to one side to cool.
- Dip one half of the cookie cakes in the melted chocolate and set on a lined tray to cool.

Chocolate, Fruit and Nut Bites

387

MAKES 24

PREPARATION TIME 10 MINUTES

COOKING TIME 5 MINUTES

INGREDIENTS

250 g / 9 oz / 1 ⅔ cups good-quality dark chocolate, chopped
250 g / 9 oz / 1 ⅔ cups good-quality milk chocolate, chopped
55 g / 2 oz / ⅓ cup walnut halves
55 g / 2 oz / ⅓ cup pistachios, shelled
55 g / 2 oz / ⅓ cup whole almonds
55 g / 2 oz / ⅓ cup hazelnuts (cob nuts)
30 g / 1 oz / 2 tbsp raisins

- Grease and line a couple of baking trays with greaseproof paper.
- Melt the dark and milk chocolate in separate heatproof bowls set over saucepans of simmering water.
- Stir occasionally until melted then remove from the heat and spoon onto the trays in rounds.
- Stud with a mixture of the nuts and raisins and chill until the chocolate rounds have set.
- Remove from the fridge after 45 minutes and peel off the trays before serving.

Dried Fruit Chocolate Bites

388

- Replace the nuts with a mixture of 100 g / 3 ½ oz / ⅔ sultanas and 55 g / 2 oz / ¼ cup currants for a nut-free option.

Mini Nut and Toffee Tarts

389

MAKES 4

PREPARATION TIME 10 MINUTES

COOKING TIME 45 MINUTES

INGREDIENTS

300 g / 10 ½ oz / 2 cups ready-made shortcrust pastry
a little plain flour, for dusting
300 g / 10 ½ oz / 1 ⅓ cups caster (superfine) sugar
150 ml / 5 fl. oz / ⅗ cup cold water
55 g / 2 oz / ¼ cup butter, cubed
150 g / 5 oz / 1 ½ cups walnut halves, roughly chopped
55 g / 2 oz / ⅓ cup cashews

- Preheat the oven to 180°C (160° fan) / 350F / gas 4.
- Roll the pastry out on a lightly floured work surface.
- Cut 4 rounds of pastry and line 4 5" pastry rings.
- Prick the bases, line with greaseproof paper and fill with baking beans. Trim any excess pastry.
- Arrange on a baking tray and blind-bake for 12-15 minutes.
- Remove and discard the greaseproof paper and beans.
- Return the pastry to the oven for 3-4 minutes.
- Combine the sugar and water in a saucepan, and cook over a medium heat, swirling occasionally, until golden-brown in colour.
- Remove from the heat and gradually stir in the butter.
- Add the nuts to the toffee sauce, stir, then spoon into the pastry tarts and serve.

Fruit and Nut Toffee Tarts

390

- Add 55 g / 2 oz / ⅓ cup of glacés cherries and 55 g / 2 oz / ⅓ cup chopped dried figs to the toffee sauce before stirring and spooning into the tarts.

391
SERVES 8
Chocolate Cake Squares

- Preheat the oven to 180°C (160° fan) / 350F / gas 4.
- Grease and line a 7" square cake tin with greaseproof paper.
- Combine the flour, margarine, sugar, salt and eggs in a large mixing bowl and beat until smooth.
- Melt the chocolate in a heatproof bowl set over a saucepan of simmering water, stirring occasionally.
- Let the chocolate cool a little before adding to the batter with the cocoa powder, folding through until incorporated.
- Spoon the batter into the tin and bake for 25-30 minutes; test with a wooden toothpick, if it comes out clean, the cake is done.
- Let the cake cool in its tin before turning out and cutting into squares.
- Garnish with rings of coloured sugar crystals on top.

PREPARATION TIME 10 MINUTES

COOKING TIME 10-15 MINUTES

INGREDIENTS

150 g / 5 oz / 1 cup self-raising flour
150 g / 5 oz / ⅔ cup margarine, softened
150 g / 5 oz / ⅔ cup golden caster (superfine) sugar
100 g / 3 ½ oz / ⅔ cup good-quality dark chocolate, chopped
3 large eggs
30 g / 1 oz / 2 tbsp cocoa powder
30 ml / 1 fl. oz / 2 tbsp whole milk
a pinch of salt

TO GARNISH
1 tbsp coloured sugar crystals

Chocolate Caramel Cake Squares
392

- Add 100 ml / 3 ½ fl. oz / ⅖ cup dulce de leche to the batter at the same time as the cocoa powder. Serve the square with extra dulce de leche if desired.

393
MAKES 24
Chocolate Truffles

- Place the chocolate in a large heatproof mixing bowl.
- Place the cream and butter in a saucepan and bring to a simmer over a moderate heat.
- Once the butter has fully melted and the mixture is simmering, remove from the heat and pour over the chocolate.
- Beat until you have a smooth mixture, then cover the bowl and chill for 4 hours.
- To make the truffles, remove the chocolate mixture from the fridge and let sit at room temperature for 10 minutes.
- Use a melon baller to take out scoops of the truffle mixture.
- Using lightly oiled hands, roll into truffle shapes then roll in the cocoa powder to lightly coat.
- Shake off any excess before serving.

PREPARATION TIME 5-10 MINUTES

COOKING TIME 10-15 MINUTES

INGREDIENTS

300 g / 10 ½ oz / 2 cups good-quality dark chocolate, chopped
300 ml / 10 ½ fl. oz / 1 ⅓ cups double (heavy) cream
55 g / 2 oz / ¼ cup unsalted butter
55 g / 2 oz / ⅓ cup cocoa powder

ALSO NEEDED
a little sunflower oil

Chocolate and Cointreau Truffles
394

- Add 65 ml / 2 ½ fl. oz / ¼ cup Cointreau to the cream and butter before bringing to a simmer.

MAKES 6

Flaky Tarts with Raspberries and Cream

Blueberry Tarts with Cream 396

- Replace the raspberries with 24 blueberries, using 4 for each tart on their tops.

Flaky Tarts with Wild Strawberries and Cream 397

- Top the tarts with wild strawberries instead of raspberries.

PREPARATION TIME 10 MINUTES

COOKING TIME 10-15 MINUTES

INGREDIENTS

200 g / 7 oz ready-made puff pastry
a little plain (all purpose) flour, for dusting
250 ml / 9 fl. oz / 1 cup whipping cream
125 g / 4 ½ oz / 1 cup icing (confectioners') sugar
1 tsp vanilla extract

TO GARNISH
12 raspberries
1 tbsp icing (confectioners') sugar

- Preheat the oven to 190°C (170° fan) / 375F / gas 5.
- Grease and line a large baking tray with greaseproof paper.
- Roll the pastry out on a lightly floured surface to 1 cm thick.
- Use a 4 cm fluted cutter to stamp out 6 rounds of pastry and a 3 cm fluted cutter to stamp out 6 rounds as well.
- Use a small 1 cm straight-sided cutter to stamp out holes from the middle of the 3 cm rounds, discarding the holes.
- Arrange the 4 cm and 3 cm rounds on the baking tray and bake for 8-10 minutes until golden and puffed.
- Remove from the oven and move to a wire rack to cool.
- Whip the cream with the icing sugar and vanilla extract in a mixing bowl until soft peaks form.
- Arrange the larger pastry rounds on a serving plate, topping with the cream.
- Sit the small rounds on top and garnish with two raspberries in the holes on top.
- Dust with icing sugar before serving.

398

SERVES 6

Raspberry Swiss Roll

- Preheat the oven to 180°C (160° fan) / 350F / gas 4.
- Grease and line a 17" x 12" x 2" jelly roll pan with greaseproof paper.
- Combine the margarine, sugar, flour, eggs and vanilla extract in a mixing bowl and beat until smooth; usually 2-3 minutes.
- Spoon the batter onto the pan and smooth until even.
- Bake for 12-15 minutes; test with a wooden toothpick, if it comes out clean, the cake is done.
- Remove from the oven and let it cool to one side.
- Remove the sponge from the pan using the greaseproof paper to help, then spread the surface with the jam.
- Roll into a log and slice into portions before serving.

PREPARATION TIME 10-15 MINUTES

COOKING TIME 10-15 MINUTES

INGREDIENTS

110 g / 4 oz / ½ cup margarine, softened
110 g / 4 oz / ½ cup caster (superfine) sugar
110 g / 4 oz / ⅔ cup self-raising flour
2 large eggs
1 tsp vanilla extract
300 g / 10 ½ oz / 1 ⅓ cups raspberry jam

Mixed Fruit Swiss Roll

399

- Replace 110 g / 4 oz / ½ cup of the raspberry jam with the same amount of blackberry jam and mix well before spreading on top of the sponge.

400

MAKES 4

Flaky Pastry Apple Pies

- Preheat the oven to 190°C (170° fan) / 375F / gas 5.
- Combine the apple, sugar, water and vanilla extract in a saucepan and bring to a simmer over a medium heat, cooking until softened to a compote.
- Remove from the heat and cool to one side.
- Grease and line a baking tray with greaseproof paper.
- Roll the pastry out on a lightly floured surface. Cut out 4 rounds approximately 10" diameter.
- Arrange the rounds on the baking tray and spoon the cooled apple compote in the centres, leaving a 2" border.
- Brush the border with a little beaten egg, fold the pastry over into a semi-circle shape, lightly crimping the edges.
- Run the tines across the top of the pastry lightly to score.
- Score the top of the pastry, then brush with a mixture of the beaten egg and milk.
- Bake for 18-20 minutes until golden-brown.

PREPARATION TIME 15 MINUTES

COOKING TIME 20 MINUTES

INGREDIENTS

225 g / 8 oz ready-made puff pastry
a little plain (all purpose) flour, for dusting
750 g / 1 lb 10 ½ oz / 3 cups cooking apples, peeled, cored and diced
110 g / 4 oz / ½ cup caster (superfine) sugar
30 ml / 1 fl. oz / 2 tbsp cold water
½ tsp vanilla extract
1 large egg, beaten
1 tbsp whole milk

Apple and Sultana Pies

401

- Add 50 g / 2 oz / ⅓ cup sultanas to the cooked apple mixture before spooning onto the pastries.

SERVES 6

Nut Brownies

PREPARATION TIME 10-15 MINUTES

COOKING TIME 15 MINUTES

INGREDIENTS

350 g / 12 oz / 2 cups good-quality dark chocolate, chopped
225 g / 8 oz / 1 cup unsalted butter, softened
250 g / 9 oz / 1 ⅓ cups light soft brown sugar
175 g / 6 oz / 1 ¾ cups pecans, chopped
110 g / 4 oz / ⅔ cup plain (all-purpose) flour
3 large eggs
1 tsp baking powder
a pinch of salt

ALSO NEEDED
1 sheet silver leaf

- Preheat the oven to 170°C (150°C fan) / 325°F / gas 3.
- Grease and line a 5" square baking tray with greaseproof paper.
- Melt the chocolate and butter in a saucepan over a medium-low heat, stirring occasionally until smooth.
- Remove from the heat and allow to cool a little.
- In a large mixing bowl, whisk the eggs until they are thick then add the sugar and continue to whisk.
- Beat in the melted chocolate mixture, then fold in the flour and baking powder until incorporated.
- Add the pecans and stir well.
- Pour into the baking tray and tap lightly a few times to release any trapped air bubbles.
- Bake for 35-40 minutes until the surface has set.
- Remove and let the brownie cool.

Cherry Brownies

403

- Add 150 g / 5 oz / 1 ½ cups dried cherries to the brownie batter before baking, omitting the pecans at the same time.

404

MAKES 24

Summer Fruit Petit Fours

INGREDIENTS

30 g / 1 oz / 2 tbsp pectin
1 tbsp tartaric acid
250 g / 9 oz / 1 cup raspberry puree
250 g / 9 oz / 1 cup strawberry puree
900 g / 2 lb / 4 cups caster (superfine) sugar
8 lemons, juiced
200 ml / 7 fl. oz / ⅘ cup glucose
125 ml / 4 ½ fl. oz / ½ cup cold water
110 g / 4 oz / ½ cup caster (superfine) sugar
sugar thermometer
24-hole round jelly mould

- Combine the pectin with 50 g of the sugar in a small bowl and mix the tartaric acid with 5 tbsp of the lemon juice in another bowl.
- Mix together the purees, 850 g of sugar, water, remaining lemon juice and glucose in a large saucepan.
- Cook over a moderate heat until boiling, removing any scum that comes to the surface.
- Add the sugar and pectin mix to the saucepan and cook, whisking constantly, until the thermometer reads 108°C.
- Once it reaches that temperature, remove the saucepan from the heat and stir in the tartaric acid mixture.
- Strain through a sieve into a clean jug.
- Pour into the moulds and let the petit fours set.
- Once set, turn out and roll in the remaining caster sugar before placing in cases and serving.

Passionfruit Petit Fours

405

- Substitute the raspberry and strawberry purees for the same weight of passionfruit puree.

406

MAKES 12

Star Mince Pies

Mincemeat and Marmalade Pies

407

- Top each mince pie with a teaspoon of good-quality marmalade instead of a dusting of icing sugar.

White Chocolate Topped Mince Pies

408

- After cooking and cooling, brush each mince pie top with melted white chocolate and omit the icing sugar.

PREPARATION TIME 10 MINUTES

COOKING TIME 15-20 MINUTES

INGREDIENTS

450 g / 1 lb ready-made sweet shortcrust pastry
a little plain (all purpose) flour, for dusting
900 g / 2 lb / 4 cups mincemeat

TO GARNISH
65 g / 2 ½ oz / ½ cup icing (confectioners') sugar

- Preheat the oven to 190°C (170° fan) / 375F / gas 5.
- Roll the pastry out on a lightly floured surface to roughly 1 cm thickness.
- Cut 12 rounds of pastry that will fit into the holes of a 12-hole cupcake tin.
- Press the pastry into the cupcake holes making sure they reach all the way to the rim.
- Gather the rest of the pastry into a ball and re-roll to roughly 1cm thickness.
- Use a small star-shaped cutter that will act as lids for the mince pies.
- Fill the base layers of pastry with the mincemeat.
- Top with the pastry lids, using a little water to moisten the rims to help them stick.
- Crimp the edges of the pastry with a fork.
- Bake for 20-25 minutes until the pastry is cooked through and lightly coloured.
- Remove from the oven and let the pies cool in the tin.
- Dust with icing sugar before serving.

409

MAKES 24

Mini Christmas Puddings

PREPARATION TIME 15-20 MINUTES

COOKING TIME 20 MINUTES

INGREDIENTS

110 g / 4 oz / ½ cup shredded suet
110 g / 4 oz / 1 cup breadcrumbs
100 g / 3 ½ oz / ⅔ cup self-raising flour
200 g / 7 oz / 1 cup brown sugar
100 g / 3 ½ oz / ⅔ cup raisins
100 g / 3 ½ oz / ⅔ cup sultanas
300 g / 10 ½ oz / 2 cups currants
30 g / 1 oz / 2 tbsp blanched almonds
1 medium Bramley apple, diced
2 large eggs
75 ml / 3 fl. oz / ⅓ cup dark rum
75 ml / 3 fl. oz / ⅓ cup stout
1 lemon, finely grated zest
½ tsp ground allspice
24 fluted butter biscuits
125 g / 4 ½ oz / 1 cup icing
(confectioners') sugar
150 ml / 5 fl. oz / 1 cup Golden Syrup
red, green sugarpaste

- Place the suet, breadcrumbs, flour, sugar and ground allspice in a large mixing bowl and mix well.
- Add the dried fruit almonds, apple and lemon zest.
- Whisk together the rum, stout and eggs.
- Add to the main mixing bowl, mixing well until you have a moist yet firm mixture. Cover the bowl with clingfilm and chill overnight.
- Take large tablespoons and shape into balls.
- Line 2 steamers with greaseproof paper and sit over saucepans of simmering water.
- Arrange the balls in the steamers, cover, and steam for 8-10 minutes.
- Arrange on biscuits and drizzle with Golden Syrup.
- Mix the icing sugar with a little boiling water.
- Spoon on top of the puddings then top with the sugarpaste icing to resemble holly and ivy.

Brandy Butter Christmas Puddings

410

- Mix together 55 ml / 2 fl. oz / ¼ cup brandy with 175 g / 6 oz / ¾ cup melted butter.

411

MAKES 24

Mini Cherry Fars

PREPARATION TIME 10-15 MINUTES

COOKING TIME 15 MINUTES

INGREDIENTS

500 ml / 18 fl. oz / 2 cups whole milk
225 g / 8 oz / 1 cup caster (superfine) sugar
150 g / 5 oz / 1 cup plain (all purpose) flour
450 g / 1 lb / 4 cups cherries, pitted and half with stems intact
75 g / 3 oz / ⅓ cup unsalted butter, melted and cooled
4 medium eggs
2 medium egg yolks
30 ml / 1 fl. oz / 2 tbsp kirsch (optional)
a pinch of salt

- Line a 24-hole mini cupcake tin with 24 mini cupcake cases.
- Preheat the oven to 180°C (160° fan) / 350F / gas 4.
- Combine everything apart from the cherries and flour in a food processor.
- Pulse until smooth, then add the flour in thirds, pulsing until just combined.
- Spoon the batter into the cases and dot with the cherries.
- Bake for 15-18 minutes until the fars are just set.
- Remove from the oven and let them cool in the tin before serving.

Mini Apricot Fars

412

- Substitute the cherries with large chunks of pitted fresh apricots.

413

MAKES 12

Simple Madeleines

- Preheat the oven to 180°C (160° fan) / 350F / gas 4.
- Grease a 12-hole madeleine tray.
- Beat together the eggs, icing sugar, salt and vanilla extract in a large mixing bowl until thick and shiny.
- Fold in the flour, 25 g at a time, as well as the baking powder.
- Once all the flour has been added, fold in the melted butter until incorporated.
- Spoon into the moulds, leaving them about three-quarters full with the batter.
- Bake for 12-14 minutes until golden and risen.
- Remove and allow them to cool in the tray for a few minutes before turning out onto a wire rack to finish cooling.
- Dust with icing sugar before serving.

PREPARATION TIME 10 MINUTES

COOKING TIME 15 MINUTES

INGREDIENTS

125 g / 4 ½ oz / 1 cup icing (confectioners') sugar, sifted
115 g / 4 oz / ½ cup unsalted butter, melted and cooled
100 g / 3 ½ oz / ⅔ cup plain (all purpose) flour, sifted
½ tsp baking powder
½ tsp vanilla extract
a pinch of salt

TO GARNISH

1 tbsp icing (confectioners') sugar

Citrus Fruit Madeleines
414

- Add 55 g / 2 oz / ⅓ cup candied mixed peel to the batter before baking.

415

SERVES 4

Churros with Thick Hot Chocolate

- Sift together the flours, salt and cornflour into a large mixing bowl.
- Add the boiling water and olive oil, mixing well until you have a soft, sticky dough; let it rest for 10 minutes.
- Combine the milk and cream in a large saucepan and heat over a medium heat until boiling.
- Remove from the heat and stir through the chocolates and Golden Syrup.
- Heat the sunflower oil in a large saucepan; the oil is hot enough as bubbles appear on a wooden spoon.
- Spoon the batter into a large piping bag and squeeze into the hot oil, cut the batter at 10 cm in length.
- Cook 2-3 at a time, frying for 3-4 minutes.
- Remove from the oil and drain on kitchen paper.
- Spoon the hot chocolate into serving glasses and serve with the churros.

Cinnamon Sugar Churros
416

- Add 1 tsp ground cinnamon to the sugar for dusting the churros with.

PREPARATION TIME 10 MINUTES

COOKING TIME 15-20 MINUTES

INGREDIENTS

1 l / 1 pint 16 fl. oz / 4 cups sunflower oil
450 ml / 16 fl. oz / 1 ¾ cups boiling water
110 g / 4 oz / ½ cup caster (superfine) sugar
100 g / 3 ½ oz / ⅔ cup plain (all purpose) flour
30 g / 1 oz / 2 tbsp cornflour (cornstarch)
100 g / 3 ½ oz / ⅔ cup self-raising flour
30 ml / 1 fl. oz / 2 tbsp olive oil
1 tsp ground cinnamon
salt
150 g / 5 oz / 1 cup dark chocolate
150 g / 5 oz / 1 cup milk chocolate
175 ml / 6 fl. oz / ¾ cup whole milk
125 ml / 4 ½ fl. oz / ½ cup double (heavy) cream
1 tbsp Golden Syrup

MAKES 12

All Chocolate Mignardises

417

Milk and White Chocolate Mignardises

418

- Substitute the dark chocolate for white chocolate, melting in separate bowls before swirling together.

Chocolate Orange Mignardises

419

- Add 1 tsp of orange extract to the chocolate mixture for a zesty twist.

PREPARATION TIME 10 MINUTES

COOKING TIME 15 MINUTES

INGREDIENTS

FOR THE MIGNARDISES
12 ready-made mini chocolate cases
150 g / 5 oz / 1 cup good-quality milk chocolate, chopped
150 g / 5 oz / 1 cup good-quality dark chocolate, chopped
250 ml / 9 fl. oz / 1 cup double (heavy) cream

TO GARNISH
55 g / 2 oz / ⅓ cup whole almonds
55 g / 2 oz / ⅓ cup hazelnuts (cob nuts)
150 g / 5 oz / ⅔ cup caster (superfine) sugar
100 ml / 3 ½ fl. oz / ⅖ cup cold water

- Grease and line a baking tray with greaseproof paper.
- Mix together the water and sugar in a saucepan for the garnish.
- Cook over a moderate heat, swirling gently, until you have a dark caramel.
- Pour the caramel onto the tray and sprinkle the nuts on top and set to one side.
- Melt the chocolates in a large heatproof bowl set over a saucepan of simmering water.
- Stir until melted then remove from the heat and cool to one side.
- Whip the cream in a separate bowl until soft peaks form then stir one third of the cream into the melted, cooled chocolate to temper it.
- Fold the remaining cream into it in 2 batches, working quickly and gently.
- Spoon into a piping bag and pipe into the mini chocolate cases.
- Chill until ready to serve.
- Break the brittle using a rolling pin and use to garnish the top of the Mignardises.

420

MAKES 24 # Chocolate Mendiants

- Preheat the oven to 190°C (170° fan) / 375F / gas 5.
- Grease and line a large baking tray; spread the almonds and hazelnuts on the tray and toast for 4-5 minutes until nutty in aroma.
- Remove from the oven and leave to cool on the tray.
- Grease and line 2 baking trays with greaseproof paper.
- Melt the chocolate in a heatproof bowl set over a saucepan of simmering water.
- Spoon the melted chocolate onto the trays in rounds, letting them set for 1 minute before studding each with 1 almond, 1 hazelnut and 2 pistachios.
- Chill until set before peeling away from the greaseproof paper.
- Serve at room temperature.

PREPARATION TIME 10 MINUTES

COOKING TIME 15 MINUTES

....

INGREDIENTS

450 g / 1 lb / 3 cups good-quality milk chocolate
100 g / 3 ½ oz / 1 cup whole almonds, toasted
75 g / 3 oz / ¾ cup hazelnuts (cob nuts), toasted
150 g / 5 oz / 1 cup shelled pistachios, chopped

Cranberry and Nut Mendiants
421

- Add a large handful of dried cranberries to the melted chocolate, stirring well before setting.

422

SERVES 4 # Banana and Chocolate Tartlets

- Preheat the oven to 190°C (170° fan) / 375F / gas 5.
- Roll the pastry out on a lightly floured surface to ½ cm thickness.
- Cut out 4 triangle shapes that are 10 cm at their base.
- Transfer to a baking tray lined with greaseproof paper.
- Cut 8 strips of pastry from the remaining pastry that are 12 cm in length.
- Brush the triangles with beaten egg and lay 2 strips 12 cm pastry from the top running down the sides.
- Prick the centres with a fork and bake for 12-14 minutes until golden and puffed around the edges.
- Remove from the oven and level the centres by cutting away any top layers of pastry.
- Spread with Nutella and let the warmth from the pastry melt it slightly before topping with banana slices and garnishing with flaked almonds.

PREPARATION TIME 10-15 MINUTES

COOKING TIME 15 MINUTES

....

INGREDIENTS

250 g / 9 oz ready-made puff pastry
a little plain (all purpose) flour, for dusting
1 large egg, beaten
250 g / 9 oz / 1 cup Nutella
1 large banana, sliced

TO GARNISH

30 g / 1 oz / ¼ cup flaked (slivered) almonds

Mango and Chocolate Tartlets
423

- Drain 400 g / 14 oz / 2 cups canned mango slices and use to replace the banana slices. Garnish with desiccated coconut.

424

SERVES 8

Chocolate, Chestnut and Walnut Squares

PREPARATION TIME 10 MINUTES

COOKING TIME 10-15 MINUTES

INGREDIENTS

150 g / 5 oz / 1 cup self-raising flour

150 g / 5 oz / ⅔ cup margarine, softened

150 g / 5 oz / ⅔ cup golden caster (superfine) sugar

100 g / 3 ½ oz / ⅔ cup good-quality dark chocolate, chopped

100 g / 3 ½ oz / 1 cup walnut halves

75 g / 3 oz / ⅓ cup sweetened chestnut puree

3 large eggs

30 g / 1 oz / 2 tbsp cocoa powder

30 ml / 1 fl. oz / 2 tbsp whole milk

a pinch of salt

TO GARNISH

55 g / 2 oz / ⅓ cup white 'hundreds and thousands'

- Preheat the oven to 180°C (160° fan) / 350F / gas 4.
- Grease and line a 7" square cake tin with greaseproof paper.
- Combine the flour, margarine, sugar, salt and eggs in a large mixing bowl and beat until smooth.
- Melt the chocolate in a heatproof bowl set over a saucepan of simmering water, stirring occasionally.
- Let the chocolate cool a little before adding to the batter with the cocoa powder, chestnut puree and walnut halves folding through until incorporated.
- Spoon the batter into the tin and bake for 25-30 minutes; test with a wooden toothpick, if it comes out clean, the cake is done.
- Remove from the oven and sprinkle the top with the hundreds and thousands.
- Let the cake cool.

Chocolate, Pecan and Sultana Cake

425

- Omit the chestnut puree and replace the walnuts with pecans. Add sultanas to the batter.

426

SERVES 8

Nut Bites

PREPARATION TIME 10-15 MINUTES

COOKING TIME 15 MINUTES

INGREDIENTS

150 g / 5 oz / 2 cups rolled oats

225 g / 8 oz / 1 cup unsalted butter, softened

110 g / 4 oz / ⅓ cup Golden Syrup

100 g / 3 ½ oz / ⅔ cup milk chocolate, chopped

100 g / 3 ½ oz / 1 cup ground almonds

100 g / 3 ½ oz / 1 cup walnuts

- Preheat the oven to 180°C (160° fan) / 350F / gas 4.
- Grease and line a 1 lb loaf tin with greaseproof paper.
- Blitz the walnuts and oats in a food processor.
- Melt the butter and syrup together in a large saucepan.
- Add the ground almonds, walnuts and oats and stir well.
- Spoon into the tin and bake for 25-30 minutes until set; test with a wooden toothpick, if it comes out clean, it's ready.
- Remove from the oven and let it cool to room temperature.
- Melt the chocolate in a heatproof bowl set atop a saucepan of simmering water, stirring occasionally.
- Remove from the heat and let it cool before pouring over the chilled nut bites.
- Let the chocolate set.

Fruit and Nut Bites

427

- Add 75 g / 3 oz / ½ cup raisins to the mixture before baking.

428

MAKES 6

Small Strawberry Jam Pies

Small Apricot Jam Pies

429

- Replace the strawberry jam with the same amount of apricot jam for a different fruit pie.

Small Raspberry Jam Pies

430

- Replace the strawberry jam with the same amount of raspberry jam.

PREPARATION TIME 10 MINUTES

COOKING TIME 15 MINUTES

INGREDIENTS

300 g / 10 ½ oz ready-made shortcrust pastry
a little plain (all purpose) flour, for dusting
1 large egg, beaten
300 g / 10 ½ oz / 1 ⅓ cups strawberry jam

TO GARNISH
2 tbsp caster (superfine) sugar

- Preheat the oven to 180°C (160° fan) / 350F / gas 4.
- Roll out 2/3 of the pastry on a lightly floured surface out to ½ cm thickness and cut out 6 rounds 4" in diameter.
- Use to line 6 holes of a cupcake tin with, then roll out the remaining pastry to ½ cm thickness.
- Cut strips of pastry to use as a lattice pattern top for the pies.
- Fill the lined pastry with strawberry jam and brush the edges with a little beaten egg.
- Top with the strips of pastry, sealing well at the rim using the tines of a fork to crimp.
- Bake for 20-25 minutes until the pastry is cooked and the filling is hot.
- Remove from the oven and dust the tops immediately with caster sugar before turning out and serving.

431

MAKES 16

Assorted Macaroons

PREPARATION TIME 10-15 MINUTES

COOKING TIME 25-30 MINUTES

INGREDIENTS

FOR THE MACAROON MIXTURE

450 g / 1 lb / 3 ¾ cups icing (confectioners') sugar, sifted
300 g / 10 ½ oz / 3 cups ground almonds
4 medium egg whites
½ tsp red food colouring
½ tsp orange food colouring
½ tsp green food colouring

FOR THE FILLINGS

110 g / 4 oz / ½ cup unsalted butter, softened
125 g / 4 ½ oz / 1 cup icing (confectioners') sugar
55 g / 2 oz / ½ cup pistachios, ground
100 g / 3 ½ oz / ⅔ cup dark chocolate
75 ml / 3 fl. oz / ⅓ cup double (heavy) cream
75 g / 3 oz / ⅓ cup strawberry jam
75 g / 3 oz / ⅓ cup passionfruit puree

- Preheat the oven to 180°C (160° fan) / 350F / gas 4. Grease and line 2 baking trays with greaseproof paper.
- Combine the ground almonds and icing sugar.
- Beat the egg whites until stiff peaks form.
- Fold the egg whites into the ground almond mixture then divide into 4 bowls.
- Colour three of the bowls with the food colourings, leave the 4th bowl uncoloured.
- Spoon into 4 piping bags fitted with 3 cm nozzles.
- Pipe 8 rounds of each mixture onto the baking trays.
- Leave for 15 minutes, then bake for 8-10 minutes.
- Remove from the oven and allow to cool.
- Heat the cream in a heatproof bowl in the microwave, then add the chocolate and stir.
- Add the butter, pistachios and icing sugar to a food processor and pulse until smooth.
- Spread half of the orange macaroon halves with passionfruit puree and half of the red macaroons with strawberry jam.
- Spread half of the green macaroons with the pistachio buttercream and half the plain macaroons with the chocolate ganache.
- Replace with the other halves to reassemble.

432

MAKES 4

Chocolate Fondants

PREPARATION TIME 15 MINUTES

COOKING TIME 25-30 MINUTES

INGREDIENTS

25 g / 1 oz / 2 tbsp butter, melted
100 g / 3 ½ oz / ⅔ cup dark chocolate, chopped
110 g / 4 oz / ½ cup unsalted butter, cubed
1 tbsp cocoa powder
2 medium eggs
2 medium egg yolks
90 g / 3 ½ oz / ⅔ cup plain (all purpose) flour

- Preheat the oven to 190°C (170° fan) / 375F / gas 5.
- Brush 4 x 200 ml ovenproof metal ramekins with some of the melted butter, then line with greaseproof paper.
- Chill the ramekins for 15 mins then brush the inside of the greaseproof with the rest of the melted butter.
- Dust the insides with the cocoa powder, tapping lightly to get rid of any excess.
- Chill until ready to fill with the batter.
- Prepare the batter by melting together the chocolate and cubed butter in a heatproof mixing bowl set over a pan of gently simmering water.
- Once melted, remove from the heat and allow to cool.
- Meanwhile, whisk together the eggs and egg yolks in a separate mixing bowl until light and thick.
- Sift the plain flour into the eggs and whisk until smooth.
- Pour the melted chocolate and butter mixture into the egg and flour mixture in thirds, mixing well between each addition.
- Divide the fondant batter evenly between the chilled moulds and arrange on a baking sheet.
- Bake in the oven for 10-12 minutes until the tops are set and the edges are starting to come away from the sides of the ramekins.
- Remove from the oven and allow to sit for 1 minute before serving.

Chocolate and Raspberry Dots

433

SERVES 4

- Melt the chocolate in a heatproof bowl set atop a saucepan of simmering water, stirring occasionally.
- Once melted, remove from the heat and leave to cool for 2 minutes.
- Line a baking tray with greaseproof paper.
- Spoon the chocolate onto the paper using a tablespoon, making 12 rounds spaced apart.
- Dot each round immediately with a raspberry and leave to set.

PREPARATION TIME 5 MINUTES

COOKING TIME 5 MINUTES

INGREDIENTS

300 g / 10 ½ oz / 2 cups good-quality milk chocolate, chopped
12 raspberries

Plum Jam Tartlet

434

MAKES 4

PREPARATION TIME 10 MINUTES

COOKING TIME 20-25 MINUTES

INGREDIENTS

250 g / 9 oz ready-made shortcrust pastry
a little plain (all purpose) flour, for dusting

450 g / 1 lb / 3 cups plums, de-stoned and chopped
175 g / 6 oz / ¾ cup caster (superfine) sugar
2 tbsp water

- Combine the plums, sugar and water in a large saucepan and cook over a moderate heat until the fruit is soft.
- Mash well and continue to cook until syrupy and thickened. Cool to one side.
- Preheat the oven to 180°C (160° fan) / 350F / gas 4.
- Roll the pastry out on a lightly floured surface to ½ cm thickness.
- Cut out 4 rounds of pastry and use to line 4 individual 4" fluted tartlet cases.
- Prick the bases and trim excess pastry.
- Line with greaseproof paper and fill with baking beans before blind-baking for 12-15 minutes until golden at the edges.
- Remove from the oven and discard the greaseproof paper and baking beans.
- Return to the oven for 3-4 minutes to brown the base.
- Once cool, fill with the plum jam and chill before serving.

Chocolate Orange Balls

435

MAKES 24

PREPARATION TIME 10 MINUTES

COOKING TIME 45 MINUTES

INGREDIENTS

300 g / 10 ½ oz / 2 cups white chocolate, chopped
300 ml / 10 ½ fl. oz / 1 ⅓ cups double (heavy) cream

55 g / 2 oz / ¼ cup unsalted butter
2-3 tsp orange flower water
1-2 tsp orange food colouring

TO GARNISH
1 orange
a few mint leaves

- Place the chocolate in a large heatproof mixing bowl.
- Place the cream and butter in a saucepan and bring to a simmer over a moderate heat.
- Once the butter has fully melted and the mixture is simmering, remove from the heat and pour over the chocolate.
- Beat until you have a smooth mixture, then add the orange flower water as necessary and orange colouring in drops, mixing until you have an orange-coloured mixture.
- Cover the bowl and chill for 4 hours.
- To make the truffles, remove the chocolate mixture from the fridge and let sit at room temperature for 10 minutes.
- Use a melon baller to take out scoops of the truffle mixture.
- Roll roughly into balls using lightly-oiled palms.
- Pare the zest from the orange and slice into thin strips before serving as a garnish for the truffles with the mint leaves.

MAKES 20-24

Chocolate Palmiers

PREPARATION TIME 10 MINUTES

COOKING TIME 45 MINUTES

INGREDIENTS

250 g / 9 oz ready-made puff pastry
a little plain (all purposes) flour, for
dusting
200 g / 7 oz / 1 ¼ cups dark
chocolate, finely chopped

- Preheat the oven to 190°C (170° fan) / 375F / gas 5.
- Roll the puff pastry out on a lightly floured surface.
- Sprinkle the finely chopped chocolate evenly all over.
- Roll the left hand side of the puff pastry so that it meets the centre of the pastry.
- Do the same with the right hand side so that it meets the rolled left hand side in the middle.
- Transfer to a baking tray and chill for 45 minutes.
- Remove after chilling and cut slices across the rolled pastry roughly 1cm thick.
- Pinch the sides of the pastry so that they form a classic Palmier shape.
- Transfer to baking trays lined with greaseproof paper.
- Bake for 12-15 minutes until golden and cooked and the chocolate is melted.
- Remove and allow to cool.

Chocolate Orange Palmiers 437

- Sprinkle a few (5-6) drops of orange extract onto the pastry before rolling out.

SERVES 4

Pine Nut and Peppercorn Meringues

PREPARATION TIME 10 MINUTES

COOKING TIME 10-15 MINUTES

INGREDIENTS

110 g / 4 oz / ½ cup golden caster
(superfine) sugar
2 large egg whites
1 tbsp cocoa powder
a pinch of salt
½ tsp cream of tartar
55 g / 2 oz / ½ cup pine nuts
1 tbsp pink peppercorns, lightly
crushed

- Preheat the oven to 130°C (110° fan) / 250F / gas ½.
- Mix together the sugar and cocoa powder in a mixing bowl.
- Whisk the egg whites in a separate, clean mixing bowl with a pinch of salt until stiff peaks form.
- Add the cream of tartar and the sugar mixture, 1 tablespoon at a time, beating thoroughly between additions until the meringue is thick and glossy.
- Spoon into a piping bag fitted with a 3 cm star-shaped nozzle.
- Grease and line a baking tray with greaseproof paper.
- Pipe blobs of meringue onto the baking tray, spaced apart, and dot with the pine nuts and crushed peppercorns.
- Bake for 2- 2 ½ hours until the meringues are dry and hollow sounding when tapped lightly.

Vanilla and Pine Nut Meringues 439

- Replace the cocoa powder with 2 tsp of vanilla extract.

440

MAKES 24 # White Sugar Truffles

- Place the chocolate in a large heatproof mixing bowl.
- Place the cream and butter in a saucepan and bring to a simmer over a moderate heat.
- Once the butter has fully melted and the mixture is simmering, remove from the heat and pour over the chocolate.
- Beat until you have a smooth mixture, then cover the bowl and chill for 4 hours.
- To make the truffles, remove the chocolate mixture from the fridge and let sit at room temperature for 10 minutes.
- Use a melon baller to take out scoops of the truffle mixture.
- Using lightly oiled hands, roll into truffle shapes then roll in the icing sugar to lightly coat.
- Shake off any excess before serving.

PREPARATION TIME 5-10 MINUTES

COOKING TIME 10-15 MINUTES

INGREDIENTS

300 g / 10 ½ oz / 2 cups good-quality dark chocolate, chopped
300 ml / 10 ½ fl. oz / 1 ⅓ cups double (heavy) cream
55 g / 2 oz / ¼ cup unsalted butter
250 g / 9 oz / 2 cups icing (confectioners') sugar

ALSO NEEDED
a little sunflower oil

Coconut Truffles

441

- Replace the icing sugar with the same weight of desiccated coconut, using it to coat the truffles.

442

SERVES 8 # Puffed Rice and Hazelnut Lollipops

- Grease and line a baking tray with greaseproof paper.
- Melt together the butter and honey in a saucepan set over a medium heat.
- Combine the puffed rice and hazelnuts in a large mixing bowl and pour over the melted butter and honey mixture.
- Stir well to coat before taking tablespoons of the mixture and shaping into balls between lightly-oiled palms.
- Leave to set on the baking tray before threading onto the lollipop sticks.
- Melt the chocolate in a heatproof bowl set atop a saucepan of simmering water, stirring occasionally until melted.
- Dip half of the lollipops into the melted chocolate before leaving to set upright in cups half-filled with M&Ms or Smarties.

PREPARATION TIME 10 MINUTES

COOKING TIME 15 MINUTES

INGREDIENTS

250 g / 9 oz / 4 cups puffed rice
110 g / 4 oz / ½ cup honey
110 g / 4 oz / ½ cup unsalted butter, melted
110 g / 4 oz / 1 cup hazelnuts (cob nuts), chopped
150 g / 5 oz / 1 cup milk chocolate, chopped

ALSO NEEDED
a little sunflower oil
thin lollipop sticks
assorted M&Ms or Smarties

Puffed Rice and
Marshmallow Lollipops

443

- Replace the hazelnuts with 75 g / 3 oz / 1 cup mini marshmallows.

444

MAKES 24

White Chocolate and Coconut Truffles

White Chocolate, Coconut and Rum Truffles

445

- Add 55 ml / 2 fl. oz / ¼ cup white rum to the truffle mixture.

White Chocolate and Malibu Truffles

446

- Add 55 ml / 2 fl. oz / ¼ cup Malibu to the truffle mixture.

PREPARATION TIME 5-10 MINUTES

COOKING TIME 10-15 MINUTES

INGREDIENTS

300 g / 10 ½ oz / 2 cups good-quality white chocolate, chopped
300 ml / 10 ½ fl. oz / 1 ⅓ cups double (heavy) cream
55 g / 2 oz / ¼ cup unsalted butter
225 g / 8 oz / 3 cups desiccated coconut

ALSO NEEDED
a little sunflower oil

- Place the chocolate in a large heatproof mixing bowl.
- Place the cream and butter in a saucepan and bring to a simmer over a moderate heat.
- Once the butter has fully melted and the mixture is simmering, remove from the heat and pour over the chocolate.
- Beat until you have a smooth mixture, then cover the bowl and chill for 4 hours.
- To make the truffles, remove the chocolate mixture from the fridge and let sit at room temperature for 10 minutes.
- Use a melon baller to take out scoops of the truffle mixture.
- Using lightly oiled hands, roll into truffle shapes then roll in the desiccated coconut to coat.

447

SERVES 8

Multicoloured Ice Lollipops

- Prepare the strawberry ice; cook strawberries in a pan until soft with 50 g caster sugar and 100 ml water. Press through sieve, then thin with water until syrupy.
- Stir in red food dye and pour into lolly moulds, until a quarter full. Freeze.
- Prepare orange layer; cook orange segments with 50 g of caster sugar and 100 ml water. Puree with a stick blender press through a sieve, then thin with water until syrupy.
- Stir in orange dye, half fill the moulds, place a lolly stick in the centre and freeze.
- Prepare the lime layer; combine lime juice with 50 g caster sugar and 50 ml water. Add food dye and fill the mould to three quarters.
- Repeat previous step for lemon layer, substituting lime juice for lemon juice, and green dye for yellow.
- Freeze until ready to serve.

PREPARATION TIME 15-20 MINUTES

COOKING TIME 25 MINUTES

INGREDIENTS

100 g / 3 ½ oz / 1 cup strawberries, hulled and halved
1 tsp red food colouring
2 oranges, segmented
1 tsp orange food colouring
2 limes, juiced
1 tsp green food colouring
2 lemons, juiced
1 tsp yellow food colouring
200 g / 7 oz / 1 cup caster (superfine) sugar

Chocolate Dipped Fruit Lollipops   448

- When frozen, dip each lollipop in cooling melted chocolate (make sure its not too hot) and re-freeze.

449

SERVES 6

Quick Ice-Cream Lollipops

- Beat together the cream, Greek yoghurt and jam in a mixing bowl until combined.
- Pour into clean, empty mini yoghurt pots and freeze for 2 hours.
- Place a lollipop stick in each after 2 hours and return to the freezer for an additional 3-4 hours until set.

PREPARATION TIME 5 MINUTES

COOKING TIME 5 MINUTES

INGREDIENTS

375 ml / 13 fl. oz / 1 ½ cups Greek yoghurt
125 ml / 4 ½ fl. oz / ½ cup whipping cream
115 g / 4 ½ oz / ½ cup strawberry jam

ALSO NEEDED
6 lollipop sticks

Dark Cherry Ice-Cream Lollipops   450

- Replace the strawberry jam with dark cherry jam.

451

MAKES 8

Raspberry Shortbread Cookies

PREPARATION TIME 10 MINUTES

COOKING TIME 15 MINUTES

INGREDIENTS

FOR THE BISCUITS
300 g / 10 ½ oz / 2 cups plain
(all purpose) flour
a little extra plain flour, for dusting
50 g / 2 oz / ⅓ cup cornflour
(cornstarch)
225 g / 8 oz / 1 cup unsalted butter,
cubed
65 g / 2 ½ oz / ½ cup icing
(confectioners') sugar
a pinch of salt

FOR THE FILLING
300 g / 10 ½ oz / 1 ⅓ cups seedless
raspberry jam, warmed

TO GARNISH
2 tbsp icing (confectioners') sugar
extra raspberry jam

- Pulse together the flour, cornflour, salt, icing sugar and butter in a food processor until it forms a dough.
- Remove the dough, knead gently and form into a ball.
- Wrap in clingfilm and chill for 60 minutes.
- Preheat the oven to 180°C (160° fan) / 350F / gas 4.
- Remove the dough from the fridge and roll out on a lightly floured surface to ½ cm thickness.
- Cut out 16 shapes using a fluted oval cutter.
- Grease and line 2 baking trays with greaseproof paper.
- Arrange on the baking trays spaced apart, then use a 1 cm straight-sided cutter to punch two holes out from 8 of the shapes.
- Bake for 12-15 minutes until they just start to colour.
- Once cool, spread the 8 biscuits without holes with the warmed jam and dust the holed biscuits with icing sugar.
- Place these on top of the jam biscuits.

Chocolate Shortbread Cookies **452**

- Replace the raspberry jam with chocolate spread, slightly warmed, inside the cookies.

453

MAKES 12

Chocolate Tuile Biscuits

PREPARATION TIME 10 MINUTES

COOKING TIME 20 MINUTES

INGREDIENTS

300 g / 10 ½ oz / 2 cups good-quality
dark chocolate
100 g / 3 ½ oz / 2 cups cornflakes
1 ½ tbsp liquid glucose

- Grease and line a large baking tray with greaseproof paper.
- Blitz the cornflakes in a food processor until very finely chopped.
- Melt the chocolate and liquid glucose together in a heatproof bowls set atop a saucepan of simmering water, stirring occasionally until melted.
- Remove from the heat and stir through the cornflakes.
- Spoon 12, 3" rounds onto the baking tray and chill until set.
- Once set, remove from the fridge and allow the chocolate tuiles to come to room temperature.
- Peel away half from the greaseproof paper and carefully mould around a rolling pin before returning to the fridge to set.
- Serve once set.

Puffed Rice Tuiles   **454**

- Stir 50 g / 2 oz / 1 cup of puffed rice into the melted chocolate instead of the cornflakes.

MAKES 4 # Individual Lime Cheesecake

Mint Cheesecakes

456

- Replace the lime juice and zest that is added after the gelatin mixture with 2 tsp peppermint extract.

White Chocolate Lime Cheesecake

457

- Mix 75 g of grated white chocolate into the cream cheese and Greek yoghurt.

PREPARATION TIME 10-15 MINUTES

COOKING TIME 15 MINUTES

INGREDIENTS

150 g / 5 oz / 1 cup digestive (graham cracker) biscuits, pulsed into fine crumbs
50 g / 2 oz / ¼ cup unsalted butter, melted
400 g / 14 oz / 2 cups cream cheese
250 g / 9 oz / 1 cup Greek yoghurt
110 g / 4 oz / ½ cup caster (superfine) sugar
2 sheets of gelatine
2 limes, juiced and finely zested
2 tbsp cold water

- Beat together the cream cheese and sugar in a mixing bowl for 2 minute until smooth and creamy.
- Soften the gelatin in 2 tbsp of lime juice and 2 tbsp of cold water, then heat in a small saucepan to dissolve the gelatin.
- Add the Greek yoghurt to the cream cheese mixture, beat well then add the gelatin mixture and beat again thoroughly.
- Add the remaining lime juice and the zest, beating well before dividing between 4 individual ramekins.
- Tap lightly to release any trapped air bubbles.
- Combine the biscuits and melted butter until they resemble wet sand.
- Spoon on top of the cheesecake mixture in the ramekins and press down gently.
- Cover and chill for 2 hours.
- When ready to serve, run a warm, wet palette knife around the inside edge of the ramekins and turn out onto serving plates.

MAKES 24

Fruit and Coconut Truffles

458

PREPARATION TIME 5-10 MINUTES

COOKING TIME 10-15 MINUTES

....

INGREDIENTS

450 g / 1 lb / 3 cups white chocolate, chopped
300 ml / 10 ½ fl. oz / 1 ⅓ cups double (heavy) cream
55 g / 2 oz / ¼ cup unsalted butter
150 g / 5 oz / 2 cups desiccated coconut
75 g / 3 oz / ⅓ cup raspberry puree
75 g / 3 oz / ⅓ cup passionfruit puree
55 ml / 2 fl. oz / ¼ cup lime cordial
a few drops of green food colouring
a few drops of red food colouring
a few drops of orange food colouring

ALSO NEEDED
a little sunflower oil

- Place the chocolate in a large heatproof mixing bowl.
- Place the cream and butter in a saucepan and simmer.
- Once the butter has melted, remove from the heat and pour over the chocolate.
- Beat until smooth, then divide between 3 bowls.
- Working quickly, add the lime cordial and a few drops of green colouring to one bowl, beating well.
- Add the passionfruit puree and a few drops of orange colouring to the second bowl, beating well.
- Add the raspberry puree and a few drops of red colouring the third bowl, beating well.
- Cover and chill all three bowls for 4 hours.
- Remove the chocolate mixture from the fridge and let sit.
- Take out scoops of the truffle mixture. Using lightly oiled hands, roll into truffle shapes then roll in the desiccated coconut to coat.

Fruit and Nut Truffles
459

- Add 150 g / 5 oz / 1 ½ cups finely chopped hazelnuts to the melted chocolate before colouring and flavouring. Omit the desiccated coconut.

SERVES 4

Lemon Meringue Tartlet

460

PREPARATION TIME 10-15 MINUTES

COOKING TIME 20 MINUTES

....

INGREDIENTS

250 g / 9 oz ready-made shortcrust pastry
a little plain (all purpose) flour, for dusting
450 g / 1 lb / 2 cups lemon curd
1 medium egg white
55 g / 2 oz / ¼ cup caster (superfine) sugar
a pinch of salt
½ tsp cream of tartar

TO GARNISH
4 cocktail cherries

- Preheat the oven to 190°C (170° fan) / 375F / gas 5.
- Roll the pastry out on a lightly floured surface.
- Cut out 4 rounds of pastry and line 4 5" fluted cases.
- Prick the bases and trim excess pastry.
- Line with greaseproof paper and fill with baking beans before blind-baking for 12-15 minutes until golden.
- Remove and discard the greaseproof paper and beans.
- Return to the oven for 3-4 minutes to brown the base.
- Whisk the egg white with the salt until stiff peaks form.
- Add the cream of tartar and the sugar, 1 tablespoon at a time, beating well between additions until thick. Spoon into a piping bag.
- Fill the pastry with lemon curd and pipe the meringue on top in swirls. Bake for 8-10 minutes.
- Remove and garnish with a cherry on top in the hole before serving.

Lime Meringue Tartlet
461

- Replace the lemon curd with lime curd.

462

MAKES 12 # Raspberry Pastry Bites

- Preheat the oven to 190°C (170° fan) / 375F / gas 5.
- Roll the pastry out on a lightly floured surface to ½ cm thickness.
- Cut out 12 rounds approximately 2" in diameter and use to line a 12-hole mini cupcake tin.
- Spoon 1 teaspoon of the ground almonds into them then top with a teaspoon of the jam and a few blueberries.
- Bake for 12-14 minutes until the pastry is cooked and the jam is hot.
- Remove from the oven and leave to cool a little before dusting with icing sugar.

PREPARATION TIME 10 MINUTES

COOKING TIME 10-15 MINUTES

INGREDIENTS

300 g / 10 ½ oz ready-made
shortcrust pastry
a little plain (all purpose) flour,
for dusting
225 g / 8 oz / 1 cup raspberry jam
100 g / 3 ½ oz / 1 cup blueberries
55 g / 2 oz / ½ cup ground almonds

TO GARNISH
2 tbsp icing (confectioners') sugar

Dark Cherry Pastry Bites 463

- Swap the raspberry jam for dark cherry jam.

464

MAKES 24 # Coconut and Chocolate Biscuits

- Preheat the oven to 170°C (150°C fan) / 325°F / gas 3.
- Grease and line a couple of baking trays with greaseproof paper.
- Cream together the butter and icing sugar in a large mixing bowl until uniform before adding the flour, desiccated coconut, egg whites and salt.
- Mix carefully until it forms a soft dough.
- Scoop into a piping bag.
- Pipe onto the baking trays in 5 cm strips.
- Bake for 12-15 minutes until golden brown and set.
- Remove from the oven and let them cool on the trays.
- Once cool, melt the chocolate in a ban marie, stirring occasionally until melted.
- Use a teaspoon to drizzle melted chocolate in a zig zag pattern on top of the biscuits.

PREPARATION TIME 10 MINUTES

COOKING TIME 25-30 MINUTES

INGREDIENTS

110 g / 4 oz / 1 stick unsalted butter,
softened
150 g / 5 oz / 1 ½ cups icing sugar
150 g / 5 oz / 1 cup plain flour
30 g / 1 oz / 2 tbsp desiccated coconut
3 medium egg whites
a pinch of salt
100 g / 3 ½ oz / ⅔ cup good-quality
dark chocolate, chopped

Coconut, Lime and Chocolate Biscuits 465

- Add 6-8 drops of lime extract when you mix the biscuit ingredients.

466

SERVES 8 # Rocky Road Squares

Dried Fruit
Chocolate Square

 467

- Replace the almonds with the same weight of chopped glacés cherries.

Cherry Chocolate
and Almond Squares

468

- Replace the raisins with 60g dried cherries.

PREPARATION TIME 10 MINUTES

COOKING TIME 10 MINUTES

INGREDIENTS

300 g / 10 ½ oz / 2 cups good-quality dark chocolate, chopped
225 g / 8 oz / ½ cups digestive (graham cracker) biscuits, chopped
110 g / 4 oz / ½ cup butter, softened
110 g / 4 oz / 1 ½ cups mini marshmallows
75 g / 3 oz / ¾ cup whole almonds, blanched and chopped
30 g / 1 oz / 2 tbsp raisins

- Grease and line a 7" square cake tin with greaseproof paper.
- Melt together the butter and chocolate in a saucepan set over a medium heat, stirring occasionally.
- Once melted, remove from the heat and stir through all the digestive biscuits and raisins.
- Stir through three-quarters of the marshmallows and almonds before pouring into the cake tin.
- Sprinkle the remaining marshmallows and almonds on top before chilling.
- Turn out once set and cut into squares.

469
MAKES 12 Chocolate and Crushed Hazelnut Lollipops

- Blitz the hazelnuts in a food processor until very finely chopped before setting to one side in a bowl.
- Place the chocolate in a large heatproof mixing bowl.
- Place the cream and butter in a saucepan and bring to a simmer over a moderate heat.
- Once the butter has melted and is simmering, remove from the heat and pour over the chocolate.
- Beat until you have a smooth mixture, then cover the bowl and chill for 3 hours.
- Remove the chocolate mixture from the fridge and let sit at room temperature for 10 minutes.
- Use an ice-cream scoop to take scoops of the mixture.
- Using lightly oiled hands, roll into round balls then roll in the finely chopped hazelnuts, coating them evenly.
- Thread onto the wooden lollipop sticks before serving in mini cupcake cases.

PREPARATION TIME 10 MINUTES

COOKING TIME 15 MINUTES

INGREDIENTS

400 g / 14 oz / 2 ⅔ cups good-quality dark chocolate, chopped
300 ml / 10 ½ fl. oz / 1 ⅓ cups double (heavy) cream
200 g / 7 oz / 2 cup hazelnuts (cob nuts)
55 g / 2 oz / ¼ cup unsalted butter

ALSO NEEDED
a little sunflower oil
12 wooden lollipop sticks

White Chocolate and Hazelnut Lollipops

470

- Replace the dark chocolate with white chocolate.

471
MAKES 6 OF EACH Melon and Mint Lollipops

- Puree the melon in a food processor then strain the juice into a jug.
- Pour 250 ml of the juice into a saucepan and add the sugar and water, stirring until the sugar has dissolved.
- Cool to one side.
- Combine the water, sugar and peppermint extract in a saucepan, stirring until the sugar has dissolved.
- Add enough green food colouring to make a 'forest green' colour, stirring well before cooling to one side.
- Pour the melon and mint liquid into a 12-hole lollipop mould, filling 6 holes with each kind.
- Freeze for 2 hours, then skewer with the lollipop sticks.
- Return to the freezer for at least 4 hours until frozen.
- Remove from the freezer and leave to thaw for a few minutes before serving with a tarragon leaf garnish.

PREPARATION TIME 10-15 MINUTES

COOKING TIME 15-20 MINUTES

INGREDIENTS

FOR THE MELON LOLLIPOPS
250 ml / 9 fl. oz / 1 cups cold water
110 g / 4 oz / ½ cup caster (superfine) sugar
½ honeydew melon, peeled and diced

FOR THE MINT LOLLIPOPS
500 ml / 18 fl. oz / 2 cups cold water
225 g / 8 oz / 1 cup caster (superfine) sugar
2-3 tsp peppermint extract
1-2 tsp green food colouring

ALSO NEEDED
12 lollipop sticks
a few tarragon leaves

Melon and Lime Lollipops

472

- Replace the peppermint extract and 100 ml of the water for the mint lollipops with 75 ml of lime cordial.

473

MAKES 6

Candied Pears

PREPARATION TIME 10 MINUTES

COOKING TIME 10 MINUTES

INGREDIENTS

6 pears, peeled with stalks intact
500 g / 1 lb 2 oz / 2 ¼ cups caster
(superfine) sugar
500 ml / 18 fl. oz / 2 cups water
2 tsp red food colouring
2 tsp green food colouring

- Combine the sugar and water in a large saucepan and cook over a medium heat, stirring until the sugar dissolves and you have a clear syrup.
- Divide the syrup into 3 small saucepans and add the green food colouring to the first and the red food colouring to the second, stirring well.
- Add 2 pears to each saucepan, laying them on their sides to submerge.
- Simmer the pears in the syrups for 50-60 minutes over a low heat until the fruit is tender.
- Drain from the syrup and serve warm or cold.

Poached Pears

474

- Omit the food colouring and replace the water with red wine. Reduce the sugar by half when making the poaching syrup.

475

MAKES 24

Raspberry Fruit Pastilles

PREPARATION TIME 10-15
MINUTES

COOKING TIME 15 MINUTES

INGREDIENTS

500 g / 18 oz / 2 cups raspberry puree
900 g / 2 lb / 4 cups caster (superfine)
sugar
200 ml / 7 fl. oz / ⅘ cup glucose
125 ml / 4 ½ fl. oz / ½ cup cold water
30 g / 1 oz / 2 tbsp pectin
8 lemons, juiced
1 tbsp tartaric acid

TO GARNISH

110 g / 4 oz / ½ cup caster
(superfine) sugar

- Grease and line a 8" x 8" cake tin with greaseproof paper.
- Combine the pectin with 50 g of the sugar in a small bowl and mix the tartaric acid with 5 tbsp of the lemon juice in another bowl.
- Mix together the puree, 850 g of sugar, water, remaining lemon juice and glucose in a large saucepan.
- Cook over a moderate heat until boiling, removing any scum that comes to the surface.
- Add the sugar and pectin mix to the saucepan and cook, whisking, until the thermometer reads 108°C.
- Once it reaches that temperature, remove the saucepan from the heat and stir in the tartaric acid mixture.
- Strain through a sieve into a clean jug.
- Pour into the cake tin and leave to set.
- Once set, turn out and cut into squares before rolling in the remaining caster sugar.

Peach Fruit Pastilles

476

- Replace the raspberry puree with peach puree.

477

SERVES 6-8 # Raspberry and Cream Meringue Nests

White Chocolate Raspberry Meringue Nests

478

- Mix 5 tbsp grated white chocolate into the cream.

White Chocolate Strawberry Meringue Nests

479

- Mix 5 tbsp grated white chocolate into the cream and replace the raspberries with strawberries.

PREPARATION TIME 10 MINUTES

COOKING TIME 60-65 MINUTES

INGREDIENTS

FOR THE MERINGUE
2 large egg whites
pinch of salt
100 g / 3 ½ oz / ½ cup caster (superfine) sugar

FOR THE CREAM AND FRUIT
300 ml / 10 ½ fl. oz / 1 ¼ cup whipping cream
25 g / 1 oz / 2 tbsp icing (confectioners') sugar
a few drops of vanilla extract
300 g / 10 ½ oz / 3 cups raspberries
1 tbsp icing sugar, for dusting

- Preheat the oven to 110°C (90° fan) / 225F / gas ¼.
- Prepare the meringue by whisking the egg whites with a pinch of salt to soft peaks in a large, clean mixing bowl.
- Add the caster sugar, a tablespoon at a time, beating well between additions until you have a thick, glossy meringue.
- Spoon the meringue into a piping bag fitted with a 2 cm straight-sided nozzle.
- Grease and line a couple of baking trays with a sheet of greaseproof paper.
- Pipe the meringue onto the baking trays in coiled rounds.
- Bake for 45-55 minutes until the meringue is cooked and uncoloured.
- Remove from the oven when ready and leave to cool on a wire rack.
- Whip the cream with the icing sugar and vanilla extract until soft peaks form.
- Spoon into a piping bag fitted with a small star-shaped nozzle.
- Pipe the cream onto the meringue nests and place the fruit on top of the cream.
- Dust lightly with the icing sugar before serving.

480

MAKES 12-14 # Biscuits Rose De Reims

PREPARATION TIME 10-15 MINUTES

COOKING TIME 40-50 MINUTES

INGREDIENTS

125 g / 4 ½ oz / ½ cup caster (superfine) sugar
75 g / 3 oz / ½ cup plain (all purpose) flour
55 g / 2 oz / ⅓ cup cornflour (cornstarch)
2 medium eggs, separated
1 tbsp baking powder
1 tsp red food colouring
55 g / 2 oz / ½ cup icing (confectioners') sugar, sifted.

- Preheat the oven to 180°C (160°C fan) / 350°F / gas 4.
- Whisk the egg yolks with 100 g of the caster sugar for 3-4 minutes until pale and thick.
- Add one of the egg whites and continue to beat.
- Add the red food colouring in drops, then add the other egg white and beat for a further 3 minutes.
- Sift in the flour, cornflour and baking powder and whisk in gently.
- Transfer the batter to a piping bag.
- Line a baking tray with parchment paper and pipe 2 inch long blobs of the batter onto the lined tray.
- Allow the batter to rest on the tray for 20 minutes until a crust starts to form.
- At this point, bake in the oven for 10-12 minutes.
- Remove from the oven and dust with the remaining caster sugar and icing sugar.

Chocolate Dipped Rose Biscuits **481**

- When cooled, dip the biscuits in melted chocolate until they are half covered, then leave to set.

482

MAKES 18 # Rolled Russian Biscuits

PREPARATION TIME 10 MINUTES

COOKING TIME 10-15 MINUTES

INGREDIENTS

110 g / 4 oz / ½ cup caster (superfine) sugar
110 g / 4 oz / ⅔ cup plain (all purpose) flour, sifted
55 g / 2 oz / ¼ cup unsalted butter, softened
4 medium egg whites
½ tsp vanilla extract
a pinch of salt

- Preheat the oven to 180°C (160°C fan) / 350F / gas 4.
- Grease and line 2 baking trays with greaseproof paper.
- Beat together the butter, vanilla extract and sugar in a mixing bowl until pale and fluffy.
- Beat in the egg whites until incorporated, then sift in the flour and beat again until smooth.
- Spoon tablespoons of the mixture onto the baking tray and use the back of the spoon to spread into circle shapes 7-8 cm in diameter. Bake for 6-8 minutes.
- Remove from the oven and let them cool on the trays for 30 seconds before carefully sliding onto a sharpening steel and shaping around into a cigarette shape.
- Slide off the steel onto a wire rack then continue in this fashion, working quickly and carefully with the other biscuits until they have all been shaped.

Lemon Rolled Russian Biscuits **483**

- Add the finely grated zest of 1 lemon and 1 tsp of lemon extract to the biscuit mixture.

484

MAKES 4

Summer Fruit Vermouth Jellies

- Combine the water, vermouth and sugar in a saucepan.
- Heat over a medium heat until the sugar dissolves, stirring occasionally.
- Remove from the heat and sprinkle over the gelatine powder.
- Let it dissolve before whisking briefly.
- Add the fruit and ladle into 4 200 ml cannele moulds.
- Chill overnight until set.

PREPARATION TIME 10 MINUTES

COOKING TIME 10 MINUTES

INGREDIENTS

500 ml / 18 fl. oz / 2 cups cold water
125 ml / 4 ½ fl. oz / ½ cup dry white vermouth
110 g / 4 oz / ½ cup caster (superfine) sugar
150 g / 5 oz / 1 ½ cups raspberries
100 g / 3 ½ oz / 1 cup blueberries
50 g / 2 oz / ½ cup blackcurrants
2 tbsp gelatine powder

Sweet Vermouth Jellies   **485**

- Replace the dry vermouth with sweet vermouth.

486

SERVES 4

Simple Chouquettes

- Sift together flour and sugar in a mixing bowl.
- Combine the butter and milk in a saucepan and heat gently until the butter melts.
- Add the flour and stir until a smooth dough forms.
- Beat the dough until it starts to pull away from the sides of the saucepan.
- Remove from the heat and add the eggs, one at a time, beating well between each addition until shiny and even.
- Spoon the dough into a piping bag fitted with a 5 cm straight-sided nozzle.
- Preheat the oven to 200°C (180° fan) / 400F / gas 6.
- Grease and line 2 baking trays with greaseproof paper.
- Pipe blobs of the pastry onto the sheets, spaced apart, then dot with the sugar nibs.
- Bake for 15-18 minutes until puffed and golden.

PREPARATION TIME 10 MINUTES

COOKING TIME 10-15 MINUTES

INGREDIENTS

110 g / 4 oz / ⅔ cup plain (all purpose) flour
110 g / 4 oz / ½ cup unsalted butter, cold and cubed
250 ml / 9 fl. oz / 1 cup whole milk
4 large eggs
50 g / 2 oz / ¼ cup sugar nibs
1 tsp caster (superfine) sugar

Cocoa Nib Chouquettes   **487**

- Replace the sugar nibs with the same weight of cocoa nibs.

488

MAKES 8

Raspberry Cookies

Shortbread Cookies with Cream and Strawberries

489

- Replace the raspberries with quartered strawberries.

Shortbread Cookies with Cream and Kiwi Fruit

490

- Replace the raspberries with pieces of kiwi fruit.

PREPARATION TIME 10-15 MINUTES

COOKING TIME 40-45 MINUTES

INGREDIENTS

200 g / 7 oz / 1 ⅓ cups plain (all purpose) flour, sifted
a little extra plain flour, for dusting
150 g/ 5 oz / ⅔ cup margarine, softened
75 g / 3 oz / ⅓ cup caster (superfine) sugar
½ tsp vanilla extract
½ tsp bicarbonate (baking) of soda
a pinch of salt
300 ml / 10 ½ fl. oz / 1 ⅓ cup double (heavy) cream
2 tbsp icing (confectioners') sugar

TO GARNISH

450 g / 1 lb / 3 cups raspberries
2 tbsp icing (confectioners') sugar
5-6 small sprigs of mint

- Preheat the oven to 150°C (130°C fan) / 300°F / gas 2.
- Grease and line a couple of baking trays with greaseproof paper.
- Cream together the margarine and sugar in a large mixing bowl until pale and fluffy.
- Beat in the flour, bicarbonate of soda and vanilla extract and knead this dough lightly for 5 minutes.
- Roll the dough out on a lightly floured surface to 1cm thickness and cut rounds out of the dough using a 7-8 cm fluted cookie cutter.
- Carefully lift onto the baking trays and space them apart.
- Bake for 12-15 minutes until set but uncoloured.
- Remove from the oven and let them cool on the baking tray for a few minutes before moving to a wire rack to cool completely.
- As the cookies are cooling, whip together the double cream with 2 tbsp of the icing sugar in a mixing bowl until it forms soft peaks.
- When the cookies are cool, spoon generous tablespoons of the whipping cream on top of them.
- Dot with 9-10 raspberries on top of each cookie and garnish most of the cookies with a sprig of mint leaves.
- Dust lightly with the remaining icing sugar just before serving.

491

MAKES 24 # Mini Financiers

- Preheat the oven to 180°C (160° fan) / 350F / gas 4.
- Brown the butter in a saucepan until nutty in aroma.
- Strain through a fine sieve into a clean bowl, allowing it to cool.
- Combine the flour, almonds and sugar in a mixing bowl.
- Gently whisk the egg whites into this mixture and then fold through the cooled, melted butter.
- Divide the batter into two bowls and colour one of them by gently whisking the red food colouring into it.
- Cover and chill the bowls for 30 minutes.
- Grease 2 12-hole mini muffin tins with unsalted butter.
- Spoon the batter into the tins and bake for 14-16 minutes until golden at the edges and risen.
- Remove from the oven and cool on a wire rack before serving in wine glasses.

PREPARATION TIME 10 MINUTES

COOKING TIME 15 MINUTES

INGREDIENTS

110 g / 4 oz / ½ cup caster (superfine) sugar
110 g / 4 oz / ½ cup slightly salted butter, softened
1 tbsp unsalted butter, softened
110 g / 4 oz / 1 cup ground almonds
30 g / 1 oz / 2 tbsp plain (all purpose) flour, sifted
3 medium egg whites
a pinch of salt
a few drops of red food colouring

Mini Financiers with Cream

492

- Whip 250 ml / 9 fl. oz / 1 cup of double (heavy) cream to soft peaks and serve with the mini financiers.

493

MAKES 8 # Shortbread Cookies with Jam Filling

- Pulse together the flour, cornflour, salt, icing sugar and butter in a food processor until it comes together to form a dough.
- Remove the dough, knead gently and form into a ball.
- Wrap in clingfilm and chill for 60 minutes.
- Preheat the oven to 180°C (160° fan) / 350F / gas 4.
- Remove the dough from the fridge and roll out on a lightly floured surface to ½ cm thickness.
- Cut out 16 shapes using a fluted round cookie cutter.
- Grease and line 2 baking trays with greaseproof paper.
- Arrange on the baking trays, then use a small star-shaped cutter to punch stars out of 8 of the rounds.
- Bake for 12-15 minutes until they just start to colour.
- Once cool, spread the 8 biscuits without holes with the warmed jam then sandwich using the remaining 8 biscuits before serving.

PREPARATION TIME 10 MINUTES

COOKING TIME 15-20 MINUTES

INGREDIENTS

FOR THE BISCUITS
300 g / 10 ½ oz / 2 cups plain (all purpose) flour
a little extra plain flour, for dusting
50 g / 2 oz / ⅓ cup cornflour (cornstarch)
225 g / 8 oz / 1 cup unsalted butter, cubed
65 g / 2 ½ oz / ½ cup icing (confectioners') sugar
a pinch of salt

FOR THE FILLING
300 g / 10 ½ oz / 1 ⅓ cups strawberry jam, warmed

Shortbread Cream Cookies

494

- Replace the strawberry jam with the same amount of whipped cream.

495

MAKES 12

Chocolate and Candied Fruit Lollipops

PREPARATION TIME 10 MINUTES

COOKING TIME 10 MINUTES

INGREDIENTS

450 g / 1 lb / 3 cups good-quality dark chocolate, chopped
30 g / 1 oz / 2 tbsp mixed candied peel, finely chopped
30 g / 1 oz / 2 tbsp candied lemon peel, sliced

TO GARNISH
1 tbsp icing (confectioners') sugar

ALSO NEEDED
12 lollipop sticks

- Grease and line 2 baking trays with greaseproof paper.
- Melt the chocolate in a large heatproof bowl set atop a saucepan of simmering water.
- Stir occasionally until melted then remove from the heat.
- Use a tablespoon to drop 12 rounds of melted chocolate onto the baking trays, spaced apart.
- Place the lollipop sticks in place in the chocolate rounds and top with the mixed peel and lemon peel.
- Leave to set until firm before dusting with icing sugar and serving.

Chocolate and Nut Lollipops
496

- Replace the candied mixed peel and lemon peel with a mixture of finely chopped nuts.

497

MAKES 4

Individual Lemon Cheesecakes

PREPARATION TIME 10-15 MINUTES

COOKING TIME 15 MINUTES

INGREDIENTS

150 g / 5 oz / 1 cup digestive (graham cracker) biscuits, pulsed into fine crumbs
50 g / 2 oz / ¼ cup unsalted butter, melted
400 g / 14 oz / 2 cups cream cheese
250 g / 9 oz / 1 cup Greek yoghurt
110 g / 4 oz / ½ cup caster (superfine) sugar
2 sheets of gelatine
2 lemons, juiced and finely zested
2 tbsp cold water

TO GARNISH
4 lime slices

- Combine the biscuits and melted butter.
- Divide between 4 individual ramekins, pressing in well then chill until needed.
- Beat together the cream cheese and sugar in a mixing bowl for 2 minute until smooth and creamy.
- Soften the gelatin in 2 tbsp of lemon juice and 2 tbsp of cold water, then heat in a small saucepan to dissolve the gelatin.
- Add the Greek yoghurt to the cream cheese mixture, beat well then add the gelatin mixture and beat again thoroughly.
- Add the remaining lemon juice and the zest, beating well until smooth.
- Spoon on top of the biscuit bases in the ramekins, cover and chill for 3 hours.
- Top each cheesecake with a lime slice.

Orange Cheesecakes
498

- Replace the lemon juice and zest with the juice of 2 oranges and zest of 1.

MAKES 12

Chocolate Whoopies

Chocolate and Pistachio Whoopies

499

500

- Add 50 g / 2 oz / ½ cup chopped pistachios to the buttercream before sandwiching the pies.

Chocolate Orange Whoopies

501

- Add 5-6 drops of orange extract and add 2 tsp of finely grated orange zest to the batter.

PREPARATION TIME 10-15 MINUTES

COOKING TIME 15-20 MINUTES

....

INGREDIENTS

FOR THE COOKIES
240 g / 8 oz / 1 ½ cups plain (all purpose) flour, sifted
a little extra plain (all purpose) flour, for dusting
175 g / 6 oz / ¾ cup margarine, softened
75 g / 3 oz / ⅓ cup caster (superfine) sugar
30 g / 1 oz / 2 tbsp cocoa powder
½ tsp bicarbonate (baking) of soda
a pinch of salt

FOR THE FILLING
225 g / 8 oz / 1 cup unsalted butter, softened
250 g / 9 oz / 2 cups icing (confectioners') sugar
110 g / 4 oz / ⅔ cup cocoa powder
55 ml / 2 fl. oz / ¼ cup whole milk

- Preheat the oven to 170°C (150°C fan) / 325F / gas 3.
- Grease and line 2 baking trays with greaseproof paper.
- Cream together the margarine and sugar in a large mixing bowl until pale and fluffy.
- Beat in the flour, bicarbonate of soda and almond extract until you have a rough dough.
- Knead the dough briefly before rolling out on a lightly floured surface to ¾ cm thickness.
- Use a 2" cookie cutter to cut out 24 rounds before carefully lifting onto the baking trays, spaced apart.
- Bake for 15-18 minutes until set and dry on top.
- Remove from the oven to a wire rack to cool.
- Blitz together the cocoa powder, icing sugar and butter in a food processor with half of the milk until smooth.
- Add a little more milk if you need to loosen the buttercream.
- Spread the underside of half of the whoopies with the buttercream and sandwich with the other halves before serving.

502

MAKES 12

Two Chocolate and Apple Whoopies

PREPARATION TIME 10-15 MINUTES

COOKING TIME 15-20 MINUTES

INGREDIENTS

240 g / 8 oz / 1 ½ cups plain (all purpose) flour, sifted
a little extra plain (all purpose) flour,
175 g / 6 oz / ¾ cup margarine, softened
75 g / 3 oz / ⅓ cup caster (superfine) sugar
1 tbsp cocoa powder
½ tsp bicarbonate (baking) of soda
a pinch of salt
300 g / 10 ½ oz / 2 cups white chocolate, chopped
250 ml / 9 fl. oz / 1 cup double (heavy) cream
250 g / 9 oz / 2 cups icing (confectioners') sugar
30 ml / 1 fl. oz / 2 tbsp Calvados
1 tsp apple extract
red food dye

- Preheat the oven to 170°C (150°C fan) / 325F / gas 3.
- Grease and line 2 baking trays with greaseproof paper.
- Cream together the margarine and sugar in a large mixing bowl until pale and fluffy.
- Beat in the flour, bicarbonate of soda and almond extract until you have a rough dough.
- Knead the dough briefly before rolling out on a lightly floured surface to ¾ cm thickness.
- Use a 2" cookie cutter to cut out 24 rounds before carefully lifting onto the baking trays, spaced apart.
- Bake for 15-18 minutes until set and dry on top.
- Remove from the oven to a wire rack to cool.
- Warm the calvados and apple extract in a small saucepan before whisking together with the icing sugar until smooth.
- Whisk in a little boiling water until you have a pouring consistency and colour with the red food colouring.
- Heat the cream in a saucepan until boiling, then remove from the heat and whisk in the chocolate until smooth.
- Let it cool and thicken before letting it cool and spreading on the underside of half of the cookies.
- Sandwich together using the remaining cookies and serve with the sauce.

503

MAKES 8

Decorated White Chocolate Cookies

PREPARATION TIME 10-15 MINUTES

COOKING TIME 15-20 MINUTES

INGREDIENTS

300 g / 10 ½ oz / 2 cups plain (all purpose) flour
a little extra plain flour, for dusting
50 g / 2 oz / ⅓ cup cornflour (cornstarch)
225 g / 8 oz / 1 cup unsalted butter, cubed
65 g / 2 ½ oz / ½ cup icing (confectioners') sugar
a pinch of salt
300 g / 10 ½ oz / 2 cups white chocolate, chopped

- Pulse together the flour, cornflour, salt, icing sugar and butter in a food processor until it forms a dough.
- Remove the dough, knead gently and form into a ball.
- Wrap in clingfilm and chill for 60 minutes.
- Preheat the oven to 180°C (160° fan) / 350F / gas 4.
- Remove the dough from the fridge and roll out on a lightly floured surface to ½ cm thickness.
- Cut out 8 shapes from the dough using a 4" round cookie cutter.
- Grease and line 2 baking trays with greaseproof paper.
- Arrange on the baking trays spaced apart and bake for 14-16 minutes until they just start to colour.
- Remove from the oven and allow them to cool on the trays.
- Melt the chocolate in a heatproof bowl set atop a saucepan of simmering water, stirring occasionally until melted.
- Let the chocolate cool for 4-5 minute before carefully pouring on top of the cookies, letting it run from the centre to the edges, making sure the chocolate stops just before the edge.
- Let the chocolate cool before using a sharp knife to lightly score patterns in the chocolate; you can also use a clean embossing stamp just before the chocolate sets.

Cherry and Mint Jelly Bites

504

SERVES 6

- Combine the water and sugar in a saucepan and warm over a medium heat, stirring until the sugar dissolves.
- Remove from the heat and whisk in the peppermint extract, gelatin and food colouring until you have a 'mint green' colour.
- Let it cool for 10 minutes before pouring into a 12-hole triangle mould.
- Place a cherry and a mint leaf in each hole before covering the mould and chilling overnight.
- Remove from the fridge and warm the outsides of the mould with a warm tea towel before turning out onto a serving plate.

PREPARATION TIME 10-15 MINUTES

COOKING TIME 10 MINUTES

INGREDIENTS

FOR THE JELLIES
300 ml / 10 ½ fl. oz / 1 ⅓ cups cold water
55 g / 2 oz / ¼ cup caster (superfine) sugar
1 tbsp gelatine powder
1 tsp peppermint extract
a few drops of green food colouring
12 mint leaves
12 cherries, stems intact

Chocolate Kiwi Lollies

505

MAKES 8

PREPARATION TIME 10 MINUTES

COOKING TIME 45 MINUTES

INGREDIENTS

4 large kiwi, skinned
300 g / 10 ½ oz / 2 cups good-quality

dark chocolate, chopped
1 tbsp liquid glucose

ALSO NEEDED
8 lollipop sticks

- Remove 1 cm from both ends of the kiwi fruit and use the middle section to cut 8 medallions roughly 1" thick.
- Arrange on a lined baking tray and skewer each with a lollipop before freezing as you prepare the coating.
- Melt the chocolate and liquid glucose together in a heatproof bowl set atop a saucepan of simmering water, stirring occasionally.
- Remove from the heat and allow it to cool for 5 minutes.
- Dip the semi-frozen kiwi fruit into the chocolate, coating well, before setting upright and chilling until set.

Mini Pancakes

506

SERVES 4

PREPARATION TIME 10 MINUTES

COOKING TIME 15 MINUTES

INGREDIENTS

FOR THE PANCAKES
125 g / 4 ½ oz / ¾ cup self-raising flour
125 ml / 4 fl. oz / ½ cup whole milk

1 medium egg
1 tbsp caster (superfine) sugar
1 tbsp butter, melted
1 tbsp sunflower oil

TO GARNISH
110 g / 4 oz / ½ cup strawberry jam
4 butter curls tbsp icing (confectioners') sugar

- Whisk together the egg, milk, butter and sunflower oil in a jug.
- Sift the flour and sugar into a mixing bowl and whisk the liquid ingredients into them, starting slowly, until you have a smooth batter.
- Heat a non-stick frying pan over a medium heat until hot and cook the pancakes, 2-3 at a time by dropping a tablespoon of the batter onto the surface until they spreads into evenly-sized rounds.
- Cook for 1 minute until set and golden, then flip and cook the other sides for 30 seconds.
- Transfer to a warm plate and cover the plate loosely with aluminium foil.
- Once all the pancakes have been cooked, serve with the jam and garnish with butter curls and a dusting of icing sugar.

507

MAKES 12

Mini Carrot Cakes

PREPARATION TIME 15 MINUTES

COOKING TIME 10 MINUTES

INGREDIENTS

450 g / 1 lb / 2 cups carrots, peeled and grated
150 g / 5 oz / ⅔ cup unsalted butter
150 g / 5 oz / 1 cup self-raising flour, sifted
110 ml / 4 fl. oz / ⅓ cup Golden syrup
55 g / 2 oz / ⅓ cup soft light brown sugar
3 medium eggs
1 tsp ground cinnamon
½ tsp ground nutmeg
a pinch of salt

- Preheat the oven to 170°C (150°C fan) / 325F / gas 3 and line a cupcake tray with 12 cupcake cases.
- Combine the butter, flour, sugar, Golden syrup, eggs, ground spices and salt in a large mixing bowl and beat using an electric mixer until smooth.
- Add the grated carrot and fold through until incorporated.
- Spoon into the cupcake cases and bake for 35-45 minutes until risen; test with a wooden toothpick, if it comes out clean, they are done.
- Remove from the oven and leave to cool in the tin before removing the cases and serving.

Carrot and Sultana Cakes

508

- Add 75 g / 3 oz / ½ cup sultanas to the batter before spooning into the cases and baking.

509

MAKES 12

Lemon and Poppy Seed Cakes

PREPARATION TIME 10 MINUTES

COOKING TIME 15 MINUTES

INGREDIENTS

150 g / 5 oz / 1 cup self-raising flour
150 g / 5 oz / ⅔ cup margarine
150 g / 5 oz / ⅔ cup caster (superfine) sugar
3 large eggs
1 lemon, juiced and zested
1 tsp lemon extract
30 g / 1 oz / ¼ cup black poppy seeds

TO GARNISH

125 g / 4 ½ oz / ½ cup icing (confectioners') sugar
2 tbsp lemon juice
2 tbsp boiling water
1 tbsp black poppy seeds

- Preheat the oven to 180°C (160° fan) / 350F / gas 4 and line a square cupcake tray with 12 square cases.
- Beat together the flour, margarine, sugar, eggs, lemon juice and zest, lemon extract and black poppy seeds in a large mixing bowl until smooth; 2-3 minutes.
- Spoon into the cases and bake for 20-25 minutes; test with a wooden toothpick, if it comes out clean, they are done.
- Remove from the oven and leave to cool in the cases.
- Whisk together the icing sugar with enough lemon juice and boiling water to produce a pourable icing.
- Let it cool and thicken a little before pouring on top of the cooled cakes and garnishing with a sprinkle of poppy seeds.

Orange and Sesame Cakes

510

- Use the juice and zest of 1 small orange and orange flower water instead of lemon extract. Substitute black sesame seeds for the poppy seeds.

SERVES 4 # Sole and Bacon Appetizer Rolls

- Preheat the grill to hot.
- Place the leek in microwave-proof bowl with 1 tbsp cold water.
- Cover and cook on high for 45 seconds.
- Remove and drain well, setting to one side to cool.
- Cut the sole fillet into 12 strips and arrange on the halved slices of bacon.
- Dot with a little butter and season well.
- Roll up and secure using toothpicks before arranging on a greaseproof paper-lined baking tray.
- Grill for 3-4 minutes, turning occasionally, until the fish is firm yet slightly springy to the touch.
- Remove from the grill and position in soup spoons, garnished with the leek.

PREPARATION TIME 10-15 MINUTES

COOKING TIME 10 MINUTES

INGREDIENTS

FOR THE ROLLS
200 g / 7 oz / 1 ⅓ cups lemon sole fillet, skinned
6 rashers of streaky bacon, halved
1 tbsp butter, softened
salt and pepper

TO GARNISH
¼ leek, sliced, washed and drained

ALSO NEEDED
12 cocktail sticks

Sole and Prosciutto Rolls

512

- Score the skin side of the sole before cutting into 12 strips. Season and grill for 3-4 minutes, turning once before removing and wrapping in slices of prosciutto.

513

SERVES 4 # Bacon and Blue Cheese Crostini

- Preheat the grill to hot.
- Toast the slices of baguette for 1 minute on both sides.
- Remove from the oven and drape a rasher of bacon across each slice.
- Return to the grill for 3 minutes until the bacon is almost cooked through, working in batches if necessary.
- Remove from the grill once the bacon is almost done and add a chunk of Roquefort on top of each slice.
- Grill for another 1-2 minutes until the cheese is melting.
- Remove from the oven and season with a pinch of crushed red peppercorns, some freshly ground black pepper and a basil leaf.
- Arrange on serving trays and garnish with sprigs of basil leaves before serving.

PREPARATION TIME 10-15 MINUTES

COOKING TIME 10 MINUTES

INGREDIENTS

½ large flute baguette, sliced at 2 cm intervals (you should have 10-12 slices)
10-12 rashers back bacon
150 g / 5 oz / 1 ½ cups Roquefort
½ tsp red peppercorns, crushed
freshly ground black pepper
small handful of basil leaves
sprigs of basil leaves, to garnish

Bacon and Raclette Crostini

 514

- Replace the blue cheese with Raclette cheese.

515

SERVES 6

Mini Seafood Gougères

Ham and Cheese Stuffed Gougères

516

- Mix the sour cream with 50 g / 2 oz / ½ cup grated Cheddar and 75 g / 3 oz / ½ cup of diced cooked ham. Use to fill the pastries.

Ham and Roquefort Stuffed Gougères

517

- Mix the sour cream with 50 g / 2 oz / ½ cup crumbled Roquefort cheese and 75 g / 3 oz / ½ cup of diced cooked ham. Use to fill the pastries.

PREPARATION TIME 15 MINUTES

COOKING TIME 15-20 MINUTES

INGREDIENTS

FOR THE GOUGERES
110 g / 4 oz / ⅔ cup plain
(all purpose) flour
110 g / 4 oz / ½ cup unsalted butter,
cold and cubed
250 ml / 9 fl. oz / 1 cup whole milk
4 large eggs
a pinch of salt

TO GARNISH
250 g / 9 oz / 1 cup sour cream
50 g / 2 oz / ⅓ cup frozen cooked
prawns, thawed
50 g / 2 oz / ⅓ cup skinless salmon
fillet, cut into small squares
1 cooked lobster tail, cut into bite-
sized portions
1 tsp pink peppercorns, crushed
a small handful of chive stalks
a few sprigs of dill

- Sift together flour and salt into a mixing bowl.
- Combine the butter and milk in a saucepan and heat gently until the butter melts.
- Add the flour and stir until a smooth dough forms.
- Beat the dough until it starts to pull away from the sides of the saucepan.
- Remove from the heat and add the eggs, one at a time, beating well between each addition until shiny and even.
- Spoon the dough into a piping bag fitted with a 5 cm straight-sided nozzle.
- Preheat the oven to 200°C (180° fan) / 400F / gas 6.
- Grease and line 2 baking trays with greaseproof paper.
- Pipe blobs of the pastry onto the sheets, spaced apart.
- Bake for 15-18 minutes until puffed and golden, then remove to a wire rack to cool before serving.
- Remove the tops once cool and fill with generous teaspoons of sour cream.
- Top with the prawns, lobster pieces and salmon square before arranging on a serving plate.
- Garnish with the herbs and a pinch of crushed peppercorns.

518

MAKES 8

Cantal Turnovers

- Preheat the oven to 180°C (160° fan) / 350F / gas 4.
- Line a large baking tray with greaseproof paper.
- Roll the pastry out on a lightly floured surface to ¾ cm thickness.
- Cut out 8 4" rounds of pastry and fill their centres with cheese and tomato.
- Wet the rim of the pastry with a little water using your fingertip before folding the bottom end over the filling and sealing with the opposite end by crimping.
- Transfer to the baking tray and brush with the beaten egg.
- Bake for 20-25 minutes until the pastry is golden and cooked.
- Remove from the oven and leave to cool a little before serving.

PREPARATION TIME 10-15 MINUTES

COOKING TIME 10 MINUTES

INGREDIENTS

350 g / 12 oz ready-made shortcrust pastry
a little plain (all purpose) flour, for dusting
2 medium eggs, beaten
150 g / 5 oz / 1 ½ cups Cantal, grated
4 vine tomatoes, cored, deseeded and diced
salt and pepper

Cantal and Chorizo Turnovers   519

- Substitute half of the diced tomato for 75 g / 3 oz / ½ cup diced chorizo in the filling.

520

SERVES 4

Bite-Sized Sausage Rolls

- Preheat the oven to 190°C (170° fan) / 375F / gas 5.
- Grease and line a large baking tray with greaseproof paper.
- Roll the pastry out on a lightly floured work surface to ½ cm thickness.
- Cut 3 cm wide strips, making sure you have 12.
- Wrap around the sausages and seal well before brushing the outsides with egg and arranging on the baking tray.
- Lightly press a large pinch of sesame seeds into the pastry and bake for 15-18 minutes until the pastry is puffed and golden-brown in colour.
- Remove to a wire rack to cool.
- Serve warm or cold.

PREPARATION TIME 5-10 MINUTES

COOKING TIME 10 MINUTES

INGREDIENTS

12 small kabanos or chipolatas
150 g / 5 oz ready-made puff pastry
75 g / 3 oz / ¾ cup sesame seeds
a little plain (all purpose) flour, for dusting
2 medium eggs, beaten

Sausage Rolls with Tzatziki   521

- Whisk together 250 g / 9 oz / 1 cup plain yoghurt with ½ grated cucumber, a few chopped mint leaves and seasoning. Serve with the sausage rolls.

522

SERVES 4

Fried Meatballs with Mint

PREPARATION TIME 10-15
MINUTES

COOKING TIME 15 MINUTES

....

INGREDIENTS

FOR THE MEATBALLS
450 g / 1 lb / 3 cups beef mince
110 g / 4 oz / 1 cup golden
breadcrumbs
75 ml / 3 fl. oz / ⅓ cup sunflower oil
1 large egg, beaten
1 tsp ground cumin
1 tsp ground coriander (cilantro)
a small handful of mint leaves,
finely chopped
salt and pepper

TO GARNISH
a pinch of ground coriander
(cilantro)
a few sprigs of mint leaves
a few mint leaves, finely sliced

ALSO NEEDED
cocktail sticks

- Preheat the oven to 190°C (170° fan) / 375F / gas 5.
- Grease and line a large baking tray with greaseproof paper.
- Mix together the beef mince, breadcrumbs, egg, ground spices, chopped mint and seasoning in a mixing bowl.
- Once the mixture is even, shape into meatballs and arrange on the baking tray.
- Bake for 25 minutes until golden on the outside.
- Heat the sunflower oil in a sauté pan set over a moderate heat until hot.
- Shallow-fry the meatballs in the oil until golden-brown in colour all over.
- Drain on kitchen paper before serving in a bowl, pricked with cocktail sticks and garnished with chopped mint, a pinch of coriander and sprigs of mint on the side.

Mint and Red Onion Meatballs 523

- Add 1 finely chopped red onion to the meatball mixture, mixing well before shaping and baking.

524

SERVES 8

Tomato Amuse Bouche

PREPARATION TIME 5-10
MINUTES

COOKING TIME 10 MINUTES

....

INGREDIENTS

FOR THE AMUSE BOUCHE
8 cherry tomatoes
½ head of broccoli, prepared into
8 small florets
55 ml / 2 fl. oz / ¼ cup lime juice
75 g / 3 oz / 1 cup desiccated coconut
30 g / 1 oz / ¼ cup flaked (slivered)
almonds
salt and pepper

ALSO NEEDED
8 cocktail sticks

- Briefly pulse together the flaked almonds and desiccated coconut with some seasoning in a food processor to combine.
- Thread one end of the cocktail sticks onto the cherry tomatoes and dip in the lemon juice before coating in the coconut and almond mixture.
- Thread the cocktail stick onto the broccoli florets and arrange in serving cups.

Spiced Tomato Amuse Bouche 525

- Add ½ tsp smoked paprika and ½ tsp mild curry powder to the coconut and almond coating.

526

SERVES 4

Ravioli Skewers

Ravioli and Blue Cheese Skewers

527

- Separate the ravioli with cubes of Gorgonzola on the skewers before grilling until the cheese starts to melt.

Ravioli and Halloumi Skewers

528

- Separate the ravioli with cubes of halloumi cheese and grill until the cheese starts to brown.

PREPARATION TIME 10-15 MINUTES

COOKING TIME 15 MINUTES

∙∙

INGREDIENTS

FOR THE SKEWERS
55 g / 2 fl. oz / ¼ cup extra-virgin olive oil
300 g / 10 ½ oz / 3 cups ready-made filled ravioli
ground pepper

TO GARNISH
1 tsp flaked sea salt
1 tbsp green pepper, finely diced
1 tbsp yellow pepper, finely diced
2 vine tomatoes, cored, deseeded and diced
a few sprigs of tarragon

ALSO NEEDED
8 wooden skewers, soaked in water for 15 minutes

- Cook the ravioli in a large saucepan of salted, boiling water until 'al dente'; usually 3-5 minutes.
- Drain and leave to steam dry before tossing with the olive oil and pepper.
- Thread onto skewers and grill under a hot grill for 1-2 minutes until the edges are golden.
- Remove from the grill and arrange on serving plates, garnish with diced peppers, tomatoes, flaked sea salt and sprigs of tarragon on the side.

529

SERVES 4

Quail Egg and Emmental Kebabs

PREPARATION TIME 5-10 MINUTES

COOKING TIME 10-15 MINUTES

INGREDIENTS

8 quail eggs
110 g / 4 oz / 1 cup Emmental,
cut into 8 even cubes

TO GARNISH
1 tbsp sesame seeds
1 tbsp shelled pistachios, crushed

ALSO NEEDED
8 cocktail sticks

- Hard boil the quail eggs in boiling water for 8 minutes.
- Drain and refresh in iced water until cool enough to handle.
- Peel and skewer onto cubes of the Emmental.
- Arrange on serving plates before garnishing with a sprinkle of sesame seeds and crushed pistachios.

Quail and Pearl Onion Kebabs   ## 530

- Substitute the cubes of Emmental for pickled, drained pearl onions.

531

SERVES 4

Fromage Frais Curried Ham Rolls

PREPARATION TIME 15 MINUTES

COOKING TIME 10 MINUTES

INGREDIENTS

250 g / 9 oz / 1 cup fromage frais
200 g / 7 oz / 1 ⅓ cups cooked ham slices
110 g / 4 oz / ½ cup mayonnaise
1 tbsp flat-leaf parsley leaves, finely chopped
1 tbsp chervil leaves, finely chopped
salt and pepper

TO GARNISH
1 tsp Madras curry powder
a few sprigs of chervil
a small handful of frisée lettuce

ALSO NEEDED
cocktail sticks

- Whisk together ¾ of the fromage frais seasoning and the chopped herbs in a mixing bowl.
- In a separate mixing bowl, whisk together the remaining fromage frais with the mayonnaise, Madras curry powder and seasoning.
- Lay the ham slices on a flat surface and spread half of them with the herb mixture and the other half with the curry mixture.
- Roll into cigars and sliced at 2" intervals.
- Secure with the cocktail sticks and arrange in a serving bowl.
- Garnish with the chervil sprigs and frisee lettuce before serving.

Cranberry and Fromage Frais Rolls   ## 532

- Substitute the chopped herbs in the fromage frais filling with a handful of chopped dried cranberries.

533

SERVES 4

Radishes Stuffed with Fromage Frais

- Remove the top ½ cm from the radishes and reserve.
- Use a small melon baller, scoop out their centres.
- Mix together the fromage frais and chives in a mixing bowl until smooth.
- Adjust the seasoning to taste before spooning into the radishes.
- Replace the tops before serving cold.

PREPARATION TIME 5 MINUTES

COOKING TIME 10-15 MINUTES

INGREDIENTS

12 radishes
175 g / 6 oz / ¾ cup fromage frais
a few chive stalks, finely chopped
salt and pepper

Cream Cheese Radishes with Bacon

 534

- Cook 2 rashers of bacon then crumble. Stir into cream cheese.

535

MAKES 8

Spicy Samosas

- Heat the sunflower oil in a large saucepan.
- Sweat the onion, ginger and chilli for 6-7 minutes until softened. Add the pork mince and cook until browned all over.
- Add the soy sauce, rice wine vinegar and sugar, stirring well until reduced by half. Season and set to one side.
- Heat the groundnut oil in a saucepan; the oil is hot enough as bubbles appear on a wooden spoon.
- Wet the rim of the wrappers with water and fold into a triangle before forming a cone around your fingers, sealing one edge, but keeping the case open.
- Fill with the pork filling before sealing well.
- Deep-fry in batches for 3-4 minutes flipping once before removing to kitchen paper to drain.
- Cut a thin section off the cucumber and finely slice as a garnish on top of the samosas with the diced carrot.

PREPARATION TIME 15 MINUTES

COOKING TIME 25-30 MINUTES

INGREDIENTS

FOR THE SAMOSAS
1 l / 1 pint 16 fl. oz / 4 cups groundnut oil
8 spring roll wrappers
55 ml / 2 fl. oz / ¼ cup sunflower oil
450 g / 1 lb / 3 cups pork mince
2 onion, finely chopped
2 cloves of garlic, minced
1 red chilli (chili), deseeded and finely chopped
55 ml / 2 fl. oz / ¼ cup dark soy sauce
55 ml / 2 fl. oz / ¼ rice wine vinegar
1 tbsp caster (superfine) sugar
salt and pepper

TO GARNISH
½ carrot, peeled and very finely diced
½ cucumber

Pork and Pea Samosas

536

- Add 100 g / 3 oz / 1 cup of thawed frozen peas to the pork before filling the wrappers.

537

SERVES 4

Cod Acra Balls

Cod and Mango Acra Balls

538

- Pulse the cod fillet with ½ diced mango in a food processor before shaping into balls.

Cod and Pineapple Acra Balls

539

- Pulse the cod fillet with 4 slices of pineapple before shaping into balls.

PREPARATION TIME 10-15 MINUTES

COOKING TIME 15-20 MINUTES

INGREDIENTS

FOR THE FRITTERS
1 l / 1 pint 16 fl. oz / 4 cups groundnut oil, for deep-frying
400 g / 14 oz / 2 ⅔ cups skinless cod fillet, cut into 1" cubes
75 g / 3 oz / ½ cup plain (all purpose) flour
salt and pepper

FOR THE BATTER
110 g / 4 oz / ⅔ cup self-raising flour
125 ml / 4 ½ fl. oz / ½ cup cold water
a small handful of flat-leaf parsley, finely chopped
salt and pepper

TO GARNISH
a small handful of green cherry tomatoes

- Heat the groundnut oil in a large, heavy-based saucepan until hot; you can tell when the oil is hot enough as bubbles appear on a wooden spoon dipped in the hot oil.
- Briefly whisk together the self-raising flour, chopped parsley, water and seasoning until you have a rough batter.
- Dry cod really well before dusting in the plain flour, shaking off any excess.
- Dip in the batter and deep-fry in batches until golden-brown in colour all over; 2-3 minutes.
- Remove with a slotted spoon to kitchen paper.
- Serve in a bowl with green cherry tomatoes as a garnish.

540

SERVES 4

Scallop and Pancetta Wraps

- Preheat the grill to hot.
- Heat the oil and butter together in a large frying pan set over a moderate heat.
- Season the scallops generously and sear in the pan in a ring, turning after 1 minute and cooking for an additional 1 minute.
- Remove to kitchen paper to drain before wrapping in pancetta.
- Grill for 2-3 minutes, turning occasionally until the pancetta is crisp and golden in colour.
- Remove to serving plates and skewer with cocktail sticks.
- Garnish with parsley on the side and a pinch of smoked paprika over the wraps.

PREPARATION TIME 5 MINUTES

COOKING TIME 10 MINUTES

INGREDIENTS

8 scallops, roe removed
8 thin slices of pancetta
1 tbsp sunflower oil
1 tbsp butter
salt and pepper

TO GARNISH
a few sprigs of flat-leaf parsley
a pinch of smoked paprika

ALSO NEEDED
8 cocktail sticks

Scallop, Pancetta and Marmalade Wraps

 541

- Brush each scallop with a little warm orange marmalade before wrapping.

542

SERVES 4

Anchovy-Stuffed Cherry Tomatoes

- Remove the top ½ cm from the cherry tomatoes and scoop out the seeds.
- Pulse together the anchovies, garlic, lemon juice and parsley in a food processor until finely ground.
- Adjust the seasoning to taste before spooning into the cherry tomatoes.
- Prick with cocktail sticks before serving.

PREPARATION TIME 10 MINUTES

COOKING TIME 10 MINUTES

INGREDIENTS

FOR THE TOMATOES
8 cherry tomatoes
110 g / 4 oz / ⅔ cup preserved anchovy fillets, drained
30 ml / 1 fl. oz / 2 tbsp extra-virgin olive oil
1 clove of garlic, crushed
1 lemon, juiced
a small handful of flat-leaf parsley, chopped
salt and pepper

ALSO NEEDED
8 cocktail sticks

Anchovy and Black Olive Tomatoes

 543

- Substitute half of the preserved anchovy fillets for pitted black olives.

544

MAKES 12

Tricolore Canapés

PREPARATION TIME 10 MINUTES

COOKING TIME 10 MINUTES

INGREDIENTS

FOR THE CANAPÉS
110 g / 4 oz / 1 cup feta, cut into
12 even cubes
12 bite-sized pieces of preserved
sundried tomato
12 picked basil leaves
¼ cucumber, peeled
salt and freshly ground black pepper

ALSO NEEDED
12 cocktail sticks

- Cut the cucumber into three even pieces and deseed each piece before cutting into 4 slices.
- Season the feta cubes in a mixing bowl with freshly ground black pepper, tossing well.
- Thread the sundried tomato onto a cocktail stick, followed by a basil leaf, cube of feta and a piece of cucumber.
- Serve chilled.

545

Pineapple, Basil and Mozzarella Skewers

- Substitute the feta for mozzarella and change the sundried tomato to pineapple.

546

SERVES 4

Vegetable-Stuffed Cherry Tomatoes

PREPARATION TIME 10 MINUTES

COOKING TIME 10 MINUTES

INGREDIENTS

225 g / 8 oz / 1 cup cottage cheese
12 vine cherry tomatoes
4 gherkins, drained and finely diced
1 small carrot, peeled and very finely diced
a small handful of basil leaves, finely chopped
salt and pepper

- Remove the tops from the cherry tomatoes and reserve.
- Deseeded and arrange on a tray.
- Mix together the cottage cheese, gherkin, carrot and basil leaves in a mixing bowl, stirring well.
- Adjust the seasoning to taste before spooning into the empty cherry tomatoes.
- Replace the tops before serving.

547

Smoked Salmon-Stuffed Cherry Tomatoes

- Finely chop smoked salmon trimmings and mix with cream cheese.

548

SERVES 4

Ham-Topped Potato Tortilla Bites

Chorizo Tortilla Bites **549**

- Substitute the pancetta for chorizo, dicing it and adding it into the beaten egg and potato mixture before baking.

Sun Dried Tomato Tortilla Bites **550**

- Substitute the pancetta for sun dried tomatoes dicing them and adding it into the beaten egg and potato mixture before baking.

PREPARATION TIME 15 MINUTES

COOKING TIME 15 MINUTES

INGREDIENTS

FOR THE TAPAS BITES
450 g / 1 lb / 3 cups floury potatoes, peeled and diced
75 g / 3 oz / ¾ cup pancetta, cut into small strips
30 ml / 1 fl. oz / 2 tbsp olive oil
1 onion, finely chopped
4 large eggs, beaten
salt and freshly ground black pepper

ALSO NEEDED
cocktail sticks

- Preheat the oven to 190°C (170° fan) / 375F / gas 5.
- Grease and line the base and sides of a 7" square cake tin with greaseproof paper.
- Cook the potato in a large saucepan of salted, boiling water for 5 minutes before draining and leaving to steam.
- Whisk the eggs with seasoning and toss the potato with the olive oil, pepper and some seasoning.
- Add the potato to the beaten egg and pour into the tin before seasoning the top.
- Bake for 10-12 minutes until the egg is set and starting to colour on top.
- Remove from the oven and leave to cool in the tin before turning out and cutting into squares.
- Preheat the grill to hot and grill the pancetta under it for 2-3 minutes until golden and crisp.
- Skewer the slices onto the tortilla squares before serving.

551

SERVES 4

Asparagus and Prosciutto Bites

PREPARATION TIME 10 MINUTES

COOKING TIME 10 MINUTES

INGREDIENTS

FOR THE BITES
½ poppy seed baguette, cut into
8 slices
125 g / 4 ½ oz / ½ cup cottage cheese
8 asparagus spears, ends removed
8 slices of prosciutto
a few chive stalks, finely chopped
salt and pepper

TO GARNISH
1 tbsp extra-virgin olive oil
freshly ground black pepper

- Blanch the asparagus spears in a saucepan of salted, boiling water for 1 ½ minutes.
- Drain and refresh in iced water.
- Stir together the cottage cheese, chopped chives and seasoning until combined.
- Spoon on top of the slices of baguette.
- Drain the asparagus and remove some of the stem so that you are left with 2" long tips.
- Wrap in the prosciutto and sit on top of the cottage cheese.
- Arrange on serving plates and garnish with black pepper and a drizzle of olive oil on the side.

Tenderstem Broccoli and Prosciutto Bites

552

- Substitute the asparagus for tenderstem broccoli, cut to 3" long pieces before blanching.

553

SERVES 8

Mushrooms with Rye Bread Stuffing

PREPARATION TIME 15-20 MINUTES

COOKING TIME 25-30 MINUTES

INGREDIENTS

50 ml / 2 fl. oz / ½ cup olive oil
400 g / 14 oz / 5 ½ cups closed cup mushrooms,
inner stalk removed
200 g / 7 oz / 2 cups rye bread, cubed
50 g / 2 oz / ½ cup Parmesan
1 large plum tomato, de-seeded and finely diced
1 small bunch parsley, finely chopped
salt and pepper

- Preheat the oven to 200°C (180° fan) / 400F / gas 6.
- Place the cubes of rye bread in a food processor and blitz until you have rye breadcrumbs.
- Transfer to a mixing bowl and combine with the Parmesan, tomato, parsley and seasoning.
- Arrange the mushrooms inverted in rows on baking trays.
- Spoon the stuffing into their centres, then drizzle with the olive oil.
- Bake for 20-25 minutes until the stuffing and mushrooms are cooked and hot.
- Remove and allow to cool for a few minutes before arranging on serving plates.
- Serve hot or cold.

Mushrooms with Pancetta Stuffing

554

- Substitute half of the mushrooms for diced pancetta.

555

SERVES 4

Chicken and Spinach Appetizers

- Preheat the oven to 190°C (170° fan) / 375F / gas 5.
- Grease and line a large baking tray with greaseproof paper.
- Blanch the spinach leaves in a saucepan of salted, boiling water for 10 seconds.
- Drain and refresh in iced water before draining again and drying well.
- Pulse together the chicken, blanched spinach, olive oil, curry powder and seasoning in a food processor until combined.
- Shape into balls and arrange on the baking tray.
- Bake for 18-20 minutes until cooked through before removing to a wire rack to cool a little.
- Prick with cocktail sticks and serve.

PREPARATION TIME 10 MINUTES

COOKING TIME 10-15 MINUTES

INGREDIENTS

FOR THE APPETIZERS
2 large skinless chicken breasts, diced
100 g / 3 ½ oz / 2 cups baby spinach leaves
30 ml / 1 fl. oz / 2 tbsp olive oil
2 tsp mild curry powder
salt and pepper

ALSO NEEDED
cocktail sticks

Breaded Chicken and Spinach Appetizers

556

- Coat the chicken balls in golden breadcrumbs before baking.

557

SERVES 4

Shrimp Toasts

- Flatten the slices of bread on a flat surface using a rolling pin.
- Pulse together the shrimp, sesame oil, lemon juice, fish sauce and chilli powder in a food processor until smooth.
- Adjust the seasoning to taste and set to one side.
- Toast the end sides of the bread slices for 1 minute under a hot grill.
- Remove and leave to cool before spreading the other side with the shrimp paste.
- Top with an even layer of sesame seeds before chilling for at least 2 hours.
- Reheat the shrimp toasts under a hot grill for 1 minute before cutting into square and serving.

PREPARATION TIME 5-10 MINUTES

COOKING TIME 10-15 MINUTES

INGREDIENTS

2 end slices from a large loaf of white sandwich bread
300 g / 10 ½ oz / 2 cups frozen cooked shrimp, thawed
55 g / 2 oz / ½ cup sesame seeds
1 tbsp sesame oil
1 tbsp fish sauce
½ lemon, juiced
a pinch of chilli (chili) powder
salt and pepper

Shrimp Toasts with Plum Sauce

558

- Serve the toasts with little pots of plum sauce on the side for dipping.

559

SERVES 4

Pigs In a Blanket

Bacon-Wrapped Prunes

560

- Substitute the chipolata sausages for 12 dried prunes, baking them for 8-10 minutes.

Leek-Wrapped Chipolatas

561

- Blanch strips of leek in boiling water for 5 seconds, refreshing in iced water. Wrap chipolatas with leek before baking.

PREPARATION TIME 5 MINUTES

COOKING TIME 45 MINUTES

INGREDIENTS

FOR THE PIGS IN BLANKETS
12 chipolata sausages, pricked
a few times
6 rashers of streaky bacon

TO GARNISH
110 g / 4 oz / ½ cup plain yoghurt
1 tbsp mayonnaise
a few spring onion (scallion) tops

ALSO NEEDED
12 cocktail sticks

- Preheat the oven to 190°C (170° fan) / 375F / gas 5.
- Grease and line a baking tray with greaseproof paper.
- Whisk together the yoghurt and mayonnaise until smooth before spooning into serving pots and chilling.
- Cut the rashers of bacon in half and wrap around the sausages, placing them seam-side down on the baking tray.
- Bake for 12-15 minutes until the sausages are cooked through and the bacon is coloured and crisp.
- Remove from the oven and skewer with cocktail sticks through the middle before serving with the yoghurt dip and a garnish of spring onions on the side.

562

SERVES 4 Swedish-Style Salmon Appetizers

- Line a flat surface with 2 sheets of cling film measuring 12" x 12".
- Cut the slices of smoked salmon into 3" x 1" strips and chop the sprigs of dill into 2" long bunches, separating them into piles.
- Sprinkle the cling film with the poppy seeds and lay the strips of salmon on top, pressing gently into the seeds to help them adhere.
- Lay small piles of dill crossways on the salmon and roll the salmon around them to secure.
- Serve cold, upright.

PREPARATION TIME 10 MINUTES

COOKING TIME 10 MINUTES

INGREDIENTS

150 g / 5 oz / 1 cup smoked salmon slices
1 tbsp white poppy seeds
a small handful of dill sprigs

Smoked Salmon and Horseradish Rolls

563

- Spread the salmon slices with a little creamed horseradish before adding the dill and rolling.

564

SERVES 4 Haddock Guacamole Tortilla Bites

- Coat the haddock in the lime juice in a mixing bowl, stir well, cover and chill for 45 minutes.
- Roughly mash the avocado with the garlic, Tabasco and seasoning.
- Stir in the cherry tomatoes and follow with the haddock and half of the lime juice from the haddock.
- Spoon onto tortilla chips and garnish with a pinch of chilli powder before serving.

PREPARATION TIME 10-15 MINUTES

COOKING TIME 15 MINUTES

INGREDIENTS

FOR THE BITES
12 large tortilla chips
2 avocados, stoned and diced
2 limes, juiced
1 clove of garlic, minced
150 g / 5 oz / 1 cup skinless haddock fillet, diced
75 g / 3 oz / ¾ cup cherry tomatoes, diced
a dash of Tabasco
salt and pepper

TO GARNISH
a pinch of chilli powder

Haddock and Salsa Tortillas

565

- Substitute the avocados for 450 g / 1 lb / 4 cups diced cherry tomatoes, mixed with 1 finely diced red onion and chopped coriander (cilantro).

566

SERVES 4

Bite-Sized Courgette with Feta

PREPARATION TIME 5-10 MINUTES

COOKING TIME 15 MINUTES

INGREDIENTS

FOR THE ROLLS
2 medium courgettes (zucchinis)
200 g / 7 oz / 2 cups feta
100 g / 3 ½ oz / ½ cup cream cheese
½ lemon, juiced
a small handful of chive stalks, chopped
salt and pepper

TO GARNISH
a few chive stalks

- Prepare the courgettes into thin ribbons using a mandolin or vegetable peeler.
- Pulse together the chives, feta, cream cheese, lemon juice and a little seasoning until smooth.
- Spread the courgette ribbons with the filling and roll into bite-sized cylinders.
- Arrange on a serving platter and garnish with chive stalks.

Feta and Red Onion Rolls

567

- Add ½ finely chopped red onion to the feta and cream cheese filling before spreading and rolling.

568

SERVES 4

Mini Croque Monsieur

PREPARATION TIME 5-10 MINUTES

COOKING TIME 10 MINUTES

INGREDIENTS

FOR THE CROQUE MONSIEUR
4 slices of white sandwich bread
55 g / 2 oz / ¼ cup butter, softened
225 g / 8 oz / 2 cups Emmental slices
150 g / 5 oz / 1 cup ham slices

ALSO NEEDED
wooden skewers

- Preheat the grill to hot and preheat the oven to 190°C (170° fan) / 375F / gas 5.
- Butter the slices of bread on one side and layer half of the cheese half of them.
- Top with ham and follow with another layer of cheese before sandwiching them with the other slices of bread.
- Arrange on a greaseproof paper-lined baking tray and bake for 8-10 minutes until the cheese starts to melt.
- Remove from the oven and remove the crusts before finishing under the grill for 1 minute on both sides until golden-brown all over.
- Cut into squares and serve with wooden skewers on the side.

Cream Cheese Mini Croque Monsieur

569

- Instead of Emmental, spread cream cheese on the bread.

570

SERVES 4

Tuna and Salmon Bites

Tuna and
Pineapples Bites

571

- Omit the salmon and double the amount of tuna, using pineapple chunks instead of papaya for the bites.

Salmon and Olive Bites

572

- Omit the tuna and double the amount of salmon, using pitted black olives instead of papaya.

PREPARATION TIME 10-15 MINUTES

COOKING TIME 15 MINUTES

....

INGREDIENTS

FOR THE BITES
55 ml / 2 fl. oz / ¼ cups sesame oil
225 g / 8 oz / 1 ½ cups tuna steak, cut into 8 pieces
225 g / 8 oz / 1 ½ cups skinless salmon fillet, cut into 8 pieces
110 g / 4 oz / ½ cup canned papaya chunks
55 g / 2 oz / ½ cup sesame seeds
4 baby onions, peeled and halved
1 tbsp butter
salt and pepper

ALSO NEEDED
cocktail sticks

- Preheat the grill to hot and grease and line 2 baking trays with greaseproof paper.
- Coat the salmon and tuna in half of the sesame oil before seasoning.
- Arrange the tuna and salmon on one tray and arrange the papaya and onions on the other tray.
- Dot the onions with butter before grilling for 5-6 minutes until they start to colour.
- Remove and set to one side.
- Grill the fish for 6-8 minutes, turning once, until they are firm yet springy to the touch.
- Remove from the oven and leave to cool a little before coating the tuna in the remaining oil.
- Crust in the sesame seeds and thread onto cocktails sticks with a piece of papaya.
- Thread the salmon and onion halves onto cocktail sticks before serving.

573

SERVES 4

Mini Corn Galettes

PREPARATION TIME 10-15 MINUTES

COOKING TIME 20-25 MINUTES

INGREDIENTS

FOR THE GALETTES
150 g / 5 oz / 1 cup self-raising flour
150 g / 5 oz / ⅔ cup canned sweetcorn
125 ml / 4 fl. oz / ½ cup whole milk
55 g / 2 oz / ¼ cup unsalted butter, for frying
2 red chillies (chilis), deseeded and finely diced
1 large egg
1 tbsp butter, melted
a small handful of flat-leaf parsley, finely chopped
salt and pepper

TO GARNISH
100 g / 3 ½ oz / ⅔ cup green olives
100 g / 3 ½ oz / ⅔ cup Kalamata olives

ALSO NEEDED
thin wooden skewers

- Whisk together the egg, milk and melted butter in a jug.
- Sift the flour into a mixing bowl and whisk the liquid ingredients into it, starting slowly, until you have a smooth batter.
- Stir through the sweetcorn, chilli and parsley before seasoning a little.
- Heat a non-stick frying pan over a medium heat until hot and add a knob of butter.
- Cook the pancakes, 2-3 at a time by dropping a tablespoon of the batter onto the surface until they spreads into evenly-sized rounds.
- Cook for 1 minute until set and golden, then flip and cook the other sides for 30 seconds.
- Transfer to a warm plate and cover the plate loosely with aluminium foil.
- Skewer the galettes and serve on a bed of olives.

574

SERVES 4

Lamb and Pine Nut Spicy Turnovers

PREPARATION TIME 20 MINUTES

COOKING TIME 50 MINUTES

INGREDIENTS

200 g / 7 oz ready-made shortcrust pastry
a little plain flour for dusting
100 g / 3 ½ oz / 1 cup pine nuts, toasted (reserve a few for garnishing)
75 g / 3 oz / ½ cup golden raisins
250 g / 9 oz / 1 ⅔ cups lamb mince
50 ml / 2 fl. oz / ¼ cup sunflower oil
1 onion, finely chopped
2 cloves garlic, minced
1 tsp ground cumin
1 tsp ground coriander
1 tsp ground cinnamon
1 egg, beaten
salt and pepper
sprig of coriander, to garnish

- In a large saucepan, heat the oil over a medium-high heat and sauté the onion and garlic for 2-3 minutes.
- Reduce the heat and add the spices and a little salt, stirring well to coat the onion and garlic.
- Sweat for a couple of minutes then add the lamb mince and increase the heat. Brown for 5-6 minutes, then reduce the heat.
- Stir in the pine nuts and raisins, cover, and cook for 10 minutes.
- Remove from the heat and spread out to cool.
- Meanwhile, preheat the oven to 180°C (160° fan) / 350F / gas 4.
- Roll the pastry out to 1cm thick on a floured surface. Cut rounds using an 8cm in diameter straight-sided cutter.
- Spoon tablespoons of the lamb filling into the centre of the pastry and wet the rims using a little water.
- Fold the pastry over to create a half-moon shape, making sure to create tips at either end.
- Arrange on a lined baking tray and brush with the beaten egg.
- Bake for 18-20 minutes.
- Remove and arrange in a serving dish.
- Garnish with the reserved pine nuts and a sprig of coriander.

575

MAKES 8

Goats' Cheese and Strawberry Balls

- Pulse the pistachios in a food processor until finely ground before tipping into a bowl.
- Divide the goats' cheese into 8 and roll into balls.
- Roll in the ground pistachios to coat evenly.
- Skewer a coriander leaf and strawberry half onto the goats' cheese balls.
- Serve cold.

PREPARATION TIME 10 MINUTES

COOKING TIME 10 MINUTES

INGREDIENTS

FOR THE BALLS
250 g / 9 oz / 2 ½ cups goats' cheese
150 g / 5 oz / 1 ½ cups shelled pistachios
4 strawberries, halved

TO GARNISH
a small handful of picked coriander (cilantro) leaves
a few sprigs of coriander (cilantro) leaves

ALSO NEEDED
cocktail sticks

Roast Tomato Croustades

576

MAKES 24

PREPARATION TIME 10 MINUTES

COOKING TIME 5-10 MINUTES

INGREDIENTS

24 mini croustades cases
12 cherry tomatoes, halved

30 ml / 1 fl. oz / 2 tbsp extra-virgin olive oil
salt and pepper

TO GARNISH
a small bunch of thyme sprigs, halved

- Preheat the oven to 190°C (170° fan) / 375F / gas 5.
- Arrange the croustade cases on a greaseproof paper-lined baking tray.
- Fill each with half of a cherry tomato and drizzle with a few drops of olive oil.
- Season and roast for 8-10 minutes until the tomato starts to colour.
- Remove from the oven and garnish with thyme sprigs before serving.

Mini Poppadoms

577

SERVES 4

PREPARATION TIME 10 MINUTES

COOKING TIME 15-20 MINUTES

INGREDIENTS

FOR THE POPPADOMS
1 l / 1 pint 18 fl. oz / 4 cups vegetable oil, for deep-frying
24 mini poppadom rounds

(available in Indian grocers)

TO GARNISH
225 g / 8 oz / 1 cup hummus
110 g / 4 oz / ½ cup mango chutney
1 green chilli (chili), deseeded and very finely diced
1 red chilli (chili), deseeded and very finely diced

- Heat the vegetable oil in a heavy-based saucepan until hot; you can tell when the oil is hot enough as bubbles appear on a wooden spoon dipped in the hot oil.
- Deep-fry the poppadom rounds using a pair of tongs, one by one, for a few seconds until they bubble and expand.
- Remove to kitchen paper to drain.
- Top the hummus with the diced chillies and serve with the poppadoms alongside the mango chutney.

578

SERVES 4

Potato and Pepper Tapas Bites

PREPARATION TIME 15 MINUTES

COOKING TIME 10-15 MINUTES

INGREDIENTS

FOR THE TAPAS BITES

675 g / 1 lb 8 oz / 4 ½ cups floury
potatoes, peeled and sliced thinly
30 ml / 1 fl. oz / 2 tbsp olive oil
4 large eggs, beaten
2 preserved red peppers, drained
and sliced
a small handful of flat-leaf parsley,
finely chopped
salt and pepper

TO GARNISH
a few sprigs of flat-leaf parsley

ALSO NEEDED
cocktail sticks

- Preheat the oven to 190°C (170° fan) / 375F / gas 5.
- Grease and line the base and sides of a 7" square cake tin with greaseproof paper.
- Cook the potato slices in a saucepan of boiling water for 5 minutes before draining and leaving to steam.
- Whisk the eggs with seasoning and parsley and toss the potato slices with the olive oil, pepper and some seasoning.
- Layer half of the potato mixture in the cake tin and add half of the egg mixture before layering the remaining slices and pouring the rest of the egg on top.
- Bake for 10-12 minutes until the egg is set and starting to colour on top.
- Remove from the oven and leave to cool in the tin before turning out and cutting into squares.
- Garnish with flat-leaf parsley and serve with cocktail

Potato and Tuna Tapas Bites 579

- Substitute the red pepper slices for 225 g / 8 oz / 1 ½ cups canned tuna, drained and flaked before stirring into the beaten egg mixture.

580

MAKES 8

Crayfish Sliders

PREPARATION TIME 10 MINUTES

COOKING TIME 10 MINUTES

INGREDIENTS

FOR THE SLIDERS

8 mini sesame seed burger buns
1 tbsp olive oil
1 tbsp butter
300 g / 10 ½ oz / 2 cups cooked
crayfish tails
110 g / 4 oz / ½ cup tomato chutney
2 gem lettuce, leaves separated and
halved
2 salad tomatoes, sliced
salt and freshly ground black pepper

ALSO NEEDED
8 wooden skewers

- Heat together the oil and butter in a sauté pan set over a moderate heat.
- Season the crayfish well and sauté for 3-4 minutes to warm through, tossing occasionally.
- Drain on kitchen paper and set to one side.
- Top the bottom halves of the burger buns with a piece of lettuce, followed by a slices of tomato.
- Top the top with a couple of crayfish tails and then a teaspoon of tomato chutney.
- Position the tops of the buns in place and skewer before serving.

Mini Chicken Sliders 581

- Grill 2 large chicken breasts and cut into strips to use in place of the crayfish in the sliders.

582

MAKES 12

Mini Tomato and Basil Quiches

- Preheat the oven to 160°C (140° fan) / 325F / gas 3.
- Arrange the tartlet cases on a greaseproof paper-lined baking tray.
- Whisk together the eggs, cream, crème fraîche and seasoning until smooth.
- Dot the tartlet cases with sundried tomato and basil before filling with the egg and cream mixture.
- Bake for 20-25 minutes until the filling is set.
- Remove to a wire rack to cool a little before serving.

PREPARATION TIME 10-15 MINUTES

COOKING TIME 10 MINUTES

INGREDIENTS

12 ready-made mini tartlet cases
125 ml / 4 ½ fl. oz / ½ cup double (heavy) cream
125 ml / 4 ½ fl. oz / ½ cup crème fraîche
3 large eggs
150 g / 5 oz / 1 cup preserved sundried tomatoes, chopped
a small handful of basil leaves, finely chopped

Tomato and Pine Nut Tartlets
 583

- Substitute the chopped basil for 2-3 toasted pine nuts in each tartlet.

584

MAKES 16

Crispy Appetizer Rolls

- Preheat the oven to 190°C (170° fan) / 375F / gas 5.
- Brush the sheets of pastry with melted butter and layer one on top of another, pressing down to seal.
- Cut into 4 squares before cutting each square into 4 and rolling into cigar shapes.
- Arrange on a large greaseproof paper-lined baking tray and bake for 14-18 minutes until golden-brown and crisp.
- Remove from the oven and leave to cool on wire racks before serving.

PREPARATION TIME 5 MINUTES

COOKING TIME 10 MINUTES

INGREDIENTS

4 sheets of filo pastry
55 g / 2 oz / ¼ cup butter, melted

Crispy Sugar Appetizer Rolls
 585

- Sprinkle each sheet with 1 tablespoon of caster (superfine) sugar before sealing, cutting and rolling.

586

SERVES 4

Serrano Ham, Egg and Pepper Canapés

Ham, Egg and Asparagus Canapés

587

- Blanch a large handful of asparagus tips in boiling, salted water for 1 minute. Drain and toss in olive oil before using instead of the green pepper.

Serrano Ham, Egg and Tomato Canapés

588

- Substitute the green pepper for strips of sundried tomato.

PREPARATION TIME 10 MINUTES

COOKING TIME 15-20 MINUTES

INGREDIENTS

FOR THE CANAPÉS
1 baguette, cut into 8 slices
1 tbsp olive oil
4 medium eggs
1 large green pepper, deseeded and cut into strips
100 g / 5 oz / ⅔ cup Serrano ham slices
salt and pepper

TO GARNISH
a pinch of flaked sea salt
a few chive stalks
a few daffodil flowers (optional)

- Cook the eggs in a saucepan of boiling water for 12 minutes.
- Drain and run under cold water for 2 minutes before peeling and halving.
- Heat the olive oil in a small frying pan set over a moderate heat until hot.
- Sauté the strips of pepper for 3-4 minutes until they start to soften and colour.
- Arrange the strips on the slices of baguette accompanied by a half of hard-boiled egg.
- Drape the ham slices on top and garnish with a pinch of salt on top with some chive stalks and daffodil flowers, if using, to the side.

589

MAKES 8

Vegetable Curry Samosas

- Heat the vegetable oil in a large, heavy-based saucepan until hot; you can tell when oil is hot enough as bubbles appear on a wooden spoon dipped in the hot oil.
- Sweat the onion, ginger and garlic for 6-7 minutes, stirring occasionally, before adding the ground spices.
- Stir well and add the potato, seasoning before covering with a lid and reducing the heat.
- Once the potato has softened, add the peas. Season and cool to one side. Heat the groundnut oil in a pan.
- Wet the rim of the wrappers with water and fold into a triangle, sealing one edge, but keeping the case open.
- Fill with the vegetable curry before sealing well.
- Deep-fry in batches for 3-4 minutes flipping once before removing to kitchen paper to drain.
- Heat the oil in a sauté pan. Add the mustard seeds, cook for 15-20 seconds before adding the onion, carrot and

Vegetable Curry Samosas with Raita

590

- Substitute the garnish for raita; stir plain yoghurt with mint, coriander, lemon juice and seasoning.

PREPARATION TIME 15-20 MINUTES

COOKING TIME 25-30 MINUTES

INGREDIENTS

FOR THE SAMOSAS
1 l / 1 pint 16 fl. oz / 4 cups vegetable oil, for deep-frying
225 g / 8 oz / 1 ½ cup plain (all purpose) flour
110 ml / 4 fl. oz / ½ cup warm water
extra plain flour, for kneading
½ tbsp dried active yeast
15-30 ml / ½-1 fl. oz / 1-2 tbsp olive oil
½ tsp salt
½ tsp caster (superfine) sugar

TO GARNISH
55 ml / 2 fl. oz / ¼ cup sunflower oil
1 onion, diced
1 carrot, peeled and thinly sliced
2 red peppers, deseeded and chopped
1 tsp brown mustard seeds
salt and pepper

591

SERVES 4

Coconut Milk Turkey Skewers

- Whisk together the coconut milk, sesame oil, fish sauce, lime juice and sugar until smooth.
- Add the turkey breast, stir well, cover and chill for at least 45 minutes.
- Preheat the grill to hot.
- Remove the turkey from the marinade and drain on kitchen paper.
- Thread onto the skewers, separated by red pepper and mango cubes.
- Brush with the marinade and grill for 8-10 minutes, turning frequently, until the turkey is coloured and firm yet slightly springy to the touch.
- Remove from the grill and serve immediately with rocket on the side.

Beef Coconut Milk Skewers

592

- Substitute the turkey breast for cubes of sirloin steak; grill for 6-10 minutes depending on desired level of cooking for the beef.

PREPARATION TIME 15 MINUTES

COOKING TIME 15-20 MINUTES

INGREDIENTS

FOR THE SKEWERS
600 g / 1 lb 5 oz / 4 cups turkey breast, cut into 1" cubes
250 ml / 9 fl. oz / 1 cup coconut milk
1 tbsp fish sauce
1 tbsp dark soy sauce
1 tbsp sesame oil
1 tsp soft light brown sugar
1 lime, juiced
1 red pepper, deseeded and cut into even squares
1 mango, destoned and cubed

TO GARNISH
a large handful of rocket (arugula)

ALSO NEEDED
8 wooden skewers, soaked in water for 15 minutes

593

SERVES 4

Mixed Vegetable Toasts

PREPARATION TIME 15 MINUTES

COOKING TIME 15-20 MINUTES

....

INGREDIENTS

FOR THE TOASTS
1 baguette, cut into 8 slices
75 ml / 3 fl. oz / ⅓ cup olive oil
1 green pepper, deseeded and
finely diced
1 red pepper, deseeded and
finely diced
1 large onion, finely diced
1 courgette (zucchini), finely diced
salt and pepper

TO GARNISH
a small handful of flat-leaf parsley,
finely chopped
a small handful of sage leaves

- Heat 2 tablespoons of the olive oil in a large sauté pan set over a moderate heat until hot.
- Sweat the onion and peppers with a little salt for 7-8 minutes, stirring and tossing occasionally.
- Transfer to a plate and set to one side.
- Wipe the pan clean before adding another 2 tablespoons of oil and sautéing the courgette for 5-6 minutes, tossing occasionally.
- Preheat the grill to hot brush the slices of baguette with the remaining olive oil and grill for 1 minute.
- Add the onion and peppers into the pan with the courgette to warm through briefly, adjusting the seasoning to taste if necessary.
- Spoon onto the baguette toasts and arrange on serving plates.
- Garnish with chopped parsley and sage leaves.

Courgette, Aubergine and Tomato Toasts   594

- Substitute peppers for vine tomatoes as well as adding ½ diced aubergine (eggplant).

595

SERVES 4

Chicken, Lettuce and Mayonnaise Canapés

PREPARATION TIME 10-15
MINUTES

COOKING TIME 15-20 MINUTES

....

INGREDIENTS

FOR THE CANAPES
1 mulitseed baguette, cut into 8 slices
30 ml / 1 fl. oz / 2 tbsp olive oil
1 tbsp butter
110 g / 4 oz / ½ cup mayonnaise
2 large skinless chicken breasts,
diced
1 tbsp plain yoghurt
½ lemon, juiced
½ small oafleaf lettuce head,
shredded
salt and pepper

TO GARNISH
a small handful of beansprouts
a few dandelion leaves (optional)

- Heat together the oil and butter in a large sauté pan set over a moderate heat.
- Season the chicken before sautéing for 7-8 minutes until golden-brown in colour on the outside and cooked through.
- Tip into a mixing bowl and leave to cool for a few minutes before adding the mayonnaise, yoghurt, lemon juice and lettuce.
- Stir well to combine before adjusting the seasoning to taste.
- Spoon onto the top of the slices of baguette before arranging on serving plates.
- Garnish with beansprouts on top and dandelion leaves if desired.

Chicken, Mayonnaise and Bacon Canapés   596

- Cook 75 g / 3 oz / ½ cup diced pancetta at the same time as the chicken; mix with the mayonnaise.

597

SERVES 4

Olive and Pesto Vol-au-Vents

Spinach Pesto Vol-au-Vents

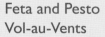

598

- Substitute the basil leaves for 75 g / 3 oz / 1 ½ cups baby spinach leaves.

Feta and Pesto Vol-au-Vents

599

- Substitute the olives with cubes of feta cheese.

PREPARATION TIME 10-15 MINUTES

COOKING TIME 10 MINUTES

INGREDIENTS

12 ready-made vol-au-vent cases
110 g / 4 oz / ⅔ cup pitted black olives
30 g / 1 oz / ½ cup picked basil leaves
125 ml / 4 ½ fl. oz / ½ cup extra-virgin olive oil
30 g / 1 oz / 2 tbsp pine nuts, toasted
55 g / 2 oz / ½ cup Parmesan, grated
1 clove of garlic, crushed
salt and pepper

- Preheat the oven to 190°C (170° fan) / 375F / gas 5.
- Grease and line a large baking tray with greaseproof paper.
- Prepare the pesto by placing the basil, pine nuts, extra-virgin olive oil, garlic and a seasoning in a food processor.
- Blitz until smooth.
- Add the Parmesan and pulse until a thicker consistency is reached.
- Arrange the vol-au-vent cases on the baking tray and spoon the pesto inside before dotting with black olive.
- Bake for 8-10 minutes until the vol-au-vents are golden at the edges.
- Remove to a wire rack to cool before serving.

Scrambled Egg and Mushroom Toasts

600

SERVES 4

PREPARATION TIME 10-15 MINUTES

COOKING TIME 10-15 MINUTES

....

INGREDIENTS

FOR THE TOASTS
1 baguette, cut into 8 slices
30 ml / 1 fl. oz / 2 tbsp olive oil
1 tbsp butter
225 g / 8 oz / 3 cups mixed wild mushrooms, brushed clean
4 large eggs, beaten
salt and pepper

TO GARNISH
a few chive stalks, finely chopped
a small handful of frisée lettuce

- Heat the olive oil and butter together in a large sauté pan set over a moderate heat.
- Sauté the mushrooms with a little seasoning, tossing occasionally, for 4-5 minutes until they start to colour.
- Reduce the heat a little and add the beaten egg, cooking until set.
- Adjust the seasoning to taste before spooning onto the slices of baguette.
- Arrange on serving plates and garnish with chopped chives and a little frisée.

Mushroom and Fried Egg Toasts

601

- Fry 8 small eggs in a little olive oil and use to top the mushrooms on the toast.

Serrano Ham and Asparagus Toasts

602

SERVES 4

PREPARATION TIME 10-15 MINUTES

COOKING TIME 15 MINUTES

....

INGREDIENTS

FOR THE TOASTS
1 flute baguette, cut into 8 slices
200 g / 7 oz / 1 cups asparagus spears, end removed and chopped
150 g / 5 oz / 1 cup Serrano ham, sliced
30 ml / 1 fl. oz / 2 tbsp olive oil
1 onion
salt and pepper

TO GARNISH
55 g / 2 oz / ½ cup Cheddar, grated
a few cherry tomatoes, halved
a small handful of frisèe lettuce

- Heat the olive oil in a large frying pan set over a medium heat until hot.
- Sweat the onion and ham with a little seasoning until the onion is soft and translucent; 5-6 minutes.
- Add the asparagus and cover the pan with a lid, reducing the heat a little as you do.
- Cook, stirring occasionally, for 3-4 minutes until the asparagus is tender.
- Adjust the seasoning to taste and set to one side to cool a little.
- Toast the baguette slices under a hot grill for 1 minute before topping with the asparagus and ham.
- Sprinkle the tops with grated Cheddar and garnish with cherry tomato and frisée before serving.

Serrano Ham and Pepper Toasts
603

- Substitute the asparagus for sliced, preserved piquillo peppers that have been drained well.

604

SERVES 4

Crab, Tomato and Rocket Toasts

- Half the slices of tomato and use to top the baguette slices.
- Combine the crab, lemon juice, olive oil and seasoning in a mixing bowl and stir well.
- Spoon on top of the tomato on the baguette slices and garnish with a few rocket leaves.
- Serve cold.

PREPARATION TIME 10 MINUTES

COOKING TIME 10 MINUTES

INGREDIENTS

FOR THE TOASTS
1 flute baguette, cut into 8 slices
2 salad tomatoes, sliced thinly
450 g / 1 lb / 3 cups white king crab meat
1 tbsp olive oil
1 lemon, juiced
salt and pepper

TO GARNISH
a large handful of rocket (arugula)

Crab, Tomato and Spinach Toasts 605

- Top the toasts with baby spinach leaves instead of using rocket.

606

SERVES 4

Banana and Bacon Mini Skewers

- Preheat the grill to hot.
- Brush the banana halves with melted butter and wrap in streaky bacon before arranging on a grilling tray.
- Grill for 4-5 minutes, turning occasionally, until the bacon is cooked and coloured all over.
- Remove to serving plates and garnish with thyme before serving.

PREPARATION TIME 5 MINUTES

COOKING TIME 10 MINUTES

INGREDIENTS

FOR THE SKEWERS
55 g / 2 oz / ¼ cup butter, melted and cooled
4 small bananas, peeled and halved
8 rashers of streaky bacon

TO GARNISH
a few sprigs of thyme

Banana, Bacon and Prune Skewers 607

- Tuck a dried prune between the bacon and banana before grilling.

608

SERVES 4

Gorgonzola and Bacon Rolls

Gorgonzola, Walnut and Bacon Rolls

 609

- Tuck a walnut half inside each roll before grilling.

Gorgonzola, Bacon and Raisin Rolls

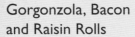 **610**

- Tuck a few raisins inside each roll before grilling.

PREPARATION TIME 5 MINUTES

COOKING TIME 10 MINUTES

INGREDIENTS

FOR THE ROLLS
175 g / 6 oz / 1 ¾ cups Gorgonzola, cut into 12 cubes
6 rashers of back bacon

TO GARNISH
12 picked flat-leaf parsley leaves

ALSO NEEDED
12 cocktail sticks

- Preheat the grill to hot before grilling the bacon for 4-5 minutes, turning once until cooked.
- Remove from the grill and half lengthways.
- Wrap a slice of bacon around the cubes of Gorgonzola and secure using a cocktail stick before arranging on a greaseproof paper-lined baking tray.
- Grill for 1 minute until the cheese starts to melt.
- Remove from the grill and arrange on a serving platter before garnishing each with a leaf of parsley.

611

SERVES 4

Cheese and Ham Croquettes

- Cook the potato in a large saucepan of salted, boiling water until tender; 15-20 minutes.
- Drain and leave to steam for 3 minutes before mashing with the butter, Cheddar,, cornflour and seasoning until smooth.
- Add the ham and stir well to incorporate.
- Preheat the oven to 190°C (170° fan) / 375F / gas 5.
- Shape into croquettes before dusting in the flour, shaking off any excess.
- Dip in the beaten egg and coat in breadcrumbs before arranging on a greaseproof paper-lined baking tray.
- Bake for 20-25 minutes until golden-brown in colour on the outside.
- Remove to a wire rack to cool before garnishing with grated Cheddar and the herbs.
- Serve with cocktail sticks.

Cheese, Chilli and Ham Croquettes

612

- Add a small handful of finely chopped jalapeño chilis to the croquette mixture.

PREPARATION TIME 15 MINUTES

COOKING TIME 20-25 MINUTES

INGREDIENTS

900 g / 2 lb / 6 cups floury potatoes, peeled and diced
225 g / 8 oz / 2 cups golden breadcrumbs
150 g / 5 oz / 1 cup cooked ham, diced
110 g / 4 oz / ½ cup butter, melted
75 g / 3 oz / ¾ cup Cheddar, grated
75 g / 3 oz / ½ cup plain (all purpose) flour
30 g / 1 oz / 2 tbsp cornflour (cornstarch)
2 large eggs, beaten
salt and pepper
30 g / 1 oz / ¼ cup Cheddar, grated
a few sprigs of thyme
a few sprigs of flat-leaf parsley, finely chopped
cocktail sticks

613

SERVES 4

Monkfish Fritters

- Heat the groundnut oil in a large, heavy-based saucepan until hot; you can tell when the oil is hot enough as bubbles appear on a wooden spoon dipped in the hot oil.
- Briefly whisk together the self-raising flour, cornflour, water and seasoning until you have a batter.
- Dry the monkfish really well before dusting in the cornflour and seasoning well.
- Dip into the batter and deep-fry in batches until golden and crisp; 2-3 minutes.
- Remove with a slotted spoon to kitchen paper to drain.
- Serve with some mixed salad leaves and lime wedges.

Monkfish and Mango Fritters

614

- Dice 2 mangoes and toss with the juice of 1 lime and some seasoning; serve alongside the fritters instead of salad leaves.

PREPARATION TIME 10-15 MINUTES

COOKING TIME 15 MINUTES

INGREDIENTS

FOR THE FRITTERS
1 l / 1 pint 16 fl. oz / 4 cups groundnut oil, for deep-frying
450 g / 1 lb / 3 cups monkfish tail, trimmed and cubed
30 g / 1 oz / 2 tbsp cornflour (cornstarch)
salt and pepper

FOR THE BATTER
125 ml / 4 ½ fl. oz / ½ cup cold water
110 g / 4 oz / ⅔ cup self-raising flour
1 tbsp cornflour (cornstarch)
salt and pepper

TO GARNISH
75 g / 3 oz / 1 cup mixed salad leaves
1 lime, cut into wedges

SERVES 4

615

Tuna and Potato Fritters

PREPARATION TIME 15 MINUTES

COOKING TIME 35 MINUTES

INGREDIENTS

450 g / 1 lb / 3 cups Maris Piper
potatoes, peeled and cut into chunks
50 g butter
200 g / 7 oz / 1 ¼ cups canned tuna,
drained
100 g / 3 ½ oz / ½ cup dried
breadcrumbs
1 l / 1 pint 16 fl. oz / 4 cups vegetable
oil for deep-frying
salt and pepper
sprigs of rosemary, to garnish
cocktail sticks, to garnish

- Cook the potatoes in a large saucepan of boiling, salted water until tender; roughly 20 minutes.
- Drain and allow to cool before mashing with the butter, tuna and seasoning.
- Heat the oil in a large, heavy-based saucepan; you can tell when the oil is hot enough as bubbles appear on a wooden spoon dipped in the hot oil.
- Take tablespoons of the mixture and roll into balls between your palms.
- Roll in the breadcrumbs to coat evenly.
- Deep-fry in batches until golden brown and crispy on the outside.
- Drain on kitchen paper and serve in small serving pots with sprigs of rosemary as a garnish and cocktail sticks alongside.

Tuna and Gruyère Fritters

616

- Stir 50 g / 2 oz / ½ cup grated Gruyère into the fritter mixture.

MAKES 8

617

Chicken and Corn Tartlet

PREPARATION TIME 10 MINUTES

COOKING TIME 15 MINUTES

INGREDIENTS

FOR THE TARTLETS
300 g / 10 ½ oz ready-made
shortcrust pastry
a little plain (all purpose) flour
2 large cooked chicken breasts, diced
150 g / 5 oz / ⅔ cup canned
sweetcorn
110 g / 4 oz / ½ cup mayonnaise
½ gem lettuce, shredded
salt and pepper

TO GARNISH
1 gem lettuce, leaves separated
4 cherry tomatoes, halved

- Preheat the oven to 180°C (160° fan) / 350F / gas 4.
- Roll the pastry out on a lightly floured surface to ½ cm thickness.
- Cut 8 rounds of pastry and use to line 8 individual 2" fluted tartlet cases.
- Trim any excess, overhanging pastry.
- Blind-bake for 12-15 minutes until golden at the edges before removing to a wire rack to cool.
- Discard the greaseproof paper and baking beans.
- Stir together the mayonnaise, sweetcorn, lettuce and diced chicken breasts in a mixing bowl, seasoning to taste.
- Spoon into the tartlet cases and serve on plates garnished with gem lettuce and cherry tomato halves.

Tuna and Sweetcorn Tartlets

618

- Substitute the chicken for 225 g / 8 oz / 1 can of canned, drained tuna chunks.

619

MAKES 4

Tomato-Topped Mini Quiches

Artichoke Mini Quiches   620

- Roughly chop 3 canned artichoke hearts that have been drained and stir into the quiche mixture instead of diced tomatoes.

Goats' Cheese-Topped   621
Mini Quiches

- Substitute the tomato tops for thin rounds of goats' cheese.

PREPARATION TIME 10-15 MINUTES

COOKING TIME 10-15 MINUTES

....

INGREDIENTS

FOR THE QUICHES
250 ml / 9 fl. oz / 1 cup whole milk
250 ml / 9 fl. oz / 1 cup crème fraîche
30 g / 1 oz / 2 tbsp butter, softened
2 spring onions (scallions), finely sliced
4 large eggs
4 vine tomatoes
salt and pepper

TO GARNISH
a large handful of rocket (arugula)

- Preheat the oven to 160°C (140° fan) / 325F / gas 3.
- Remove the tops from the tomatoes and reserve to one side.
- Deseed two of the tomatoes and finely dice before mixing with the spring onions.
- Whisk the eggs in a large mixing bowl with the milk, crème fraîche and seasoning.
- Stir in the diced tomato and spring onion mixture.
- Grease 4 holes of a large muffin tin with the butter before pouring in the quiche mixture.
- Bake for 25-30 minutes until the quiches are set and golden on top.
- Remove from the oven and turn out before topping with the reserved tomato tops and serving.

622

MAKES 4

Ham, Tomato and Mozzarella Tartlets

PREPARATION TIME 10-15
MINUTES

COOKING TIME 10-15 MINUTES

INGREDIENTS

FOR THE TARTLETS
250 g / 9 oz ready-made shortcrust
pastry
a little plain (all purpose) flour,
for dusting
100 g / 3 ½ oz / 1 cup cherry
tomatoes, halved
50 g / 2 oz / ⅓ cup ham slices
a large handful of picked basil leaves
8 baby mozzarella balls, drained
salt and pepper

TO GARNISH
a few sprigs of flat-leaf parsley

- Preheat the oven to 180°C (160° fan) / 350F / gas 4.
- Roll the pastry out on a lightly floured surface to ½ cm thickness.
- Cut 4 rounds of pastry and use to line 4 individual 4" tartlet cases.
- Prick the bases with a fork and trim some of the excess pastry.
- Line with greaseproof paper and fill with baking beans.
- Blind-bake for 12-15 minutes until golden-brown in colour at the edges.
- Remove from the oven to a wire rack and discard the greaseproof paper and baking beans.
- Once cool, fill with the ham, mozzarella and cherry tomato halves before tucking basil leaves amongst the filling.
- Garnish with parsley before serving.

Chorizo, Tomato and Cheddar Tartlets

623

- Substitute the ham for diced, cooked chorizo and the mozzarella for Cheddar.

624

SERVES 4

Sundried Tomato-Stuffed Chicken Breasts

PREPARATION TIME 10 MINUTES

COOKING TIME 20 MINUTES

INGREDIENTS

FOR THE ROLLS
225 g / 8 oz / 1 cup plain (all purpose)
flour
2 large skinless chicken breasts,
butterflied
110 g / 4 oz / ⅔ cup preserved
sundried tomatoes, drained
a small handful of basil leaves
salt and pepper

TO GARNISH
a handful of basil leaf sprigs

ALSO NEEDED
cocktail sticks

- Lay the chicken breasts on a square of cling film and season.
- Place a few basil leaves in the centre and top with sundried tomatoes.
- Roll the chicken breast over to enclose before rolling into a cylinder inside the cling film.
- Tie one end securely with kitchen string and holding that end, roll the other end on a flat surface to tighten.
- Secure the untied end with kitchen string and place in a heavy-based saucepan.
- Cover with cold water and heat over a moderate heat.
- Reduce the heat and cook for 15 minutes before turning off the heat and letting the chicken cool in the water.
- Chill for 2 hours.
- Unwrap and slice into portions before pricking with cocktail sticks and garnishing with basil sprigs.

Mozzarella-Stuffed Chicken Breasts

625

- Substitute the sundried tomato with slices of mozzarella cheese before wrapping.

626

SERVES 4

Salmon and Herb Appetizers

- Sift together the flours and baking powder.
- Combine the egg yolk, milk and yeast in a jug.
- Add the wet ingredients to the dry and whisk. Add the melted butter and stir well.
- Whisk the egg whites with a pinch of salt until soft peaks form then fold into the batter.
- Coat a frying pan with sunflower oil and heat.
- Cook generous tablespoons of the batter in the pan until set on the bottom and you start to see bubbles on top.
- Flip and fry for 15 seconds. Heat vegetable oil in a pan.
- Season the salmon and cook skin-side first until the dish is opaque. Flip and cook for a further 2-3 minutes. Remove skin and cut into 8.
- Stir together the chopped dill, gherkin and sour cream before spooning on top of the blinis.
- Top with salmon, dill sprigs and pink peppercorns.

Tuna and Herb Appetizers

627

- Substitute the salmon fillet for tuna steak, seared in a hot pan for 2 minutes on both sides.

PREPARATION TIME 15 MINUTES

COOKING TIME 20-25 MINUTES

INGREDIENTS

175 ml / 6 fl. oz / ⅔ cup whole milk, warmed
75 g / 3 oz / ½ cup plain (all purpose) flour
75 g / 3 oz / ½ cup buckwheat flour
30 ml / 1 fl. oz / 2 tbsp sunflower oil
1 tbsp butter, melted and cooled
½ tsp dried active yeast
½ tsp baking powder
1 medium egg yolk
1 medium egg white
a pinch of salt
30 ml / 1 fl. oz / 2 tbsp sunflower oil
225 g / 9 oz salmon fillet
125 g / 4 ½ oz / ½ cup sour cream
4 baby gherkins in vinegar, drained and diced
a few sprigs of dill, chopped
½ tsp pink peppercorns, crushed

628

SERVES 4

Lobster, Duck and Pineapple Skewers

- Cook the lobster in a saucepan of boiling water for 12 minutes before draining and refreshing in iced water.
- Remove once cool enough to handle and crack the lobster shell to extract the claw, body and tail meat.
- Cut the tail meat into 6 and reserve with the claws.
- Heat a dry frying pan over a medium heat, season the duck and place skin-side down in the pan.
- Render the fat until the skin is golden, thin and crisp before flipping and cooking for a further 8-10 minutes.
- Remove from the pan and leave to rest for 5 minutes before cutting into 8 chunks.
- Preheat the grill to hot.
- Thread two chunks of pineapple onto the skewers with the duck and lobster between them.
- Grill for 2-3 minutes until the pineapple starts to caramelise. Remove and garnish with chopped dill.

Lobster, Duck and Mango Skewers

629

- Substitute the pineapple for 1" cubes of mango on the skewers.

PREPARATION TIME 10-15 MINUTES

COOKING TIME 25 MINUTES

INGREDIENTS

FOR THE SKEWERS
1 pineapple, peeled, cored and cut into 16 1" cubes
2 lb fresh lobster, frozen beforehand for 10 minutes
225 g / 8 oz duck breast, trimmed, scored and cut into 8
salt and pepper

TO GARNISH
a few sprigs of dill, chopped

ALSO NEEDED
8 wooden skewers, soaked in water for 15 minutes

630

SERVES 4

Majorcan Quail Egg Canapés

Duck and Prosciutto Canapés

631

- Use duck eggs instead of quail eggs and substitute the chorizo for folded slices of prosciutto.

Quail and Black Pudding Canapés

632

- Substitute the slices of chorizo for slices of black pudding, grilling them separately for 2 minutes before using.

PREPARATION TIME 10 MINUTES

COOKING TIME 10 MINUTES

....

INGREDIENTS

FOR THE CANAPÉS
½ flute baguette, cut into 8 slices
30 ml / 1 fl. oz / 2 tbsp olive oil
8 quail eggs
8 slices of chorizo
salt and pepper

TO GARNISH
a large handful of alfalfa sprouts

- Preheat the grill to hot and top the slices of baguette with a slice of chorizo.
- Toast for 1 minute until the chorizo starts to curl upwards.
- Remove from the grill and set on a plate covered with the alfalfa sprouts.
- Heat 1 tablespoon of the oil in a frying pan set over a medium heat.
- Fry 4 eggs of the eggs with some seasoning, covering with a lid once the white has set underneath and starts to crisp.
- Remove the lid after 45 seconds and move the fried eggs to kitchen paper to drain.
- Add another tablespoon of oil to the pan and fry the remaining eggs in the same manner, draining on kitchen paper.
- Sit the fried eggs on top of the chorizo before serving.

633

MAKES 6

Anchovy and Potato Mini Quiches

- Preheat the oven to 160°C (140° fan) / 325F / gas 3.
- Roll the pastry out on a lightly floured surface.
- Cut 6 rounds of pastry and line 6 3" fluted cases.
- Arrange the tartlet cases on a baking tray and place the new potatoes on it as well.
- Whisk together the cream, creme fraîche, eggs and seasoning in a mixing bowl.
- Divide the diced potato between the tartlet cases and fill with the egg filling.
- Bake the new potatoes and quiches for 45-50 minutes until the filling is deep-golden brown in colour.
- Remove from the oven before turning out the quiches and arranging on a platter.
- Slice the new potatoes and arrange on the platter.
- Top with the halved anchovy fillets, lime zest and chilli flakes before serving.

Anchovy, Potato and Chorizo Quiches

634

- Add 55 g / 2 oz / ⅓ cup diced chorizo to the quiches before baking.

PREPARATION TIME 15 MINUTES

COOKING TIME 15-20 MINUTES

INGREDIENTS

FOR THE QUICHES
300 g / 10 ½ oz ready-made shortcrust pastry
a little plain (all purpose) flour, for dusting
250 ml / 9 fl. oz / 1 cup double (heavy) cream
250 ml / 9 fl. oz / 1 cup crème fraîche
225 g / 8 oz / 1 ½ cups white potatoes, finely diced
3 medium eggs
salt and potato

TO GARNISH
3-4 new potatoes
6 preserved anchovy fillets, halved
1 lime, zest pared and julienned
½ tsp red chilli (chili) flakes

ALSO NEEDED
cocktail sticks

635

SERVES 4

Prosciutto and Cream Cheese Rolls

- Stir two thirds of the chopped herbs for the garnish into the olive oil and set to one side.
- Overlap two slices of prosciutto together on a flat surface and sprinkle with a little of the chopped herbs.
- Spoon a generous tablespoon of cream cheese in the centre and season well.
- Roll into a cylinder making sure the cream cheese is evenly distributed inside.
- Cut in half and arrange on a serving platter, garnish with chopped herbs, chive stalks and the herb olive oil.

Cream Cheese and Pesto Rolls

636

- Stir 30 g / 1 oz / 2 tbsp basil pesto into the cream cheese before using as a filling for the rolls.

PREPARATION TIME 15 MINUTES

COOKING TIME 10-15 MINUTES

INGREDIENTS

FOR THE ROLLS
16 slices of prosciutto
225 g / 8 oz / 1 cup cream cheese
a few chive stalks, finely chopped
a few sprigs of chervil, chopped
a few sprigs of sage, chopped
salt and pepper

TO GARNISH
175 ml / 6 fl. oz / ⅔ cup extra-virgin olive oil
a few chive stalks, half of them finely chopped, half left whole
a few sprigs of flat-leaf parsley, finely chopped
a few sprigs of chervil, finely chopped

ALSO NEEDED
wooden skewers

637

SERVES 4

Bacon-Wrapped Mango Cubes

PREPARATION TIME 10-15
MINUTES

COOKING TIME 5 MINUTES

INGREDIENTS

FOR THE CUBES
4 slices of streaky bacon, halved
1 large mango, destoned and cut
into 8 1" cubes
½ orange, segmented

ALSO NEEDED
cocktail sticks

- Preheat the grill to hot.
- Wrap the mango cubes in pieces of streak bacon and arrange on a grilling tray.
- Grill until the bacon is cooked and coloured all over.
- Cut 4 orange segments in half and thread onto the wrapped mango cubes using a cocktail stick.
- Serve immediately.

Mango and Grape Bacon Wraps **638**

- Substitute the orange segment on top for a seedless red or black grape.

639

SERVES 4

Squid with Garlic and Parsley

PREPARATION TIME 10 MINUTES

COOKING TIME 10 MINUTES

CHILLING TIME 30 MINUTES

INGREDIENTS

FOR THE SQUID BROCHETTES
55 ml / 2 fl. oz / ¼ cup olive oil
2 frozen squid tubes, thawed
1 frozen squid tentacle, thawed
and chopped
2 cloves of garlic, minced
1 tbsp honey
½ tsp dried parsley
salt and pepper

TO GARNISH
75 g / 3 oz / 1 cup frisée lettuce
30 g / 1 oz / 2 tbsp flaked (slivered)
almonds

ALSO NEEDED
8 wooden skewers, soaked in water
for 15 minutes

- Cut the squid tubes in half so that you have 4 flat pieces before cutting those pieces in half.
- Whisk the dried parsley, garlic and olive oil in a mixing bowl before adding the squid tube and tentacles.
- Cover and chill for 30 minutes.
- Preheat the grill to hot and line a baking tray with greaseproof paper.
- Remove the squid from the marinade.
- Thread on the wooden skewers and brush the tentacle parts with honey before threading onto the skewers.
- Top with flaked almonds and arrange flat on the baking tray.
- Grill for 3-4 minutes, until the squid tubes are coloured on top.
- Remove from the grill and serve with frisée lettuce in bowls.

Squid and Chilli Brochettes **640**

- Add 2 deseeded and finely diced red chillies (chilis) to the marinade before threading onto the skewers and grilling.

641

MAKES 6

Cheese and Spinach Mini Tartlets

Mixed Pepper and Cheese Tartlets

642

- Substitute the spinach with a mixture of ½ a diced green, red and yellow pepper.

Three Cheese Tartlets

643

- Substitute the spinach for the same weight of grated Gruyère and Cheddar.

PREPARATION TIME 10 MINUTES

COOKING TIME 15-20 MINUTES

INGREDIENTS

300 g / 10 ½ oz ready-made shortcrust pastry
a little plain (all purpose) flour, for dusting
250 ml / 9 fl. oz / 1 cup whole milk
250 ml / 9 fl. oz / 1 cup crème fraîche
200 g / 7 oz / 2 cups feta, cubed
50 g / 2 oz / 1 cup baby spinach leaves
3 large eggs
salt and pepper

- Preheat the oven to 180°C (160° fan) / 350F / gas 4.
- Roll the pastry out on a lightly floured surface to ½ cm thickness.
- Cut 6 rounds of pastry and use to line 6 individual 3" mince pie or fluted tartlet cases.
- Prick the bases with a fork and trim some of the excess pastry.
- Line with greaseproof paper and fill with baking beans.
- Blind-bake for 12-14 minutes until golden-brown in colour at the edges.
- Remove from the oven and discard the greaseproof paper and baking beans.
- Reduce the oven to 160°C (140° fan) / 325F / gas 3.
- Whisk together the eggs, milk and creme fraîche with seasoning in a mixing bowl.
- Arrange the feta and spinach in the cases and fill with the egg mixture.
- Bake for 25-30 minutes until the tops are golden-brown in colour and the filling is set.
- Remove to a wire rack to cool before turning out and serving.

644

SERVES 4

Lamb and Cumin Keftas

PREPARATION TIME 10 MINUTES

COOKING TIME 20 MINUTES

INGREDIENTS

500 g / 1 lb 2 oz / 3 ⅓ cups minced lamb
1 tsp ground coriander
2 tsp ground cumin
½ tsp chilli (chili) powder
1 egg yolk
small handful mint leaves, chopped
salt and black pepper
sprig of mint leaves, to garnish
lemon wedges, to garnish
1 tbsp sesame seeds, to garnish
wooden skewers, soaked in water for 30 minutes beforehand

- Preheat the oven to 220°C (200° fan) / 425F / gas 7.
- Line a baking sheet with baking parchment.
- In a large bowl, combine the lamb, spices, seasoning, chopped mint and egg yolk until well combined.
- Using oiled hands, take tablespoons of the mixture and roll between your palms to make balls.
- Thread two balls onto two skewers, piercing the balls through their centres with the skewers.
- Bake the skewers for 12-15 minutes until golden brown in colour.
- Remove and allow to rest for a few minutes before placing in serving bowls.
- Sprinkle with the sesame seeds and garnish with lemon wedges and a sprig of mint leaves before serving.

645

MAKES 12

Potato, Chive and Ham Appetizers

PREPARATION TIME 10-15 MINUTES

COOKING TIME 20-25 MINUTES

INGREDIENTS

FOR THE APPETIZERS
675 g / 1 lb / 8 oz / 4 ½ cups floury potatoes, peeled and diced
110 g / 4 oz / ½ cup butter, melted
100 g / 3 ½ oz / ⅔ cup cooked ham, diced
1 tbsp cornflour
a small bunch of chives, finely chopped
salt and pepper

TO GARNISH
a few chive stalks

ALSO NEEDED
cocktail sticks

- Cook the potatoes in a saucepan of salted, boiling water until tender; 15-20 minutes usually.
- Preheat the oven to 190°C (170° fan) / 375F / gas 5.
- Drain the potatoes and leave to steam dry for 3 minutes before mashing with the butter and cornflour until smooth.
- Add the ham, chives and seasoning and stir well to incorporate.
- Shape into cakes between your palms and arrange in a 12-hole cupcake tray.
- Bake for 15-18 minutes until golden and crisp before removing to a wire rack to cool.
- Serve with chive stalks and cocktail sticks on the side.

MAKES 12

Savoury Vegetable Madeleines

- Preheat the oven to 180°C (160° fan) / 350F / gas 4.
- Grease a 12-hole madeleine tray.
- Beat together the eggs, Parmesan, salt and pepper in a large mixing bowl until thick and shiny.
- Fold in the flour, 25 g at a time, as well as the baking powder.
- Once all the flour has been added, fold in the melted butter until incorporated.
- Spoon into the moulds, leaving them about three-quarters full with the batter.
- Bake for 12-14 minutes until golden and risen.
- Remove and allow them to cool in the tray for a few minutes before turning out onto a wire rack to finish cooling.
- Garnish with a sprig of bay leaves.

PREPARATION TIME 15 MINUTES

COOKING TIME 15 MINUTES

INGREDIENTS

125 g / 4 ½ oz / 1 ¼ cups Parmesan, finely grated
115 g / 4 oz / ½ cup unsalted butter, melted and cooled
100 g / 3 ½ oz / ⅔ cup plain (all purpose) flour, sifted
50 g / 2 oz / ⅓ cup pitted black olives, chopped
½ courgette (zucchini), diced
½ carrot, peeled and diced
½ tsp baking powder
salt and pepper
a sprig of bay leaves

Butifarra and Rose Appetizers

647

SERVES 4

PREPARATION TIME 5-10 MINUTES

COOKING TIME 5-10 MINUTES

INGREDIENTS

FOR THE SAUSAGE
300 g / 10 ½ oz / 2 cups raw butifarra sausage

a large handful of red rose petals

ALSO NEEDED
cocktail sticks

- Preheat the oven to 190°C (170° fan) / 375F / gas 5.
- Roast the sausage on a baking tray for 18-20 minutes until golden on the outside.
- Remove and cut into bite-sized pieces before tossing with the rose petals in a mixing bowl.
- Spoon into serving dishes and skewer with cocktail sticks before serving.

Stuffed Cherry Tomatoes

648

SERVES 4

PREPARATION TIME 15 MINUTES

COOKING TIME 10 MINUTES

INGREDIENTS

FOR THE TOMATOES
8 vine cherry tomatoes, tops removed and reserved
110 g / 4 oz / ½ cup cream cheese

½ cucumber, peeled and cut into 8 slices
a small handful of basil leaves, cut chiffonade
salt and pepper

TO GARNISH
30 g / 1 oz / ¼ cup pine nuts, toasted
30 g / 1 oz / ¼ cup flaked (slivered) almonds, toasted

- Beat the cream cheese until soft in a mixing bowl before adding the basil and seasoning.
- Stir briefly and set to one side.
- Deseeded the tomatoes before filling with the cream cheese.
- Sit on top of the cucumber slices and garnish with the pine nuts and flaked almonds.
- Replace half of the tomato tops before serving.

649

SERVES 4

Strawberry and Almond Celery

PREPARATION TIME 10 MINUTES

COOKING TIME 10 MINUTES

INGREDIENTS

FOR THE CELERY
4 celery stalks, peeled and halved
250 ml / 9 fl. oz / 1 cup whipping cream
150 g / 5 oz / 1 ½ cups strawberries, hulled and diced

TO GARNISH
30 g / 1 oz / 2 tbsp flaked (slivered) almonds
a few strawberries, hulled and diced

- Whip the cream until soft peaks form then stir through the diced strawberries.
- Cover and chill for 15 minutes before spooning into the celery stalks.
- Arrange on a serving plate and scatter the flaked almonds on top of the celery before garnishing the plate with diced strawberries.

Celery with Raisin Cream

650

- Fold 75 g / 3 oz / ½ cup raisins into the whipped cream before chilling.

651

SERVES 4

Goats' Cheese-Stuffed Cherry Tomatoes

PREPARATION TIME 10 MINUTES

COOKING TIME 10 MINUTES

INGREDIENTS

12 vine cherry tomatoes, tops removed and reserved
225 g / 8 oz / 2 cups goats' cheese log
30 g / 1 oz / ¼ cup sesame seeds, toasted
1 tbsp cumin seeds
1 tbsp curry powder
1 tbsp poppy seeds
1 tbsp harissa
1 tsp cornflour (cornstarch)

- Deseed the cherry tomatoes and set to one side.
- Divide the goats' cheese into 12 and roll into small balls.
- Roll roll of the balls in the sesame seeds to coat, roll 2 in the poppy seeds, roll another 2 in cumin seeds and another 2 in curry powder.
- Dust the final two in cornflour before rolling in harissa paste to coat.
- Place the goats' cheese balls in the empty cherry tomatoes and replace the tops before serving.

Goats' Cheese and Rocket Tomatoes

652

- Serve the stuffed tomatoes with a small handful of rocket (arugula) leaves on the side.

653

SERVES 16-18 Bacon and Mushroom Choux Buns

- Preheat the oven to 220°C (200° fan) / 425F / gas 7.
- Sift flour, salt and pepper into a mixing bowl.
- Combine butter and milk in a pan and heat gently until melted. Add the flour and stir until smooth dough starts to form. Beat until it pulls away from the pan.
- Remove from the heat and gradually add eggs, beating well until the dough is shiny. Transfer to a piping bag.
- Pipe onto a baking tray and bake for 10 minutes. Reduce the heat to 150°C (130° fan) / 300F / gas 2 and bake for 5-7 minutes until risen. Remove and allow to cool.
- Melt butter, then whisk in flour, cook for 1-2 minutes.
- Pour in the milk and whisk until incorporated. Fold in the diced bacon and mushroom.
- Simmer until thickened. Season to taste, then set aside.
- Remove tops of the buns with a knife, hollow the centres and spoon in filling. Replace the tops and serve.

Bacon and Feta Choux Buns 654

- Substitute the mushroom for diced feta.

PREPARATION TIME 20-25 MINUTES

COOKING TIME 30 MINUTES

....

INGREDIENTS

FOR THE CHOUX PASTRY
120 g / 4 ½ oz / ¾ cup plain (all purpose) flour
120 g / 4 ½ oz / ½ cup butter, cubed
250 ml / 9 fl. oz / 1 cup semi-skimmed milk
6 medium eggs
1 tsp salt
pepper

FOR THE FILLING
30 g / 1 oz / 2 tbsp butter
30 g / 1 oz / 2 tbsp plain (all purpose) flour
500 ml / 18 fl. oz / 2 cups semi-skimmed milk
100 g / 3 ½ oz / 1 ⅓ cups button mushrooms, diced
2 rashers bacon, finely diced
salt and pepper

655

SERVES 4 Turmeric Chicken Brochettes

- Whisk together the sugar, turmeric, yoghurt and seasoning in a mixing bowl.
- Add the chicken strips and stir to coat well in the marinade.
- Cover and chill for at least 45 minutes.
- Remove from the bowl after marinading and shake off any excess marinade before threading onto skewers.
- Cook under a hot grill for 6-8 minutes, turning once, until the chicken is cooked through and starting to colour.
- Remove from the grill and serve immediately in glasses.

PREPARATION TIME 5-10 MINUTES

COOKING TIME 10 MINUTES

....

INGREDIENTS

FOR THE BROCHETTES
2 large skinless chicken breasts, cut into strips
125 g / 4 ½ oz / ½ cup plain yoghurt
¾ tsp ground turmeric
½ tsp caster (superfine) sugar
salt and pepper

ALSO NEEDED
wooden skewers, soaked in cold water for 15 minutes

Curried Chicken Brochettes 656

- Substitute the turmeric in the marinade for 1 tsp Madras curry powder.

657

MAKES 16

Mini Cucumber Sandwiches

Cucumber and Mint Mini Sandwiches

658

- Toss the sliced cucumber with a small handful of sliced mint leaves and the juice of 1 lime before assembling.

Cucumber and Dill Sandwiches

659

- Toss the cucumber with a small bunch of chopped dill and the juice of ½ lemon before assembling.

PREPARATION TIME 10-15 MINUTES

COOKING TIME 10 MINUTES

INGREDIENTS

FOR THE SANDWICHES
8 slices of wholewheat sandwich bread
55 g / 2 oz / ¼ cup butter, softened
2 small cucumbers, peeled and thinly sliced
salt and pepper

TO GARNISH
4-5 sprigs of mint leaves

- Spread the slices of bread with a light coating of butter and top half with 3-4 layers of cucumber slices.
- Arrange the other slices of bread on top and remove the crusts.
- Cut into quarters and stack on a serving platter, garnishing with mint sprigs before serving.

660

SERVES 4

Gouda and Cumin Accras

- Briefly whisk together the self-raising flour, cornflour, cumin, chilli pepper, chervil, water and seasoning until you have a rough batter.
- Stir in the Gouda, cover and chill for 30 minutes.
- Heat the groundnut oil in a large, heavy-based saucepan until hot; you can tell when the oil is hot enough as bubbles appear on a wooden spoon dipped in the hot oil.
- Shape into balls and dust in the plain flour, shaking off any excess.
- Deep-fry in batches for 2-3 minutes until golden-brown in colour and crisp.
- Remove with a slotted spoon to a kitchen paper to drain.
- Serve in bowls garnish with chervil, parsley and chive and wooden skewers.

Cheddar and Cumin Accras   661

- Substitute the Gouda with grated vintage Cheddar.

PREPARATION TIME 10-15 MINUTES

COOKING TIME 15 MINUTES

INGREDIENTS

FOR THE ACCRAS
1 l / 1 pint 16 fl. oz / 4 cups groundnut oil, for deep-frying
200 g / 7 oz / 2 cups Gouda, grated
110 g / 4 oz / ⅔ cup self-raising flour
110 g / 4 oz / ⅔ cup cornflour (cornstarch)
50 g / 2 oz / ⅓ cup plain (all purpose)
175 ml / 6 fl. oz / ⅔ cup cold water
1 red chilli (chili) pepper, deseeded and finely diced
1 tbsp chervil leaves, finely chopped
2 tsp ground cumin, salt and pepper

TO GARNISH
a few sprigs of chervil leaves
a few sprigs of flat-leaf parsley
a few chive stalks

662

SERVES 4

Goats' Cheese and Peanut Appetizers

- Preheat the oven to 190°C (170° fan) / 375F / gas 5.
- Cut the filo pastry into 8 even rectangles and spread a teaspoon of peanut butter on the centre of each.
- Top the peanut butter with a slice of goats' cheese before folding the ends in and wrapping the goats' cheese in the pastry.
- Arrange on a greaseproof paper-lined baking tray and brush the tops with a little melted butter.
- Sprinkle the sesame and poppy seeds on top and bake for 12-15 minutes until the pastry is golden and cooked.
- Remove from the oven and serve immediately with a pot of soy sauce and sesame seeds on the side.

Goats' Cheese and   663
Pear Appetizers

- Top the slices of goats' cheese with a little finely diced pear before wrapping and baking.

PREPARATION TIME 10 MINUTES

COOKING TIME 20-25 MINUTES

INGREDIENTS

FOR THE APPETIZERS
2 sheets of ready-made filo pastry, kept under a damp cloth
225 g / 8 oz / 2 cups goats' cheese log, cut into 8 slices
75 g / 3 oz / ⅓ cup peanut butter
30 g / 1 oz / 2 tbsp butter, melted and cooled
30 g / 1 oz / ¼ cup poppy seeds
1 tbsp sesame seeds

TO GARNISH
55 ml / 2 fl. oz / ¼ cup dark soy sauce
1 tsp sesame seeds

664

SERVES 4

Coconut Fish Fried Appetizers

PREPARATION TIME 10-15 MINUTES

COOKING TIME 15 MINUTES

INGREDIENTS

FOR THE APPETIZERS
1 l / 1 pint 16 fl. oz / 4 cups groundnut oil, for deep-frying
450 g / 1 lb / 3 cups skinless cod fillet, cut into chunks
50 g / 2 oz / ⅓ cup plain (all purpose) flour
150 g / 5 oz / 2 cups desiccated coconut
75 g / 3 oz / ⅓ cup golden breadcrumbs
2 large eggs
a few sprigs of coriander (cilantro), finely chopped
salt and pepper
1 lemon, cut into thin wedges
55 g / 2 oz / ¼ cup tomato ketchup
a few sprigs of coriander (cilantro)

- Heat the oil in a large, heavy-based saucepan; you can tell when the oil is hot enough as bubbles appear on a wooden spoon dipped in the hot oil.
- Toss together the coconut, breadcrumbs, chopped coriander and seasoning in a bowl and set to one side.
- Dust the cod in the flour, shaking off the excess before dipping in the egg and coating in the coconut breadcrumb mixture.
- Deep-fry in batches until golden-brown in colour.
- Remove with a slotted spoon to kitchen paper to drain.
- Serve with lemon wedges, pots of ketchup and sprigs of coriander.

Coconut and Peanut Cod Appetizers

665

- Substitute half of the desiccated coconut for chopped peanuts in the breadcrumb mixture.

666

SERVES 4

Salmon and Goats' Cheese Rolls

PREPARATION TIME 10 MINUTES

COOKING TIME 20 MINUTES

INGREDIENTS

FOR THE ROLLS
2 large skinless salmon fillets
150 g / 5 oz / 1 ½ cups goats' cheese
a few sprigs of dill
salt and pepper

TO GARNISH
a few sprigs of dill
a few sprigs of mint leaves

ALSO NEEDED
cocktail sticks

- Pulse together the goats' cheese, half of the dill and some seasoning in a food processor.
- Place the salmon fillets on a flat surface and lightly flatten using a rolling pin covered with cling film.
- Sprinkle the remaining chopped dill on 2 separate sheets of cling film and lay the salmon fillets on top.
- Spread the goats' cheese evenly on top of the salmon, leaving at least a 1 cm border at the edges.
- Roll tightly into a cylinder inside the cling film and tie the ends well using kitchen string.
- Cook in a steamer sat atop a saucepan of gently simmering water for 6-10 minutes, depending on thickness until the salmon is just cooked.
- Remove from the steamer and chill before unwrapping and slicing into rolls.
- Serve with dill sprigs, mint and cocktail sticks.

Salmon, Walnut and Cheese Rolls

667

- Incorporate 30 g / 1 oz / 2 tbsp finely chopped walnut halves into the goats' cheese and dill filling before rolling.

SERVES 4

Cucumber and Fish Roe Appetizers

Cucumber and Flaked Almond

669

- Top the cucumber pieces with a teaspoon of flaked (slivered) almonds.

Cucumber and Pink Peppercorn

670

- Top the cucumber pieces with a few crushed pink peppercorns.

PREPARATION TIME 10 MINUTES

COOKING TIME 10 MINUTES

INGREDIENTS

FOR THE APPETIZERS
2 cucumbers, peeled and cut into 4
125 g / 4 ½ oz / ½ cup fromage frais
8 chive stalks

TO GARNISH
30 g / 1 oz / 2 tbsp fish roe, chilled
a few chive stalks, chopped

- Blanch the chive stalks in a saucepan of boiling water for 10 seconds.
- Refresh in iced water and set to one side.
- Tie the blanched chive stalks around the cucumber pieces and spoon a scant tablespoon of fromage frais on top.
- Garnish with a teaspoon of fish roe on top and a sprinkle of chopped chive before serving.

671

SERVES 4

Camembert and Hazelnut Appetizers

PREPARATION TIME 5-10
MINUTES

COOKING TIME 10-15 MINUTES

INGREDIENTS

250 g / 9 oz / 2 ½ cups Camembert
wheel
75 g / 3 oz / ¾ cup hazelnuts
(cob nuts), roughly chopped

- Preheat the oven to 180°C (160° fan) / 350F / gas 4.
- Arrange the wheel of camembert on a lined baking tray and warm for 10 minutes in the oven.
- Remove and leave to cool for 5 minutes before cutting into generous slices and topping with the chopped hazelnuts.
- Serve immediately.

Camembert and Hazelnut Crostini Appetizers

672

- Place the slices of Camembert and hazelnuts on slices of toasted ciabatta to make crostinis.

673

SERVES 4

Cheese and Walnut Appetizers

PREPARATION TIME 5 MINUTES

COOKING TIME 10 MINUTES

INGREDIENTS

FOR THE APPETIZERS
300 g / 10 ½ oz / 3 cups goats'
cheese log, chilled
16 walnut halves
a pinch of ground pepper

TO GARNISH
a few lettuce leaves

ALSO NEEDED
8 cocktail sticks

- Divide the goats' cheese into 8 before rolling into balls.
- Place a walnut half on opposite ends of the balls and skewer with cocktail sticks.
- Line a plate with lettuce leaves and sit the appetizers on top before serving.

Cheese, Walnut and Cranberry Appetizers

674

- Mix 30 g / 1 oz / 2 tbsp dried cranberries into the goats' cheese before shaping into balls.

675

SERVES 4

Deep-Fried Rigotte Appetizers

- Heat the oil in a large, heavy-based saucepan; you can tell when the oil is hot enough as bubbles appear on a wooden spoon dipped in the hot oil.
- Dust the Rigotte in the flour, shaking off the excess before dipping in the egg and coating in breadcrumbs.
- Deep-fry in batches for 2 minutes until golden-brown and crisp.
- Remove with a slotted spoon to kitchen paper to drain.
- Top with folded slices of cucumber and some radish before skewering with cocktail sticks and serving.

PREPARATION TIME 10-15 MINUTES

COOKING TIME 15 MINUTES

INGREDIENTS

FOR THE APPETIZERS
1 l / 1 pint 16 fl. oz / 4 cups groundnut oil, for deep-frying
300 g / 10 ½ oz / 3 cups Rigotte (use another goats' milk cheese if not available), cut into large cubes
225 g / 8 oz / 2 cups golden breadcrumbs
50 g / 2 oz / ⅓ cup plain (all purpose) flour
2 large eggs, beaten

TO GARNISH
½ cucumber, thinly sliced
2 radish, thinly sliced

ALSO NEEDED
cocktail sticks

Rigotte Appetizers with Tomato Chutney

676

- Serve the appetizers with little pots of tomato chutney on the side.

677

SERVES 4

Tuna, Caper and Coriander Crostinis

- Preheat the grill to hot.
- Coat the tuna steak in half of the groundnut oil and then season and crust with the sesame seeds.
- Heat a large frying pan over a moderate heat until hot.
- Sear the tuna for 2 minutes on both sides before removing to a warm plate.
- Brush the slices of ciabatta with the olive oil and top with pepper before grilling until the pepper softens.
- Cut the tuna into 8 and sit on top of the pepper before garnishing with a caper, some lemon zest, sliced coriander and a sprig of coriander leaves.

PREPARATION TIME 10-15 MINUTES

COOKING TIME 10 MINUTES

INGREDIENTS

1 red pepper, deseeded and cut into 8 slices
½ ciabatta loaf, cut into 8 slices
50 ml / 2 fl. oz / ¼ cup groundnut oil
50 ml / 2 fl. oz / ¼ cup olive oil
50 g / 2 oz / ⅓ cup sesame seeds
250 g / 9 oz / 1 ⅔ cups tuna steak
salt and pepper

TO GARNISH
½ lemon, zest pared and cut into strips
a few coriander (cilantro) leaves, finely sliced
8 preserved capers, drained
8 small sprigs of coriander (cilantro) leaves

Tuna, Ginger and Pepper Crostinis

678

- Substitute the lemon zest for julienned strips of fresh ginger.

679

MAKES 8

Shrimp and Mango Brochettes

Shrimp, Mango and Peanut Brochettes

 680

- Add a small handful of chopped peanuts to the bowl when you toss the shrimp and mango together.

Shrimp and Pineapple Brochettes

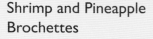 **681**

- Substitute the cubes of mango for pineapple.

PREPARATION TIME 10-15 MINUTES

COOKING TIME 10 MINUTES

INGREDIENTS

FOR THE BROCHETTES
30 ml / 1 fl. oz / 2 tbsp groundnut oil
8 shrimp, peeled with tails intact
1 large mango, peeled and diced
1 lime, juiced
a large handful of coriander (cilantro) leaves, chopped
flaked sea salt and freshly ground black pepper

ALSO NEEDED
8 bamboo skewers

- Preheat the grill to hot.
- Toss the shrimp with the groundnut oil and a little seasoning in a mixing bowl.
- Grill for 3 minutes, turning once, until pink and tender.
- Remove from the grill and toss in a bowl with the lime juice, mango, coriander and a little more seasoning.
- Thread two cubes of mango with one shrimp between onto the skewers and serve immediately.

682

MAKES 12

Mushroom and Serrano Ham Tartlets

- Heat the olive oil and butter together in a large frying pan set over a moderate heat until hot.
- Sauté the mushrooms for 5-6 minutes with some seasoning, tossing occasionally.
- Add the ham and garlic and continue to cook for a few minutes, before adding the parsley.
- Stir well before spooning into the tartlet cases.
- Garnish with frisée before serving.

PREPARATION TIME 10-15 MINUTES

COOKING TIME 10 MINUTES

INGREDIENTS

FOR THE TARTLETS
12 ready-made shortcrust pastry mini tartlets
30 ml / 1 fl. oz / 2 tbsp olive oil
1 tbsp butter
2 cloves of garlic, finely chopped
110 g / 4 oz / ⅔ cup Serrano ham, chopped
75 g / 3 oz / 1 cup button mushrooms, halved
1 tbsp picked flat-leaf parsley leaves, finely chopped
salt and pepper

TO GARNISH
a few sprigs of frisée lettuce

Mushroom and Pine Nut Tartlets　683

- Substitute the chopped ham for toasted pine nuts that have been lightly crushed.

684

MAKES 8

Salt Cod and Pepper Tartlets

- Heat the olive oil in a large frying pan set over a medium heat and sweat the onion and pepper with a little seasoning until translucent; 8-10 minutes, stirring occasionally, before removing to one side.
- Preheat the grill to hot.
- Strain the salt cod and dry well before dividing into 8 small portions.
- Spoon the onion and pepper into the tartlet cases and top with salt cod.
- Grill for 2 minutes on a baking tray to warm through the salt cod.
- Meanwhile, whisk together the mayonnaise, garlic and seasoning until smooth then spoon a teaspoon on top of the salt cod tartlets and return to the grill to glaze for 1 minute.
- Remove and serve immediately.

PREPARATION TIME 10-15 MINUTES

COOKING TIME 15-20 MINUTES

INGREDIENTS

FOR THE TARTLETS
8 ready-made square mini tartlet cases
30 ml / 1 fl. oz / 2 tbsp olive oil
225 g / 8 oz / 1 ½ cups salt cod, rinsed in cold water overnight
2 green pepper, deseeded and thinly sliced
2 onions, finely sliced
salt and pepper

FOR THE AIOLI
100 g / 3 ½ oz / ½ cup mayonnaise
2 cloves of garlic, minced
salt and pepper

Crunchy Cod and Vegetable Tartlets　685

- Substitute the aioli for a teaspoon of panko breadcrumbs on each tartlet before grilling.

686

SERVES 4

Smoked Salmon and Apple Rolls

PREPARATION TIME 10 MINUTES

COOKING TIME 10-15 MINUTES

INGREDIENTS

FOR THE ROLLS

150 g / 5 oz / 1 cup smoked salmon slices, trimmed at the edges
2 Granny Smith apples, cored and halved
1 lemon, juiced
a pinch of caster (superfine) sugar
a pinch of ground white pepper

ALSO NEEDED
cocktail sticks

- Grate the apples on a mandolin set to the julienne setting.
- Toss the julienned apple with the lemon juice, sugar and pepper in a mixing bowl.
- Lay the slices of salmon on a flat, clingfilm-lined surface and arrange the apple evenly in the centre.
- Roll well before cutting in half, skewering and serving immediately.

Apple and Walnut Salmon Rolls **687**

- Add 1 tbsp finely chopped walnut halves to the apple when you toss in the mixing bowl.

688

SERVES 4

Ham, Cheese and Spinach Rolls

PREPARATION TIME 5-10 MINUTES

COOKING TIME 15 MINUTES

INGREDIENTS

FOR THE ROLLS

55 g / 2 oz / ¼ cup butter
8 large eggs
110 g / 4 oz / ⅔ cup prosciutto
110 g / 4 oz / 1 cup Gruyère, thinly sliced
a small handful of flat-leaf parsley, finely chopped
salt and pepper

TO GARNISH
a few baby spinach leaves

ALSO NEEDED
cocktail sticks

- Whisk together the eggs with seasoning and chopped parsley in a large mixing bowl.
- Heat knobs of butter in a frying pan set over a medium heat.
- Pour one quarter of the beaten egg into the pan and allow it to set before flipping to cook the other side.
- Once cooked and golden-brown, remove to one side and cook the remaining beaten egg, using a knob of butter each time, until you have 4 egg pancakes.
- Lay the pancakes on a flat surface before topping with slices of cheese and then prosciutto.
- Roll into cylinders before cutting and skewering with cocktail sticks.
- Serve with a garnish of baby spinach leaves.

Salami and Cheese Egg Rolls **689**

- Substitute the prosciutto for slices of salami inside the egg rolls.

690

SERVES 4

Pistachio Appetizers

Pork, Pistachio and Apple Appetizers

691

- Substitute the lamb mince for pork mince and serve with sliced green apple.

Lamb and Walnut Appetizers

692

- Substitute the pistachios for chopped walnut halves.

PREPARATION TIME 10-15 MINUTES

COOKING TIME 10 MINUTES

....

INGREDIENTS

FOR THE APPETIZERS
450 g / 1 lb / 3 cups lamb mince
175 g / 6 oz / 1 ½ cups shelled pistachios, chopped
30 g / 1 oz / ¼ cup hazelnuts (cob nuts), finely chopped
½ tsp ground cumin
½ tsp ground oregano
salt and pepper

TO GARNISH
110 g / 4 oz / 1 cup pistachios
30 ml / 1 fl. oz / 2 tbsp light soy sauce

ALSO NEEDED
wooden skewers

- Preheat the oven to 190°C (170° fan) / 375F / gas 5.
- Grease and line a large baking tray with greaseproof paper.
- Mix together the lamb mince, hazelnuts, cumin, oregano, seasoning and one thirds of the pistachios in a large mixing bowl.
- Roll the balls in the remaining pistachios and arrange on the baking tray.
- Bake for 18-20 minutes until golden brown in colour.
- Remove from the oven and serve in bowls with a little soy sauce.
- Serve with wooden skewers and pistachios on the side.

Grated Carrot and Herring Canapés

693

SERVES 8

PREPARATION TIME 10-15 MINUTES

COOKING TIME 10 MINUTES

INGREDIENTS

8 slices of rye bread
375 g / 13 oz / 2 ½ cups carrots, peeled and grated
225 g / 8 oz / 1 ½ cups smoked herring fillets, sliced
1 lemon, juiced
1 tsp caster (superfine) sugar
1 tbsp picked coriander (cilantro) leaves, finely chopped
salt and pepper

TO GARNISH

a few sprigs of coriander (cilantro) leaves

- Whisk together the lemon juice, sugar and a little seasoning with the chopped coriander.
- Add the carrot to the dressing and toss well to coat lightly.
- Cut out 8 rounds from the slices of rye bread using a straight-sided 4" cookie cutter.
- Top with generously tablespoons of the carrot and follow with a couple of slices of herring.
- Garnish with some picked coriander leaves and a sprig of coriander to the side.

Carrot, Cabbage and Herring Canapés

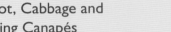

694

- Finely shred a quarter of a small white cabbage and use in place of half of the grated carrot.

Crab and Espelette Pepper Appetizers

695

SERVES 4

PREPARATION TIME 15 MINUTES

COOKING TIME 10 MINUTES

INGREDIENTS

FOR THE APPETIZERS
8 mini blinis
2 Espelette peppers, tops removed
225 g / 8 oz / 1 ½ cups white crab meat
110 g / 4 oz / ⅔ cup smoked salmon slices
55 g / 2 oz / ¼ cup mayonnaise
a few chive stalks, finely chopped
a pinch of cayenne pepper
1 lemon, juiced
salt and pepper

TO GARNISH

225 g / 8 oz / 1 cup canned mango slices
1 tbsp olive oil
8 baby spinach leaves, stems trimmed

- Puree the mango slices in a food processor until smooth before covering and chilling.
- Blanch the peppers in a saucepan of boiling water for 10 seconds before refreshing in iced water.
- Quarter then peel off the skins and reserve to one side before deseeding the quarters and setting to one side.
- Mix the crab meat, mayonnaise, lemon juice, cayenne pepper and seasoning in a mixing bowl.
- Stamp out 8 rounds of smoked salmon.
- Toss the spinach leaves with the olive oil.
- Arrange the blinis in the base of a metal pastry ring.
- Top with the quarter of pepper, cutting them to size if necessary, before spooning the crab on top.
- Place a round of smoked salmon on top and follow with a piece of pepper skin. Sit a leaf of spinach on top, spoon a little mango puree on top.

Crab and Avocado Timbales

696

- Add 1 diced avocado to the crab meat when you mix with the mayonnaise, lemon juice, cayenne pepper and seasoning.

697

SERVES 4

Goats' Cheese and Pesto Turnovers

- Prepare the pesto by placing the spinach, extra-virgin olive oil, pine nuts, garlic and a little salt and pepper in a food processor. Blitz until smooth.
- Add the goats' cheese and pulse until a thick consistency is reached.
- Cover and chill until needed.
- Roll the pastry out on a lightly floured surface to ¾ cm thickness.
- Cut out 8 strips that are 5 cm x 2 cm x ¾ cm in dimension.
- Spoon a little of the pesto onto the bottom half of the strips of pastry before folding the other half on top, sealing the edges well.
- Brush the tops with beaten egg before arranging on the baking tray, spaced apart.
- Bake for 12-15 minutes until golden and puffed.

PREPARATION TIME 10 MINUTES

COOKING TIME 15-20 MINUTES

INGREDIENTS

250 g / 9 oz ready-made puff pastry
a little plain (all purpose) flour,
for dusting
1 large egg, beaten
100 g / 3 ½ oz / 1 cup pine nuts,
toasted
75 g / 3 oz / 1 cup baby spinach leaves
55 ml / 2 fl. oz / ¼ cup extra-virgin
olive oil
75 g / 3 oz / ¾ cup goats' cheese,
crumbled
2 cloves of garlic
salt and pepper

Cheddar and Pesto Turnovers

698

- Use finely grated Cheddar in place of the goats' cheese in the pesto.

699

SERVES 4

Toasted Tuna Bites

- Mix together the tuna, mayonnaise, lemon juice and seasoning in a mixing bowl.
- Toast the slices of bread under a hot grill until golden in colour on both sides.
- Spread the tuna on 4 of the slices, before placing the other toasted slices on top to assemble toasted sandwiches.
- Remove the crusts using a bread knife and cut into squares.
- Skewer cucumber balls and cherry tomato halves on top of the squares using cocktail sticks before serving.

PREPARATION TIME 10 MINUTES

COOKING TIME 10 MINUTES

INGREDIENTS

4 slices of white sandwich bread
½ cucumber, balled using a
melon baller
4 cherry tomatoes, halved
300 g / 10 ½ oz / 2 cups canned
tuna, drained
1 tbsp mayonnaise
½ lemon, juiced
salt and pepper

ALSO NEEDED
cocktail sticks

Tuna and Jalapeño Squares

700

- Add 6 finely chopped, pickled jalapenos to the tuna filling.

701

SERVES 4

Camembert and Ham Appetizers

Camembert and Raspberry Jam Appetizers

 702

- Spoon a teaspoon of raspberry jam on top of the appetizers just before serving.

Brie and Ham Appetizers

703

- Substitute the Camembert for Brie.

PREPARATION TIME 10 MINUTES

COOKING TIME 5 MINUTES

....

INGREDIENTS

FOR THE APPETIZERS
½ flute baguette, cut into 8 slices
250 g / 9 oz / 2 ½ cups Camembert, cut into 8 even pieces
50 g / 2 oz / ½ cup Parma ham, cut into 8 strips

TO GARNISH
4 chive stalks, halved

- Preheat the grill to hot.
- Wrap the pieces of Camembert in the Parma ham and sit on top of the slices of baguette.
- Grill for 1-2 minutes until the cheese starts to melt.
- Remove from the oven and garnish the tops with chive stalks before serving.

Roquefort and Walnut-Stuffed Apricots

704

SERVES 4

- Butterfly the apricot halves with a sharp knife.
- Pulse the Roquefort and walnuts in a food processor until they come together.
- Spoon the mixture into the butterflied apricot halves before serving with skewers on the side.

PREPARATION TIME 5-10 MINUTES

COOKING TIME 5-10 MINUTES

INGREDIENTS

8 large apricot halves
200 g / 7 oz / 2 cups Roquefort, crumbled
100 g / 3 ½ oz / 1 cup walnut halves, chopped

ALSO NEEDED
wooden skewers

Pistachio and Gorgonzola-Stuffed Apricots

705

- Replace the walnut halves with shelled pistachios and use Gorgonzola instead of the Roquefort.

Mini Meat Pies

706

MAKES 8

- Mix together the beef mince, Worcestershire sauce and seasoning in a mixing bowl.
- Preheat the oven to 190°C (170° fan) / 375F / gas 5.
- Grease and line a baking tray with greaseproof paper.
- Roll the pastry out on a lightly floured surface.
- Stamp out 16 rounds of pastry 3" in diameter and arrange half on the baking tray.
- Divide the beef mixture into 8 and roll into balls.
- Sit on top of the pastry halves on the tray and lightly brush the edges with the beaten egg.
- Lay the other pastry rounds on top, sealing the edges well.
- Brush the tops with the remaining egg and bake for 18-20 minutes until golden and risen.
- Remove from the oven and leave to cool before serving.

PREPARATION TIME 10 MINUTES

COOKING TIME 10-15 MINUTES

INGREDIENTS

400 g / 14 oz ready-made puff pastry
450 g / 1 lb / 3 cups beef mince
a little plain (all purpose) flour
2 medium eggs, beaten
2 tsp Worcestershire sauce
salt and pepper

Mini Pork Pies

707

- Substitute the beef mince for pork mince instead.

708

SERVES 4

Cucumber and Cream Cheese Bites

PREPARATION TIME 10 MINUTES

COOKING TIME 10-15 MINUTES

INGREDIENTS

1 cucumber
200 g / 7 oz / 1 cup cream cheese
1 clove of garlic, minced
a small bunch of chive stalks,
finely chopped
a pinch of red pepper flakes
salt and pepper

ALSO NEEDED
cocktail sticks

- Mix together the cream cheese, chives, garlic, red pepper flakes and seasoning until smooth and creamy.
- Spoon into a piping bag fitted with a straight-sided nozzle and set to one side.
- Remove one end of the cucumber and remove the seeds from the centre using a corer.
- Pipe the cream cheese mixture into the centre and cut slices using a warm, wet knife.
- Skewer onto the cocktail sticks and serve upright in shot glasses.

Cream Cheese and Bacon Bites

709

- Crumble 4 rashers of cooked streaky bacon and incorporate into the cream cheese before piping into the cucumber and slicing.

710

MAKES 8

Cheese Mini Pizzas

PREPARATION TIME 10 MINUTES

COOKING TIME 10-15 MINUTES

INGREDIENTS

FOR THE PIZZAS
300 g / 10 ½ oz ready-made dough
a little plain (all purpose) flour
55 ml / 2 fl. oz / ¼ cup extra-virgin
olive oil
110 g / 4 oz / 1 cup grated mozzarella
1 clove of garlic, minced
salt and pepper

TO GARNISH
a small bunch of flat-leaf parsley,
finely chopped

- Preheat the oven to 200°C (180° fan) / 400F / gas 6.
- Grease and line a large baking tray with greaseproof paper.
- Mix the olive oil with the garlic in a small jug.
- Divide the dough into 8 balls and roll out on a lightly floured work surface to 1 cm thickness, with various widths.
- Move to the baking tray and brush with the garlic olive oil.
- Top with grated mozzarella and seasoning before baking for 12-14 minutes until golden at the edges.
- Remove from the oven and sprinkle with parsley before serving.

Anchovy Mini Pizzas

711

- Top the pizzas with preserved anchovy fillets before baking.

712

MAKES 8

Mushroom and Ham Mini Pizzas

Aubergine and Chorizo Mini Pizzas

713

- Substitute the sliced mushroom for finely diced aubergine (eggplant) and diced chorizo instead of diced ham.

Pancetta and Pepper Mini Pizzas

714

- Substitute the ham and mushroom for diced pancetta and diced red pepper.

PREPARATION TIME 10 MINUTES

COOKING TIME 15-20 MINUTES

INGREDIENTS

300 g / 10 ½ oz ready-made pizza dough
a little plain (all purpose) flour, for dusting
1 tbsp olive oil
150 g / 5 oz / 1 cup gammon steak, finely diced
110 g / 4 oz / 1 cup mozzarella, sliced
110 g / 4 oz / ½ cup passata
75 g / 3 oz / 1 cup button mushrooms, sliced

TO GARNISH

a small handful of rocket (arugula)
a few sprigs of thyme

- Preheat the oven to 200°C (180° fan) / 400F / gas 6.
- Divide the dough into 8 small balls and roll out on a lightly floured surface to 3" in diameter.
- Arrange on baking trays and drizzle with a little olive oil.
- Spread a teaspoon of passata on top, then top with sliced mushrooms, slices of mozzarella and some diced ham.
- Bake for 10-12 minutes until the dough is cooked and the cheese has melted.
- Remove the tips of the thyme sprigs and use to garnish the pizzas as well as a few rocket leaves.

715

SERVES 8

Cheese and Chive Savoury Popcakes

PREPARATION TIME 10 MINUTES

COOKING TIME 15-20 MINUTES

INGREDIENTS

FOR THE POPCAKES

120 g / 4 ½ oz / ¾ cup plain
(all purpose) flour
110 g / 4 oz / ½ cup butter, cubed
250 ml / 9 fl. oz / 1 cup whole milk
100 g / 3 ½ oz / 1 cup Cheddar,
finely grated
4 large eggs
1 red pepper, deseeded and finely
diced
salt and pepper

TO GARNISH

55 g / 2 oz / ¼ cup butter, melted
and cooled
a large bunch of chive stalks,
finely chopped

ALSO NEEDED

24 wooden skewers

- Preheat the oven to 200°C (180° fan) / 400F / gas 6.
- Mix together the flour and seasoning in a bowl.
- Heat together the butter and milk in a saucepan until melted together.
- Add the flour and stir until a smooth dough comes together.
- Continue to beat the dough until it starts to pull away from the sides of the saucepan.
- Remove from the heat and add the eggs, one at a time, beating well between each addition, until the dough is shiny and even.
- Beat in the Cheddar and red pepper until incorporated before transferring the dough to a piping bag fitted with a 2-3 cm straight-sided nozzle.
- Pipe 24 blobs onto a lined baking tray, spaced apart, and bake in the oven for 12-15 minutes until golden and set.
- Remove from the oven and leave to cool before skewering each with a skewer.
- Dip in the melted butter then roll in the chopped chives before leaving to dry.
- Serve upright in cups.

716

SERVES 4

Gingerbread and Foie Gras Popcakes

PREPARATION TIME 10 MINUTES

COOKING TIME 10 MINUTES

INGREDIENTS

FOR THE PIZZA DOUGH

350 g / 12 oz / 3 cups ready-made
gingerbread cake, chopped
75 g / 3 oz / ½ cup foie gras,
deveined and finely chopped
75 g / 3 oz / ¾ cup hazelnuts
(cob nuts), finely chopped
1 medium egg, beaten
1 tbsp Madeira (optional)
salt and pepper

ALSO NEEDED

12 wooden skewers

- Preheat the oven to 190°C (170° fan) / 375F / gas 5.
- Grease and line a large baking tray with greaseproof paper.
- Pulse the gingerbread in a good processor until it resembles breadcrumbs.
- Tip into a bowl and add the foie gras, hazelnuts, egg, Madeira (if using) and seasoning.
- Mix well with you hands until you have a homogenous ball before shaping into 12 smaller balls between your palms.
- Arrange on the baking tray and bake for 15-18 minutes until deep golden-brown in colour.
- Remove from the oven and skewer with the wooden skewers as they cool.
- Serve warm or cold.

717
SERVES 4

Parmesan, Ham and Chive Bites

- Fold the ham slices on themselves a few times until coiled and skewer onto the Parmesan using the wooden skewers.
- Thread the chive stalks onto the wooden skewers and garnish with extra chive before serving.

PREPARATION TIME 5-10 MINUTES

COOKING TIME 5 MINUTES

INGREDIENTS

110 g / 4 oz / 1 cup Parmesan, diced
100 g / 3 ½ oz / 1 cup Serrano ham slices
8 chive stalks, halved

TO GARNISH
a few extra chive stalks, halved

ALSO NEEDED
8 wooden skewers

Chicory and Ham Appetizers

718
SERVES 8

PREPARATION TIME 10 MINUTES

COOKING TIME 10 MINUTES

INGREDIENTS

FOR THE APPETIZERS
4 chicory (endive) bulbs
400 g / 14 oz / 2 ⅔ cups cooked ham, diced
125 g / 4 ½ oz / ½ cup plain yoghurt

1 tbsp mayonnaise
1 tsp Dijon mustard
a small bunch of flat-leaf parsley, finely chopped
a few chive stalks, finely chopped
salt and pepper

TO GARNISH
a few extra chive stalks
a few sprigs of flat-leaf parsley, roughly chopped

- Remove the outer leaves of the chicory bulbs so that you have 16 large leaves.
- Mix together the diced ham, yoghurt, mayonnaise, mustard, herbs and seasoning, stirring well.
- Spoon the mixture into 8 of the leaves, then replace the other leaves on top to mimic a chicory bulb.
- Arrange upright in a serving dish before serving.

Crayfish Toasts

719
SERVES 4

PREPARATION TIME 5-10 MINUTES

COOKING TIME 5 MINUTES

INGREDIENTS

12 round rye toasts
250 g / 9 oz / 1 2/3 cups cooked crayfish tails, drained

125 g / 4 1/2 oz / 1/2 cup plain yoghurt
1 tbsp mayonnaise
1/2 lemon, juiced
a pinch of cayenne pepper
salt and pepper

TO GARNISH
a handful of pea shoots

- Whisk together the yoghurt, mayonnaise, lemon juice, cayenne pepper and seasoning in a mixing bowl until smooth.
- Gently stir in the crayfish tails before spooning onto the rye toasts.
- Garnish with pea shoots before serving.

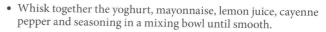

720

SERVES 4

Tomato and Herb Mini Tartlets

Tomato and Bacon
Mini Tartlets

721

- Substitute the capers and basil leaves for 100 g / 3 ½ oz / ⅔ cup finely diced pancetta, spooning into the cases before baking.

Tomato and Feta
Mini Tartlets

722

- Substitute the capers and basil for small chunks of feta cheese.

PREPARATION TIME 10 MINUTES

COOKING TIME 10 MINUTES

INGREDIENTS

16 vol-au-vent cases
8 cherry tomatoes, halved
16 picked basil leaves
30 ml / 1 fl. oz / 2 tbsp extra-virgin olive oil
1 tbsp preserved baby capers, drained
salt and pepper

- Preheat the oven to 200°C (180° fan) / 400F / gas 6.
- Grease and line a large baking tray with greaseproof paper.
- Toss the cherry tomato halves with the olive oil and some seasoning.
- Arrange the vol-au-vent cases on it and spoon two cherry tomato halves into each.
- Dot with a few capers before baking for 6-8 minutes until the cherry tomatoes are coloured.
- Remove from the oven and tuck a basil leaf into case before serving.

723
SERVES 8

Capocollo and Pepper Canapés

- Use a 3" cookie cutter to stamp out rounds from the bread slices.
- Spread with onion marmalade and top each with a caper and a slice of capocollo.
- Finish with a slice of preserved red pepper and a slice of jalapeño before serving.

PREPARATION TIME 10-15 MINUTES

COOKING TIME 5-10 MINUTES

....

INGREDIENTS

1 sandwich loaf, sliced 1" thick with crusts removed
225 g / 8 oz / 1 cup onion marmalade
8 capers
8 slices of capocollo (use prosciutto if not available)
100 g / 3 ½ oz / ½ cup preserved red pepper, sliced
1 green jalapeño, deseeded and sliced

Brie and Walnut Canapes   724

- Substitute the capocollo with Brie and use walnut halves in place of the pepper slices.

725
SERVES 4

Citrus and Merguez Canapes

- Heat the olive oil in a sauté pan set over a medium heat.
- Sauté the carrot with a little salt and pepper for 6-7 minutes, stirring frequently until softened.
- Add the chopped tomatoes, stir and simmer for another 6-7 minutes until thickened before adjusting the seasoning to taste.
- Toast the slices of baguette under a hot grill then top with some of the carrot and tomato stew.
- Top with slices of lemon, merguez and olives before garnishing with dill.

PREPARATION TIME 10 MINUTES

COOKING TIME 15-20 MINUTES

....

INGREDIENTS

FOR THE PIZZA DOUGH
½ flute baguette, sliced
1 tbsp olive oil
2 preserved lemons, sliced into wedges
250 g / 9 oz / 1 ⅔ cups cooked merguez, sliced
400 g / 14 oz / 2 cups canned chopped tomatoes
2 carrots, peeled and diced
a small handful of pitted green olives, halved
salt and pepper

TO GARNISH
a few sprigs of dill, chopped

Bacon and Olive Canapes   726

- Substitute the lemon with black olives and use cooked streaky bacon instead of the merguez.

MAKES 8

Artichoke and Ham Mini Pizzas

PREPARATION TIME 10-15
MINUTES

COOKING TIME 10 MINUTES

....

INGREDIENTS

300 g / 10 ½ oz ready-made pizza
dough
a little plain (all purpose) flour,
for dusting
1 tbsp olive oil
110 g / 4 oz / 1 cup grated mozzarella
110 g / 4 oz / ½ cup passata
50 g / 2 oz / ⅓ cup Parma ham, sliced
2 preserved artichoke hearts, drained
and sliced
8 pitted black olives
8 cherry tomatoes, chopped
1 tsp dried oregano

- Preheat the oven to 200°C (180° fan) / 400F / gas 6.
- Divide the dough into 8 small balls and roll out on a lightly floured surface to 3" in diameter.
- Arrange on baking trays and drizzle with a little olive oil.
- Spread a teaspoon of passata on top, then sprinkle the mozzarella on top.
- Follow with the tomato, ham, artichoke, tomato and olives then sprinkle with a pinch of oregano.
- Bake for 10-12 minutes until the dough is risen and the cheese has melted.
- Remove from the oven and serve immediately.

Chicken Mini Pizzas

728

- Use cooked diced chicken breast instead of ham on the pizzas.

SERVES 4

Duck, Beetroot and Apple Sandwiches

PREPARATION TIME 15-20
MINUTES

COOKING TIME 10 MINUTES

....

INGREDIENTS

FOR THE SANDWICHES
8 slices of wholewheat sandwich
bread
200 g / 7 oz / 1 cup cooked duck leg,
shredded
75 g / 3 oz / ⅓ cup butter, salted
2 Granny Smith apples, cored and
thinly sliced
1 tbsp mayonnaise
1 tbsp plain yoghurt
salt and pepper

TO GARNISH
2 beetroot, cooked, peeled and sliced
thinly on a mandolin

ALSO NEEDED
wooden skewers

- Mix together the duck, mayonnaise, yoghurt and seasoning in a bowl, stirring well.
- Spread the slices of bread evenly with butter and top half with the duck mixture.
- Lay slices of apple on top and place the remaining slices of bread on top to make 4 sandwiches.
- Cut each sandwiches into 4 triangles and skewer a beetroot slice on top of each before serving.

Duck and Cream Cheese Sandwiches

730

- Replace the mayonnaise and yoghurt with cream cheese.

731

SERVES 4

Ham-Wrapped Figs

Fig and Pepper Wraps   731

- Replace the Brie with slices of preserved red pepper before grilling and wrapping.

Prune and Fig Wraps   733

- Substitute the brie for dried prunes before grilling and wrapping.

PREPARATION TIME 10 MINUTES

COOKING TIME 5 MINUTES

INGREDIENTS

4 ripe green figs, halved
125 g / 4 ½ oz / 1 ¼ cups Brie, sliced
110 g / 4 oz / ⅔ cup prosciutto slices
salt and freshly ground black pepper

ALSO NEEDED
cocktail sticks

- Preheat the grill to hot.
- Place a slice of Brie on top of the cut side of the fig halves and season well.
- Grill for 1 minute until the cheese starts to melt, then wrap with a slice of ham and secure using a cocktail stick.
- Serve immediately.

734

SERVES 4

Courgette Tempura with Mango Chutney

PREPARATION TIME 10-15
MINUTES

COOKING TIME 15-20 MINUTES

INGREDIENTS

1 l / 1 pint 16 fl. oz / 4 cups
groundnut oil, for deep-frying
150 g / 5 oz / 1 cup plain (all purpose)
flour
1 tbsp cornflour (cornstarch)
a little extra plain (all purpose) flour,
250 ml / 9 fl. oz / 1 cup sparkling
water, ice cold
1 tbsp fish sauce
2 courgettes (zucchinis), sliced
1 tbsp sunflower oil
2 large mangoes, diced
4" knob of ginger, grated
125 ml / 4 ½ fl. oz / ½ cup distilled
vinegar
75 g / 3 oz / ⅓ cup caster (superfine)
sugar
1 stick of cinnamon
½ tsp ground ginger, ½ tsp turmeric
salt and pepper

- Heat the sunflower oil in a saucepan set over a medium heat until hot, then add the ginger, turmeric, cinnamon and sugar.
- Stir once before carefully adding the vinegar, stirring well.
- Add the mangoes and grated ginger and cover with a lid, reducing the heat at the same time.
- Cook for 15-20 minutes until the mango is soft.
- Remove from the heat and stir to break up the fruit a little before seasoning to taste and setting to one side.
- Heat the groundnut oil in a large, heavy-based saucepan until hot; you can tell when the oil is hot enough as bubbles appear on a wooden spoon dipped in the hot oil.
- Roughly whisk the sparkling water into the flour and cornflour in a mixing bowl.
- Add the fish sauce and whisk again briefly.
- Dust the courgette slices with a little flour before dipping in the tempura batter and deep-frying for 2 minutes until golden and crisp.
- Remove with a slotted spoon and drain on kitchen paper.
- Skewer with toothpicks and serve with the chutney.

735

SERVES 8

Lamb Meatballs with Tzatziki

PREPARATION TIME 10-15
MINUTES

COOKING TIME 10-15 MINUTES

INGREDIENTS

FOR THE MEATBALLS
675 g / 1 lb 8 oz / 4 ½ cups lamb
mince
1 tsp ground cumin
1 tsp ground coriander
½ tsp smoked paprika
½ tsp dried oregano
½ tsp dried basil
salt and pepper

FOR THE TZATZIKI
250 g / 9 oz / 1 cup Greek yoghurt
1 clove of garlic, minced
½ lemon, juiced
¼ cucumber, peeled and grated
salt and pepper

TO GARNISH
16 small mint leaves

- Mix together all the ingredients for the meatballs in a large mixing bowl.
- Cover and chill for 30 minutes.
- Preheat the oven to 190°C (170° fan) / 375F / gas 5.
- Shape the lamb mixture into 16 small meatballs and arrange on a large baking tray lined with greaseproof paper.
- Bake for 20-25 minutes until golden-brown in colour.
- Meanwhile, mix together all the ingredients for the tzatziki in a mixing bowl, adjusting the seasoning to taste.
- Spoon into 8 shot glasses and chill until ready to serve.
- Remove the meatballs from the oven when ready and skewer with cocktail sticks.
- Place 2 mint leaves in each shot glass and sit the meatballs over the rim before serving.

736

SERVES 8

Cheesy Bites

- Preheat the oven to 190°C (170° fan) / 375F / gas 5.
- Grease and line 2 large baking trays with greaseproof paper.
- Butter the squares of loaf and arrange spaced slightly apart on the baking trays.
- Sprinkle the cheese evenly on top over the squares and sprinkle ½ teaspoon of black poppy seeds on top of each square.
- Bake for 10-12 minutes until the cheese is golden and melted.
- Remove from the oven and leave to cool a little before serving.

PREPARATION TIME 10 MINUTES

COOKING TIME 10-15 MINUTES

INGREDIENTS

1 small ciabatta loaf, crusts removed and cut into 32 squares
350 g / 12 oz / 3 ½ cups Comté, grated
110 g / 4 oz / ½ cup butter, softened
110 g / 4 oz / 1 cup black poppy seeds

Mushroom & Pepper Tempura

737

SERVES 4

PREPARATION TIME 10 MINUTES

COOKING TIME 10-15 MINUTES

INGREDIENTS

1 l / 1 pint 16 fl. oz / 4 cups groundnut oil, for deep-frying
150 g / 5 oz / 1 cup plain (all purpose) flour
1 tbsp cornflour (cornstarch)

a little extra plain (all purpose) flour,
250 ml / 9 fl. oz / 1 cup sparkling water, ice cold
1 tbsp fish sauce
2 red peppers, deseeded and sliced
150 g / 5 oz / 2 cups mixed wild mushrooms
125 ml / 4 ½ fl. oz / ½ cup dark soy sauce
125 ml / 4 ½ fl. oz / ½ cup sesame oil

- Whisk together the sesame oil and soy sauce and set to one side.
- Heat the groundnut oil in a large, heavy-based saucepan until hot; you can tell when the oil is hot enough as bubbles appear on a wooden spoon dipped in the hot oil.
- Roughly whisk the sparkling water into the flour and cornflour in a mixing bowl.
- Add the fish sauce and whisk again briefly.
- Dust the vegetables with a little flour before dipping in the tempura batter and deep-frying for 2 minutes until golden and crisp.
- Remove with a slotted spoon and drain on kitchen paper.
- Skewer with toothpicks and serve with the soy sauce and sesame oil mixture.

Seafood Canapes

738

SERVES 4

PREPARATION TIME 10-15 MINUTES

COOKING TIME 10-15 MINUTES

INGREDIENTS

1 flute baguette, sliced
300 g / 10 ½ oz / 2 ½ cups frozen squid tentacles, thawed and cut to size

250 g / 9 oz / 2 cups cooked and peeled prawns
55 g / 2 oz / ½ cup glass noodles, cut in half
8 preserved anchovy fillets, drained and patted dry
1 small carrot, peeled and julienned
100 g / 3 ½ oz / 1 cup grape tomatoes
baby spinach leaves

- Place the noodles in a bowl and cover with boiling water.
- Let the noodles sit for 2 minutes before stirring and running under cold water.
- Dry well and set to one side.
- Preheat the oven to 180°C (160° fan) / 350F / gas 4.
- Arrange the slices of baguette on a baking tray and bake for 5 minutes.
- Remove and top each with an anchovy fillet, a prawn and a piece of squid.
- Arrange on platters and garnish with a piece of noodle and carrot before decorating the platters with spinach leaves and tomatoes.

SAVOURY

739

MAKES 6

Olive and Thyme Mini Cakes

PREPARATION TIME 10-15
MINUTES

COOKING TIME 15 MINUTES

INGREDIENTS

FOR THE MINI LOAFS
250 g / 9 oz / 1 ⅔ cups self-raising
flour, sifted
125 ml / 4 ½ fl. oz / ½ cup olive oil
110 g / 4 oz / 1 cup Parmesan,
finely grated
1 tsp dried thyme
a few sprigs of thyme,
roughly chopped
2 large eggs, beaten
salt and pepper

TO GARNISH
a few sprigs of thyme
a small handful of green olives

- Preheat the oven to 170°C (150°C fan) / 325°F / gas 3.
- Grease and line 6 mini loaf tins with greaseproof paper.
- Whisk together the eggs and olive oil in a jug.
- Combine the flour, dried thyme and Parmesan in a mixing bowl.
- Add the wet ingredient to the dry and fold until combined.
- Add the olives and chopped thyme, folding gently, before seasoning the batter.
- Spoon into the loaf tins and bake for 35-40 minutes; test with a wooden toothpick, if it comes out clean, the loafs are done.
- Remove from the oven and leave to cool before turning out and garnishing with thyme sprigs and olives.

Olive and Sundried Tomato Loaves

 740

- Omit the thyme and replace with 75 g / 3 oz / ½ cup sliced sundried tomato.

741

SERVES 4

Breaded Cod Acras

PREPARATION TIME 10-15
MINUTES

COOKING TIME 15-20 MINUTES

INGREDIENTS

FOR THE FRITTERS
1 l / 1 pint 16 fl. oz / 4 cups
groundnut oil, for deep-frying
400 g / 14 oz / 2 ⅔ cups skinless cod
fillet, cut into 1" cubes
1 large eggs
75 g / 3 oz / ½ cup plain
(all purpose) flour
salt and pepper

FOR THE BATTER
75 g / 3 oz / ½ cup self-raising flour
55 g / 2 oz / ½ cup golden
breadcrumbs
125 ml / 4 ½ fl. oz / ½ cup cold water
a small handful of coriander
(cilantro), finely chopped
salt and pepper
coriander (cilantro)

- Heat the groundnut oil in a large, heavy-based saucepan until hot; you can tell when the oil is hot enough as bubbles appear on a wooden spoon dipped in the hot oil.
- Briefly whisk together the self-raising flour, chopped coriander, breadcrumbs, water and seasoning until you have a rough batter.
- Dry cod really well before pulsing in a food processor with the egg, 1 tbsp plain flour and seasoning.
- Shape into balls and dust in the remaining plain flour, shaking off any excess.
- Dip in the batter and deep-fry in batches until golden-brown in colour all over; 2-3 minutes.
- Remove with a slotted spoon to kitchen paper.
- Serve with wooden skewers and a sprig of coriander on the side.

Cod and Chorizo Acras

742

- Substitute 75 g / 3 oz / ½ cup cod fillet for diced chorizo, pulsing it with the cod in the food processor.

743

SERVES 4 Courgette Rolls

- Slice the courgette into thin ribbons on a mandolin.
- Beat together the olive oil, fromage frais, cottage cheese, garlic and seasoning in a mixing bowl.
- Place the ribbons of courgette on a flat surface covered with cling film and spoon a tablespoon of the filling before rolling the courgette around it.
- Secure using cocktail sticks before flipping on their sides and seasoning with salt and plenty of coarsely ground black pepper.
- Garnish with rosemary before serving.

PREPARATION TIME 10 MINUTES

COOKING TIME 10-15 MINUTES

INGREDIENTS

FOR THE ROLLS
1 large courgette (zucchini)
125 g / 4 ½ oz / ½ cup fromage frais
125 g / 4 ½ oz / ½ cup cottage cheese
30 ml / 1 fl. oz / 2 tbsp olive oil
1 clove of garlic, minced
salt and coarsely ground black pepper

TO GARNISH
a few sprigs of rosemary

ALSO NEEDED
cocktail sticks

Courgette Goats' Cheese Rolls   744

- Substitute the cottage cheese for herbed goats' cheese.

745

MAKES 8 Spanish Empanadas

- Heat the olive oil in a large sauté pan.
- Sweat the onion and garlic for 4-5 minutes.
- Add the chopped tomatoes, capers, sweetcorn, paprika and seasoning and simmer for 5 minutes.
- Preheat the oven to 190°C (170° fan) / 375F / gas 5. Grease and line a baking tray with greaseproof paper.
- Pulse the flour, salt and butter in a food processor.
- Add the egg and half of the water and pulse again until it forms a dough, adding more water if necessary.
- Turn the dough out and knead gently before rolling out on a lightly floured work surface to 1/2 cm thickness.
- Cut out 8 3" rounds of pastry and fill with scant tablespoons of the vegetable filling.
- Fold one end over the filling and seal well.
- Arrange on a greaseproof paper-lined baking tray and bake for 20-25 minutes. Serve with sprigs of mint leaves.

PREPARATION TIME 15 MINUTES

COOKING TIME 20-25 MINUTES

INGREDIENTS

FOR THE PASTRY
250 g / 9 oz / 1 ⅔ cups wholewheat flour
a little plain (all purpose) flour, for dusting
110 g / 4 oz / ½ cup unsalted butter, cold and cubed
1-2 tbsp iced water
1 small egg, a pinch of salt

FOR THE FILLING
30 ml / 1 fl. oz / 2 tbsp olive oil
200 g / 7 oz / 1 cup canned chopped tomatoes
100 g / 3 ½ oz / ½ cup canned sweetcorn
1 large onion, sliced
1 clove of garlic, minced
1 tbsp baby capers, drained
1 tsp paprika, salt and pepper
a few sprig of mint leaves

Manchego and Vegetable Empanadas   746

- Add 75 g / 3 oz / ¾ cup diced Manchego to the vegetable mixture for the filling.

747

SERVES 4

Caramelised BBQ Chicken Drumsticks

Bourbon BBQ Chicken Drumsticks

748

- Substitute the soy sauce in the recipe for good-quality bourbon.

Treacle BBQ Chicken Drumsticks

749

- Substitute the dark brown sugar for the same amount of treacle.

PREPARATION TIME 5-10 MINUTES

COOKING TIME 10 MINUTES

....

INGREDIENTS

8 chicken drumsticks
125 g / 4 ½ oz / ½ cup tomato ketchup
55 ml / 2 fl. oz / ¼ cup sunflower oil
55 ml / 2 fl. oz / ¼ cup dark soy sauce
30 g / 1 oz / 2 tbsp soft dark brown sugar
30 ml / 1 fl. oz / 2 tbsp white wine vinegar
1 tbsp honey
½ tsp garlic powder
salt and pepper

- Make a few slashes in each drumstick and place in a shallow dish.
- Whisk together the sunflower oil, ketchup, soy sauce, sugar, honey and garlic powder in a mixing bowl until smooth.
- Adjust the seasoning to taste before pouring over the chicken.
- Rub the marinade into the chicken, cover, and chill for at least 30 minutes.
- Preheat the oven to 190°C (170° fan) / 375F / gas 5.
- Remove the chicken from the marinade and place in a roasting tray.
- Bake for 35-45 minutes until the juices run clear when the thickest part of the drumstick is pierced.
- Remove from the oven and leave to cool for a few minutes before serving.

750
SERVES 4
Goats' Cheese and Duck Canapés

- Preheat the grill to hot and line a baking tray with greaseproof paper.
- Cut the smoked duck breast into 1/2 cm thick slices
- Use a 3" cookie cutter to cut out rounds of bread from the slices.
- Toast for 30 seconds before removing.
- Top with half of the duck, then follow with a slice of goats' cheese and the rest of the duck slices on top.
- Grill for 1-2 minutes until the cheese starts to melt.
- Remove to a serving plate and garnish with thyme before serving.

PREPARATION TIME 10 MINUTES

COOKING TIME 10 MINUTES

INGREDIENTS

FOR THE CANAPÉS
8 slices of sandwich bread
150 g / 5 oz / 1 ½ cups goats' cheese cut into slices
150 g / 5 oz / 1 cup smoked, cured duck breast

TO GARNISH
a few small sprigs of thyme

Duck, Apple and Cheese Rounds
751

- Substitute half of the duck for 1 tbsp finely diced apple on top before grilling.

752
SERVES 4
Spinach and Parmesan Crostini

- Heat the olive oil in a large sauté pan set over a moderate heat.
- Sauté the garlic for 30 seconds before adding the spinach leaves.
- Cook until wilted, tossing and stirring occasionally.
- Toast the slices of sourdough under a hot grill for 1 minute before removing and topping with the spinach.
- Garnish with shaved Parmesan and a drizzle of cream before serving.

PREPARATION TIME 10 MINUTES

COOKING TIME 10 MINUTES

INGREDIENTS

FOR THE CROSTINIS
1 small sourdough loaf, cut into 8 thin slices
200 g / 7 oz / 4 cups baby spinach leaves
30 ml / 1 fl. oz / 2 tbsp olive oil
salt and pepper

TO GARNISH
55 g / 2 oz / ½ cup Parmesan, shaved
55 ml / 2 fl. oz / ¼ cup double (heavy) cream

Spicy Spinach Crostini
753

- Add 1 finely chopped red chilli to the pan at the same time as the garlic. Omit the Parmesan garnish.

754

MAKES 8

Mushroom Burger

PREPARATION TIME 10-15 MINUTES

COOKING TIME 15-20 MINUTES

INGREDIENTS

450 g / 1 lb / 3 cups beef mince
16 large button mushrooms, stems removed
1 onion, finely sliced
1 beef tomato, sliced
a small handful of baby spinach leaves
4 slices of burger cheese, quartered
salt and pepper

TO GARNISH
1 tbsp sesame seeds

- Preheat the oven to 190°C (170° fan) / 375F / gas 5.
- Mix the beef mince with seasoning in a mixing bowl before dividing in 8 and shaping into mini patties.
- Arrange the patties on a greaseproof paper-lined baking tray and bake for 10-12 minutes until coloured all over.
- Remove from the oven and pat dry using kitchen paper.
- Turn half of the button mushrooms upside down and layer a few spinach leaves, then sliced of onion and tomato.
- Top with the patties, then a piece of cheese and finally the remaining mushrooms.
- Sprinkle the tops with sesame seeds before serving.

Pork and Soy Burgers

755

- Substitute the beef mince for pork mince and add 30 ml / 1 fl. oz / 2 tbsp dark soy sauce when mixing. Omit the salt.

756

MAKES 8

Mini Artichoke Pizzas

PREPARATION TIME 20 MINUTES

COOKING TIME 20-25 MINUTES

INGREDIENTS

FOR THE PIZZAS
8 Globe artichokes, peeled and trimmed
1 tbsp olive oil
110 g / 4 oz / 1 cup Cheddar, grated
110 g / 4 oz / ½ cup passata
8 pitted black olives
8 preserved anchovy fillets, drained
1 lemon, juiced

TO GARNISH
8 red chillies (chilis)

- Preheat the oven to 190°C (170° fan) / 375F / gas 5.
- Grease and line a baking tray with greaseproof paper.
- Prepare a bowl of cold water and lemon juice.
- Remove any purple leaves and hairy portions from the centre of the artichokes before cutting off their bases to leave you with a flat mushroom shape, transferring each prepared artichoke to the lemon and water mixture.
- Simmer the artichokes in a saucepan of boiling water until tender; 10-12 minutes.
- Drain and dry well before arranging on the baking tray.
- Drizzle with olive oil, spread their tops with passata.
- Sprinkle the Cheddar on top before topping with olive and anchovy.
- Arrange the chillies on the tray as well and bake everything for 12-15 minutes.

Basil and Artichoke Mini Pizzas

757

- Top the artichoke pizzas with basil leaves half way through baking.

758

SERVES 4

Cream Cheese-Stuffed Ratte Potatoes

Goats' Cheese and Grape Potatoes

759

- Substitute the cream cheese for goats' cheese and the tomatoes for a large handful of diced grapes. Garnish with walnut halves on top.

Cream Cheese and Chive Potatoes

760

- Substitute the basil leaves for chopped chives in the stuffing.

PREPARATION TIME 10-15 MINUTES

COOKING TIME 20-25 MINUTES

INGREDIENTS

FOR THE STUFFED POTATOES
450 g / 1 lb / 3 cups Ratte potatoes (use Charlotte if not available), one end removed
225 g / 8 oz / 1 cup cream cheese
2 vine tomatoes, cored, deseeded and finely diced
a few sprigs of basil leaves, finely chopped
salt and pepper

TO GARNISH
a large handful of basil leaf sprigs

- Peel the potatoes and use a sharp turning knife or a small baller to scoop out the insides, leaving at least a ½ cm border of potato.
- Arrange upright in a steamer and sit over a saucepan of simmering water.
- Cover and steam for 12-15 minutes until fork tender.
- Once tender and cooked, remove from the steamer and leave to dry and cool.
- Beat the cream cheese in a mixing bowl until smooth before adding the chopped basil, tomatoes and seasoning.
- Stir well and spoon into the potatoes before arranging upright on a serving plate.
- Garnish with sprigs of basil leaves.

761

SERVES 4

Smoked Salmon-Stuffed Potato Appetizers

PREPARATION TIME 15 MINUTES

COOKING TIME 20-25 MINUTES

....

INGREDIENTS

FOR THE APPETIZERS

250 g / 9 oz / 1 ⅔ cups new potatoes
110 g / 4 oz / ⅔ cup smoked salmon slices, diced
30 ml / 1 fl. oz / 2 tbsp extra-virgin olive oil
1 red chilli (chili) pepper, deseeded and finely diced
1 green chilli (chili) pepper, deseeded and finely diced
1 lime, juiced
½ shallot, finely chopped
a small handful of flat-leaf parsley, finely chopped
salt and pepper

TO GARNISH
½ tsp smoked paprika

- Cook the potatoes in a saucepan of boiling water until tender; 15-18 minutes.
- Drain and leave to steam dry until cool enough to handle.
- Meanwhile, stir together the salmon, olive oil, chilli peppers, shallot, lime juice and parsley in a mixing bowl.
- Adjust the seasoning to taste and set to one side.
- Remove the tops of the potatoes and remove a little of the cooked potato before filling with the smoked salmon mixture.
- Arrange on serving plates and garnish with a pinch of smoked paprika before serving.

Bacon and Sour Cream Potatoes   762

- Stuff the potatoes with tablespoons of sour creme, topping them with chopped, cooked crispy bacon pieces. Garnish with chopped chives.

763

SERVES 4

Salmon and Crème Fraîche Blinis

PREPARATION TIME 10-15 MINUTES

COOKING TIME 15 MINUTES

....

INGREDIENTS

FOR THE BLINIS

175 ml / 6 fl. oz / ⅔ cup whole milk, warmed
75 g / 3 oz / ½ cup plain (all purpose) flour
75 g / 3 oz / ½ cup buckwheat flour
30 ml / 1 fl. oz / 2 tbsp sunflower oil
1 tbsp butter, melted and cooled
½ tsp dried active yeast
½ tsp baking powder
1 egg yolk, 1 egg white
a pinch of salt

TO GARNISH
175 ml / 6 fl. oz / ¾ cup crème fraîche
150 g / 5 fl. oz / 1 cup skinless salmon fillet, cut into 8 even squares
8 redcurrants
a large handful of chervil sprigs
freshly ground black pepper

- Sift together the flours and baking powder into a large mixing bowl.
- Combine the egg yolk, milk and yeast in a jug.
- Add the wet ingredients to the dry and whisk. Add the melted butter and stir well.
- Whisk the egg whites with a pinch of salt until soft peaks form then fold into the batter.
- Coat a non-stick frying pan with a little sunflower oil and heat over a medium heat.
- Cook generous tablespoons of the batter in the pan until set on the bottom. Flip and cook for 30 seconds.
- Top with a chervil sprig before spooning a small tablespoon of creme fraîche on top.
- Sit a square of salmon on top before garnishing with black pepper and a redcurrant.

Smoked Salmon and Cheese Blinis   764

- Substitute the crème fraîche for goats' cheese and use small folded slices of smoked salmon.

765

MAKES 8

Roquefort and Walnut Mini Pizzas

- Preheat the oven to 200°C (180° fan) / 400F / gas 6.
- Divide the dough into 8 small balls and roll out on a lightly floured surface to 3" in diameter.
- Arrange on baking trays and drizzle with a little olive oil.
- Spread a small tablespoon of chopped tomato on top before topping with Roquefort.
- Bake for 10-12 minutes until the dough is risen and the cheese has melted.
- Remove from the oven and garnish with a walnut half and sprigs of thyme on top, with more thyme and chopped walnuts on the side.

PREPARATION TIME 10 MINUTES

COOKING TIME 10 MINUTES

INGREDIENTS

FOR THE PIZZAS
300 g / 10 ½ oz ready-made pizza dough
a little plain (all purpose) flour, for dusting
1 tbsp olive oil
110 g / 4 oz / 1 cup Roquefort, cubed
110 g / 4 oz / ½ cup canned chopped tomatoes

TO GARNISH
8 walnut halves
a few sprigs of thyme
a few walnut halves, chopped

Gorgonzola and Leek Mini Pizzas   766

- Sweat ½ chopped leek in butter until soft; spoon on top of the pizzas and use Gorgonzola instead of Roquefort.

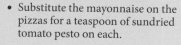

767

MAKES 8

Mini Pizzas with Goats' Cheese

- Preheat the oven to 200°C (180° fan) / 400F / gas 6.
- Divide the dough into 8 small balls and roll out on a lightly floured surface to 3" in diameter.
- Arrange on baking trays and drizzle with a little olive oil.
- Pulse together the black olives, lemon juice, extra-virgin olive oil and garlic until spreadable.
- Spread on top of the rounds of dough and top with goats' cheese and mayonnaise.
- Arrange a few rocket and radicchio leaves on top before baking for 10-12 minutes until the dough is cooked and the leaves are coloured at the edges.
- Remove from the oven and serve immediately.

PREPARATION TIME 15 MINUTES

COOKING TIME 15 MINUTES

INGREDIENTS

FOR THE PIZZAS
300 g / 10 ½ oz ready-made pizza dough
a little plain (all purpose) flour, for dusting
1 tbsp olive oil
150 g / 5 oz / 1 ½ cups goats' cheese
100 g / 3 ½ oz / ⅔ cup pitted black olives
75 g / 3 oz / ⅓ cup mayonnaise
30 ml / 1 fl. oz / 2 tbsp extra-virgin olive oil
1 radicchio, leaves separated
1 clove of garlic, crushed
½ lemon juiced
a small handful of rocket (arugula)

Tapenade and Pesto Pizzas   768

- Substitute the mayonnaise on the pizzas for a teaspoon of sundried tomato pesto on each.

769

SERVES 4

Breaded Meatballs

Lamb and Mint Breaded Meatballs

770

- Substitute the dried herbs for a small bunch of chopped mint, added to the lamb mince before shaping into balls.

Beef and Onion Meatballs

771

- Use beef mince instead of lamb and add 1 diced onion to the mixture.

PREPARATION TIME 10-15 MINUTES

COOKING TIME 20 MINUTES

....

INGREDIENTS

FOR THE MEATBALLS
1 l / 1 pint 18 fl. oz / 4 cups groundnut oil, for deep-frying
450 g / 1 lb / 3 cups lamb mince
225 g / 8 oz / 2 cups golden breadcrumbs
75 g / 3 oz / ½ cup plain (all purpose) flour
3 large eggs, beaten
1 tsp dried oregano
1 tsp dried basil
salt and pepper

TO GARNISH
1 lemon, zest julienned

- Heat the oil in a heavy-based saucepan until hot; you can tell when the oil is hot enough as bubbles appear on a wooden spoon dipped in the hot oil.
- Combine the lamb mince, dried herbs and seasoning in a bowl, mixing well with your hands.
- Shape into meatballs and arrange on a greaseproof paper-lined baking tray.
- Dust in the flour, shaking off any excess before dipping in the egg and coating in breadcrumbs.
- Deep-fry in batches until golden-brown in colour; 4-5 minutes.
- Remove to kitchen paper to drain before serving in a bowl garnished with lemon zest.

772
SERVES 4 Olive and Walnut Beef Meatballs

- Preheat the oven to 190°C (170° fan) / 375F / gas 5.
- Grease and line a large baking tray with greaseproof paper.
- Pulse the walnuts in a food processor until finely chopped.
- Add to the beef mince, chopped olives, ground cumin and seasoning in a mixing bowl.
- Mix well with your hands before shaping into meatballs.
- Arrange on the baking tray and bake for 20-25 minutes until golden-brown on the outside.
- Serve in bowls, garnished with green olives and pricked with cocktail sticks.

PREPARATION TIME 10 MINUTES

COOKING TIME 10 MINUTES

INGREDIENTS

FOR THE MEATBALLS
450 g / 1 lb / 3 cups beef mince
100 g / 3 ½ oz / ⅔ cup pitted green olives, chopped
50 g / 2 oz /⅓ cup walnut halves
½ tsp ground cumin
salt and pepper

TO GARNISH
a few green olives

ALSO NEEDED
cocktail sticks

Chilli Beef Meatballs
773

- Substitute the olives for 2 finely chopped red chillies (chilis).

774
SERVES 4 Toasted Chorizo and Ham Sandwiches

- Preheat the grill to hot and preheat the oven to 190°C (170° fan) / 375F / gas 5.
- Butter the slices of bread on one side and layer with chorizo layers.
- Top with ham slices before sandwiching them with the other slices of bread.
- Arrange on a greaseproof paper-lined baking tray and bake for 8-10 minutes until the bread is golden in colour.
- Remove from the oven and finish under a hot grill for 1 minute on both sides until golden-brown all over.
- Cut into squares and prick with skewers before serving.

PREPARATION TIME 5-10 MINUTES

COOKING TIME 10 MINUTES

INGREDIENTS

FOR THE SANDWICHES
4 slices of white sandwich bread
55 g / 2 oz / ¼ cup butter, softened
110 g / 4 oz / ⅔ cup chorizo slices
110 g / 4 oz / ⅔ cup ham slices

ALSO NEEDED
wooden skewers

Chorizo and Sundried Tomato Toasties
775

- Substitute the ham for 100 g / 3 ½ oz / ½ cup sundried tomato pesto.

776

SERVES 4

Fromage Frais Daussade on Toast

PREPARATION TIME 10 MINUTES

COOKING TIME 15 MINUTES

....

INGREDIENTS

1 baguette, cut into 8 slices
250 g / 9 oz / 1 cup fromage frais
½ leek, green top removed
½ white onion, finely sliced
55 ml / 2 fl. oz / ¼ cup vinegar
1 tsp caster (superfine) sugar
salt and pepper

- Finely slice the leek white and set to one side.
- Whisk together the sugar, seasoning and vinegar in a bowl before adding the onion.
- Stir well and leave at room temperature for 10 minutes before adding the leek.
- Stir again and spoon the leek and onion into a separate mixing bowl.
- Add the fromage frais and stir well before adjusting the seasoning to taste.
- Toast the slices of bread under a hot grill for 1 minute before removing and topping with the daussade.

Parsley Daussade on Toast

777

- Add a small handful of finely chopped flat-leaf parsley to the daussage before using on the toasts.

778

SERVES 4

Two Pepper-Stuffed Mussels

PREPARATION TIME 10-15 MINUTES

COOKING TIME 15 MINUTES

....

INGREDIENTS

250 ml / 9 fl. oz / 1 cup dry white wine
1 tbsp olive oil
14 large mussels, beards removed
2 cloves of garlic, finely chopped
1 yellow pepper, deseeded and diced
1 red pepper, deseeded and diced
a small bunch of flat-leaf parsley, finely chopped
salt and pepper

TO GARNISH
1 tbsp saffron threads

- Discard any mussels that are open.
- Heat the wine in a saucepan set over a moderate until it starts to boil.
- Add the mussels and cove with a lid, letting the steam cook the mussels.
- Shake the pan occasionally and cook for 3-4 minutes before checking; discard any that haven't opened.
- Remove the meat from 12 of the mussels and retain half of their shells.
- Heat the olive oil in a large frying pan over a medium heat and sauté the garlic and peppers with a little seasoning for 1 minute.
- Remove from the heat and stir through the parsley.
- Spoon into the mussel shells and sit the mussel meat on top.
- Garnish with a pinch of saffron threads before serving.

Creamy Two Pepper Mussels

779

- Add 55 ml / 2 fl. oz / ¼ cup crème fraîche to the sautéed peppers before spooning into the shells and serving.

Curried Leek Individual Quiches

Curried Leek and Potato Quiches

781

- Add 1 tablespoon of diced, cooked white potato the quiches at the same time as the leek.

Curried Leek and Apple Quiches

782

- Add 1 diced apple to the quiche mixture before baking.

PREPARATION TIME 10-15 MINUTES

COOKING TIME 20-25 MINUTES

INGREDIENTS

FOR THE MINI QUICHES
300 g / 10 ½ oz ready-made shortcrust pastry
a little plain (all purpose) flour, for dusting
1 medium egg, beaten
30 g / 1 oz / 2 tbsp butter
½ leek, trimmed and finely sliced (keep trimmings)
250 ml / 9 fl. oz / 1 cup whole milk
250 ml / 9 fl. oz / 1 cup crème fraîche
3 large eggs
2 tsp mild curry powder
salt and pepper

TO GARNISH
½ tsp mild curry powder
a large handful of sliced leek trimmings

- Preheat the oven to 180°C (160° fan) / 350F / gas 4.
- Roll the pastry out on a lightly floured surface.
- Cut 4 rounds of pastry and use to line 6 individual 3" fluted tartlet cases.
- Prick the bases and trim the excess pastry.
- Line with greaseproof paper and fill with baking beans.
- Blind-bake for 12-15 minutes until golden-brown.
- Remove from the oven and discard the greaseproof paper and baking beans.
- Brush the bases with the beaten egg and leave to one side.
- Reduce the oven to 160°C (140° fan) / 325F / gas 3.
- Melt the butter in a large sauté pan and sweat the leek for 6-8 minutes until softened.
- Stir in the curry power and season to taste.
- Whisk together the eggs, milk and creme fraîche with seasoning.
- Arrange the sweated leek in the pastry cases and fill with the quiche filling.
- Baking for 25-30 minutes.
- Remove from the oven and garnish with a pinch of curry powder on top and the reserved leek trimmings.

783

SERVES 4

Shrimp Fritters

PREPARATION TIME 10-15 MINUTES

COOKING TIME 15 MINUTES

INGREDIENTS

FOR THE FRITTERS

1 l / 1 pint 16 fl. oz / 4 cups groundnut oil, for deep-frying
8 large prawns, peeled with tails intact
30 g / 1 oz / 2 tbsp cornflour (cornstarch)
salt and pepper

FOR THE BATTER

125 ml / 4 ½ fl. oz / ½ cup cold water
110 g / 4 oz / ⅔ cup self-raising flour
1 tbsp cornflour (cornstarch)
1 tbsp fish sauce
salt and pepper

TO GARNISH

a few sprigs of basil leaves

- Heat the groundnut oil in a large, heavy-based saucepan until hot; you can tell when the oil is hot enough as bubbles appear on a wooden spoon dipped in the hot oil.
- Briefly whisk together the self-raising flour, cornflour, water, fish sauce and seasoning until you have a batter.
- Dry the prawns really well before dusting in the cornflour and seasoning well.
- Dip into the batter and deep-fry in batches until golden and crisp; 2-3 minutes.
- Remove with a slotted spoon to kitchen paper to drain.
- Serve garnished with basil sprigs.

Chilli Shrimp Fritters

784

- Add 1 diced red chilli (chili) to the batter before dipping the prawns in it. Serve with pots of sweet chilli sauce as well.

785

MAKES 8

Roquefort and Grape Brioche Rolls

PREPARATION TIME 5 MINUTES

COOKING TIME 10 MINUTES

INGREDIENTS

8 ready-made brioche rolls
110 g / 4 oz / 1 cup Roquefort, cut into 8 thin slices
16 seedless black grapes
16 seedless green grapes

- Remove the top inch from the brioche rolls and reserve.
- Cut out some of the centre of the rolls and discard.
- Toast the rolls and their tops under a hot grill for 1 minute.
- Remove and position the slices of Roquefort across the rolls.
- Sit 2 grapes of each variety on top and follow with the brioche tops before serving.

Roquefort and Pear-Stuffed Brioche

786

- Crumble the Roquefort and mix with 2 cored and diced pears. Spoon into the rolls.

787

SERVES 4 Cucumber and Basil Mini Soufflés

- Preheat the oven to 200°C (180°C fan) / 400°F / gas 6.
- Brush the insides of 4 ramekins with half of the butter using a pastry brush. Chill until needed.
- Melt the rest of the butter in a saucepan over a medium heat, then whisk in the flour. Cook for 1-2 minutes.
- Whisk in the milk then whisk in the egg yolks, mustard, basil and the grated Cheddar until smooth.
- Simmer the sauce for 5-6 minutes, season, then remove it from the heat and stir through the cucumber.
- Whisk the egg whites in a clean mixing bowl with a pinch of salt until soft peaks form.
- Whisk a third of the whites into the cheese sauce, then fold the remaining egg whites in.
- Run the tip of your finger around rim of the ramekins then bake for 12-15 minutes until golden and risen.
- Turn out and garnish with marjoram sprigs on top.

Tuna and Cucumber Mini Soufflés   788

- Stir 110 g / 4 oz / ½ cup drained, canned tuna flakes into the sauce at the same time as the cucumber.

PREPARATION TIME 10-15 MINUTES

COOKING TIME 20 MINUTES

INGREDIENTS

FOR THE SOUFFLÉS
55 g / 2 oz / ½ stick butter, softened
30 g / 1 oz / 2 tbsp plain (all purpose) flour
250 ml / 9 fl. oz / 1 cup whole milk
100 g / 3 ½ oz / 1 cup Cheddar, grated
4 large eggs, separated
1 tsp Dijon mustard
½ cucumber, peeled, deseeded and finely diced
1 tsp dried basil
salt and pepper

TO GARNISH
a few sprigs of marjoram

789

MAKES 12 Goats' Cheese and Ham Canapés

- Snip the ends of the chive stalks to leave you with 3" stalks.
- Top the crackers with a tablespoon of goats' cheese before placing folded slices of air-dried ham on top.
- Garnish with a snipped chive stalk before serving cold.

PREPARATION TIME 5 MINUTES

COOKING TIME 10 MINUTES

INGREDIENTS

FOR THE TOPPINGS
12 round cheese crackers
175 g / 6 oz / 1 ¾ cups goats' cheese
150 g / 5 oz 1 cup air-dried ham slices

TO GARNISH
12 chive stalks

Goats' Cheese and Walnut Canapés   790

- Stud the goats' cheese with a walnut half before placing the folded ham on top and garnishing.

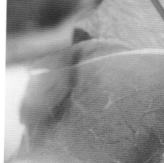

791

SERVES 4

Piperade on Toast

Cheesy Piperade on Toast

792

- Stir 50 g / 2 oz / ½ cup feta cubes into the piperade before spooning onto the toasts.

Smoked Salmon Piperade Toasts

793

- Add 50 g / 2 oz / ⅓ cup smoked salmon trimmings to the egg before serving.

PREPARATION TIME 15 MINUTES

COOKING TIME 15 MINUTES

....

INGREDIENTS

FOR THE PIPERADE
4 slices of wholemeal bread, halved
100 g / 3 ½ oz / ⅔ cup cooked ham, diced
30 ml / 1 fl. oz / 2 tbsp olive oil
6 medium eggs, beaten
2 red peppers, deseeded and diced
2 vine tomatoes, cored, deseeded and diced
salt and pepper

TO GARNISH
1 red pepper, deseeded and sliced
a small handful of chive stalks
a few sprigs of thyme, roughly chopped

- Heat the olive oil in a large sauté pan set over a moderate heat.
- Sauté the red pepper for 2-3 minutes, tossing occasionally before adding the ham.
- Cook for a further 2-3 minutes, stirring occasionally, before reducing the heat and adding the eggs.
- Stir the eggs occasionally until they are set and creamy then add the diced tomato and adjust the seasoning to taste.
- Toast the slices of bread under a hot grill for 1 minute before arranging on plates.
- Top with the piperade and garnish with chopped thyme on top and slices of pepper and chive stalks to one side.

Curried Scallops on Crispy Potatoes

794

SERVES 4

- Cook the potatoes in a saucepan of salted, boiling water until tender; 10-12 minutes.
- Drain and leave to steam dry and cool.
- Cut in half and season well.
- Heat the olive oil in a frying pan set over a medium heat and sauté the potatoes until golden-brown in colour.
- Meanwhile, heat the sunflower oil in a large frying pan set over a moderate heat until hot.
- Dust the scallops in curry powder and seasoning before pan-frying in a ring until coloured underneath; usually 2 minutes.
- Flip and cook the other side for a further minute until firm yet slightly springy to the touch.
- Drain the potatoes and flatten slightly with a fork.
- Arrange slices of apple on top of the potato before topping with a scallop and serving immediately.

PREPARATION TIME 10 MINUTES

COOKING TIME 15-20 MINUTES

INGREDIENTS

8 scallops, roe removed
4 Charlotte potatoes
30 ml / 1 fl. oz / 2 tbsp olive oil
30 ml / 1 fl. oz / 2 tbsp sunflower oil
2 tsp mild curry powder
1 Gala apple, cored, quartered and thinly sliced
salt and pepper

Curried Scallops, Raisins and Potatoes

795

- Sit the curried scallop on top of the crispy potato halves and garnish the top with 3-4 raisins.

Camembert and Broccoli Quiches

796

MAKES 4

- Preheat the oven to 180°C (160° fan) / 350F / gas 4.
- Roll the pastry out on a lightly floured surface.
- Cut 4 rounds of pastry and line 4 4" tartlet cases.
- Prick the bases and trim the excess pastry.
- Line with greaseproof paper and fill with baking beans.
- Blind-bake for 12-15 minutes until golden-brown.
- Remove and discard the greaseproof paper and beans.
- Reduce the oven to 160°C (140° fan) / 325F / gas 3.
- Brush the bases with the beaten egg.
- Whisk the eggs, milk and creme fraîche with seasoning.
- Arrange the broccoli and camembert in the pastry cases and fill with the quiche filling. Bake for 25-30 minutes.
- Remove from the oven leave to cool a little before garnishing with a pink of peppercorns.

PREPARATION TIME 10 MINUTES

COOKING TIME 20 MINUTES

INGREDIENTS

FOR THE QUICHES
250 g / 9 oz ready-made shortcrust pastry
a little plain (all purpose) flour, for dusting
250 ml / 9 fl. oz / 1 cup whole milk
250 ml / 9 fl. oz / 1 cup crème fraîche
125 g / 4 ½ oz / 1 ¼ cups Camembert, diced
3 large eggs
1 small egg, beaten
½ small head of broccoli, prepared into small florets
salt and pepper

TO GARNISH
½ tsp crushed pink peppercorns

Camembert and Dried Cranberry Quiches

797

- Substitute the broccoli florets for 1 tablespoon of dried cranberries in each quiche before baking.

MAKES 12

Rocket, Parmesan and Pine Nut Pizzas

798

PREPARATION TIME 15-20
MINUTES

COOKING TIME 25-40 MINUTES

....

INGREDIENTS

200 g / 7 oz / 1 ⅓ cups plain (all purpose) flour
a little plain flour, for dusting
3.5g dried active yeast
½ tsp salt
½ tbsp caster (superfine) sugar
25 ml / 1 fl. oz / 2 tbsp olive oil
110 ml / 4 ½ fl. oz / ⅓ cup warm water (roughly 45 degrees)
500 g / 1 lb 2 oz / 2 ½ cups canned chopped tomatoes
2 cloves garlic, minced
1 tbsp olive oil
1 tsp sugar, salt and pepper
150 g / 5 oz / 3 cups rocket (arugula) leaves
75 g / 3 oz / ¾ cup Parmesan
50 g / 2 oz / ½ cup pine nuts, toasted
50 ml extra-virgin olive oil

- Prepare the sauce by heating the olive oil for it in a saucepan over a moderate heat.
- Sauté the garlic for a minute, then add the chopped tomatoes, sugar and seasoning.
- Bring to a simmer and cook for 4-5 minutes.
- Remove from the heat and leave to one side.
- Preheat the oven to 220°C (200° fan) / 425F / gas 7.
- Combine the flour, salt, yeast and sugar.
- Mix in the oil and water to form a dough, then kneading gently on a floured surface for a minute.
- Divide the dough into small balls and roll out on a lightly floured work surface to roughly ½cm thickness.
- Arrange on trays and drizzle with the olive oil. Top with a little of the tomato sauce. Bake for 15-20 minutes.
- Remove and top with a combination of rocket leaves, some pine nuts and shaved Parmesan.

Rocket and Cherry Tomato Pizzas

799

- Substitute the pine nuts for 2 cherry tomato halves on the pizzas before baking.

SERVES 4

Olive Tapenade and Anchovy Toasts

800

PREPARATION TIME 10-15
MINUTES

COOKING TIME 15 MINUTES

....

INGREDIENTS

FOR THE TOASTS
1 flute baguette, cut into 8 slices
225 g / 8 oz / 1 ½ cup pitted black olives
55 ml / 2 fl. oz / ¼ cup extra-virgin olive oil
2 preserved anchovy fillets, drained
2 cloves of garlic, crushed
½ lemon, juiced
salt and pepper

TO GARNISH
30 ml / 1 fl. oz / 2 tbsp balsamic vinegar
16 preserved anchovy fillets, drained
1 large red pepper, deseeded and cut into 16 strips
a small handful of chive stalks, finely chopped

- Pulse together the olives, 2 anchovy fillets, garlic, olive oil and lemon juice in a food processor until smooth.
- Adjust the seasoning to taste and set to one side.
- Toast the slices of baguette under a hot grill for 1 minute.
- Remove and spread with a tablespoon of the tapenade.
- Top with 2 anchovy fillets and 2 strips of red pepper before returning to the grill for 1-2 minutes to soften the red pepper.
- Remove to serving plates and garnish with chopped chives and a drizzle of balsamic vinegar.

Two Olive Tapenade Anchovy Toasts

801

- Substitute half of the black olives for pitted green olives in the tapenade.

SERVES 4

Tricolore Crostinis

Goats' Cheese and Balsamic Crostinis

803

- Replace the basil leaf garnish with a drizzle of good-quality balsamic vinegar on top.

Goats' Cheese and Walnut Crostinis

804

- Substitute the tomato slices for 1 tablespoon of walnut halves on each.

PREPARATION TIME 10 MINUTES

COOKING TIME 10 MINUTES

INGREDIENTS

FOR THE CROSTINIS
1 wholemeal baguette, cut into
8 thin slices
250 g / 9 oz / 2 ½ cups goats' cheese
2 salad tomatoes
salt and freshly ground black pepper

TO GARNISH
8 sprigs of basil leaves

- Toast the slices of baguette under a hot grill for 1-2 minutes until they are golden-brown in colour.
- Remove to one side to cool.
- Spoon the goats' cheese onto the slices and use a fork to mash a little across the baguette slices.
- Season generously before topping with a slice of tomato.
- Garnish with a sprig of basil leaves before serving.

805

SERVES 4

Creamed Salmon Crostinis

PREPARATION TIME 10 MINUTES

COOKING TIME 20 MINUTES

INGREDIENTS

FOR THE CROSTINIS
1 small white loaf, cut into
8 thin slices
450 g / 1 lb / 3 cups skinless
salmon fillet
225 g / 8 oz / cup cream cheese
125 ml / 4 ½ fl. oz / ½ cup dry
white wine
1 bay leaf
1 tsp black peppercorns
a few chive stalks, finely chopped
salt and pepper

TO GARNISH
75 g / 3 oz / ½ cup smoked
salmon slices
8 asparagus spears, ends removed
1 red chilli (chili), deseeded and
cut into thin rings

- Place the salmon in a saucepan and cover with the wine, bay leaf, peppercorns and cold water.
- Cook covered over a medium heat until the salmon is firm yet springy to the touch; 6-8 minutes.
- Drain the salmon and discard the bay leaf and peppercorns.
- Pulse with the cream cheese and chives in a food processor until you have a smooth paté texture.
- Adjust the seasoning to taste and set to one side.
- Blanch the asparagus in a saucepan of salted, boiling water for 1 minute before draining and drying.
- Cut in half lengthways and set to one side.
- Toast the slices of bread under a hot grill until golden.
- Spread with the creamed salmon, garnish with a slice of smoked salmon, a couple of pieces of asparagus and a chilli ring on top.

Creamed Salmon and Gherkin Crostinis

806

- Top the creamed salmon with thin slices of pickled gherkins, omitting the smoked salmon as well.

807

MAKES 8

Mini Seafood Pizzas

PREPARATION TIME 15 MINUTES

COOKING TIME 10-15 MINUTES

INGREDIENTS

FOR THE PIZZAS
300 g / 10 ½ oz ready-made
pizza dough
a little plain (all purpose) flour,
for dusting
1 tbsp olive oil
1 fennel bulb, trimmed and
thinly sliced
150 g / 5 oz / 1 cup frozen baby
shrimp, thawed
100 g / 3 ½ oz / ⅔ cup cooked
mussel meat
8 cherry tomatoes, halved
salt and pepper

TO GARNISH
a few sprigs of flat-leaf parsley,
finely chopped

- Preheat the oven to 200°C (180° fan) / 400F / gas 6.
- Divide the dough into 8 small balls and roll out on a lightly floured surface to 3" in diameter.
- Arrange on baking trays and drizzle with a little olive oil.
- Top the dough rounds with a sliced fennel, cherry tomato halves, 3-4 baby shrimp and finally the mussel meat on top.
- Bake for 10-12 minutes until the dough is risen and golden.
- Remove from the oven and garnish with chopped parsley on top before serving.

Seafood and Goats' Cheese Pizzas

808

- Substitute the mussel meat for a small round of goats' cheese on top of each pizza before baking.

809

SERVES 4 # Pear and Roquefort Tartlets

- Preheat the oven to 200°C (180° fan) / 400F / gas 6.
- Roll the pastry out on a lightly floured surface to ½cm thickness.
- Cut out tartlet shapes using a fluted 7cm cookie cutter.
- Arrange on a baking tray, spaced apart.
- Arrange the crumbled Roquefort on top of the pastry, leaving a slight border at the perimeter.
- Overlap the slices of pear laying on their sides on top of the Roquefort.
- Bake for 15-18 minutes until the pastry is risen and puffed and the cheese and pear are golden.
- Remove and allow to cool on a wire rack for a few minutes before stacking on a serving plate.
- Eat hot or cold.

PREPARATION TIME 15-20 MINUTES

COOKING TIME 20-25 MINUTES

INGREDIENTS

250 g / 9 oz / ready-rolled puff pastry
a little plain (all purpose) flour, for dusting
200 g / 7 oz / 2 cups Roquefort, crumbled
4 Williams pears, cored and sliced into thin wedges
salt and pepper

Roquefort and Peach Tartlets

810

- Substitute the pears for slices of peach.

811

SERVES 4 # Rolled Omelette

- Beat the eggs together with the chopped chervil and seasoning.
- Heat small knobs of butter in a small frying pan until melted before adding a quarter of the egg mixture.
- Let it set and turn golden underneath before flipping and cooking for a further 30 seconds.
- Transfer to a plate and cook the remaining pancakes in this way.
- Lay the pancakes on a flat surface and top with a ham slices in a single layer before rolling up into a cylinder shape.
- Cut into bite-sized pieces and serve on plates garnished with chervil.

PREPARATION TIME 10 MINUTES

COOKING TIME 15 MINUTES

INGREDIENTS

FOR THE ROLLS
30 g / 1 oz / 1 tbsp
110 g / 4 oz / ⅔ cup ham slices
4 large eggs
a small handful of chervil, finely chopped
salt and pepper

TO GARNISH
a few sprigs of chervil

Mixed Herb Omelette Rolls

812

- Substitute half of the chopped chervil for a mixture of chopped tarragon and chopped flat-leaf parsley.

SERVES 4

Chick Liver and Spinach Crostini

PREPARATION TIME 15 MINUTES

COOKING TIME 15 MINUTES

INGREDIENTS

½ sourdough loaf, cut into
4 thin slices
30 ml / 1 fl. oz / 2 tbsp olive oil
30 g / 1 oz / 2 tbsp butter
150 g / 5 oz / 1 cup chicken livers,
washed and dried
150 g / 5 oz / 3 cups baby spinach
leaves
110 g / 4 oz / ½ cup canned chickpeas
(garbanzo beans), drained
a few sprigs of flat-leaf parsley,
finely chopped
salt and pepper

- Toast the slices of bread under a hot grill until golden-brown in colour.
- Remove and cut in half.
- Heat the butter in a sauté pan set over a moderate heat until the butter stops foaming.
- Season the chicken livers and sauté for 3-4 minutes, tossing occasionally until they are firm yet slightly springy on the outside.
- Stir in the parsley and tip onto a plate, leaving them to rest as you add the oil to the pan.
- Add the chickpeas and sauté for 2-3 minutes with a lid on top before removing it and adding the spinach.
- Cook, stirring occasionally, until the spinach wilts.
- Adjust the seasoning to taste before spooning onto the toasts.
- Top with chicken livers before serving.

MAKES 4

Spinach Tartlets

PREPARATION TIME 10 MINUTES

COOKING TIME 15-20 MINUTES

INGREDIENTS

250 g / 9 oz ready-made
shortcrust pastry
a little plain (all purpose) flour,
for dusting
250 g / 9 oz / 5 cups baby spinach
250 ml / 9 fl. oz / 1 cup double
(heavy) cream
125 ml / 4 ½ fl. oz / ½ cup crème
fraîche
3 medium eggs
salt and pepper

- Preheat the oven to 180°C (160° fan) / 350F / gas 4.
- Roll the pastry out on a lightly floured surface to ½ cm thickness.
- Cut 4 rounds of pastry and use to line 4 individual 4" fluted tartlet cases.
- Prick the bases with a fork and trim some of the excess pastry.
- Line with greaseproof paper and fill with baking beans.
- Blind-bake for 12-15 minutes until golden-brown in colour at the edges.
- Remove from the oven to a wire rack and discard the greaseproof paper and baking beans.
- Reduce the oven to 160°C (140° fan) / 325F / gas 3.
- Combine the eggs, cream, crème fraîche and 200 g of the spinach in a food processor with seasoning.
- Pulse until smooth.
- Pour into the tartlet cases and arrange the remaining spinach in the centre.
- Bake for 25-30 minutes until the filling is set.
- Remove from the oven to a wire rack to cool before serving.

Salmon Pierogies

815

MAKES 8

- Preheat the oven to 190°C (170° fan) / 375F / gas 5.
- Heat the butter in a sauté pan set over a medium heat and sweat the onion with a little seasoning for 4-5 minutes, until it softens and turns translucent.
- Add the salmon fillet and stir well, cooking for a further 3 minutes.
- Stir through the dill and remove from the heat.
- Roll the pastry out on a lightly floured surface. Cut out 8 rounds of pastry 3" in diameter.
- Spoon a little salmon filling into their centres and wet the rims with a little water using your fingertip.
- Fold one end over the other and seal well.
- Arrange on a greaseproof paper-lined baking tray and brush with the beaten egg before sprinkling the poppy seeds on top.
- Bake for 15-18 minutes.

PREPARATION TIME 10-15 MINUTES

COOKING TIME 15-20 MINUTES

INGREDIENTS

250 g / 9 oz ready-made puff pastry
a little plain (all purpose) flour,
for dusting
30 g / 1 oz / 2 tbsp butter
2 small skinless salmon fillets, diced
1 small onion, finely chopped
1 large egg, beaten
1 tbsp black poppy seeds
a few sprigs of dill, chopped
salt and pepper

816

SERVES 4

Pork Nems

PREPARATION TIME 10-15 MINUTES

COOKING TIME 20-25 MINUTES

INGREDIENTS

1 l / 1 pint 18 fl. oz / 4 cups
groundnut oil, for deep-frying
30 ml / 1 fl. oz / 2 tbsp vegetable oil
8 spring roll wrappers

450 g / 1 lb / 3 cups pork mince
2 large onions, finely chopped
2 cloves of garlic, minced
a small handful of red chard
4 spring onions (scallions), sliced
1 medium egg, beaten
1 tbsp rice wine vinegar
1 tbsp dark soy sauce
salt and pepper
55 ml / 2 fl. oz / ¼ cup sweet
chilli sauce

- Heat the groundnut oil in a large, heavy-based saucepan until hot; the oil is hot enough as bubbles appear on a wooden spoon dipped in the hot oil.
- Heat the vegetable oil in a large sauté pan.
- Sweat the onion and garlic until the onion turns translucent.
- Add the pork mince and spring onion, stir well, and continue cooking for 3 minutes before stirring through the soy sauce, red chard and rice wine vinegar.
- Brush the rims of the wrappers with the beaten egg.
- Spoon the pork and vegetable filling into the middle of the wrappers and fold the ends in and over the filling.
- Roll up tightly into cylinders and arrange on a baking tray.
- Deep-fry in batches for 2-3 minutes.
- Drain on kitchen paper before serving with pots of sweet chilli sauce.

817

SERVES 4

Baked Beans and Spinach Toasts

PREPARATION TIME 5-10 MINUTES

COOKING TIME 10-15 MINUTES

INGREDIENTS

FOR THE TOASTS
1 flute baguette, cut into 8 slices
400 g / 14 oz / 2 cups canned baked beans

225 g / 8 oz / 4 ½ cups baby
spinach leaves
30 ml / 1 fl. oz / 2 tbsp olive oil
1 tbsp butter

TO GARNISH
a small handful of basil leaves,
chopped

- Preheat the grill to hot.
- Warm the beans in a saucepan set over a medium heat, stirring occasionally until the beans have softened a little.
- Heat together the olive oil and butter in a large sauté pan and wilt the spinach with seasoning, tossing and stirring frequently.
- Drain on kitchen paper and set to one side.
- Grill the baguette slices for 1 minute before removing and topping with the spinach.
- Spoon the beans on top before garnishing with basil and serving.

818

MAKES 24

Chilli Con Carne Tacos

PREPARATION TIME 10-15
MINUTES

COOKING TIME 30-35 MINUTES

INGREDIENTS

24 round tortilla chips
450 g / 1 lb / 3 cups beef mince
200 g / 7 oz / 1 cup canned
chopped tomatoes
200 g / 7 oz / 1 cup canned
kidney beans, drained
75 g / 3 oz / ⅔ cup Red Leicester
(or similar), grated
30 ml / 1 fl. oz / 2 tbsp olive oil
1 onion, diced
1 clove of garlic, minced
1 tsp paprika
1 tsp ground cumin
1 tsp ground coriander
½ tsp ground cinnamons
salt and pepper

- Heat the olive oil in a saucepan set over a medium heat.
- Sweat the onion and garlic for 4-5 minutes until softened and translucent.
- Add the ground spices, stir well, then add the beef mince and brown well over.
- Add the chopped tomatoes and kidney beans, stir well, and cover with a lid.
- Cook over a reduced heat for 20-25 minutes until the kidney beans are softened.
- Adjust the seasoning to taste and preheat the grill to hot.
- Arrange the tortilla chips on a lined baking tray and top with a scant tablespoon of the chilli.
- Sprinkle the grated cheese on top and grill for 1-2 minutes until melted.
- Remove and serve immediately.

Chilli Sour Cream Tacos

819

- Substitute the melted cheese on top for a small dollop of sour cream and a small preserved jalapeño.

820

SERVES 4

Filled Mini Blini Sandwiches

PREPARATION TIME 20-25
MINUTES

COOKING TIME 20-25 MINUTES

INGREDIENTS

175 ml / 6 fl. oz / ⅔ cup whole milk,
warmed
75 g / 3 oz / ½ cup plain
(all purpose) flour
75 g / 3 oz / ½ cup buckwheat flour
30 ml / 1 fl. oz / 2 tbsp sunflower oil
1 tbsp butter, melted and cooled
½ tsp dried active yeast
½ tsp baking powder
1 egg yolk, 1 egg white
a pinch of salt
4 medium eggs, hard-boiled,
peeled and halved
2" fresh ginger, peeled and julienned
2 black radish, thinly sliced
1 tbsp pink micro salad leaves
1 tbsp salmon roe
1 tbsp mayonnaise
chive stalks, finely chopped
salt and pepper

- Sift together the flours and baking powder into a large mixing bowl.
- Combine the egg yolk, milk and yeast in a jug.
- Add the wet ingredients to the dry and whisk until you have a smooth batter. Add the melted butter and stir well.
- Whisk the egg whites with a pinch of salt until soft peaks form then fold into the batter.
- Coat a frying pan with sunflower oil and heat.
- Cook generous tablespoons of the batter in the pan until set on the bottom and you start to see bubbles on top.
- Flip and cook for 30 seconds.
- Remove the egg yolk from the eggs and mash with the mayonnaise and seasoning.
- Spread the blinis with the paste before topping with radish slices, ginger, salmon roe, micro salad and chive. Sandwich together.

Cream Cheese Blini Sandwiches

821

- Fold the salmon roe and chives into 175 g / 6 oz / ¾ cup softened cream cheese and use as the only filling for the sandwiches.

822

SERVES 4

Flaky Pastry Vegetable Tart

- Preheat the oven to 190°C (170° fan) / 375F / gas 5.
- Prepare the courgette into ribbons using a vegetable peeler or mandolin.
- Roll the pastry out on a lightly floured surface to ½ cm thickness and cut out 4 5" rounds.
- Arrange on a greaseproof paper-lined baking tray and spread the centre with a little basil pesto.
- Top with courgette ribbons and seasoning and bake for 10-12 minutes.
- Remove from the oven and add the artichoke and cherry tomatoes before returning to the oven for 6-8 minutes until the pastry is golden in colour.
- Remove from the oven and garnish with rocket on top before serving.

PREPARATION TIME 10 MINUTES

COOKING TIME 10-15 MINUTES

INGREDIENTS

FOR THE TARTS
250 g / 9 oz ready-made puff pastry
a little plain (all purpose) flour, for dusting
150 g / 5 oz / 1 cup canned artichoke hearts, drained and chopped
75 g / 3 oz / ⅓ cup basil pesto
55 ml / 2 fl. oz / ¼ cup extra-virgin olive oil
8 vine cherry tomatoes
½ courgette (zucchini)
salt and pepper

TO GARNISH
a large handful of rocket (arugula)

Flaky Pastry Pine Nut Tarts

823

- Substitute the rocket leaves on top for a sprinkling of pine nuts, adding them on top of the tarts at the same time as the artichoke and tomatoes.

824

SERVES 4

Roquefort Cream Canapés

- Pulse together the Roquefort, cream and cream cheese in a food processor until smooth.
- Chill until ready to serve.
- Toast the slices of bread under a hot grill until golden in colour on both sides.
- Use a 3" in diameter cookie cutter to cut rounds out of the centre of the pieces of toast.
- Top with generous tablespoons of the Roquefort cream and garnish with a slice of pear, a walnut half and radicchio or saffron.

PREPARATION TIME 10-15 MINUTES

COOKING TIME 15 MINUTES

INGREDIENTS

FOR THE CANAPÉS
8 slices of white sandwich bread
225 g / 8 oz / 2 cups roquefort, crumbled
110 g / 4 oz / ½ cup cream cheese
1 tbsp double (heavy) cream

TO GARNISH
8 walnut halves
1 ripe pear, cored and cut into 8 slices
a pinch of saffron threads
a handful of picked watercress leaves
a few radicchio leaves, torn

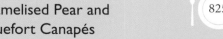

Caramelised Pear and Roquefort Canapés

825

- Sauté the pear slices in 1 tbsp melted butter until golden in colour on the outsides.

826

MAKES 8

Smoked Salmon Appetizer Rolls

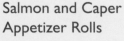

Salmon and Gherkin Appetizer Rolls

827

- Line the base of the smoked salmon with gherkins instead of asparagus.

Salmon and Caper Appetizer Rolls

828

- Garnish the tops of the rolls with baby capers instead of dill.

PREPARATION TIME 5-10 MINUTES

COOKING TIME 15-20 MINUTES

INGREDIENTS

FOR THE APPETIZER ROLLS
8 melba toasts
300 g / 10 ½ oz / 1 ½ cups cream cheese
250 g / 9 oz / 1 ⅔ cups smoked salmon slices
3 asparagus spears, ends and tips removed
1 tbsp extra-virgin olive oil

TO GARNISH
8 sprigs of dill

- Blanch the asparagus in a saucepan of salted, boiling water for 1 minute before refreshing in iced water.
- Cover a flat surface with cling film and layer the smoked salmon slices on it to cover in an even layer.
- Toss the asparagus spears in the olive oil and arrange in a line at the base of smoked salmon.
- Warm the cream cheese briefly in a microwave to loosen before stirring well.
- Spread on top of the remaining area of smoked salmon before rolling up the smoked salmon over the filling into a cylinder.
- Wrap tightly in cling film, tying the ends with kitchen string and chill for at least 2 hours.
- Remove from the fridge and unwrap before cutting into 8 portions.
- Sit flat on the melba toasts and garnish with dill sprigs before serving.

829

SERVES 4 | # Goats' Cheese and Chilli Crostinis

- Preheat the grill to hot.
- Whisk together the olive oil and chilli pepper in a small bowl.
- Grill the slices of baguette for 1 minute before removing and top the slices with goats' cheese triangles.
- Return to the grill for 1-2 minutes to glaze the cheese before removing and arranging on serving plates.
- Spoon the chilli oil on top before garnishing with rocket leaves.

PREPARATION TIME 10 MINUTES

COOKING TIME 10 MINUTES

INGREDIENTS

FOR THE ROSTINIS
1 flute baguette, cut into 8 slices
55 ml / 2 fl. oz / ¼ cup extra-virgin olive oil
225 g / 8 oz / 1 ½ cups goats' cheese, cut into triangles
2 red chilli (chili) peppers, deseeded and finely diced
salt and freshly ground black pepper

TO GARNISH
a large handful of rocket (arugula)

Goats' Cheese and Honey Crostinis

830

- Substitute the dressing for a teaspoon of honey on top of the crostinis.

831

SERVES 4 | # Prosciutto, Spinach and Mozzarella Bruschetta

- Preheat the grill to hot.
- Arrange the slices of bread on a grilling tray and toast for 1 minute.
- Remove and top each with a couple of baby spinach leaves, a ball of mozzarella in the middle and a folded slice of prosciutto on top.
- Sprinkle with a little grated mozzarella and season well before grilling for 1-2 minutes until the cheese melts.
- Remove and serve immediately.

PREPARATION TIME 10 MINUTES

COOKING TIME 5-10 MINUTES

INGREDIENTS

1 sourdough loaf, cut into 8
1" thick slices
8 baby mozzarella balls, drained
100 g / 3 ½ oz / ⅔ cup prosciutto slices
55 g / 2 oz / ½ cup grated mozzarella
a small handful of baby spinach leaves
salt and freshly ground black pepper

Fig, Ham and Cheese Bruschetta

832

- Substitute the mozzarella for rounds of goats' cheese; and use fresh fig halves on top of the ham before grilling.

833

SERVES 4

Seafood Bruschetta

PREPARATION TIME 15 MINUTES

COOKING TIME 15-20 MINUTES

....

INGREDIENTS

1 sourdough loaf, cut into 8
1" thick slices
75 ml / 3 fl. oz / ⅓ cup extra-virgin
olive oil
75 ml / 3 fl. oz / ⅓ cup olive oil
250 g / 9 oz / 1 ⅔ cups peeled prawns
200 g / 7 oz / 1 cup canned chopped
tomatoes
150 g / 5 oz / 1 cup frozen calamari
rings, thawed
150 g / 9 oz / 1 cup small scallops
100 g / 3 ½ oz / ½ cup basil pesto
2 cloves of garlic, minced
a small handful of Kalamata
olives, pitted
a small handful of flat-leaf
parsley, finely chopped
salt and pepper
sprigs of chervil
basil leaves

- Preheat the grill to hot.
- Heat half of the olive oil in a large sauté pan until hot.
- Season the prawns and sauté for 3-4 minutes until pink.
- Transfer to a plate then add the remaining olive oil.
- Season the calamari and scallops and sauté for 3-4 minutes, tossing occasionally.
- Stir in the chopped parsley before adding to the prawns.
- Warm the chopped tomatoes over a low heat.
- Mix together the extra-virgin olive oil and garlic before using to brush the sourdough with.
- Grill for 1 minute before removing and spreading half of the slices with pesto and the other half with chopped tomatoes.
- Top with a mixture of seafood and olive before garnishing with the herbs and serving.

Seafood and Chorizo Bruschetta   **834**

- Substitute the scallops for the same weight of sliced chorizo, grilling them before serving on the bruschetta.

835

SERVES 4

Coriander and Crushed Tomato Crostinis

PREPARATION TIME 15 MINUTES

COOKING TIME 10 MINUTES

....

INGREDIENTS

1 flute baguette, cut into 8 thin slices
1 small bunch of coriander (cilantro),
roughly chopped
450 g / 1 lb / 3 cups vine tomatoes,
cored and finely diced
110 ml / 4 fl. oz / ½ cup extra-virgin
olive oil
salt and pepper

- Stir together the tomato and chopped coriander with three-quarters of the olive oil and a little seasoning.
- Cover and leave at room temperature for 10 minutes.
- Drizzle the remaining olive oil on the slices of baguette before topping with the tomato and coriander salad.
- Serve immediately.

Tomato, Parsley and   **836**
Garlic Crostini

- Substitute the coriander for chopped flat-leaf parsley and add 1 minced clove of garlic.

837

SERVES 4

Pitta Bread with Hummus

Hummus and Onion Marmalade Toasts

838

- Top the hummus with teaspoons of ready-made onion marmalade.

Hummus and Almond Pittas

839

- Top the hummus with flaked (slivered) almonds.

PREPARATION TIME 10 MINUTES

COOKING TIME 10 MINUTES

INGREDIENTS

FOR THE PITTA BREADS
8 mini white pitta breads
400 g / 14 oz / 2 cups canned chickpeas (garbanzo beans), drained
55 ml / 2 fl. oz / ¼ cup extra-virgin olive oil
55 ml / 2 fl. oz / ¼ cup tahini
2 cloves of garlic, minced
½ lemon, juiced
salt and pepper

TO GARNISH
30 g / 1 oz / 2 tbsp raisins
1 tbsp sesame seeds
a few chive stalks, chopped
a few sprigs of flat-leaf parsley

- Toast the pitta breads under a hot grill for 1 minute.
- Pulse together the olive oil, chickpeas, tahini, lemon juice, garlic and seasoning until smooth.
- Spoon generous tablespoons of the hummus on top of the pitta breads.
- Garnish with raisins, chive and sesame seeds on top with parsley on the side.

840

SERVES 4

Duck and Vegetable Canapés

PREPARATION TIME 15 MINUTES

COOKING TIME 5-10 MINUTES

INGREDIENTS

FOR THE CANAPÉS
1 baguette, cut into 8 slices
100 g / 4 ½ oz / ⅔ cup smoked,
cured duck breasts slices
55 g / 2 oz / ½ cup pine nuts, toasted
30 ml / 1 fl. oz / 2 tbsp extra-virgin
olive oil
1 tbsp sherry vinegar
2 gem lettuce, finely shredded
2 vine tomatoes, deseeded and
finely diced
1 stick of celery, peeled and
finely diced
salt and pepper

TO GARNISH
a small handful of basil sprigs
a small handful of alfalfa sprouts

- Toss together the pine nuts, tomato, celery, lettuce, olive oil, vinegar and seasoning in a mixing bowl.
- Spoon on top of the slices of baguette and arrange on serving plates.
- Sit a slice of duck breasts on top before garnishing with a sprig of basil leaves and some alfalfa sprouts to the side.

Duck, Walnut and Raisin Canapés

841

- Use 75 g / 3 oz / ¾ cup chopped walnut halves and add a small handful of raisins into the topping.

842

SERVES 4

Cod, Tomato and Pepper Slices

PREPARATION TIME 15 MINUTES

COOKING TIME 15-20 MINUTES

INGREDIENTS

FOR THE SLICES
1 baguette, cut into 8 slices
55 ml / 2 fl. oz / ¼ cup olive oil
225 g / 8 oz / 1 ½ cups skinless cod
fillet, diced
2 large red peppers, deseeded and
thinly sliced
2 vine tomatoes, skinned and
thinly sliced
½ green pepper, deseeded and
thinly sliced
½ onion, thinly sliced
salt and pepper

TO GARNISH
a small handful of flat-leaf
parsley, finely chopped
a few sprigs of dill
a few sprigs of flat-leaf parsley

- Preheat the oven to 190°C (170° fan) / 375F / gas 5.
- Heat half of the olive oil in a heatproof sauté pan set over a medium heat until hot.
- Sauté the peppers with a little seasoning for 6-7 minutes until they start to soften.
- Add the cod, sliced tomato and the remaining olive oil, stirring well before transferring to the oven for 8-10 minutes until the cod is firm yet springy to the touch.
- Remove from the oven and adjust the seasoning to taste.
- Stack 2 slices of bread of plates and top with the cod and vegetables before garnishing with chopped parsley, dill sprigs and sprigs of flat-leaf parsley on the side.

Cod, Pepper and Olive Slices

843

- Substitute the slices tomato for 75 g / 3 oz / ½ cup pitted, chopped black olives in the stew mixture.

844

SERVES 4 # Two Pepper and Sausage Toasts

- Preheat the grill to hot and arrange the red peppers on a grilling tray.
- Grill until blackened and blistered before removing to a plastic bag and securing well.
- Leave for 10 minutes before removing, halving, deseeding and peeling away the skins.
- Grill the sausages for 10-12 minutes, turning occasionally until golden-brown in colour all over.
- Remove from the grill and cut in half before grilling the baguette slices for 1 minute.
- To assemble the toasts, arrange a red pepper half on top of the baguette, then follow with a half of sausage.
- Skewer a green chilli pepper on top before arranging on serving plates and garnishing with sage leaves.

PREPARATION TIME 10 MINUTES

COOKING TIME 20-25 MINUTES

INGREDIENTS

FOR THE TOASTS
1 multiseed baguette, cut into 8 slices
4 large good-quality pork sausages
(at least 80% pork meat)
8 preserved green chilli (chili)
peppers, drained
4 red peppers

TO GARNISH
a large handful of sage leaves

ALSO NEEDED
8 wooden skewers

Two Pepper and Shrimp Toasts   845

- Substitute the sausage for a large, peeled and deveined shrimp, grilling them until pink and tender.

846

SERVES 4 # Creamy Spanish Pepper Canapés

- Combine the mayonnaise, yoghurt, paprika and seasoning in a mixing bowl, stirring well.
- Stir in the diced pepper and ham coating them well in the sauce.
- Spoon on top of the baguette slices and arrange on serving plates.
- Garnish with a pinch of smoked paprika and sage leaves.

PREPARATION TIME 15 MINUTES

COOKING TIME 10 MINUTES

INGREDIENTS

FOR THE CANAPÉS
1 multiseed baguette, cut into 8 slices
1 green pepper, deseeded and very finely diced
1 red pepper, deseeded and very finely diced
150 g / 5 oz / 1 cup Serrano ham, finely diced
150 g / 5 oz / ⅔ cup plain yoghurt
55 g / 2 oz / ¼ cup mayonnaise
½ tsp paprika
salt and pepper

TO GARNISH
½ tsp smoked paprika
8 picked sage leaves

Creamy Pepper and Manchego Toasts   847

- Substitute the Serrano ham for the same amount of diced Manchego.

848

SERVES 4

Sobrasada and Honey Canapés

Sobrasada and Olive Canapés

849

- Add 75 g / 3 oz / ½ cup pitted black olives to the sobrasada mixture.

Sobrasada and Crème Fraîche Canapés

850

- Top the canapés with a teaspoon of crème fraîche.

PREPARATION TIME 10-15 MINUTES

COOKING TIME 15-20 MINUTES

INGREDIENTS

FOR THE CANAPÉS
8 slices of white sandwich bread
30 ml / 1 fl. oz / 2 tbsp olive oil
225 g / 8 oz / 1 ½ cups sobrasada, ground
200 g / 7 oz / 1 cup canned chopped tomatoes
30 g / 1 oz / 2 tbsp honey
salt and pepper

TO GARNISH
a large handful of friseé lettuce
a few chive stalks
4 cherry tomatoes, halved

- Heat the olive oil in a large frying pan set over a moderate heat until hot.
- Sauté the sobrasada until browned all over before adding the chopped tomatoes and honey.
- Adjust the seasoning to taste and set to one side.
- Preheat the grill to hot.
- Toast the slices of bread until golden-brown on both sides before removing the crusts.
- Cut half of the slices into triangles and cut out rounds from the other half using a 4" cookie cutter.
- Arrange stacks of toast on plates and top with the sobrasada mixture.
- Garnish with frisée, chives and cherry tomatoes before serving.

851

SERVES 4 Crushed Potatoes and Anchovy Toasts

- Cook the potatoes in a large saucepan of salted, boiling water until very tender; usually 18-22 minutes.
- Drain and leave to steam dry for 5 minutes before crushing with olive oil and seasoning using a fork.
- Toast the slices of baguette under a hot grill for 1 minute before removing.
- Top the slices of toast with the crushed potatoes and follow with a preserved anchovy fillet.
- Arrange on serving plates and garnish with cherry tomato halves, rocket leaves and alfalfa sprouts on the side.

PREPARATION TIME 10 MINUTES

COOKING TIME 25 MINUTES

INGREDIENTS

FOR THE TOASTS
1 multiseed baguette, cut into 8 slices
450 g / 1 lb / 3 cups new potatoes
75 ml / 3 fl. oz / ⅓ cup extra olive oil
8 preserved anchovy fillets, drained
salt and pepper

TO GARNISH
4 cherry tomatoes, halved
a small handful of rocket (arugula)
a small handful of alfalfa sprouts

Crushed Potato and Pesto Toasts   852

- Spread each of the toasts with a teaspoon of basil pesto before topping with the crushed potatoes.

853

SERVES 4 Scrambled Egg and Seafood Toasts

- Melt the butter in a large sauté pan set over a medium heat.
- Season the cod and shrimp and sauté in the butter for 5-6 minutes, stirring occasionally until the cod is opaque and the shrimp are pink and tender.
- Add the beaten egg, reduce the heat and cook until the egg is set yet creamy.
- Gently flake the cod pieces and adjust the seasoning to taste before spooning onto the baguette slices.
- Finely chop some of the chive stalks and sprinkle on top before garnishing with chive stalks and some parsley.

PREPARATION TIME 10-15 MINUTES

COOKING TIME 15 MINUTES

INGREDIENTS

FOR THE TOASTS
½ multiseed baguette, cut into 8 thin slices
30 g / 1 oz / 2 tbsp butter
6 large eggs, beaten
150 g / 5 oz / 1 cup skinless cod fillet, diced
8 peeled prawns, deveined
salt and pepper

TO GARNISH
a small bunch of chive stalks
a few sprigs of flat-leaf parsley

Egg, Chorizo and Cod Toasts   854

- Dice 100 g / 3 ½ oz / ⅔ cup chorizo and sauté with the cod in butter before adding the egg.

855

SERVES 4

Chorizo and Quail Egg Canapés

PREPARATION TIME 10-15 MINUTES

COOKING TIME 15 MINUTES

INGREDIENTS

FOR THE TOASTS
½ flute baguette, cut into 8 pieces
55 ml / 2 fl. oz / ¼ cup olive oil
110 g / 4 oz / ⅔ cup chorizo, diced
100 g / 3 ½ oz / ½ cup mayonnaise
100 g / 3 ½ oz / ½ cup tomato
ketchup
½ tsp smoked paprika
½ clove of garlic, minced
8 quail eggs
4 preserved red peppers, drained,
skinned and halved
salt and pepper

TO GARNISH
a few chive stalks

- Whisk together the mayonnaise, tomato ketchup, garlic, paprika and seasoning until smooth.
- Spread on top of the baguette slices and top with a slice of red pepper before setting to one side.
- Heat half of the olive oil in a frying pan until hot.
- Fry the quail eggs for 2-3 minutes.
- Drain on kitchen paper and cook the remaining eggs.
- Preheat the grill to hot.
- Drain the oil from the pan so that you have 1 tbsp left and fry the chorizo in it for 2 minutes, tossing occasionally.
- Pop a fried egg on top of the pepper on the canapés, top with some chorizo and flash under the grill for 30-45 seconds.
- Remove from the grill and serve on platters garnished with chive stalks.

Salami and Quail Egg Canapés

856

- Substitute the chorizo for slices of salami, placed on top of the peppers before the quail egg.

857

SERVES 4

Cecina and Blue Cheese Canapés

PREPARATION TIME 10 MINUTES

COOKING TIME 5-10 MINUTES

INGREDIENTS

FOR THE CANAPÉS
1 flute baguette, cut into 8 slices
225 g / 8 oz / 1 ½ cups cecina
(use air-dried ham if not available),
thinly sliced
125 g / 4 ½ oz / 1 ¼ cups
Gorgonzola, cubed

TO GARNISH
50 g / 2 oz / ½ cup Gorgonzola,
cubed

- Toast the slices of baguette under a hot grill for 1 minute.
- Remove and arrange on platters before topping with slices of ham and cubes of Gorgonzola.
- Garnish with extra Gorgonzola on the side.

Cecina, Walnut and Roquefort Canapés

858

- Add walnut halves to each toast and substitute the Gorgonzola for Roquefort.

859

SERVES 4

Serrano Ham and Mushroom Toasts

Ham, Mushroom and Brie Toasts

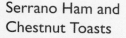
860

- Top the toasts with slices of Brie, glazing them under the grill for 1 minute before garnishing with parsley.

Serrano Ham and Chestnut Toasts

861

- Substitute the mushrooms for cooked, diced chestnuts.

PREPARATION TIME 10-15 MINUTES

COOKING TIME 10-15 MINUTES

INGREDIENTS

FOR THE TOASTS
1 small sourdough loaf, cut into 8 slices
30 ml / 1 fl. oz / 2 tbsp olive oil
225 g / 8 oz / 1 ½ cups Serrano ham, sliced
300 g / 10 ½ oz / 4 cups mixed wild mushrooms, brushed clean
salt and pepper

TO GARNISH
a small handful of flat-leaf parsley, finely chopped

- Heat the olive oil and butter together in a large sauté pan set over a moderate heat.
- Sauté the ham for 2 minutes, tossing occasionally, before adding the mushrooms and continuing to cook for 3-4 minutes.
- Adjust the seasoning to taste before spooning onto slices of the bread.
- Garnish with chopped parsley before serving.

862

SERVES 4

Mushroom, Shrimp and Aioli Toasts

PREPARATION TIME 15 MINUTES

COOKING TIME 15 MINUTES

INGREDIENTS

FOR THE TOASTS
225 g / 8 oz / 1 ½ cups frozen peeled shrimp, thawed
150 g / 5 oz / 2 cups button mushrooms, quartered
150 g / 5 oz / ⅔ cup mayonnaise
30 ml / 1 fl. oz / 2 tbsp olive oil
1 tbsp butter
1 flute baguette, cut into 8 slices
2 cloves of garlic, minced
salt and pepper

TO GARNISH
a small handful of beansprouts

- Heat the olive oil and butter together in a large sauté pan set over a moderate heat.
- Sauté the mushrooms with seasoning for 3-4 minutes, tossing occasionally until they start to colour.
- Add the shrimp and continue to sauté for a further 3-4 minutes until they are pink and tender.
- Meanwhile, stir together the mayonnaise, garlic and seasoning until smooth.
- Spoon on top of the slices of baguette before topping with mushrooms and shrimp.
- Garnish with beansprouts before serving.

Mushroom, Cheese and Aioli Toasts

 863

- Instead of using sautéed shrimp, use crumbled goats' cheese over the toasts.

864

SERVES 4

Cheese, Walnut and Date Toasts

PREPARATION TIME 10 MINUTES

COOKING TIME 10 MINUTES

INGREDIENTS

FOR THE TOASTS
1 multiseed baguette, cut into 8 slices
225 g / 8 oz / 1 cup cream cheese, softened
24 walnut halves
12 pitted dates
a few chive stalks, finely chopped

TO GARNISH
a few chive stalks

- Toast the slices of baguette under a hot grill for 1 minute.
- Remove and arrange on a serving platter before spreading with cream cheese.
- Dot with dates and walnut halves before sprinkling the tops with chopped chives.
- Garnish with chive stalks before serving.

Cheese, Walnut and Tomato Toasts

865

- Substitute the pitted dates with a piece of preserved sundried tomato.

866

SERVES 4

Shrimp, Lettuce and Ham Toasts

- Toast the slices of bread under a hot grill until golden-brown in colour on both sides.
- Remove the crusts and cut into triangular halves.
- Melt the butter in a saucepan set over a medium heat.
- Cook the beaten egg with seasoning, stirring until the egg is set but still creamy.
- Remove from the heat and stir through the pepper.
- Stack the toast triangles on serving plates and spoon the egg on top.
- Follow with slices of ham and a shrimp on top before serving with the frisée and oak leaf lettuce.

PREPARATION TIME 10-15 MINUTES

COOKING TIME 15 MINUTES

INGREDIENTS

6 slices of white sandwich bread
100 g / 3 ½ oz / ⅔ cup ham slices
30 g / 1 oz / 2 tbsp butter
5 large eggs, beaten
4 peeled and cooked shrimp
1 large red pepper, deseeded and finely diced
a large handful of oak leaf lettuce, torn
a large handful of frisée lettuce, torn
salt and pepper

Shrimp and Black Pudding Toasts   867

- Substitute the ham slices with 75 g / 3 oz / ½ cup cooked, diced black pudding.

868

SERVES 4

Fish Fingers

- Heat the groundnut oil in a large, heavy-based saucepan until hot; you can tell when the oil is hot enough as bubbles appear on a wooden spoon dipped in the hot oil.
- Pulse together the cod and cornflour with a little seasoning in a food processor until smooth.
- Shape the cod into finger shapes and dust in the plain flour, shaking off any excess.
- Dip in the beaten egg and coat in breadcrumbs before deep-frying in batches until golden-brown and crisp; 3-4 minutes.
- Drain on kitchen paper before serving with the herbs as a garnish.

PREPARATION TIME 10 MINUTES

COOKING TIME 15-20 MINUTES

INGREDIENTS

FOR THE FISH FINGERS
1 l / 1 pint 18 fl. oz / 4 cups groundnut oil, for deep-frying
450 g / 1lb / 3 cups skinless cod fillet, trimmed and diced
225 g / 8 oz / 2 cups golden breadcrumbs
75 g / 3 oz / ½ cup plain (all purpose) flour
30 g / 1 oz / 2 tbsp cornflour (cornstarch)
2 large eggs, beaten
salt and pepper

TO GARNISH
a few sprigs of chervil
a few tarragon leaves

Fish Fingers with Tartare Sauce   869

- Stir together mayonnaise with a little lemon juice, baby capers and chopped gherkins to serve with the fish fingers.

870

SERVES 4

Scrambled Egg and Bacon Blinis

Scrambled Egg and Cheese Blinis

871

- Top the scrambled egg on the blinis with a teaspoon of goats' cheese instead of bacon.

Scrambled Egg and Olive Blinis

872

- Top the scrambled egg with pitted green olives instead of bacon.

PREPARATION TIME 15 MINUTES

COOKING TIME 20-25 MINUTES

INGREDIENTS

FOR THE BLINIS
175 ml / 6 fl. oz / ⅔ cup whole milk, warmed
75 g / 3 oz / ½ cup plain (all purpose) flour
75 g / 3 oz / ½ cup buckwheat flour
30 ml / 1 fl. oz / 2 tbsp sunflower oil
1 tbsp butter, melted and cooled
½ tsp dried active yeast
½ tsp baking powder
1 medium egg yolk
1 medium egg white
a pinch of salt

FOR THE TOPPING
30 g / 1 oz / 2 tbsp butter
6 medium eggs, beaten
4 rasher of streaky bacon
salt and pepper
8 sprigs of chervil leaves

- Sift together the flours and baking powder into a large mixing bowl.
- Combine the egg yolk, milk and yeast in a jug, mixing well.
- Add the wet ingredients to the dry and whisk until you have a smooth batter.
- Add the melted butter and stir well.
- Whisk the egg whites with a pinch of salt until soft peaks form then fold into the batter.
- Coat a non-stick frying pan with a little sunflower oil and heat over a medium heat.
- Cook generous tablespoons of the batter in the pan until set on the bottom and you start to see bubbles on top.
- Flip and cook for 30 seconds before transferring to a warm plate.
- Cook the bacon under a hot grill for 3-4 minutes, turning once until golden in colour and crisp.
- Drain on kitchen paper and cut in half.
- Melt the butter in a large saucepan set over a medium heat and add the beaten eggs and seasoning, stirring until the eggs are set yet creamy.
- Spoon on top of the blinis and top with bacon.
- Garnish with chervil sprigs before serving.

873

SERVES 4

Chicken, Ham and Pepper Canapés

- Heat the olive oil in a large sauté pan set over a moderate heat until hot.
- Sauté the pancetta and chicken for 5-6 minutes until coloured on the outside.
- Add the vegetables, reduce the heat, and cook until softened.
- Stir through the vinegar and honey and adjust the seasoning to taste.
- Toast the bread under a hot grill before using a 2" cookie cutter to cut out 8 rounds of toast.
- Top with the chicken mixture, arrange on serving plates before topping with sour cream and garnishing with frisée.

PREPARATION TIME 15 MINUTES

COOKING TIME 15-20 MINUTES

INGREDIENTS

FOR THE CANAPÉS
4 thick slices of white sandwich bread
30 ml / 1 fl. oz / 2 tbsp olive oil
30 g / 1 oz / 2 tbsp pancetta, diced
1 large onion, sliced
1 large red pepper, deseeded and sliced
4 small skinless chicken breasts, diced
30 ml / 1 fl. oz / 2 tbsp balsamic vinegar
1 tbsp honey
salt and pepper

TO GARNISH
30 g / 1 oz / 2 tbsp sour cream
a small handful of frisée lettuce

Chicken, Artichoke and Pepper Canapés

874

- Substitute the pancetta for 2 diced, preserved artichoke hearts.

875

SERVES 4

Tuna Paté and Caper Canapés

- Toast the slices of bread under a hot grill until golden-brown on both sides.
- Remove the crusts and cut into triangular quarters.
- Stir together the tuna and capers in a mixing bowl before spooning onto the toast quarters.
- Top with slices of pepper and garnish with frisée and extra capers before serving.

PREPARATION TIME 10 MINUTES

COOKING TIME 10 MINUTES

INGREDIENTS

FOR THE CANAPÉS
4 slices of white sandwich bread
400 g / 14 oz / 2 cups canned tuna steak, drained
55 g / 2 oz / ⅓ cup baby capers, drained
salt and pepper

TO GARNISH
2 preserved red peppers, drained and sliced
1 tbsp baby capers, drained
a small handful of frisée lettuce

Tuna and Cream Cheese Canapés

876

- Spread the toast triangles with a teaspoon of cream cheese before topping with tuna and garnishing.

MAKES 12

Cecina and Pepper Tartlet

PREPARATION TIME 15 MINUTES

COOKING TIME 10-15 MINUTES

INGREDIENTS

FOR THE TARTLETS
12 ready-made vol-au-vent cases
55 ml / 2 fl. oz / ¼ cup olive oil
100 g / 3 ½ oz / ⅔ cup cecina
(use air-dried ham if not available),
finely chopped
1 onion, chopped
1 clove of garlic, minced
2 green peppers, deseeded and
finely diced
1 preserved red pepper, drained
and finely diced
1 tbsp flaked (slivered) almonds
salt and pepper

TO GARNISH
a few sprigs of rosemary

- Preheat the oven to 190°C (170° fan) / 375F / gas 5.
- Heat the olive oil in a large frying pan set over a medium heat until hot.
- Sauté the onion, peppers and garlic for 5-6 minutes until softened.
- Add the cecina and stir well before adjusting the seasoning to taste.
- Spoon into the vol-au-vent cases and arrange on a greaseproof paper-lined baking tray.
- Bake for 6-8 minutes until the cases are warmed through.
- Remove and serve on rosemary-lined platters.

Three Pepper Mini Tartlets
878

- Substitute the ham for a diced yellow pepper for a vegetarian version.

SERVES 4

Shrimp, Cod and Mushroom Tartlet

PREPARATION TIME 10-15
MINUTES

COOKING TIME 20-25 MINUTES

INGREDIENTS

150 g / 5 oz ready-made puff pastry
a little plain (all purpose) flour, for
dusting
1 small egg, beaten
55 ml / 2 fl. oz / ¼ cup olive oil
150 g / 5 oz / 1 cup raw prawns
(shrimps), peeled and de-veined with
tails intact
150 g / 5 oz / 1 cup skinless cod fillet,
cut into chunks
100 g / 3 ½ oz / 1 ⅓ cups closed cup
mushrooms, quartered
1 small onion, finely chopped
½ green pepper, de-seeded
and sliced
salt and pepper
a few sprigs of thyme, to garnish

- Preheat the oven to 200°C (180° fan) / 400F / gas 6.
- Lightly flour a work surface and lay down the pastry.
- Cut out 4 rounds of pastry. Arrange on baking sheets.
- Make a circular indent on the rounds of pastry so that you leave roughly a 1 inch border.
- Place a weight that covers the inner circle of the 4 rounds. Brush the outer rim with the beaten egg.
- Bake the pastry for 12-15 minutes until the outer border has puffed up and is risen.
- Heat the olive oil in a frying pan.
- Sweat the onion, green pepper and mushrooms for 7-8 minutes then increase the heat and add the prawns and cod.
- Cook for 3-4 minutes. Season.
- Spoon the filling into the pastry. Garnish with a few sprigs of thyme.

Shrimp, Cod and Caper Tartlets
880

- Substitute the mushrooms with baby capers.

881

MAKES 4

Broccoli Quiche Mini Soufflés

Pepper Quiche Mini Soufflés

882

- Substitute the broccoli with 2 diced red peppers in the pastry cases before adding the soufflé mixture.

Asparagus Quiche Mini Soufflés

883

- Substitute the broccoli for blanched, chopped asparagus spears.

PREPARATION TIME 15 MINUTES

COOKING TIME 15-20 MINUTES

INGREDIENTS

FOR THE SOUFFLÉS
250 g / 9 oz ready-made shortcrust pastry
a little plain (all purpose) flour, for dusting
1 small head of broccoli, prepared into small florets
125 ml / 4 ½ fl. oz / ½ cup whipping cream
125 ml / 4 ½ fl. oz / ½ cup crème fraîche
2 medium egg yolks
2 medium egg whites
salt and pepper

TO GARNISH
½ tsp flaked sea salt

- Preheat the oven to 180°C (160° fan) / 350F / gas 4.
- Roll the pastry out on a lightly floured surface.
- Cut 4 rounds of pastry and line 4 4" fluted cases.
- Prick the bases and trim the excess pastry.
- Line with greaseproof paper and fill with baking beans.
- Blind-bake for 12-15 minutes until golden-brown.
- Remove from the oven and discard the greaseproof paper and baking beans.
- Reduce the oven to 160°C (140° fan) / 325F / gas 3.
- Cook most of the florets in a saucepan of boiling, salted water for 3 minutes.
- Drain and cool to one side.
- Whisk together the egg yolks, cream, crème fraîche and seasoning in a bowl.
- Whisk the egg whites with a pinch of salt until soft peaks form before carefully folding into the cream mixture.
- Arrange the cooked florets in the pastry before spooning in the egg white mixture.
- Bake for 25-30 minutes until the filling is risen and golden on top.
- Remove to a wire rack to cool before turning out and garnishing with the reserved florets and sea salt.

MAKES 6

Seafood and Salmon Roe Tartlet

884

PREPARATION TIME 10 MINUTES

COOKING TIME 15-20 MINUTES

INGREDIENTS

FOR THE QUICHES

300 g / 10 ½ oz ready-made
shortcrust pastry
a little plain (all purpose) flour,
for dusting
225 g / 8 oz / 1 ½ cups frozen baby
shrimp, thawed
110 g / 4 oz / ⅔ cup white crab meat
55 g / 2 oz / ¼ cup plain yoghurt
55 g / 2 oz / ¼ cup mayonnaise
30 g / 1 oz / 2 tbsp tomato ketchup
½ lemon, juiced
a pinch of paprika
salt and pepper

TO GARNISH

1 tbsp salmon roe
a small handful of frisée lettuce

- Preheat the oven to 180°C (160° fan) / 350F / gas 4.
- Roll the pastry out on a lightly floured surface to ½ cm thickness.
- Cut 6 rounds of pastry and use to line 6 individual 3" fluted tartlet cases.
- Trim any excess, overhanging pastry.
- Blind-bake for 12-15 minutes until golden at the edges before removing to a wire rack to cool.
- Discard the greaseproof paper and baking beans.
- Stir together the yoghurt, mayonnaise, ketchup, lemon juice, paprika and seasoning in a mixing bowl until smooth.
- Stir through the crab meat and shrimp before spooning into the tartlet cases.
- Top with frisée and ½ a teaspoon of salmon roe before serving.

Seafood and Caviar Tartlets

885

- Top the tartlets with a little black caviar on top instead of the salmon roe.

886

MAKES 4

Shrimp and Vegetable Tartlet

PREPARATION TIME 15-20
MINUTES

COOKING TIME 15-20 MINUTES

INGREDIENTS

FOR THE TARTLETS

250 g / 9 oz ready-made shortcrust
pastry
a little plain (all purpose) flour,
for dusting
55 ml / 2 fl. oz / ¼ cup olive oil
8 shrimp, peeled with tails intact
1 courgette (zucchini), finely diced
1 yellow pepper, deseeded and diced
1 red pepper, deseeded and diced
1 clove of garlic, minced
2 vine tomatoes, deseeded and diced
salt and pepper

TO GARNISH

sprigs of flat-leaf parsley

- Preheat the oven to 180°C (160° fan) / 350F / gas 4.
- Roll the pastry out on a lightly floured surface.
- Cut 4 rounds of pastry and line 4 4" tartlet cases.
- Prick the bases and trim the excess pastry.
- Line with greaseproof paper and fill with baking beans.
- Blind-bake for 12-15 minutes until golden-brown.
- Remove and discard the greaseproof paper and beans.
- Heat the olive oil in a large saucepan.
- Sweat the peppers, courgette and garlic with a little salt until softened.
- Add the shrimp and tomatoes and continue to cook for 5-6 minutes until the shrimp are cooked.
- Turn out the tartlets from the cases and adjust the seasoning of the shrimp and vegetables to taste before spooning into the tartlet cases.
- Garnish with parsley before serving.

Shrimp and Goats' Cheese Tartlets

887

- Top the shrimp tartlets with a tablespoon of crumbled goats' cheese before serving.

888

SERVES 4

Ham, Emmental and Pineapple Sandwiches

- Preheat the grill to hot.
- Split the mini rolls in half and spread the bases with mayonnaise and top with pineapple ring halves and then a slice of Emmental.
- Season with black pepper and grill for 1 minute.
- Remove and top with folded slices of ham and then the roll tops.
- Garnish with frisée and chive before serving.

PREPARATION TIME 10 MINUTES

COOKING TIME 10 MINUTES

INGREDIENTS

FOR THE SANDWICHES
110 g / 4 oz / ½ cup canned pineapple rings, drained and halved
110 g / 4 oz / ½ cup mayonnaise
110 g / 4 oz / ⅔ cup thin ham slices
110 g / 4 oz / 1 cup Emmental slices
8 seeded mini rolls
salt and pepper

TO GARNISH
a few chive stalks
a small handful of frisée lettuce

Ham and Cream Cheese Rolls   889

- Substitute the Emmental slices with a scant tablespoon of cream cheese.

890

SERVES 4

Rice Cakes Topped with Tomatoes

- Combine the diced tomato, sliced basil, olive oil and a generous amount of seasoning in a mixing bowl, stirring well.
- Spread the tops of the rice cakes with a tablespoon of fromage frais before topping with a generous tablespoon of the tomato mixture.
- Garnish with a sprig of basil leaves on top before serving.

PREPARATION TIME 10 MINUTES

COOKING TIME 10 MINUTES

INGREDIENTS

FOR THE RICE CAKES
8 rice cakes
125 g / 4 ½ oz / ½ cup fromage frais
55 ml / 2 fl. oz / ¼ cup extra-virgin olive oil
4 large vine tomatoes, cored and finely diced
a small handful of basil leaves, sliced
salt and freshly ground black pepper

TO GARNISH
8 sprigs of basil leaves

Tomato and Onion Rice Cakes   891

- Substitute 1 of the tomatoes for ½ finely diced white onion.

892

MAKES 4

Veal and Cumin Burgers

PREPARATION TIME 10 MINUTES

COOKING TIME 10-15 MINUTES

INGREDIENTS

FOR THE BURGERS

4 mini sesame seed burger buns,
halved
450 g / 1 lb / 3 cups veal mince
2 tsp ground cumin
½ white onion, thinly sliced
2 salad tomatoes, sliced
a small bunch of coriander (cilantro),
roughly chopped
a pinch of chili flakes
a large handful of purple alfalfa
sprouts
salt and pepper

TO GARNISH

a sprig of flat-leaf parsley
1 vine tomato
a few slices of white onion

- Preheat the grill to hot.
- Combine the veal mince, chopped coriander, chilli flakes, cumin and seasoning in a mixing bowl.
- Mix well with your hands before shaping into 4 even-sized balls.
- Flatten into patties and arrange on a grilling tray.
- Grill for 10-12 minutes, turning once, until coloured on top and cooked through.
- Remove from the grill and leave to rest for 2 minutes as you grill the burger buns.
- Top the bottom halves with onion and tomato slices before sitting the patties on top.
- Top with alfalfa sprouts before arranging on serving plates and garnishing with tomato, onion slices and parsley.

893

SERVES 4

Thai Beef Skewers with Potatoes

PREPARATION TIME 15-20
MINUTES

COOKING TIME 20-25 MINUTES

INGREDIENTS

675 g / 1 lb 8 oz / 4 ½ cups sirloin
steak, trimmed and cubed
55 ml / 2 fl. oz / ¼ cup sesame oil
1" piece of ginger, peeled and
finely chopped
1 tbsp fish sauce
1 tbsp rice wine vinegar
1 lime, juiced
1 tbsp soft light brown sugar
300 g / 10 ½ oz / 2 cups new potatoes
30 ml / 1 fl. oz / 2 tbsp olive oil
2 limes, sliced
1 habanero chilli (chili), half sliced
and half finely chopped
2-3 mint leaves, chopped
3-4 coriander (cilantro) leaves,
chopped
salt and pepper

- Whisk together the sugar, lime juice, fish sauce, vinegar, ginger and sesame oil in a mixing bowl.
- Add the beef, stir well to coat before covering and leaving for 15 minutes.
- Cook the potatoes in a large saucepan of salted, boiling water until tender; 15-18 minutes.
- Drain and leave to steam dry for 3 minutes before tossing with olive oil and seasoning.
- Preheat the grill to hot and thread the beef onto the skewers.
- Grill for 8-10 minutes, turning occasionally; heat the reserved marinade in a small saucepan until boiling.
- Remove the skewers and let them rest for 5 minutes.
- Divide the potatoes between 2 serving bowls and garnish with lime slices.
- Sit 2 skewers on top of each bowl and brush with the marinade.
- Garnish with chopped and sliced chilli as well as the herbs.

894

MAKES 4

Beef Empanadas

- Heat the olive oil in a large frying pan.
- Sauté the beef mince with the oregano, basil, paprika and seasoning until well browned.
- Add the chopped tomatoes, stir well, and continue to cook over a reduced heat for 5 minutes.
- Tip the mixture into a colander and drain.
- Preheat the oven to 180°C (160° fan) / 350F / gas 4. Line a large baking tray with greaseproof paper.
- Roll the pastry out on a lightly floured surface.
- Cut out 4 8" rounds and spoon the filling into the centres.
- Wet the rim of the pastry with a little water using your fingertip before folding the bottom end over the filling and sealing with the opposite end by crimping.
- Transfer to the baking tray and bake for 22-25 minutes.
- Stir together the cinnamon and sugar in a small pot.
- Sprinkle the sugar mixture on top and serve.

PREPARATION TIME 10 MINUTES

COOKING TIME 20 MINUTES

INGREDIENTS

350 g / 12 oz ready-made shortcrust pastry
a little plain (all purpose) flour
30 ml / 1 fl. oz / 2 tbsp olive oil
450 g / 1 lb / 3 cups beef mince
200 g / 7 oz / 1 cup chopped tomatoes
30 ml / 1 fl. oz / 2 tbsp olive oil
1 tbsp soft light brown sugar
1 tsp ground cinnamon
1 tsp paprika
½ tsp dried oregano
½ tsp dried basil
salt and pepper

Broccoli and Tuna Mini Quiches

895

MAKES 4

PREPARATION TIME 10-15 MINUTES

COOKING TIME 20 MINUTES

INGREDIENTS

250 g / 9 oz ready-made shortcrust pastry
a little plain (all purpose) flour, for dusting

250 ml / 9 fl. oz / 1 cup whole milk
250 ml / 9 fl. oz / 1 cup crème fraîche
225 g / 8 oz / 1 ½ cups canned tuna chunks, drained
3 large eggs
1 small egg, beaten
1 small head of broccoli, prepared into small florets
salt and pepper

- Preheat the oven to 180°C (160° fan) / 350F / gas 4.
- Roll the pastry out on a lightly floured surface to ½ cm thickness.
- Cut 4 rounds of pastry and use to line 4 individual 4" tartlet cases.
- Prick the bases with a fork and trim some of the excess pastry.
- Line with greaseproof paper and fill with baking beans.
- Blind-bake for 12-15 minutes until golden-brown in colour at the edges.
- Remove from the oven and discard the greaseproof paper and baking beans.
- Brush the bases with the beaten egg and leave to one side.
- Whisk together the eggs, milk and creme fraîche with seasoning before using to fill the pastry cases.
- Dot with broccoli florets and tuna chunks before baking for 25-30 minutes until the filling is set and golden on top.

Avocado and Cheese Crackers

896

SERVES 4

PREPARATION TIME 10-15 MINUTES

COOKING TIME 5-10 MINUTES

INGREDIENTS

8 cream crackers
225 g / 8 oz / 1 cup cream cheese
2 ripe avocados, destoned and thinly sliced

1 red pepper, deseeded and finely diced
1 tbsp extra-virgin olive oil
a few chive stalks, finely chopped
salt and freshly ground black pepper

- Spread the crackers evenly with cream cheese before topping with the avocado slices.
- Sprinkle the tops with red pepper, chopped chives and black pepper.
- Drizzle with olive oil before serving.

897

SERVES 4

Crab and Apple Avocado Creams

PREPARATION TIME 15 MINUTES

COOKING TIME 10 MINUTES

....

INGREDIENTS

FOR THE CREAMS
2 large Granny Smith apples,
cored and finely diced
½ lemon, juiced
½ lime, juiced
225 g / 8 oz / 1 ½ cups white crab
meat
2 ripe avocados, destoned and diced
55 ml / 2 fl. oz / ¼ cup whipping
cream
salt and pepper

TO GARNISH
1 tbsp flat-leaf parsley leaves

- Puree the avocado, lime juice, cream and seasoning in a food processor until smooth.
- Toss the apple with the lemon juice and a little seasoning before spooning into the base of 4 individual serving jars.
- Top with the avocado cream and follow with the crab meat, flaking it as you do.
- Garnish with parsley on top before serving.

Seafood and Avocado Cream Appetizers

 898

- Substitute half of the crab meat for 75 g / 3 oz / ½ cup cooked and peeled prawns.

899

SERVES 4

Apple and Foie Gras Appetizers

PREPARATION TIME 10-15
MINUTES

COOKING TIME 20-25 MINUTES

....

INGREDIENTS

FOR THE APPETIZERS
8 slices of Bayonne ham
8 star-shaped crackers
2 Golden Delicious apples,
peeled and cored
225 g / 8 oz / 1 ½ cups goose foie
gras, deveined
55 ml / 2 fl. oz / ¼ cup double
(heavy)cream
55 g / 2 oz / ¼ cup butter, diced
1 tbsp dry sherry
2 tsp caster (superfine) sugar
salt and pepper

TO GARNISH
8-12 sprigs of chervil leaves
salt and freshly ground black pepper

ALSO NEEDED
8 cocktail sticks

- Heat a frying pan over a moderate heat until very hot. Season the foie gras and sear in the pan until golden.
- Remove to a food processor and deglaze pan using sherry before tipping into the food processor as well.
- Add cream, half of the butter, seasoning before blitzing until smooth. Cover and chill. Slice apples into 1 cm rings, preparing 8 slices that are 2" in diameter.
- Melt the remaining butter in a clean frying pan and sauté the apple with sugar for 2-3 minutes.
- Grease and line a baking tray with greaseproof paper before placing 8 2" metal rings on it.
- Line the base with apple before spooning the foie gras pate on top. Cover and chill for 1 hour.
- Transfer carefully onto a serving platter before removing the rings. Top with folded ham slices and star cracker. Garnish with chervil and a little more seasoning.

Pear and Foie Gras Appetizers

900

- Substitute the apple slices for slices of pear, caramelising them in the same way.

901

MAKES 4 Spinach and Shrimp Mini Tartlets

- Preheat the oven to 180°C (160° fan) / 350F / gas 4.
- Roll the pastry out on a lightly floured surface.
- Cut 4 rounds of pastry and line 4 4" ceramic moulds.
- Prick the bases and trim the excess pastry. Chill.
- Heat the olive oil in a large frying pan set over a moderate heat until hot.
- Wilt the spinach with a little seasoning before draining, chopping and dividing between the pastry cases.
- Whisk together the milk, creme fraîche and eggs with seasoning before pouring over the spinach into the cases.
- Top with the grated cheese and bake for 22-25 minutes until the pastry is golden-brown at the edges and the filling is set.
- Remove to a wire rack to cool a little before serving with a cooked prawn on top.

Spinach and Scallop Mini Tartlets   902

- Substitute the shrimp for 4 small scallops, cooked until golden-brown and firm yet springy to the touch on both sides.

PREPARATION TIME 10 MINUTES

COOKING TIME 15-20 MINUTES

INGREDIENTS

FOR THE TARTLETS
250 g / 9 oz ready-made puff pastry
a little plain (all purpose) flour, for dusting
55 ml / 2 fl. oz / ¼ cup olive oil
250 g / 9 oz / 5 cups baby spinach leaves
250 ml / 9 fl. oz / 1 cup whole milk
125 ml / 4 ½ fl. oz / ½ cup crème fraîche
50 g / 2 oz / ½ cup Cheddar, finely grated
3 medium eggs
salt and pepper

TO GARNISH
4 frozen cooked shrimp, thawed

903

SERVES 4 Artichoke and Parsley Dip

- Warm together the artichoke hearts and cream in a saucepan set over a low heat.
- Tip into a food processor and add the mayonnaise, lemon juice and parsley.
- Blitz until smooth before adjusting the seasoning to taste.
- Preheat a griddle pan over a moderate heat until hot.
- Brush one side of the slices of bread with olive oil and griddle on the pan until lightly charred, then rotating by 90° and griddling for another 1-2 minutes until you have a cross-hatch pattern.
- Serve the dip warm or cold on the toasts, sprinkling a little chopped parsley on top.

Artichoke and Olive Dip   904

- Stir 75 g / 3 oz / ½ cup pitted black olives into the dip before serving.

PREPARATION TIME 10 MINUTES

COOKING TIME 10-15 MINUTES

INGREDIENTS

FOR THE DIP
350 g / 12 oz / 2 ⅓ cups canned artichoke hearts, drained and chopped
75 ml / 3 fl. oz / ⅓ cup whipping cream
1 tbsp mayonnaise
½ lemon, juiced
a small bunch of flat-leaf parsley leaves, chopped
salt and pepper

TO GARNISH
55 ml / 2 fl. oz / ¼ cup extra-virgin olive oil
4 large slices of sourdough
a small handful of flat-leaf parsley leaves, finely chopped

905

MAKES 8

Chickpea Flour Mini Pizzas

Chickpea Flour Vegetarian Pizzas

906

- Substitute the chicken for cubes of tofu.

Red Onion Chickpea Flour Pizzas

907

- Substitute the mushrooms for sliced red onion.

PREPARATION TIME 10-15 MINUTES

COOKING TIME 15 MINUTES

....

INGREDIENTS

100 g / 3 ½ oz / ⅔ cup plain (all purpose) flour
100 g / 3 ½ oz / ⅔ cup chickpea (gram) flour
a little plain (all purpose) flour, for dusting
125 ml / 4 ½ fl. oz / ½ cup warm water (at 40°C)
125 g / 4 ½ oz / ½ cup passata
75 g / 3 oz / 1 cup button mushrooms, sliced
30 ml / 1 fl. oz / 2 tbsp olive oil
2 cooked chicken breasts, cubed
1 onion, thinly sliced
½ tbsp caster (superfine) sugar
1 tsp dried active yeast
½ tsp salt
freshly ground black pepper
sage leaves

- Preheat the oven to 220°C (200° fan) / 425F / gas 7.
- Combine the flours, salt, yeast and sugar in a large mixing bowl.
- Mix in the oil and water to form a dough, bringing it together with your hands, then kneading gently on a lightly floured surface for 1 minute until even.
- Divide into 8 balls and roll out to ½ cm thick.
- Arrange on baking trays and spread the tops with a scant tablespoon of passata.
- Arrange the mushroom, chicken and onion on top before baking for 10-12 minutes until the dough is cooked and coloured.
- Remove from the oven and garnish with sage and freshly ground pepper before serving.

908

SERVES 4

Chicken Liver Paté with Capers

- Heat 1 tablespoon of the butter in a large frying pan set over a moderate heat.
- Sauté the livers with the thyme and seasoning for 2 minutes, tossing occasionally, until browned on the outside.
- Deglaze the pan with the madeira, letting it reduce by half.
- Tip in a food processor and add the cream and allspice.
- Blitz until smooth before adding the remaining butter.
- Adjust the seasoning to taste before scraping into a bowl and stirring in the capers.
- Chill for 2 hours until ready to serve with the bread.

PREPARATION TIME 10-15 MINUTES

COOKING TIME 10-15 MINUTES

INGREDIENTS

FOR THE PATÉ
300 g / 10 ½ oz / 2 cups chicken livers, cleaned and diced
110 g / 5 oz / ⅔ cup butter, diced
75 ml / 3 fl. oz / ⅓ cup double (heavy) cream
55 ml / 2 fl. oz / ¼ cup madeira
30 g / 1 oz / 2 tbsp baby capers, drained
½ tsp ground thyme
½ tsp ground allspice

TO GARNISH
½ crust white loaf, cut into slices

Chicken Liver Paté with Paprika   909

- Add 1 tsp of paprika to the chicken livers as you blitz them in the food processor.

910

MAKES 8

Tomato-Onion Savoury Tatin Tartlets

- Preheat the oven to 190°C (170°C fan) / 375°F / gas 5.
- Line a baking tray with greaseproof paper.
- Roll the pastry out on a lightly floured work surface to ½ cm thickness.
- Cut out 8 rounds of pastry 5-6 cm in diameter and transfer to the lined baking tray.
- Prick each a few times with a fork.
- Arrange the sliced onion and the tomatoes on top of each pastry.
- Drizzle with the olive oil and the balsamic vinegar, then sprinkle with the sugar and some seasoning.
- Bake in the oven for 10-12 minutes until the pastry is puffed and golden and the vegetables are softened.
- Remove from the oven and serve immediately.

PREPARATION TIME 10 MINUTES

COOKING TIME 15-20 MINUTES

INGREDIENTS

160 g / 5 ½ oz ready-made puff pastry
a little plain (all purpose) flour, for dusting
55 ml / 2 fl. oz / ¼ cup extra-virgin olive oil
25 ml / 1 fl. oz / 2 tbsp balsamic vinegar
320 g / 11 oz / 2 cups vine cherry tomatoes
1 large onion, sliced
1 tsp caster (superfine) sugar
salt and pepper

Tomato and Goats' Cheese Tatins   911

- Substitute the onion for cubes of goats' cheese.

MAKES 6

Olive and Thyme Mini Cakes

912

PREPARATION TIME 10 MINUTES

COOKING TIME 10-15 MINUTES

....

INGREDIENTS

FOR THE CAKES

250 g / 9 oz / 1 ⅔ cups self-raising flour, sifted

125 ml / 4 ½ fl. oz / ½ cup extra-virgin olive oil

110 g / 4 oz / 1 cup Parmesan, finely grated

75 g / 3 oz / ½ cup pitted green olives

50 g / 2 oz / ⅓ cup pitted black olives

a few sprigs of thyme, leaves stripped

1 tbsp buttermilk

2 large eggs, beaten

salt and pepper

TO GARNISH

30 g / 1 oz / ¼ cup green olives

a few sprigs of thyme

- Preheat the oven to 170°C (150°C fan) / 325°F / gas 3.
- Grease and line 6 mini loaf tins with greaseproof paper.
- Whisk together the eggs and olive oil in a jug.
- Combine the flour and Parmesan in a mixing bowl.
- Add the wet ingredient to the dry ones and fold until combined.
- Add the green olives and stripped thyme leaves, stirring well, before spooning into the loaf tins.
- Stud with the black olives and bake for 35-40 minutes; test with a wooden toothpick, if it comes out clean, the cakes are done.
- Remove from the oven and leave to cool before turning out and slicing.
- Garnish with green olives and thyme.

Rosemary and Thyme Mini Cakes 913

- Omit the olives from the recipe and add 2 tsp dried rosemary to the batter before baking.

MAKES 6

Salmon and Dill Savoury Cakes

914

PREPARATION TIME 10 MINUTES

COOKING TIME 10-15 MINUTES

....

INGREDIENTS

FOR THE MINI LOAFS

250 g / 9 oz / 1 ⅔ cups self-raising flour, sifted

125 ml / 4 ½ fl. oz / ½ cup olive oil

110 g / 4 oz / 1 cup Parmesan, finely grated

2 skinless salmon fillets, diced

1 tbsp black poppy seeds

1 tsp dried dill

2 large eggs, beaten

salt and pepper

TO GARNISH

a few sprigs of dill

- Preheat the oven to 170°C (150°C fan) / 325°F / gas 3.
- Grease and line 6 mini loaf tins with greaseproof paper.
- Whisk together the eggs and olive oil in a jug.
- Combine the flour, salmon, dried dill and Parmesan in a mixing bowl.
- Add the wet ingredient to the dry ones and fold until combined.
- Add some seasoning before spooning into the loaf tins before sprinkling the tops with poppy seeds.
- Bake for 40-45 minutes; test with a wooden toothpick, if it comes out clean, the cakes are done.
- Remove from the oven and leave to cool before turning out.
- Garnish with dill before serving.

Salmon and Sundried Tomato Loafs 915

- Substitute half of the diced salmon fillet with 75 g / 3 oz / ½ cup chopped sundried tomato.

916
MAKES 12

Onion and Tuna Mini Pizzas

Onion and Goats' Cheese Pizzas
917

- Substitute the black olives and tuna for 175 g / 6 oz / 1 ¾ cups crumbled goats' cheese as a topping.

Tuna and Caper Mini Pizzas
918

- Substitute the black olives for baby capers.

PREPARATION TIME 10 MINUTES

COOKING TIME 15-20 MINUTES

INGREDIENTS

300 g / 10 ½ oz ready-made pizza dough
a little plain (all purpose) flour, for dusting
1 tbsp olive oil
225 g / 8 oz / 1 cup ready-made onion marmalade/chutney
225 g / 8 oz / 1 ½ cups canned tuna, drained and flaked
75 g / 3 oz / ½ cup pitted black olives, roughly chopped
salt and pepper

- Preheat the oven to 200°C (180° fan) / 400F / gas 6.
- Divide the dough into 12 small balls and roll out on a lightly floured surface to 2" in diameter.
- Arrange on baking trays and drizzle with a little olive oil.
- Top with a tablespoon of onion marmalade followed by flaked tuna and olives.
- Bake for 8-10 minutes until the pizza dough is cooked through.
- Remove from the oven and serve immediately.

919

MAKES 4

Tomato and Basil Crème Brûlées

PREPARATION TIME 10-15 MINUTES

COOKING TIME 15-20 MINUTES

CHILLING TIME 3 HOURS

INGREDIENTS

FOR THE CRÈME BRÛLÉES

250 ml / 9 fl. oz / 1 cup whole milk
250 ml / 9 fl. oz / 1 cup whipping cream
4 medium eggs
salt and pepper

TO GARNISH

75 g / 3 oz / ½ cup preserved sundried tomatoes, drained
55 ml / 2 fl. oz / ¼ cup balsamic vinegar
a few basil leaves, cut chiffonade
a sprig of basil leaves

ALSO NEEDED

chef's blowtorch

- Preheat the oven to 150°C (130° fan) / 300F / gas 2.
- Line a roasting tray with a tea towel and position 4 individual ceramic ramekins in it.
- Whisk together the eggs, milk and cream in a saucepan before cooking over a low heat, stirring all the time until it reaches a coating consistency.
- Pour into the dishes and fill the roasting tray with boiling water that comes halfway up the dishes.
- Bake for 1 hour 10-20 minutes until just set; they should wobble slightly in the centres when they are done.
- Remove from the oven and chill for 3 hours until set.
- Top the brûlée with sundried tomato, cut basil and a tablespoon of balsamic vinegar before caramelising with a blowtorch.
- Serve with a sprig of basil leaves on the side.

Tomato and Mushroom Crème Brûlées

920

- Sauté 75 g / 3 oz / 1 cup chanterelle mushrooms and use as a topping instead of the vinegar.

921

MAKES 4

Shrimp and Coconut Crème Brûlées

PREPARATION TIME 10-15 MINUTES

COOKING TIME 15-20 MINUTES

CHILLING TIME 3 HOURS

INGREDIENTS

FOR THE CRÈME BRÛLÉES

250 ml / 9 fl. oz / 1 cup whole milk
250 ml / 9 fl. oz / 1 cup whipping cream
4 medium eggs
salt and pepper

TO GARNISH

25 g / 1 oz / ⅓ cup desiccated coconut
1 tbsp coconut flakes
4 coriander (cilantro) leaves
1 tbsp olive oil
4 peeled shrimp
salt and pepper

ALSO NEEDED

chef's blowtorch

- Preheat the oven to 150°C (130° fan) / 300F / gas 2.
- Line a roasting tray with a tea towel and position 4 individual ceramic ramekins in it.
- Whisk together the eggs, coconut milk and cream in a saucepan before cooking over a low heat, stirring all the time until it reaches a coating consistency.
- Pour into the dishes and fill the roasting tray with boiling water that comes halfway up the dishes.
- Bake for 1 hour 15-25 minutes until just set. Remove from the oven and chill for 3 hours until set.
- Coat the shrimp in the olive oil and season well.
- Cook under a hot grill for 4-5 minutes. Remove and dry on kitchen paper.
- Stud the brulées with a shrimp before sprinkling with the desiccated coconut.
- Toast with a blowtorch, garnish with coconut flakes and coriander.

Coconut and Chilli Crème Brûlées

922

- Substitute the coconut topping with a teaspoon of finely chopped green chilli (chili).

923

MAKES 4

Pepper Crumble Crème Brûlées

- Preheat the oven to 150°C (130° fan) / 300F / gas 2.
- Line a roasting tray with a tea towel and position 4 individual ceramic ramekins in it.
- Whisk together the eggs, milk and cream in a saucepan before cooking over a low heat, stirring all the time until it reaches a coating consistency.
- Pour into the dishes and fill the roasting tray with boiling water that comes halfway up the dishes.
- Bake for 1 hour 10-20 minutes until just set; they should wobble slightly in the centres when they are done.
- Remove from the oven and chill for 3 hours until set.
- Rub together the oats, flour and butter in a mixing bowl until they resemble breadcrumbs.
- Dot the brulées with the peppers and follow with a tablespoon of the crumble mixture.
- Toast the crumble briefly with a blowtorch.

Pepper and Olive Crème Brûlées 924

- Substitute the crumble topping with 75 g / 3 oz / ½ cup chopped mixed olives.

PREPARATION TIME 10-15 MINUTES

COOKING TIME 15-20 MINUTES

CHILLING TIME 3 HOURS

INGREDIENTS

FOR THE CRÈME BRÛLÉES
250 ml / 9 fl. oz / 1 cup whole milk
250 ml / 9 fl. oz / 1 cup whipping cream
4 medium eggs
salt and pepper

TO GARNISH
1 yellow pepper, deseeded and diced
1 red pepper, deseeded and diced
50 g / 2 oz / ⅔ cup rolled oats
50 g / 2 oz / ⅓ cup plain (all purpose) flour
50 g / 2 oz / ¼ cup butter, cold and cubed

ALSO NEEDED
chef's blowtorch

925

MAKES 4

Smoked Salmon Crème Brûlées

- Preheat the oven to 150°C (130° fan) / 300F / gas 2.
- Line a roasting tray with a tea towel and position 4 individual brûlée dishes in it.
- Whisk together the eggs, milk and creme fraîche in a saucepan before cooking over a low heat, stirring all the time until it reaches a coating consistency.
- Pour into the dishes and fill the roasting tray with boiling water that comes halfway up the dishes.
- Bake for 1 hour 10-20 minutes until just set; they should wobble slightly in the centres when they are done.
- Remove from the oven and chill for 3 hours until set.
- Just before serving, to with smoked salmon slices and sprinkle with caster sugar.
- Caramelise with a blowtorch, before topping with sesame seeds and a sprig of dill.

Salmon and Leek Crème Brûlées 926

- Add ½ finely sliced leek to the custard mixture before baking.

PREPARATION TIME 10 MINUTES

COOKING TIME 45 MINUTES

INGREDIENTS

FOR THE CRÈME BRULÉES
110 g / 4 oz / ⅔ cup smoked salmon, sliced
250 ml / 9 fl. oz / 1 cup whole milk
250 ml / 9 fl. oz / 1 cup double (heavy) cream
4 medium eggs
salt and pepper

TO GARNISH
75 g / 3 oz / ⅓ cup caster (superfine) sugar
30 g / 1 oz / 2 tbsp sesame seeds
4 sprigs of dill

ALSO NEEDED
chef's blowtorch

927

SERVES 4

Mini Avocado and Onion Hamburgers

Avocado and Fried Egg Hamburger

928

- Top the burgers with a fried quail's egg instead of caramelised onions.

Mini Avocado Cheeseburgers

929

- Substitute the caramelised onions for a slice of Swiss cheese on top.

PREPARATION TIME 10-15 MINUTES

COOKING TIME 20-25 MINUTES

INGREDIENTS

FOR THE HAMBURGERS
½ flute baguette, cut into 8 slices
2 onions, finely sliced
2 medium, ripe avocados, destoned and sliced
450 g / 1 lb / 3 cups beef mince
30 g / 1 oz / 2 tbsp butter
1 tbsp olive oil
1 tsp dried thyme
1 tsp caster (superfine) sugar
salt and pepper

TO GARNISH
30 ml / 1 fl. oz / 2 tbsp extra-virgin olive oil
a few sprigs of thyme, chopped

- Mix together the olive oil and thyme for the garnish in a mixing bowl before setting to one side.
- Melt together the butter and oil in a large frying pan set over a medium heat.
- Sweat the onion with seasoning until translucent before adding the sugar and continuing to cook until caramelised.
- Remove from the heat and set to one side.
- Mash together the mince, dried thyme and seasoning in a large mixing bowl.
- Shape into 8 small patties and arrange on a greaseproof paper-lined baking tray.
- Grill for 3-4 minutes on both sides until coloured on both sides.
- To assemble the burgers, sit a burger patty on top of a slice of baguette and top with a slice of avocado.
- Arrange on serving plates and spoon a scant tablespoon of the caramelised onion on top before drizzling with the thyme olive oil.
- Serve immediately.

930

MAKES 4

Salmon and Spinach Filo Tartlets

- Preheat the oven to 190°C (170° fan) / 375F / gas 5.
- Grease and line a baking tray with greaseproof paper.
- Brush the sheets of pastry with melted butter before layering one on top of another.
- Cut into 4 even squares and drape over upturned individual dariole moulds.
- Bake for 12-15 minutes until golden and crisp.
- Remove to a wire rack to cool.
- Heat the olive oil in a large frying pan set over a moderate heat until hot.
- Wilt the spinach with a little seasoning before transferring to kitchen paper to drain.
- Combine with the smoked salmon, pine nuts, crème fraîche and seasoning in a mixing bowl, stirring well.
- Spoon into the filo pastry tartlets before serving.

PREPARATION TIME 10-15 MINUTES

COOKING TIME 25-30 MINUTES

....

INGREDIENTS

4 sheets of ready-made filo pastry
55 ml / 2 fl. oz / ¼ cup olive oil
300 g / 10 ½ oz / 6 cups baby spinach leaves
75 g / 3 oz / ½ cup smoked salmon, sliced
75 g / 3 oz / ⅓ cup crème fraîche
30 g / 1 oz / 2 tbsp pine nuts
30 g / 1 oz / 2 tbsp butter, melted and cooled
salt and pepper

Smoked Salmon and Almond Tartlets

931

- Substitute the pine nuts for the same weight of flaked (slivered) almonds in the filling.

932

SERVES 4

Beef, Rocket and Parmesan Canapés

- Freeze the beef for 10 minutes before slicing thinly into 8 slices.
- Chill the slices for 10 minutes before arranging on top of slices of baguette.
- Top with a few rocket leaves, a little shaved Parmesan and some black pepper.
- Serve immediately.

PREPARATION TIME 10 MINUTES

COOKING TIME 5-10 MINUTES

FREEZING TIME 10 MINUTES

CHILLING TIME 10 MINUTES

....

INGREDIENTS

½ poppy seed baguette, cut into 8 slices
110 g / 4 oz / ⅔ cup beef fillet, trimmed
30 g / 1 oz / ¼ cup Parmesan, shaved
a small handful of rocket (arugula)
freshly ground black pepper

Beef, Rocket and Pepper Canapés

933

- Substitute the Parmesan for thin strips of preserved red peppers that have been drained.

Duck and Orange Mini Sandwiches

934

SERVES 4

PREPARATION TIME 10 MINUTES

COOKING TIME 20-25 MINUTES

INGREDIENTS

FOR THE SANDWICHES
4 slices of granary bread, crusts removed
55 g / 2 oz / ¼ cup butter, softened
30 g / 1 oz / 2 tbsp cup caster (superfine) sugar
2 duck breasts, trimmed and scored on the fat
1 orange
salt and pepper

TO GARNISH
½ orange, zest pared and julienned

ALSO NEEDED
wooden skewers

- Preheat the oven to 190°C (170° fan) / 375F / gas 5.
- Heat an ovenproof saucepan over a medium heat.
- Season the duck breasts and render the fat in the hot pan, placing them skin-side down first.
- Cook until the skin is thin, golden and crisp before turning and transferring to the oven for 10-12 minutes.
- Remove from the oven and leave to rest for 5 minutes.
- Thinly pare the zest from the orange and finely chop before thinly slicing the duck breasts and tossing with the zest.
- Spread 2 of the slices of bread with butter and top with the duck.
- Place the remaining slices of bread on top and cut into quarters.
- Secure with skewers and transfer to plates, garnishing with julienned orange zest before serving.

Duck and Raspberry Mini Sandwiches

935

- Spoon half a teaspoon of raspberry jam on top of the duck before completing the sandwiches.

Individual Fish and Vegetable Pies

936

SERVES 4

PREPARATION TIME 10-15 MINUTES

COOKING TIME 15 MINUTES

INGREDIENTS

300 g / 10 ½ oz ready-made puff pastry
a little plain (all purpose) flour, for dusting
225 g / 8 oz / 1 ½ cups canned tuna, drained
55 ml / 2 fl. oz / ¼ cup olive oil
1 large egg, beaten
1 aubergine (eggplant), finely diced
1 green pepper, deseeded and finely diced
1 red pepper, deseeded and finely diced
salt and pepper

- Preheat the oven to 190°C (170° fan) / 375F / gas 5.
- Grease and line a baking tray with greaseproof paper.
- Heat the olive oil in a large frying pan set over a moderate heat and sauté the vegetables with a little seasoning for 4-5 minutes, tossing occasionally.
- Drain in a colander before mixing with the tuna.
- Roll the pastry out to ½ cm thickness and cut out 8 shapes using a fish-shaped cutter.
- Arrange half of them on the baking tray and spoon the filling onto them, leaving at least a 2 cm border.
- Brush the rims with a little egg, then lay the other pastry halves on top and crimp well with the tines of a fork to seal.
- Brush the tops with the remaining egg and bake for 18-22 minutes until puffed and golden in colour.
- Remove to a wire rack to cool before serving.

Chorizo and Vegetable Fish Pies

937

- Replace the tuna with diced chorizo in the filling.

938

MAKES 24

Tzatziki on Toast

Green Olive Tzatziki on Crackers

939

- Substitute the pitted black olives for pitted green olives.

Red Onion Tzatziki on Crackers

940

- Add ½ minced red onion to the Tzatziki.

PREPARATION TIME 15 MINUTES

COOKING TIME 10 MINUTES

INGREDIENTS

100 g / 3 ½ oz dark rye crackers
100 g / 3 ½ oz mini Ryvita crackers
½ large cucumber, sliced thinly into discs
small handful of mint sprigs
150 g / 5 oz / 1 cup pitted black olives, drained
black pepper

FOR THE TZATZIKI

300 g / 10 ½ oz / 1 ¼ cups Greek yoghurt
½ large cucumber, finely diced
juice of ½ lemon
1 clove of garlic
salt and pepper

- Prepare the tzatziki by whisking together the Greek yoghurt, lemon juice, minced garlic and finely diced cucumber in a mixing bowl until smooth.
- Season to taste, then cover and chill until needed.
- When ready to assemble the canapés, place a slice of cucumber on top of each mini cracker.
- Top with a teaspoon of the tzatziki then garnish with a sprig of mint leaves and a pitted black olive.
- Season with black pepper and arrange the canapés on top of the dark rye crackers, using them as a platter of sorts.

941

SERVES 4

Anchovy and Pepper Pancake Rolls

PREPARATION TIME 10 MINUTES

COOKING TIME 15-20 MINUTES

....

INGREDIENTS

FOR THE PANCAKES
250 ml / 9 fl. oz / 1 cup whole milk
50 g / 2 oz / ⅓ cup buckwheat flour
50 g / 2 oz / ⅓ cup plain (all purpose) flour
30 ml / 1 fl. oz / 2 tbsp sunflower oil
30 g / 1 oz / 2 tbsp butter, melted and cooled
2 small eggs
salt and pepper

FOR THE FILLING
225 g / 8 oz / 1 ⅓ cup preserved Piquillo peppers, drained
150 g / 5 oz / 1 cup preserved anchovy fillets, drained

ALSO NEEDED
cocktail sticks

- Whisk together the eggs, milk and butter in a large mixing bowl.
- Add the flours and gradually whisk until you have a smooth batter.
- Add a little seasoning then cover and chill for 30 minutes.
- Set to one side to be reheated later.
- Remove the pancake batter and heat teaspoons of the sunflower oil in a frying pan set over a medium heat.
- Add a ladle of the batter once hot and fry the pancakes for 1 minute before flipping and cooking the other side for 1 minute.
- Lay the cooked pancakes on a flat surface and top with the peppers and anchovies before rolling.
- Cut into bite-sized pieces and serve in glasses with cocktail sticks on the side.

Pepper and Cheese Pancake Rolls   942

- Substitute the anchovy fillets for 150 g / 5 oz / 1 ½ cups grated Gruyère.

943

MAKES 8

Oriental Pancake and Lamb Appetizers

PREPARATION TIME 10-15 MINUTES

COOKING TIME 35-40 MINUTES

....

INGREDIENTS

250 ml / 9 fl. oz / 1 cup whole milk
100 g / 3 ½ oz / ⅔ cup buckwheat flour
30 ml / 1 fl. oz / 2 tbsp sunflower oil
30 g / 1 oz / 2 tbsp butter, melted and cooled
2 small eggs
salt and pepper
30 ml / 1 fl. oz / 2 tbsp sunflower oil
450 g / 1 lb / 3 cups lamb mince
1 onion, finely chopped
2 cloves of garlic, minced
2" piece of ginger, minced
1 tsp ground cumin
½ tsp ground Chinese 5 spice
salt and pepper

TO GARNISH
1 tbsp flat-leaf parsley leaves

- Whisk together the eggs, milk and butter.
- Add the flour and gradually whisk until you have a smooth batter.
- Season then cover and chill for 30 minutes.
- Heat the over a moderate heat before sweating the onion, garlic and ginger with seasoning.
- Once translucent, add the lamb mince and ground spices, sautéing until the lamb is browned all over. Set to one side to be reheated later.
- Remove the pancake batter and heat teaspoons of the sunflower oil in a frying pan set over a medium heat.
- Add a ladle of the batter and fry the pancakes for 1 minute before flipping and cooking the other side.
- Reheat the lamb filling at the same time.
- Line 8 silicone cupcake cases with the pancakes and spoon the lamb into them. Garnish with parsley.

Beef and Chickpea   944
Pancake Appetizers

- Substitute the lamb mince for beef mince and add 110 g / 4 oz / ½ cup cooked chickpeas.

945
SERVES 4 Shrimp, Pepper and Mushroom Appetizers

- Preheat the grill to hot.
- Grill the pepper until blackened and blistered, then remove to a plastic bag and seal well.
- Leave for 5 minutes before peeling, deseeded and cutting into strips.
- Arrange the mushrooms and shrimp on a baking tray, drizzle with olive oil and season generously.
- Grill for 5 minutes, turning once after 3 minutes.
- Remove from the grill and reheat the peppers quickly.
- Arrange the peppers on the centre of serving plates and top with a mushroom.
- Sit two shrimp on top of the mushroom and secure with a wooden skewer.
- Garnish with sage, a cherry tomato half and a pinch of flaked sea salt before serving.

PREPARATION TIME 10-15 MINUTES

COOKING TIME 15 MINUTES

INGREDIENTS

FOR THE APPETIZERS
30 ml / 1 fl. oz / 2 tbsp olive oil
8 large shrimp, peeled and deveined
4 small field mushrooms, peeled with stems removed
1 red pepper
salt and pepper

TO GARNISH
4 sprigs of sage leaves
2 cherry tomatoes, halved
a pinch of flaked sea salt

ALSO NEEDED
wooden skewers

Shrimp, Pepper and Courgette Appetizers
946

- Use 1" thick discs of courgette (zucchini) instead of mushrooms.

947
SERVES 4 Beef Meatballs Coated in Breadcrumbs

- Preheat the oven to 190°C (170° fan) / 375F / gas 5.
- Mix together the breadcrumb and chopped parsley in a shallow bowl.
- Mix together the dried parsley, dried basil, beef mince and seasoning in a mixing bowl.
- Shape into balls before rolling in the breadcrumbs to coat, pressing them in well if necessary.
- Arrange on a greaseproof paper-lined baking tray and bake for 22-25 minutes until the breadcrumbs are golden-brown in colour.
- Remove from the oven and serve immediately with parsley leaves and wooden skewers on the side.

PREPARATION TIME 10 MINUTES

COOKING TIME 10 MINUTES

INGREDIENTS

FOR THE MEATBALLS
450 g / 1 lb / 3 cups beef mince
225 g / 8 oz / 2 cups panko breadcrumbs
a small handful of flat-leaf parsley leaves, finely chopped
1 tsp dried parsley
1 tsp dried basil
salt and pepper

TO GARNISH
a small handful of flat-leaf parsley leaves

ALSO NEEDED
wooden skewers

Breaded Beef and Ginger Meatballs
948

- Add 1 tablespoon of finely chopped ginger to the meatball mixture before shaping.

949

SERVES 4

Chorizo and Almond Toasted Appetizers

Chorizo and Black Olive Toasties

950

- Substitute the flaked almonds for halved, pitted black olives.

Chorizo and Brie Toasties

951

- Substitute the flaked almonds for thin slices of Brie.

PREPARATION TIME 10-15 MINUTES

COOKING TIME 15-20 MINUTES

....

INGREDIENTS

55 ml / 2 fl. oz / ¼ cup olive oil
½ white sandwich loaf, cut into
2 cm thick slices, crusts removed
75 g / 3 oz / ⅓ cup sun dried tomato
pasta sauce
100 g / 3 ½ oz / ⅔ cup chorizo, cut
into 8 even discs
25 g / 1 oz / 2 tbsp flaked (slivered)
almonds
wooden skewers

- Preheat the grill to hot.
- Brush the slices of bread with the olive oil on one side.
- Toast the bread with the olive oil side facing up for 2 minutes, then turn and toast the other side for 1 minute.
- Remove and cut into 16 even squares.
- Spread 8 of pieces of toast with some of the sun dried pasta sauce on the non olive oil side.
- Top with a disc of chorizo and a few flaked almonds.
- Flash under the grill for another minute.
- Remove and top with the remaining 8 pieces of toast.
- Secure with the wooden skewers and serve on plates.

952

SERVES 8

Cream of Mushroom Soup

- Melt the unsalted butter in a saucepan set over a medium heat and sauté the mushrooms and shallot with a little seasoning until they start to brown at the edges.
- Once browned, add the stock and bay leaf, stirring well.
- Bring the mixture to a simmer, cooking for 25-30 minutes before removing the bay leaf.
- Puree the mixture using a hand blender or food processor before stirring through the cream.
- Adjust the seasoning to taste and keep warm over a low heat.
- Heat the butter in a small frying pan over a moderate heat until melted then add the sliced mushroom and seasoning, sautéing until brown at the edges.
- Ladle the soup into 8 small serving glasses and top with a sliced piece of mushroom and a chive stalk.

Creamy Mushroom and Chestnut Soup   953

- Add 50 g / 2 oz / ⅓ cup cooked, chopped chestnuts to the saucepan as you add the stock.

PREPARATION TIME 15 MINUTES

COOKING TIME 50-55 MINUTES

INGREDIENTS

FOR THE SOUP
225 g / 8 oz / 3 cups wild mushrooms, sliced
225 g / 8 oz / 3 cups white button mushrooms, sliced
30 g / 1 oz / 2 tbsp unsalted butter
1 shallot, finely chopped
1 bay leaf
1 l / 1 pint 16 fl. oz / 4 cups light chicken stock
125 ml / 4 fl. oz / ½ cup double (heavy) cream
salt and pepper

TO GARNISH
1 tbsp butter
1 large button mushroom
8 small chive stalks
salt and pepper

954

MAKES 12

Mini Tomato Savoury Cakes

- Preheat the oven to 180°C (160° fan) / 350F / gas 4.
- Brown the butter in a saucepan until nutty in aroma.
- Strain through a fine sieve into a clean bowl.
- Combine the flour, almonds and Parmesan.
- Gently whisk the egg whites into this mixture and then fold through the cooled, melted butter. Chill for 30 minutes.
- Grease a 12-hole tin with unsalted butter.
- Spoon the batter into the tin, filling the holes three-quarters of the way before topping with a slice of tomato.
- Sprinkle the tops with the dried mixed herbs and seasoning before baking for 15-18 minutes until golden at the edges.
- Remove to a wire rack to cool before turning out and serving.

Mini Olive Savoury Cakes   955

- Replace the tomato slices with chopped black and green olives on top.

PREPARATION TIME 10-15 MINUTES

COOKING TIME 10 MINUTES

INGREDIENTS

3 large tomatoes, cut into 12 slices
110 g / 4 oz / ½ cup butter, softened
75 g / 3 oz / ¾ cup Parmesan, grated
1 tbsp unsalted butter, softened
110 g / 4 oz / 1 cup ground almonds
30 g / 1 oz / 2 tbsp plain (all purpose) flour, sifted
3 medium egg whites
2 tsp mixed dried herbs
salt and freshly ground black pepper

956

SERVES 4

Taco Boats with Tuna

PREPARATION TIME 10-15 MINUTES

COOKING TIME 10 MINUTES

INGREDIENTS

225 g / 8 oz / 1 ½ cups tuna steak, diced
4 taco boat shells
2 large avocados, destoned and diced
1 clove of garlic minced
2 limes, juiced
1 carrot, peeled and grated
½ red chilli (chili), deseeded and finely chopped
a few sprigs of coriander (cilantro) leaves, chopped
salt and pepper

- Toss the tuna with the chilli, seasoning and half of the lime juice.
- Mash the avocados with the garlic, seasoning and the remaining lime juice until you have a smooth guacamole.
- Spoon into the taco shells and top with the diced tuna, grated carrot and chopped coriander before serving.

Tuna and Sour Cream Tacos

957

- Sear the tuna and sit on top of guacamole-filled taco shells, topping them with a little sour cream.

958

MAKES 8

Ham and Olive Mini Savoury Cakes

PREPARATION TIME 10-15 MINUTES

COOKING TIME 30-35 MINUTES

INGREDIENTS

25 ml / 1 fl. oz / 2 tbsp sunflower oil
4 medium eggs
300 g / 10 ½ oz / 2 cups plain (all purpose) flour
2 tsp baking powder
40 g / 1 ½ oz / 2 tbsp butter, melted
225 g / 8 oz / 2 cups Gruyère, grated
75 g / 3 oz / ½ cup cooked ham, diced
75 g / 3 oz / ½ cup pitted green olives, diced
½ red pepper, de-seeded and finely diced
salt and black pepper
parsley leaves, to garnish

- Preheat the oven to 180°C (160° fan) / 350F / gas 4.
- In a large mixing bowl, beat the eggs until light and frothy.
- Add the flour, melted butter and baking powder and beat again until smooth.
- Fold in the Gruyère, red pepper, ham and olives, mixing thoroughly.
- Season the batter well and mix again.
- Spoon the batter into 8 individual non-stick loaf tins.
- Bake for 20-25 minutes until a cake tester comes out clean from their centres.
- Remove from the oven and allow them to cool in their tins for 5 minutes before turning out onto a wire rack to cool completely.
- Serve warm or cold with a parsley leaf garnish.

Ham and Herb Mini Cakes

959

- Substitute the olives for a mixture of chopped herbs.

960

SERVES 4

Chorizo and Pepper Tortilla

Ham and Pepper Tortilla

961

- Substitute the chorizo for diced, cooked ham.

Almond and Pepper Tortilla

962

- Substitute chorizo for 50 g / 2 oz / ½ cup flaked (slivered) almonds.

PREPARATION TIME 10 MINUTES

COOKING TIME 15 MINUTES

INGREDIENTS

1 red pepper, de-seeded and diced
1 green pepper, de-seeded and diced
3 medium potatoes, peeled and sliced to 2 cm thickness
1 small chorizo sausage, sliced
55 ml / 2 fl. oz / ¼ cup olive oil
6 large eggs
100 ml / 3 ½ fl. oz / ½ cup whole milk
salt and pepper
sprig of parsley, to garnish
cocktail sticks, to garnish

- Preheat the oven to 180°C (160° fan) / 350F / gas 4.
- Heat the olive oil in a large frying pan over a medium-high heat and fry the chorizo and peppers together for 3-4 minutes, stirring occasionally.
- Remove and drain on kitchen paper, then add the potato slices to the pan and reduce the heat and cover the pan, allowing them to cook for 8-10 minutes.
- Make sure the potatoes cover the base of the pan, then remove the cover and increase the heat so that they bottoms are browned and crispy.
- Meanwhile, whisk together the eggs, milk and seasoning.
- Arrange the peppers and chorizo in and around the potato.
- Pour the eggs into the frying pan and transfer to the oven.
- Let it bake in the until puffed and set; usually 10-12 minutes.
- Remove from the oven and allow to sit for a few minutes before turning out onto a chopping board.
- Slice into square portions and serve on greaseproof paper, with a sprig of parsley and some cocktail sticks as a garnish.

963

SERVES 4

Mini Greek Sandwiches

PREPARATION TIME 10-15 MINUTES

COOKING TIME 10 MINUTES

INGREDIENTS

FOR THE SANDWICHES
1 small sourdough loaf, cut into 8 slices
½ cucumber, deseeded and diced
30 ml / 1 fl. oz / 2 tbsp extra-virgin olive oil (preferably Greek)
2 vine tomatoes, deseeded and diced
150 g / 5 oz / 1 ½ cups feta, diced
½ tsp dried oregano
½ red onion, finely sliced

TO GARNISH
4 sprigs of flat-leaf parsley
½ red onion, finely sliced

ALSO NEEDED
4 cocktail sticks

- Mix the feta, cucumber, tomato and oregano in a mixing bowl, tossing well.
- Brush one side of the slices of bread with a little olive oil.
- Top with feta mixture and follow with some sliced red onion.
- Place the other slices of bread on top before skewering with a cocktail stick and garnishing with a sprig of parsley.

Feta and Preserved Lemon Sandwiches

964

- Substitute the red onion for very thinly sliced preserved lemon in the sandwiches.

965

SERVES 4

Saint-Albray and Pistachio Appetizers

PREPARATION TIME 10 MINUTES

COOKING TIME 5 MINUTES

INGREDIENTS

FOR THE APPETIZERS
1 brioche loaf, cut into 8 slices
50 g / 2 oz / ½ cup shelled pistachios, chopped
225 g / 8 oz / 2 cups Saint-Albray (use Camembert if not available), cut into 8 pieces

TO GARNISH
a small handful of mixed salad leaves
1 tbsp balsamic vinegar

- Preheat the grill to hot.
- Use a round 3-4" cookie cutter to cut 8 rounds of brioche out of the slices.
- Top with a piece of cheese before grilling until the cheese melts.
- Remove from the oven and sprinkle with pistachios.
- Serve with salad leaves and a drizzle of balsamic vinegar on the side.

Brie and Cranberry Appetizers

966

- Substitute the Saint-Albray for Brie and use 3-4 dried cranberries on top of each instead of pistachio.

967

SERVES 4 # Serrano Ham and Seafood Crostini

- Cook the eggs in a large saucepan of boiling water for 12 minutes before refreshing in iced water.
- Peel once cool enough to handle and remove the top and bottom ½ cm of egg white.
- Halve the eggs and remove the cooked yolk from half, finely chopping it and reserving to one side.
- Preheat the grill to hot.
- Brush the slices of crostini with olive oil and grill until golden-brown and toasted.
- Remove from the oven and top with a piece of Serrano ham before returning to the grill for 1 minute.
- Remove and top with a folded piece of smoked salmon, half of egg then a teaspoon of mayonnaise.
- Top with half a cooked shrimp and sprinkle with the chopped yolk before skewering.
- Serve with lime halves and a sprig of dill.

Serrano Ham and Scallop Crostini   968

- Pan-fry 4 scallops until golden-brown and firm yet spring to the touch. Halve and use instead of the egg and shrimp on the crostini.

PREPARATION TIME 10-15 MINUTES

COOKING TIME 15-20 MINUTES

INGREDIENTS

½ flute baguette, cut into 8 slices
4 slices of Serrano ham, halved
4 small slices of smoked salmon, halved
8 small eggs
4 peeled and cooked shrimp, halved
55 g / 2 oz / ¼ cup mayonnaise
30 ml / 1 fl. oz / 2 tbsp extra-virgin olive oil

TO GARNISH
2 limes, halved
a few sprigs of dill

ALSO NEEDED
wooden skewers

969

SERVES 4 # Egg, Spinach and Gruyère Toasts

- Cook the eggs in a saucepan of boiling water for 10 minutes.
- Heat the olive oil and butter in a large frying pan set over a moderate heat before flash-frying the spinach for 1-2 minutes with seasoning until wilted.
- Remove from the pan and drain on kitchen paper.
- Refresh the eggs in iced water before peeling and carefully removing the top ½ cm with a sharp knife.
- Toast the slices of bread under a hot grill and remove the crusts before quartering into triangles.
- Half the eggs then top the triangles with a tablespoon of wilted spinach.
- Sit a halved egg on top of the spinach and sprinkle a little gruyère and pepper on top.
- Glaze for 20-30 seconds under the grill to melt the cheese before serving.

Egg, Spinach and Chorizo Toasts   970

- Slice 55 g / 2 oz / ⅓ cup chorizo and grill before topping the egg on the toasts.

PREPARATION TIME 15-10 MINUTES

COOKING TIME 10 MINUTES

INGREDIENTS

4 slices of white sandwich bread
4 medium eggs
30 ml / 1 fl. oz / 2 tbsp olive oil
1 tbsp butter
150 g / 5 oz / 3 cups baby spinach leaves
55 g / 2 oz / ½ cup Gruyère, finely grated
salt and freshly grated black pepper

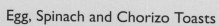

971

MAKES 8

Basil and Olive Waffle Cookies

PREPARATION TIME 10-15
MINUTES

COOKING TIME 15-20 MINUTES

INGREDIENTS

150 g / 5 oz / 1 cup plain (all purpose)
flour, sifted
a little extra plain (all purpose) flour,
for dusting
55 g / 2 oz / ½ cup Parmesan,
finely grated
55 ml / 2 fl. oz / ¼ cup extra-virgin
olive oil
1 medium egg yolk
2 tsp dried basil
½ tsp salt
150 g / 5 oz / 1 cup sundried
tomatoes, chopped
55 ml / 2 fl. oz / ¼ cup olive oil
salt and pepper
basil leaves, finely chopped

- Combine the flour, Parmesan, dried basil and salt in a food processor.
- Pulse until the mixture resembles fine breadcrumbs.
- Add the egg yolk and the olive oil and pulse until a dough forms; add a little warm water if the mixture looks dry.
- Turn the mixture out onto a work surface and form into a ball.
- Wrap in cling film and chill for 15 minutes.
- Preheat the oven to 180°C (160°C) / 350°F / gas 4.
- Grease and line 2 baking trays with greaseproof paper.
- Remove the dough from the fridge and roll out on a lightly floured work surface to ¾ cm thickness.
- Use a waffle-embossed cookie cutter to cut out 2 rounds of dough before carefully lifting onto the baking trays.
- Bake for 12-15 minutes until golden-brown and set.
- Reconstitute the sundried tomato in boiling water before draining and blitzing with olive oil and seasoning until you have a thick puree.
- Remove the cookies from the oven and leave to cool before spreading half with the sundried tomato puree and sandwiching using the remaining half.
- Arrange and garnish with chopped basil leaves.

972

SERVES 4

Carrot Soup with Savoury Balls

PREPARATION TIME 15-20
MINUTES

COOKING TIME 20-25 MINUTES

INGREDIENTS

30 ml / 1 fl. oz / 2 tbsp olive oil
450 g / 1 lb / 3 cups carrots, peeled
and grated
1 onion, finely chopped
1 clove of garlic, minced
½ tsp ground coriander
500 ml / 18 fl. oz / 2 cups vegetable
stock
30 ml / 1 fl. oz / 2 tbsp double
(heavy) cream
salt and pepper
175 g / 6 oz / 1 ½ cups ready-made
gingerbread cake, chopped
150 g / 5 oz / 1 cup foie gras, chopped
30 g / 1 oz / ¼ cup hazelnuts (cob
nuts), very finely chopped
1 tbsp cornflour (cornstarch)
1 medium egg, beaten
1 tbsp Madeira
salt and pepper

- Preheat the oven to 190°C (170° fan) / 375F / gas 5.
- Pulse the gingerbread in a good processor until it resembles breadcrumbs.
- Tip half into a bowl and add the foie gras, cornflour, hazelnuts, egg, Madeira and seasoning.
- Mix well until before shaping into 8 balls between your palms and rolling in the reserved gingerbread crumbs.
- Arrange on a greaseproof paper-lined baking tray and bake for 15-18 minutes until deep golden-brown in colour.
- Remove and leave to cool to one side.
- Heat the olive oil in a large saucepan set over a medium heat before sweating the onion and garlic for 4-5 minutes until translucent.
- Add the carrot, ground coriander, carrot and stock and heat until simmering, stirring occasionally.
- Simmer for 15 minutes before pureeing with a stick blender.
- Stir through the cream and adjust the seasoning to taste.
- Reheat the balls in the oven before skewering; pour the soup into 8 glasses and sit the balls over the rim before serving.

SERVES 4

Steamed Potatoes with Black Pudding

- Place the potatoes in a steamer and cook over a saucepan of gently simmering water for 12-15 minutes.
- Preheat the oven to 190°C (170° fan) / 375F / gas 5.
- Arrange the black pudding on a baking tray and roast for 15 minutes.
- Remove and leave to cool before peeling and chopping.
- Place the calvados in a pan and reduce by half.
- Add the cream and bring to the boil before reducing the heat to a gentle simmer.
- Pour into the nitrous oxide siphon and set to one side.
- Arrange the potato halves on a serving platter and top with finely chopped black pudding.
- Remove the tips from 8 sprigs of thyme and garnish on top of the black pudding before finishing with some espuma from the nitrous oxide siphon.
- Garnish with sprigs of thyme.

PREPARATION TIME 10-15 MINUTES

COOKING TIME 20 MINUTES

INGREDIENTS

4 potatoes, peeled, halved lengthways
1 tbsp extra-virgin olive oil
300 g / 10 ½ oz / 2 cups black pudding
salt and pepper
125 ml / 4 ½ fl. oz / ½ cup double (heavy) cream
75 ml / 3 fl. oz / ⅓ cup calvados
thyme sprigs
paprika
nitrous oxide siphon

Roquefort and Leek Mini Quiches

MAKES 4

PREPARATION TIME 10-15 MINUTES

COOKING TIME 20-25 MINUTES

INGREDIENTS

FOR THE MINI QUICHES
250 g / 9 oz ready-made shortcrust pastry
a little plain (all purpose) flour, for dusting

1 medium egg, beaten
30 g / 1 oz / 2 tbsp butter
½ leek, trimmed and finely sliced (keep trimmings)
250 ml / 9 fl. oz / 1 cup whole milk
250 ml / 9 fl. oz / 1 cup crème fraîche
110 g / 4 oz / 1 cup Roquefort, grated
3 large eggs
salt and pepper

TO GARNISH
reserved leek trimmings, julienned

- Preheat the oven to 180°C (160° fan) / 350F / gas 4.
- Roll the pastry out on a lightly floured surface to ½ cm thickness. Cut 4 rounds of pastry and use to line 4 individual 4" tartlet cases.
- Prick the bases and trim the excess pastry. Line with greaseproof paper and fill with baking beans. Blind-bake for 12-15 minutes until golden-brown.
- Remove and discard the greaseproof paper and beans. Brush the bases with the beaten egg.
- Reduce the oven to 160°C (140° fan) / 325F / gas 3.
- Melt butter in a pan and sweat the leek for 6-8 minutes.
- Whisk the eggs, milk and creme fraîche with seasoning.
- Arrange the sweated leek in the pastry cases and fill with the quiche filling.
- Dot with Roquefort before baking for 25-30 minutes.
- Garnish with julienned leek.

Mini Broccoli Pizzas

MAKES 8

PREPARATION TIME 10 MINUTES

COOKING TIME 10-15 MINUTES

INGREDIENTS

300 g / 10 ½ oz ready-made pizza dough
a little plain (all purpose) flour, for dusting

1 tbsp olive oil
110 g / 4 oz / 1 cup mozzarella, drained and sliced
4 vine tomatoes
1 small head of broccoli, prepared into florets
salt and pepper

- Preheat the oven to 200°C (180° fan) / 400F / gas 6.
- Divide the dough into 8 small balls and roll out on a lightly floured surface to 3" in diameter.
- Arrange on baking trays and drizzle with a little olive oil.
- Quarter and deseed the tomatoes, finely dicing half of them.
- Top half of the dough rounds with diced tomato and top the other half with tomato quarters.
- Follow with slices of mozzarella, then broccoli florets and seasoning.
- Bake for 10-12 minutes until the dough is risen and the cheese has melted.
- Remove from the oven and serve immediately.

976

SERVES 4

Courgette, Ham and Rice Appetizers

PREPARATION TIME 10-15 MINUTES

COOKING TIME 40-50 MINUTES

....

INGREDIENTS

1 large courgette (zucchini), sliced thinly using a mandolin
8 slices of Parma ham
100 g / 3 ½ oz / ½ cup arborio rice
30 ml / 1 fl. oz / 2 tbsp olive oil
1 tbsp butter
1 shallot, finely chopped
1 clove of garlic, minced
55 ml / 2 fl. oz / ¼ cup dry white wine
500 ml / 18 fl. oz / 2 cups vegetable stock, kept hot on the stove
8 chive stalks
salt and freshly ground black pepper

- Heat together the oil and butter in a saucepan.
- Sauté the shallots gently for 4-5 minutes then add the garlic to cook for a further 2 minutes.
- Add the rice and coat in the butter, mixture and cook until the grains start to turn translucent.
- Add the white wine and increase the heat to reduce.
- Add one ladle of hot vegetable stock to the risotto.
- Continue adding one ladle of stock until the rice is soft yet still defined; usually 25-30 minutes.
- Adjust the seasoning to taste before cooling.
- Blanch the chive stalks in boiling water for 5 seconds before refreshing in iced water.
- Lay slices of the courgette on a chopping board and lay slices of Parma ham on top.
- Spoon a tablespoon of the risotto on top before rolling up and securing with a chive stalk.

Sundried Tomato Risotto Rolls

977

- Add 50 g / 2 oz / ⅓ cup chopped sundried tomatoes to the risotto before seasoning.

978

MAKES 4

Two Salmon and Leek Turnover

PREPARATION TIME 10 MINUTES

COOKING TIME 15 MINUTES

....

INGREDIENTS

FOR THE TURNOVERS
300 g / 10 ½ oz ready-made puff pastry
a little plain (all purpose) flour, for dusting
30 ml / 1 fl. oz / 2 tbsp olive oil
½ leek, halved, sliced and washed
2 skinless salmon fillets, sliced
75 g / 3 oz / ½ cup smoked salmon, sliced
a few sprigs of dill, chopped
1 medium egg, beaten
salt and pepper

TO GARNISH
a few sprigs of dill, chopped

- Heat the olive oil in a large frying pan.
- Sweat the sliced leek with a little seasoning until softened; 5-6 minutes. Drain on kitchen paper and slice.
- Preheat the oven to 180°C (160° fan) / 350F / gas 4.
- Line a large baking tray with greaseproof paper.
- Roll the pastry out on a lightly floured surface.
- Cut out 4 8" rounds of pastry and arrange the leek in the centre, followed by the salmon fillet, the smoked salmon and then the dill.
- Wet the rim of the pastry with a little water before folding the bottom end over the filling and sealing with the opposite end by crimping.
- Transfer to the baking tray little score using a sharp knife.
- Brush with the beaten egg and bake for 18-22 minutes.
- Serve with extra dill.

Sea Bass and Leek Turnover

979

- Slice 3 skinless sea bass fillets and use instead of the salmon fillet and smoked salmon on top of the sweated leek.

Italian Turnovers

980
MAKES 4

- Heat the olive oil in a large frying pan.
- Sauté the mushrooms with a little salt and pepper until they are golden brown in colour.
- Drain on kitchen paper before mixing in a bowl with the prosciutto, mozzarella, dried herbs and a little more seasoning.
- Preheat the oven to 180°C (160° fan) / 350F / gas 4.
- Line a large baking tray with greaseproof paper.
- Roll the pastry out on a lightly floured surface to ¾ cm thickness.
- Cut out 4 8" rounds of pastry and spoon the filling into their centres.
- Wet the rim of the pastry with a little water using your fingertip before folding the bottom end over the filling and sealing with the opposite end by crimping.
- Transfer to the baking tray and bake for 22-25 minutes.

PREPARATION TIME 10 MINUTES

COOKING TIME 15 MINUTES

INGREDIENTS

350 g / 12 oz ready-made shortcrust pastry
a little plain (all purpose) flour, for dusting
30 ml / 1 fl. oz / 2 tbsp olive oil
150 g / 5 oz / 2 cups chestnut mushrooms, sliced
100 g / 3 ½ oz / ⅔ cup prosciutto, sliced
100 g / 3 ½ oz / 1 cup mozzarella, sliced
½ tsp dried oregano
½ tsp dried basil
salt and pepper

Artichoke and Prosciutto Turnovers

981

- Replace the mushrooms with the same amount of chopped artichoke hearts.

982
MAKES 8

Tomato, Olive and Anchovy Turnover

- Preheat the oven to 180°C (160° fan) / 350F / gas 4.
- Grease and line a large baking tray with greaseproof paper.
- Roll the pastry out on a lightly floured surface to ½ cm thickness.
- Cut out 8 ovals of pastry 10 cm x 8 cm x ½ cm in dimension.
- Mix together the anchovy, tomato, olive and dried herbs in a bowl.
- Spoon the filling into the centre of the rounds and wet the rims with a little water using your fingertip.
- Fold one end of the pastry over the filling and crimp with the other end, sealing well.
- Transfer to the tray and bake for 18-20 minutes until the pastry is lightly golden in colour.
- Serve warm, garnished with a pinch of thyme.

PREPARATION TIME 10 MINUTES

COOKING TIME 15 MINUTES

INGREDIENTS

FOR THE TURNOVERS
400 g / 14 oz ready-made shortcrust pastry
a little plain (all purpose) flour, for dusting
100 g / 3 ½ oz / ⅔ cup preserved anchovy fillets, drained and chopped
8 cherry tomatoes, halved
a small handful of pitted black olives, sliced
½ tsp dried oregano
½ tsp dried basil

TO GARNISH
1 tsp thyme, finely chopped

Tomato, Olive and Tuna Turnover

983

- Use 200 g / 7 oz / 1 ½ cups canned tuna flakes in place of the anchovy fillets.

984

SERVES 4

Sundried Tomato and Cheese Canapés

Pesto and Cream Cheese Crostini

985

- Mix together 225 g / 8 oz / 1 cup cream cheese with 1 tbsp pesto and use to top the melba toasts.

Cream Cheese and Walnut Canapés

986

- Substitute the sundried tomato for a large handful of walnut halves.

PREPARATION TIME 10 MINUTES

COOKING TIME 10 MINUTES

INGREDIENTS

FOR THE CROSTINI
8 round Melba toasts
110 g / 4 oz / ⅔ cup preserved sundried tomato, chopped
300 g / 10 ½ oz / 1 ⅓ cups cottage cheese
1 tsp baby capers, drained
2 vine tomatoes, quartered and deseeded
salt and pepper

TO GARNISH
8 picked basil leaves

- Pulse together the cottage cheese, capers and sundried tomato in a food processor until just combined.
- Preheat the grill to hot.
- Grill the tomato petals skin-side up until the skins start to wrinkle.
- Top the melba toasts with the sundried tomato mixture before topping with a tomato petal and garnishing with a basil leaf.
- Serve immediately.

Lamb and Gouda Mini Pies

987

SERVES 4

- Preheat the oven to 200°C (180° fan) / 400F / gas 6.
- Grease and line a baking tray with greaseproof paper.
- Heat the olive oil in a frying pan seat over a medium heat until hot before adding the caraway seeds.
- Add the onion and carrot and sweat for 6-8 minutes, stirring frequently until softened.
- Add the lamb and brown well all over before adjusting the seasoning to taste.
- Set to one side to cool a little.
- Cut the sheets of filo in half so you have 8 in total.
- Working quickly, fill the centre of the sheets of filo pastry with the lamb filling before bringing the edges of the pastry out and around into a pouch shape.
- Arrange on the baking tray and bake for 12-15 minutes until the pastry is cooked and golden.
- Serve with rocket, Gouda and a pinch of caraway seeds.

PREPARATION TIME 10 MINUTES

COOKING TIME 15-20 MINUTES

INGREDIENTS

4 sheets of filo pastry, kept under
a damp tea towel
1 tbsp olive oil
1 tbsp unsalted butter
300 g / 10 ½ oz / 2 cups lamb mince
1 carrot, peeled and diced
1 onion, finely chopped
1 tsp caraway seeds
salt and pepper

TO GARNISH

125 g / 4 ½ oz / 1 ¼ cups Gouda,
cut into batons
a large handful of rocket leaves
a pinch of caraway seeds

Lamb and Cheddar Mini Pies

988

- Replace the Gouda with batons of Cheddar cheese when you serve the pies.

Fig, Ham and Tomato Cakes

989

MAKES 6

- Preheat the oven to 170°C (150°C fan) / 325°F / gas 3.
- Grease 6 disposable mini loaf tins.
- Whisk together the eggs and olive oil in a jug.
- Combine the flour, figs, sundried tomato and half of the ham and Parmesan.
- Add the wet ingredient to the dry ones and fold until combined.
- Add some seasoning before spooning into the loaf tins.
- Sprinkle the remaining Parmesan on top and lay the remaining slices of ham on top.
- Bake for 40-50 minutes; test with a wooden toothpick, if it comes out clean, the cakes are done.
- Remove from the oven and leave to cool before serving.

PREPARATION TIME 10 MINUTES

COOKING TIME 10 MINUTES

INGREDIENTS

250 g / 9 oz / 1 ⅔ cups self-raising
flour, sifted
125 ml / 4 ½ fl. oz / ½ cup olive oil
110 g / 4 oz / 1 cup Parmesan, finely
grated
100 g / 3 ½ oz / ⅔ cup Parma ham
slices
100 g / 3 ½ oz / ⅔ cup dried figs,
chopped
50 g / 2 oz / ⅓ cup sundried tomato,
chopped
2 large eggs, beaten
salt and pepper

Ham, Olive and Gorgonzola Cakes

990

- Substitute the figs for diced Gorgonzola and the sundried tomato for chopped black olives.

991

MAKES 4

Mini Pepper Pizzas

PREPARATION TIME 10 MINUTES

COOKING TIME 20-25 MINUTES

INGREDIENTS

250 g / 9 oz ready-made pizza dough
a little plain (all purpose) flour,
for dusting
30 ml / 1 fl. oz / 2 tbsp olive oil
2 onions, sliced
2 red peppers, deseeded and sliced
150 g / 5 oz / 1 cup sea bass,
pin-boned and diced
salt and pepper

TO GARNISH

a small handful of picked basil leaves

- Preheat the oven to 220°C (200° fan) / 425F / gas 7.
- Divide the dough into 8 small balls and roll out on a lightly floured surface to 1 cm thickness.
- Arrange on 2 baking trays line with greaseproof paper.
- Heat the olive oil in a large frying pan and sweat the onion and peppers with a little salt until softened; 5-7 minutes, stirring frequently.
- Spoon the vegetables on top of the dough and top with diced sea bass.
- Bake for 8-10 minutes until the fish is cooked and the dough is golden at the edges and firm underneath.
- Remove from the oven and serve with basil leaves on top.

Chorizo Mini Pizzas

992

- Substitute the sea bass with diced chorizo on top of the pizzas.

993

SERVES 4

Tomato Soup

PREPARATION TIME 10-15 MINUTES

COOKING TIME 30-35 MINUTES

INGREDIENTS

30 ml / 1 fl. oz / 2 tbsp olive oil
1 kg / 2 lb 4 oz / 4 cups ripe vine tomatoes, washed, cored and quartered
1 medium onion, finely chopped
1 medium carrot, finely chopped
1 stick of celery, finely chopped
1 tbsp tomato puree
1 tsp caster (superfine) sugar
1 tsp dried basil
1 l / 1 pint 16 fl. oz / 4 cups vegetable stock, hot
125 ml / 4 ½ fl. oz / ½ cup double (heavy) cream
salt and pepper
a small bunch of picked basil leaves
30 ml / 1 fl. oz / 2 tbsp double (heavy) cream
1 tbsp extra-virgin olive oil

- Heat the olive oil in a large saucepan over a medium-low heat for 1-2 minutes.
- Add the onion, carrot and celery and sweat for 8-10 minutes with a little salt until they just start to colour.
- Stir in the tomato puree, then add the tomatoes and mix well.
- Add the sugar, dried basil, stock and seasoning and simmer for 20 minutes.
- Blend the soup using a stick blender until smooth, then stir through the double cream and adjust the seasoning to taste.
- Ladle into warm soup bowls and garnish with a swirl of double cream, a drizzle of olive oil and a few of basil leaves.
- Serve immediately.

Tomato and Mixed Olive Soup

994

- Garnish the soup with 1 tablespoon of chopped green and black olives.

995

MAKES 4 Individual Beef Pies

- Preheat the oven to 180°C (160° fan) / 350F / gas 4.
- Divide the pastry in two and roll both out on a lightly floured surface to ½ cm thickness.
- Cut 4 rounds from one piece and line 4" fluted cases.
- Prick the base a few times with a fork then chill.
- Use a 4" fluted cutter to cut 4 rounds from the other pastry and cut thin strips from the leftover pastry.
- Heat the oil in a large frying pan and season the steak before frying for 2-3 minutes.
- Remove from the pan and drain on kitchen paper.
- Arrange some of the cheese in the base of the pastry and top with steak strips.
- Lay the pastry lids on top and brush with egg before arranging the strips of pastry on top in a lattice pattern.
- Bake for 20-25 minutes. Serve with chopped dill on top.

PREPARATION TIME 10-15 MINUTES

COOKING TIME 15 MINUTES

INGREDIENTS

FOR THE PIES
350 g / 12 oz / ready-made shortcrust pastry
a little plain (all purpose) flour
30 ml / 1 fl. oz / 2 tbsp groundnut oil
200 g / 7 oz / 2 cups Halloumi, thinly sliced
250 g / 9 oz / 1 ⅔ cups sirloin steak, cut into strips
1 large egg, beaten
salt and pepper

TO GARNISH
a few dill sprigs, finely chopped

Steak and Olive Pies 996

- Use chopped black olives in place of the cheese as a filling for the pies.

997

SERVES 4 Creole-Style Eggs

- Cook the eggs in a saucepan of boiling water for 8 minutes.
- Drain and refresh the eggs in iced water.
- Once cool enough to handle, peeled and half, scooping out the yolk into a small bowl.
- Mix the yolk with the cayenne pepper, creme fraîche, desiccated coconut and seasoning then spoon back into the egg white halves.
- Dress a serving platter with chard leaves and top with the filled egg halves.
- Garnish with the chives and grated Cheddar, serving alongside the carrot sticks.

PREPARATION TIME 10-15 MINUTES

COOKING TIME 10 MINUTES

INGREDIENTS

FOR THE EGGS
4 quail eggs
125 g / 4 ½ oz / ½ cup creme fraîche
1 tbsp desiccated coconut
a pinch of cayenne pepper
salt and pepper

TO GARNISH
100 g / 3 ½ oz / 1 ⅓ cups baby red chard
50 g / 2 oz / ½ cup Cheddar, grated
2 carrots, peeled and cut into sticks
a few chive stalks, finely chopped

Cheese and Mustard Eggs 998

- Replace the desiccated coconut with 1 tsp Dijon mustard and use the Cheddar in the egg yolk mixture instead of as a garnish.

999

SERVES 4

Vermicelli Minestrone

PREPARATION TIME 15-20
MINUTES

COOKING TIME 20-25 MINUTES

INGREDIENTS

55 ml / 2 fl. oz / ¼ cup olive oil
2 cloves garlic, minced
2 white potatoes, peeled and diced
2 large sticks of celery, diced
2 large carrots, peeled and diced
1 small courgette (zucchini), diced
½ Hispi cabbage, shredded
110 g / 4 oz / 1 ¼ cups vermicelli
pasta
750 ml / 1 pint 7 fl. oz / 3 cups
vegetable stock
400 g / 14 oz / 2 cups canned
chopped tomatoes
100 g / 3 ½ oz / 1 cup green (string)
beans, sliced
75 g / 3 oz / ¾ cup frozen petit pois
salt and pepper
chopped parsley

- Heat the olive oil in a large casserole dish over a medium heat until hot.
- Sweat the potatoes, garlic, courgette, carrot and celery with a little salt for 8-10 minutes until they have softened, stirring occasionally.
- Add the chopped tomatoes, cabbage and beans and stir well.
- Simmer for 3 minutes before adding the vermicelli and simmering for 10-12 minutes until tender.
- Add the peas and let them thaw in the soup for 2-3 minutes before adjusting the seasoning to taste.
- Spoon into serving bowls and garnish with chopped parsley before serving.

Beef Minestrone

1000

- Add 300 g / 10 ½ oz / 2 cups minced beef after sweating the vegetables for 8-10 minutes, stirring well to break up.

1001

SERVES 4

Tomato and Seafood Soup

PREPARATION TIME 10-15
MINUTES

COOKING TIME 20-25 MINUTES

INGREDIENTS

150 g / 5 oz / 1 cup cooked and
peeled prawns (shrimps)
150 g / 5 oz / 1 cup cooked mussels
75 g / 3 oz / ½ cup frozen calamari
rings, thawed
30 ml / 1 fl. oz / 2 tbsp olive oil
400 g / 14 oz / 2 cups canned
chopped tomatoes
150 g / 5 oz / 1 ½ cups cherry
tomatoes, diced
250 ml / 9 fl. oz / 1 cup vegetable
stock
30 ml / 1 fl. oz / 2 tbsp double
(heavy) cream
1 clove of garlic, minced
a pinch of dried oregano
a pinch of dried basil
salt and pepper
oregano sprigs, chopped
flat-leaf parsley

- Heat the olive oil in a large saucepan set over a medium heat.
- Sauté the garlic briefly before adding the canned chopped tomatoes, cherry tomatoes, dried herbs and stock.
- Simmer for 15 minutes, then puree using a stick blender until smooth.
- Add the calamari rings and let them gently cook in the soup for 5 minutes, then add the cooked mussels and prawns to let them warm through for 3 minutes.
- Stir in the cream and simmer for 1 minute before adjusting the seasoning to taste.
- Spoon into serving bowls and arrange the seafood in the middle.
- Garnish with parsley and chopped oregano.

Creamy Tomato and Garlic Soup

1002

- Omit the seafood from the recipe and use 3 cloves of garlic instead of one.

1003

SERVES 4

Potato Omelette Appetizers

Potato and Olive Tomato

1004

- Add a small handful of chopped, pitted green olives to the eggs as you beat them.

Potato and Sundried Tomato Appetizers

1005

- 150 g / 5 oz / 1 cup of potato with 100 g / 3 ½ oz / ⅔ cup sundried tomatoes.

PREPARATION TIME 10-15 MINUTES

COOKING TIME 10-15 MINUTES

INGREDIENTS

FOR THE OMELETTE
3 slices of white sandwich bread, 1" thick
450 g / 1 lb / 3 cups white potatoes, peeled and halved
55 g / 2 oz / ¼ cup butter, softened
30 ml / 1 fl. oz / 2 tbsp extra-virgin olive oil
8 large eggs
salt and pepper

TO GARNISH
a small handful of frisée lettuce

ALSO NEEDED
cocktail sticks

- Cook the potatoes halves in a large saucepan of salted, boiling water until tender; 20-25 minutes.
- Drain and leave to steam dry until cool enough to handle before slicing.
- Toss the potato slices with the olive oil and seasoning.
- Preheat the oven to 190°C (170° fan) / 375F / gas 5.
- Grease and line a 7" square springform cake tin with greaseproof paper.
- Butter the slices of bread before removing the crusts and arranging across the base of the cake tin, cutting to size if necessary.
- Beat the eggs in a mixing bowl with seasoning before layering the slices of potato on top of the bread.
- Pour the egg on top and bake for 12-15 minutes until golden-brown in colour on top.
- Remove from the oven and leave to cool a little before turning out and cutting into slices.
- Skewer with cocktail sticks before serving.

1006

SERVES 4

Tomato and Goats' Cheese Puddings

PREPARATION TIME 10-15
MINUTES

COOKING TIME 15 MINUTES

·····························

INGREDIENTS

4 vine cherry tomatoes
50 g / 2 oz / ¼ cup butter, softened
25 g / 1 oz / 2 tbsp plain (all purpose)
flour
250 ml / 9 fl. oz / 1 cup whole milk
4 medium egg whites
4 medium egg yolks
1 tsp Dijon mustard
75 g / 3 oz / ¾ cup goats' cheese,
diced
salt and pepper

- Preheat the oven to 200°C (180° fan) / 400F / gas 6.
- Brush the insides of 4 mini casserole dishes with half of the butter.
- Chill until needed.
- Melt the remaining butter in a saucepan set over a medium heat, then whisk in the flour until you have a smooth roux.
- Cook the roux for 1-2 minutes, whisking occasionally.
- Whisk in the milk in a slow, steady stream until you have a thickened sauce, then whisk in the egg yolks, mustard and most of the goats' cheese.
- Simmer for 2-3 minutes, adjusting the seasoning to taste, then removing to one side.
- Whisk the egg whites in a clean mixing bowl with a pinch of salt until soft peaks form.
- Whisk a third of the whites into the cheese sauce, then fold the remaining egg whites in.
- Spoon into the dishes and top with the remaining cheese and place a cherry tomato in the centre.
- Run the tip of your finger around the rim of the ramekins then bake for 12-15 minutes until golden and risen.
- Remove from the oven once risen and golden.

1007

SERVES 4

Shrimp and Tomato Gratins

PREPARATION TIME 10 MINUTES

COOKING TIME 15 MINUTES

·····························

INGREDIENTS

400 g / 14 oz / 2 cups canned
chopped tomatoes
300 g / 10 ½ oz / 2 cups shrimp,
peeled and deveined
50 g / 2 oz / ½ cup Parmesan,
finely grated
1 tbsp olive oil
1 clove of garlic, minced
a pinch of caster (superfine) sugar
salt and pepper

TO GARNISH
4 sprigs of thyme

- Preheat the oven to 190°C (170° fan) / 375F / gas 5.
- Heat the olive oil in a small saucepan set over a medium heat.
- Sauté the garlic for 30 seconds, stirring frequently, before adding the chopped tomatoes, sugar and seasoning.
- Stir well and simmer for 10 minutes until thickened slightly.
- Add the shrimp and half of the Parmesan, stirring well.
- Spoon into 4 mini casserole dishes and arrange on a baking tray.
- Bake for 12-15 minutes until bubbling at the sides, then remove and sprinkle the remaining Parmesan on top.
- Remove the tops of the thyme sprigs and place on top of the casseroles before serving.

Tomato and Olive Mini Pizzas

1008

MAKES 12

- Preheat the oven to 200°C (180° fan) / 400F / gas 6.
- Divide the dough into 12 small balls and roll out on a lightly floured surface to 2" in diameter.
- Arrange on baking trays and drizzle with a little olive oil.
- Toss together the olives, tomato, garlic, basil and seasoning and spoon on top of the pizza dough.
- Sprinkle with Parmesan and bake for 8-10 minutes until golden-brown on top.
- Remove from the oven and drizzle with extra-virgin olive oil before serving.

PREPARATION TIME 10 MINUTES

COOKING TIME 10 MINUTES

INGREDIENTS

300 g / 10 ½ oz ready-made pizza dough
a little plain (all purpose) flour
1 tbsp olive oil
2 vine tomatoes, finely diced
1 clove of garlic, minced
110 g / 4 oz / ⅔ cup pitted Kalamata olives, finely chopped
handful of basil leaves, chopped
1 tbsp Parmesan, finely grated
salt and pepper
30 ml / 1 fl. oz / 2 tbsp olive oil

Crab and Potato Mini Casseroles

1009

MAKES 4

PREPARATION TIME 10-15 MINUTES

COOKING TIME 20-25 MINUTES

INGREDIENTS

450 g / 1 lb / 3 cups Maris Piper potatoes, peeled and diced evenly

450 g / 1 lb / 3 cups white crab meat
250 ml / 9 fl. oz / 1 cup whole milk
50 g / 2 oz / ¼ cup butter
50 g / 2 oz / ½ cup Cheddar, grated
1 tbsp creme fraîche
salt and pepper

- Cook the potatoes in a large saucepan of salted, boiling water until tender: 15-20 minutes.
- Drain and leave to cool and dry for a few minutes before mashing with most of the butter, the creme fraîche, cheddar and seasoning until smooth.
- Preheat the oven to 190°C (170° fan) / 375F / gas 5.
- Use the remaining butter to grease the inside of 4 mini casserole dishes.
- Warm the milk and crab meat in a saucepan set over a medium heat.
- Season to taste before spooning into the casseroles dishes.
- Top with the mashed potato and smooth the top level with the rims.
- Place on a baking tray and bake for 15-18 minutes until golden-brown on top.
- Remove from the oven and leave to stand for 5 minutes before serving.

Bean Puree with Chorizo

1010

SERVES 4

PREPARATION TIME 10 MINUTES

COOKING TIME 20-25 MINUTES

INGREDIENTS

FOR THE PUREE
450 g / 1 lb / 4 cups broad (fava) beans, shelled

250 ml / 9 fl. oz / 1 cup whole milk
125 ml / 4 ½ fl. oz / ½ cup double (heavy) cream
110 g / 4 oz / ⅔ cup chorizo, peeled and diced
salt and pepper

TO GARNISH
a few chive stalks, chopped

- Combine the broad beans, milk and half of the cream in a saucepan and cook over a low-medium heat for 15-20 minutes until the broad beans are very soft.
- Strain the broad beans from the cooking liquor, making sure you reserve it.
- Puree the broad beans with some of the cooking liquor in a food processor until smooth.
- Finish with the remaining cream and adjust the seasoning to taste.
- Place back in a small saucepan set over a low heat to keep warm.
- Heat a dry frying pan over a moderate heat until hot and sauté the chorizo until golden-brown in colour.
- Spoon the warm puree into serving pots and top with the chorizo and some of its oil.
- Garnish with chive on top before serving.

1011
SERVES 4

Lime and Dill Salmon Tartare

PREPARATION TIME 10 MINUTES

COOKING TIME 10 MINUTES

INGREDIENTS

400 g / 14 oz / 2 ⅔ cups skinless
salmon fillet
1 shallot, finely chopped
2 limes, juiced
salt and pepper

TO GARNISH
1 lime, cut into wedges
a few sprigs of dill, chopped

- Finely dice the salmon using a sharp knife.
- Toss in a bowl with the lime juice, shallot and seasoning.
- Cover and chill for 30 minutes.
- Spoon into serving pots and garnish with dill on top and lime wedges on the side.

Tuna Tartare with Chilli   1012

- Replace the salmon with tuna fillet and use finely chopped red chilli instead of dill.

1013
SERVES 4

Goats' Cheese and Shallot Crostini

PREPARATION TIME 10 MINUTES

COOKING TIME 15-20 MINUTES

INGREDIENTS

FOR THE CROSTINI
55 ml / 2 fl. oz / ¼ cup olive oil
110 g / 4 oz / 1 cup goats' cheese
round, sliced
1 small ciabatta loaf, sliced
2 tomatoes, sliced
6 shallots, sliced
1 tsp caster (superfine) sugar
salt and freshly ground black pepper

TO GARNISH
30 ml / 1 fl. oz / 2 tbsp extra-virgin
olive oil

- Heat the olive oil in a large frying pan set over a medium heat.
- Sweat the shallots with a little salt and pepper until they soften and turn translucent.
- Add the sugar and reduce the heat, continuing to cook until caramelised.
- Preheat the grill to hot.
- Arrange the slices of ciabatta on a lined baking tray and top with the shallot.
- Lay two slices of tomato on top, then two rounds of goats' cheese.
- Season well and grill for 2-3 minutes until the cheese starts to melt a little.
- Remove from the grill and drizzle with extra-virgin olive oil before serving.

Fontina and Shallot Crostini   1014

- Substitute the goats' cheese with cubed fontina before grilling.

Courgette Caviar on Toast

1015

SERVES 4

- Preheat the grill to hot.
- Toss the courgette with half of the olive oil, salt and pepper and arrange on a baking tray.
- Grill for 6-8 minutes, turning once, until golden at the edges.
- Remove from the grill and leave to cool for 5 minutes before pulsing with the Parmesan, garlic and parsley in a food processor until you have a thick spreading consistency.
- Add a little more olive oil to loosen if necessary and adjust the seasoning to taste.
- Toast the ciabatta slices under the grill until lightly brown in colour then remove and spread with the courgette caviar.
- Garnish with the seeds on top before serving.

PREPARATION TIME 10-15 MINUTES

COOKING TIME 15 MINUTES

INGREDIENTS

1 small ciabatta loaf, sliced
125 ml / 4 ½ fl. oz / ½ cup olive oil
50 g / 2 oz / ½ cup Parmesan, grated
2 courgettes (zucchinis), diced
1 clove of garlic, crushed
a small bunch of flat-leaf parsley, chopped
salt and pepper

TO GARNISH
2 tbsp pumpkin seeds
1 tbsp sunflower seeds

Aubergine Caviar on Toast

1016

- Substitute the courgette for 2 diced aubergines (eggplants).

Pear and Blue Cheese Cakes

1017

MAKES 8

- Preheat the oven to 180°C (160° fan) / 350F / gas 4.
- Combine the flour, sugar, salt and baking powder in a large mixing bowl.
- In a separate mixing bowl, whisk together the butter, yoghurt, eggs and vanilla extract until smooth.
- Add to the dry ingredients and mix until just incorporated.
- Fold through the pear and blue cheese before spooning into 8 square silicone cupcake cases.
- Arrange on a baking tray and bake 22-25 minutes until golden and risen; test with a wooden toothpick, if it comes out clean, they are ready.
- Remove and transfer to a wire rack to cool before serving.

PREPARATION TIME 10-15 MINUTES

COOKING TIME 10 MINUTES

INGREDIENTS

250 g / 9 / 1 ⅔ cups plain (all purpose) flour, sifted
110 g / 4 oz / ½ cup caster (superfine) sugar
125 ml / 4 ½ fl. oz / ½ cup plain yoghurt
110 g / 4 oz / 1 cup blue cheese (e.g. Roquefort), diced
75 g / 3 oz / ⅓ cup butter, melted and cooled
2 pears, diced
1 medium egg
1 tsp vanilla extract
1 tsp baking powder
a pinch of salt

Blue Cheese and Cranberry Cakes

1018

- Substitute the pear with 100 g / 3 ½ oz / ⅔ cup dried cranberries.

Index

Index

Index

Index